T0320477

# Securing Government Information and Data in Developing Countries

Saleem Zoughbi
*UN APCICT, UN ESCAP, South Korea*

A volume in the Advances in Information Security, Privacy, and Ethics (AISPE) Book Series

www.igi-global.com

Published in the United States of America by
    IGI Global
    Information Science Reference (an imprint of IGI Global)
    701 E. Chocolate Avenue
    Hershey PA 17033
    Tel: 717-533-8845
    Fax: 717-533-8661
    E-mail: cust@igi-global.com
    Web site: http://www.igi-global.com

Library of Congress Cataloging-in-Publication Data


Names: Zoughbi, Saleem, 1950- editor.
Title: Securing government information and data in developing countries /
  Saleem Zoughbi, editor.
Description: Hershey, PA : Information Science Reference, 2017.
Identifiers: LCCN 2016053173| ISBN 9781522517030 (hardcover) | ISBN
  9781522517047 (ebook)
Subjects: LCSH: Electronic government information--Security
  measures--Developing countries. | Internet in public
  administration--Developing countries.
Classification: LCC JF1525.A8 S44 2017 | DDC 352.3/8028558--dc23 LC record available at
https://lccn.loc.gov/2016053173


This book is published in the IGI Global book series Advances in Information Security, Privacy, and Ethics (AISPE) (ISSN: 1948-9730; eISSN: 1948-9749)


British Cataloguing in Publication Data
A Cataloguing in Publication record for this book is available from the British Library.

All work contributed to this book is new, previously-unpublished material. The views expressed in this book are those of the authors, but not necessarily of the publisher.

# Advances in Information Security, Privacy, and Ethics (AISPE) Book Series

ISSN:1948-9730
EISSN:1948-9749

## MISSION

As digital technologies become more pervasive in everyday life and the Internet is utilized in ever increasing ways by both private and public entities, concern over digital threats becomes more prevalent.

The **Advances in Information Security, Privacy, & Ethics (AISPE) Book Series** provides cutting-edge research on the protection and misuse of information and technology across various industries and settings. Comprised of scholarly research on topics such as identity management, cryptography, system security, authentication, and data protection, this book series is ideal for reference by IT professionals, academicians, and upper-level students.

## COVERAGE

- Internet Governance
- Access Control
- Cookies
- CIA Triad of Information Security
- Security Information Management
- Cyberethics
- Security Classifications
- IT Risk
- Risk Management
- Network Security Services

IGI Global is currently accepting manuscripts for publication within this series. To submit a proposal for a volume in this series, please contact our Acquisition Editors at Acquisitions@igi-global.com or visit: http://www.igi-global.com/publish/.

The Advances in Information Security, Privacy, and Ethics (AISPE) Book Series (ISSN 1948-9730) is published by IGI Global, 701 E. Chocolate Avenue, Hershey, PA 17033-1240, USA, www.igi-global.com. This series is composed of titles available for purchase individually; each title is edited to be contextually exclusive from any other title within the series. For pricing and ordering information please visit http://www.igi-global.com/book-series/advances-information-security-privacy-ethics/37157. Postmaster: Send all address changes to above address. Copyright © 2017 IGI Global. All rights, including translation in other languages reserved by the publisher. No part of this series may be reproduced or used in any form or by any means – graphics, electronic, or mechanical, including photocopying, recording, taping, or information and retrieval systems – without written permission from the publisher, except for non commercial, educational use, including classroom teaching purposes. The views expressed in this series are those of the authors, but not necessarily of IGI Global.

# Titles in this Series

*For a list of additional titles in this series, please visit: www.igi-global.com*

*Cybersecurity Breaches and Issues Surrounding Online Threat Protection*
Michelle Moore (George Mason University, USA)
Information Science Reference • copyright 2017 • 408pp • H/C (ISBN: 9781522519416)
• US $195.00 (our price)

*Security Solutions and Applied Cryptography in Smart Grid Communications*
Mohamed Amine Ferrag (Guelma University, Algeria) and Ahmed Ahmim (University of Larbi Tebessi, Algeria)
Information Science Reference • copyright 2017 • 464pp • H/C (ISBN: 9781522518297)
• US $215.00 (our price)

*Threat Mitigation and Detection of Cyber Warfare and Terrorism Activities*
Maximiliano E. Korstanje (University of Palermo, Argentina)
Information Science Reference • copyright 2017 • 315pp • H/C (ISBN: 9781522519386)
• US $190.00 (our price)

*Online Banking Security Measures and Data Protection*
Shadi A. Aljawarneh (Jordan University of Science and Technology, Jordan)
Information Science Reference • copyright 2017 • 312pp • H/C (ISBN: 9781522508649)
• US $215.00 (our price)

*Developing Next-Generation Countermeasures for Homeland Security Threat Prevention*
Maurice Dawson (University of Missouri-St. Louis, USA) Dakshina Ranjan Kisku (National Institute of Technology, India) Phalguni Gupta (National Institute of Technical Teachers' Training & Research, India) Jamuna Kanta Sing (Jadavpur University, India) and Weifeng Li (Tsinghua University, China)
Information Science Reference • copyright 2017 • 428pp • H/C (ISBN: 9781522507031)
• US $210.00 (our price)

*Security Solutions for Hyperconnectivity and the Internet of Things*
Maurice Dawson (University of Missouri-St. Louis, USA) Mohamed Eltayeb (Colorado Technical University, USA) and Marwan Omar (Saint Leo University, USA)
Information Science Reference • copyright 2017 • 347pp • H/C (ISBN: 9781522507413)
• US $215.00 (our price)

*Managing Security Issues and the Hidden Dangers of Wearable Technologies*
Andrew Marrington (Zayed University, UAE) Don Kerr (University of the Sunshine Coast, Australia) and John Gammack (Zayed University, UAE)
Information Science Reference • copyright 2017 • 345pp • H/C (ISBN: 9781522510161)
• US $200.00 (our price)

www.igi-global.com

701 E. Chocolate Ave., Hershey, PA 17033
Order online at www.igi-global.com or call 717-533-8845 x100
To place a standing order for titles released in this series,
contact: cust@igi-global.com
Mon-Fri 8:00 am - 5:00 pm (est) or fax 24 hours a day 717-533-8661

# Table of Contents

**Preface**................................................................................................................xii

**Introduction**........................................................................................................xiii

**Chapter 1**
Managing Software Architecture in Domains of Security-Critical Systems:
Multifaceted Collaborative eGovernment Projects ...............................................1
> *Jesus Cano, UNED University, Spain & IEEE CS eGovernment, Spain*
> *& San Pablo CEU University, Spain*
> *Roberto Hernández, UNED University, Spain*

**Chapter 2**
Big Data on E-Government ....................................................................................27
> *Mohd. Shahid Husain, Integral University, India*
> *Neha Khan, Integral University, India*

**Chapter 3**
Hybrid Biometrics and Watermarking Authentication ..........................................37
> *Kareem Kamal A. Ghany, BeniSuef University, Egypt*
> *Hossam M. Zawbaa, Babes-Bolyai University, Romania*

**Chapter 4**
An Empirical Investigation of M-Government Acceptance in Developing
Countries: A Case of Kenya...................................................................................62
> *Gilbert Bundi Mwirigi, Ministry of Interior and Coordination of*
> *National Government, South Korea*
> *Hangjung Zo, Korea Advanced Institute of Science and Technology,*
> *South Korea*
> *Jae Jeung Rho, Korea Advanced Institute of Science and Technology,*
> *South Korea*
> *Min Jae Park, Korea Advanced Institute of Science and Technology,*
> *South Korea*

**Chapter 5**
A Smart Government Framework for Mobile Application Services in
Mongolia..............................................................................................90
    *Tumennast Erdenebold, Global Information Telecommunications*
       *Technology Program, South Korea*

**Chapter 6**
Cloud Computing in E-Governance: Indian Perspective ...................104
    *Mohd. Shahid Husain, Integral University, India*
    *M. Akheela Khanum, Integral University, India*

**Chapter 7**
Major Issues Affecting Government Data and Information in Developing
Countries.............................................................................................115
    *Saleem Zoughbi, Bethlehem University, Palestine*

**Chapter 8**
Major Technology Trends Affecting Government Data in Developing
Countries.............................................................................................127
    *Saleem Zoughbi, Bethlehem University, Palestine*


**Related References**............................................................................ 136

**Compilation of References** ........................................................... 212

**About the Contributors** ................................................................. 303

**Index**................................................................................................ 305

# Detailed Table of Contents

**Preface** ................................................................................................................ xii

**Introduction** .......................................................................................................... xiii

**Chapter 1**
Managing Software Architecture in Domains of Security-Critical Systems:
Multifaceted Collaborative eGovernment Projects ................................................. 1
    *Jesus Cano, UNED University, Spain & IEEE CS eGovernment, Spain*
        *& San Pablo CEU University, Spain*
    *Roberto Hernández, UNED University, Spain*

This chapter describes the management and technological considerations on software architecture and the executive approach to projects that need security-critical and multifaceted requirements. This results in several agreements, one of which is to promote measures regarding the exchange of information from the private sector through public networks. The authors put forward ways to approach these issues and their difficulties from the perspective that there are technical-administrative e-Government models that can be applied to developing countries and encourage a global alliance - in line with the United Nations Millennium Goals (MDG) - for development that will help attain the remaining goals in the immediate future.

**Chapter 2**
Big Data on E-Government ....................................................................................... 27
    *Mohd. Shahid Husain, Integral University, India*
    *Neha Khan, Integral University, India*

All aspects of big data need to be thoroughly investigated, with emphasis on e-governance, needs, challenges and its framework. This chapters recognizes that e-governance needs big data to be reliable, fast and efficient. Another principle is that the trust of a citizen is the main concern. The extraction of meaningful data from large variety of data is a critical issue in big data hence new approaches must be developed. This chapter basically discusses the key concepts of veracity in big data on e-governance. Its main aim is to provide the comprehensive overview big data in e-governance. E-government is still struggling to move advanced level of development. Current e-government applications handle only structured data and sharing between the applications is also difficult.

## Chapter 3

Hybrid Biometrics and Watermarking Authentication .......................................37
*Kareem Kamal A. Ghany, BeniSuef University, Egypt*
*Hossam M. Zawbaa, Babes-Bolyai University, Romania*

There are many tools and techniques that can support management in the information security field. In order to deal with any kind of security, authentication plays an important role. In biometrics, a human being needs to be identified based on some unique personal characteristics and parameters. In this book chapter, the researchers will present an automatic Face Recognition and Authentication Methodology (FRAM). The most significant contribution of this work is using three face recognition methods; the Eigenface, the Fisherface, and color histogram quantization. Finally, the researchers proposed a hybrid approach which is based on a DNA encoding process and embedding the resulting data into a face image using the discrete wavelet transform. In the reverse process, the researchers performed DNA decoding based on the data extracted from the face image.

## Chapter 4

An Empirical Investigation of M-Government Acceptance in Developing
Countries: A Case of Kenya...............................................................................62
*Gilbert Bundi Mwirigi, Ministry of Interior and Coordination of*
*National Government, South Korea*
*Hangjung Zo, Korea Advanced Institute of Science and Technology,*
*South Korea*
*Jae Jeung Rho, Korea Advanced Institute of Science and Technology,*
*South Korea*
*Min Jae Park, Korea Advanced Institute of Science and Technology,*
*South Korea*

Technological development in the past decade has motivated governments in developing countries to focus on leveraging new technologies for efficient and effective public service delivery. M-government has been singled out as one of the fundamental aspect for socio-economic growth in developing countries. Therefore, this study aims at investigating the factors that influence individuals in adoption of new technology, specifically m-government in the context of developing countries. Precisely, this study was to present and empirically validate a research model based on user behavior that examine m-government acceptance in developing countries and inspect the moderating role of facilitating conditions on m-government adoption. The research model was tested using data from 248 respondents from Kenya, surveyed between August and September 2011. The results indicated that the proposed model explained a variance of 60.5 percent of behavior intention to use m-government. In addition, facilitating conditions were found to be a crucial spur to m-government acceptance in developing countries.

**Chapter 5**

A Smart Government Framework for Mobile Application Services in
Mongolia ................................................................................................................ 90
*Tumennast Erdenebold, Global Information Telecommunications
Technology Program, South Korea*

The Smart Government is the advanced e-Government which has been indicated as an emerging global trend in public service delivery. The utilization of Smart Government mobile service is having various numbers of challenges including complexity of different technologies, and reducing duplication among existing and new systems in the application field. In order to get over these challenges, an integrated, an innovative and common system architecture is required to design for the mobile services of Smart Government. Hence, this study designed and proposed "A Smart Government framework for mobile application services" to integrate common parts of the application service. The research covered mobile application service components, and centered on mobile G2C and C2G interactions in the front-office application domain. In addition, the Federal Enterprise Architecture Framework is used, and designed architecture followed up recommendations are proposed for decision makers, government officials, researchers who related to ICT and e-Government.

**Chapter 6**

Cloud Computing in E-Governance: Indian Perspective .................................... 104
*Mohd. Shahid Husain, Integral University, India
M. Akheela Khanum, Integral University, India*

Cloud Computing is becoming a rapidly accepted and deployed paradigm both by individuals and organizations alike. The government of various countries is also moving its services to cloud to offer better and just in time services to the users. This chapter explores the basic concepts of Cloud Computing, which includes the main features of Cloud Computing, the cloud deployment models, the services offered by the cloud, motivations behind adoption of cloud by organizations, in general and by the Government, in particular. We also lay an insight into the various Cloud Computing initiatives taken by the Government of India to facilitate its citizens with easy access to information/services.

**Chapter 7**

Major Issues Affecting Government Data and Information in Developing
Countries ...........................................................................................................115

*Saleem Zoughbi, Bethlehem University, Palestine*

The ever-developing technology is multifaceted, not only in technical specifications, but also in mode, type and characteristics. New technologies are designed and produced, new ways of using these technologies also are being suggested, tested and adopted. Telecommunications and digital technology provide today remarkable smart technologies that enable people to capture, process, maintain, disseminate and store efficiently all kinds of information at very fast speed, with high degree of efficiency and correctness. Much of government data collected are continuously affected by the development in such technology. Recent trends of technology currently and for 2017 and beyond have shown that the impact of such trends will enhance the impact on the way governments handle data. This chapter presents an overview of such trends. However, a common strategy for government data should be developed in a concise way that will guide the process of dealing with the trends of modern technologies. Therefore government data platform will adopt new technologies, new hardware and software but essentially the way government data is kept and managed still remain the same, just new tools have been adopted.

**Chapter 8**

Major Technology Trends Affecting Government Data in Developing
Countries ...........................................................................................................127

*Saleem Zoughbi, Bethlehem University, Palestine*

The success of government data platforms and systems do not depend only on technology. There are other issues that affect this progress. Some of these are very essential to the continuity and not only the implementation, such as leadership. Other issues are the absence of a clear well adopted policy and legal framework that governs its data, security of data, cyber legislation and laws. The government-provided ICT resources and the infrastructure would also be an important issue that would affect government data. Financing is also another critical issue. For developing countries, sustainability of development is a necessity for best impact of development projects. As it is adopted by the United Nations, sustainable development goals (SDG's for the agenda of 2030) have substantial dependency on information and communications technology. All goals practically require government data in one way or another, and hence sustainable development is directly related to government data should successful development is sought. Other issues include open data, open government. This chapter discusses such issues and sheds light on ways of handing them.

**Related References** ........................................................................................ 136

**Compilation of References** ........................................................................... 212

**About the Contributors** ................................................................................ 303

**Index** .............................................................................................................. 305

# Preface

In any developing country, the national priority of developing information and communication technology is paramount, intrinsic and would have a vital role in the national development agenda. This role is more of a means for developing other sectors of socioeconomic development of the country rather than actual end.

This role not only generates several sources of information and data, but spreads over different sectors. Stakeholders, with the government as the main one, become directly involved in the tasks of not only generating and publishing or granting access to data, but managing it in terms of maintaining its integrity, validity, correctness and most of all its privacy and security. Therefore, *security* of government information and data can extend to a larger definition, with integrated qualities, such as the following:

1.  Data and information is correct, updated continuously;
2.  Validation rules exists and applied periodically or whenever data is added;
3.  Proper control of activity issues based on proper authorization of access, reporting features, and monitoring software in the background;
4.  Identification of privacy-level classifications including through protection means and methods;
5.  Detection of malicious agents for misuse of government information and data, be they actual hackers and people or dubious software;
6.  Adapting real-time continuous monitoring and reporting agents of unusual and suspected efforts to access, change or use such data.

This book had a focus on determining what issues are most relevant to the design, implantation, and maintenance of secure government information and data through examining case studies of some developing countries.

I am grateful to the authors who contributed chapters in this book, and I am sure these chapters contain ideas that trigger further research on the development of secure government information and data.

*Saleem Zoughbi*
*Bethlehem University, Palestine*

# Introduction

## INTRODUCTION

The concept of "Government Information and Data" can be a very ambiguous one if not properly defined. What is the relevance of data and information to government agencies if it's not tightly connected with governance on one side and the citizens on the other? Issues that are pertinent to the proper ownership and usage of government data could vary, however basic ones can be well identified:

1.  Validity of data is of primary concern. This implies a lot of operations to sustain it. This is not only based on the initial time of generating and capturing data by the proper government authority, but its ability to secure it well such that vulnerability to attackers, malicious elements (be human or software) becomes almost impossible.
2.  Ability to sustain rapid growth with whatever that implies. It is not the storage area that is alarming, rather the operations and tasks needed to manage and protect this growing data become more complex, even in a non-linear way. Hence the issue of big data is overarching.
3.  The efficiency of access to data, not only in terms of regulations and access control, but rather the environment in which it is saved. This means that data and information of the government should be present "everywhere", i.e. can be reached anytime from anywhere. This implies in fact also the speed of access should be well catered to and latency access time is minimized.
4.  One other important issue is the heterogeneous formats in which data and information can be transported from and to, thus allowing ease of usage of data once accessed.

Certainly other issues can be decisive in the successful usage of government information and data. The "usage" here refers to all operations and tasks that such data is subjected to. A general layout of such usage is outlined in Figure 1.

*Figure 1. Usage of secure government information and data*

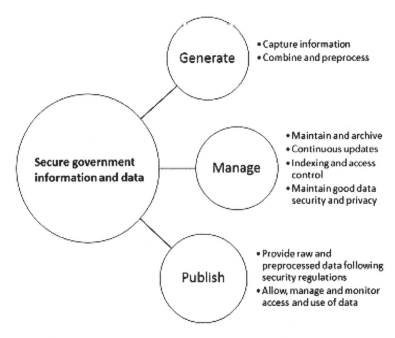

## ISSUES ADDRESSED IN THIS BOOK

Once discussion about securing government information and data starts, the task and operations indicated in Figure 1 form an integral part of the definition of security. The term "secure" is used here not only in the context of preventing illegal use, but also in the sense of making sure that such data is used properly, legally, efficiently and in a fast way. One should recall always the concept of "*access legally and safely anytime, from anywhere and in any format*". The significant issues that control the security of government information and data in this definition are many, but the major ones are being addressed by authors of chapters in this book.

This book is intended to provide an overall view of the most relevant issues that affect the success of securing government information and data. In no way this book was intended as a conclusive review of case studies, although selected cases were provided.

### Software Architecture (Chapter 1)

The operations and tasks referred to earlier form the backbone of any information system that is designed to manage government information and data in a secure way.

Information systems are designed to implement automated and efficient management in a technically secure and successful manner. A proper software architecture would make the critical factor in this security, no matter the content of the information and data is certified and acknowledged as valid, correct and maintained properly. Intelligent methods of developing information systems and executive procedures are needed to be designed to the specifications, needs and requirements of the government information and data with the full definition of "security". For example, enterprise architecture provides an efficient way of developing such systems. Consequently, one of the approaches required is to encourage measures regarding information exchange by the private sector through public networks.

## Big Data (Chapter 2)

As indicated earlier, huge amounts of data impose certain challenges. With government information and data piling continuously, the growth of data become a real concern. The term *Big Data* is associated with such growth of data. In fact the concept of big data was firstly started by Google and Yahoo. The objective is to make relevant information available for the user from the huge amount of data. Using big data strategy secures efficient results, speed and better delivery of services. The role of big data in government information and data management includes also the consideration of big data in e-government by objectives, challenges and comparative study of both traditional and big data e-government.

## Biometrics Technology in Security (Chapter 3)

An example of security tasks that is vital to the security of government information and data is the authentication process. Authentication makes sure that the only approved users and proper data processes are cleared to be active. This guarantees security of government information and data.

In order to deal with any kind of security, authentication plays an important role. In this book a mathematical model is presented as an example, in biometrics, a human-being needs to be identified based on some unique personal characteristics and parameters. Technical methods and tools are needed can be used efficiently for authentication of identities. Examples of such methods include automatic Face Recognition and Authentication Methodology (FRAM). The most significant contribution of this work is using three face recognition methods; the Eigenface, the Fisherface, and color histogram quantization.

## M-Government Acceptance (Chapter 4)

The increasing attention to developing the infrastructure for communications and mobile computing in developing countries have been a major reason for investing heavily on information technology. Such development does not only provide the capability that provides extensive and proactive electronic services to their citizens, but also provides an important opportunity for smart technology applications which in turn provide extensive data and information generated by the public, the private sector and by the officials of the government. Weather this data is real time or archival in nature, mobile governed applications and mobile technology has led to growth of government information and data, which in turn requires being "secure" in the integral definition as explained earlier. Chapter 4 provides an insight into this issue.

## Smart Government and Smart Data (Chapter 5)

All trends in electronic governance are leading to an enriched "smart governance" in the sense of increasing dependence on mobile and smart technologies data acquisition generation, transmission and access. The utilization of Smart Government mobile service is having various numbers of challenges including complexity of different technologies, and reducing duplication among existing and new systems in the application field. These are essential challenges to secure government information and data. In-depth research is needed to shed light on such issue and hence align the security to the basic framework of secure government information and data. Chapter 5 presents shares a research.

## Cloud Computing (Chapter 6)

Whatever the challenges presented in the issues discussed, that affect the achievement of secure government information and data, the ever-present need for dealing with huge data from anywhere, anytime with proper access modes and formats implies that clouds have to be used.

Cloud Computing is becoming a rapidly accepted and deployed paradigm both by individuals and organizations alike. The governments of various countries are also moving its services to government clouds to offer better and just in time services to the users. Chapter 6 explores the basic concepts of Cloud Computing, and looking at developing countries that use cloud computing within the concept of secure government information and data.

## Major Issues Affecting Government Data and Information (Chapter 7)

In securing government data, there are many factors and issues to consider, which some of these are of high concern. Among these are some of primary dimensions such as leadership, policies and legal framework, government data ecosystems, national technology infrastructure, human resources and of course financing. Other issues of concern are the sustainable development goals (SDGs) of the United Nations, with what they imply form using government data for development. This also implies the search for continuous and sustained architecting trends of government data.

This chapter addresses in broad terms the kind of issues that can be of great impact on the performance and success of government data environments. This is a result of observation and close monitoring of trends rather than research results.

## Technology Trends Affecting Government Data and Information (Chapter 8)

The ever going, and increasing, growth of technology develop has been providing the world with very efficient means of technology, be that software or hardware. Telecommunications and digital technology provides today remarkable smart technologies that enable people to capture, process, maintain, disseminate and store efficiently all kinds of information at very fast speed, with high degree of efficiency and correctness. Much of government data collected are continuously affected by the development in such technology.

Chapter 8 reviews latest trends of technology for 2017 and beyond, this highlighting the impact of such development on the way governments handle data.

## CONCLUSION

Serious issues form critical pathways for development of secure government information and data in developing countries. Two important facts appear:

1.  The technical and strategic progress in these issues are normally separate and independent. They could overlap and proceed with varying progress levels. In this case security for such government information and data would be difficult to control, not alone to achieve completely.

2.  The lack of balancing and harmonization between these solutions (technical or otherwise) in all issues would become counterproductive, and it may raise additional challenges that are not foreseen in different societies of developing countries.

Examining cases in different developing countries, observing the effect of such imbalance and comparing reasons and impacts along different technical progress in government information and data systems, practices and content would provide a clear indication and effective guidelines for better and more security for government information and data.

*Saleem Zoughbi*
*UN APCICT, UN ESCAP, South Korea*

# Chapter 1
# Managing Software Architecture in Domains of Security– Critical Systems:
## Multifaceted Collaborative eGovernment Projects

**Jesus Cano**
*UNED University, Spain & IEEE CS eGovernment, Spain & San Pablo CEU University, Spain*

**Roberto Hernández**
*UNED University, Spain*

## ABSTRACT

*This chapter describes the management and technological considerations on software architecture and the executive approach to projects that need security-critical and multifaceted requirements. This results in several agreements, one of which is to promote measures regarding the exchange of information from the private sector through public networks. The authors put forward ways to approach these issues and their difficulties from the perspective that there are technical-administrative e-Government models that can be applied to developing countries and encourage a global alliance - in line with the United Nations Millennium Goals (MDG) - for development that will help attain the remaining goals in the immediate future.*

DOI: 10.4018/978-1-5225-1703-0.ch001

## INTRODUCTION

Managing information systems in security-critical architectural environments requires a stable and well-defined context in all sectors if the goals are to be achieved. However, as the vast majority of managers only know too well and of which they are fully aware, this stability in the best of circumstances is highly relative. Those in charge of information technologies (CIOs) need to adapt to the changing visions of those in charge of business (CEOs), which is being brought about by the new business models that are usually linked to the emergence of new technologies in companies' day-to-day routine.

One of the challenges that is emerging in the national security of many countries is that of protecting people and critical infrastructures, particularly in the area of industrial cybersecurity, which has a massive impact on the population. Governments are raising awareness regarding these threats, drawing up national legislation or improving current legislation to strengthen collaboration among government agencies, companies and citizens. Although efforts are being made to destroy the myths surrounding the complexity of cybersecurity, as in (Talbot, Frincke, & Bishop, 2010), there are no clear criteria as to how to build information systems to avoid global security risks when different countries, different industrial sectors and citizens of different nationalities are involved.

This work reviews the literature on systems and architectures linked to international public safety, the protection of people and infrastructures. We put forward a collaborative global security model where the industrial sectors and public organizations can come together. We will set out a practical case study together with the experience and the lessons learned in the development of eGovernment for trading in hazardous industrial goods. In the discussion, we will evaluate the model from an eGovernment point of view and improve citizen collaboration and involve the businesses and industries affected. This could include the control, prevention and protection of hazardous chemical substances, power supplies or basic supplies for the population, as well as improving control to prevent any criminal or antisocial use. We will describe the technical aspects to be borne in mind, the difficulties arising from their supra-national scope and the peculiarities deriving from merging eGovernment and private enterprise in a distributed information system for collective security.

This chapter describes the management and technological issues of software architecture and the executive approach for a project that needs security-critical and multifaceted requirements. Consequently, one of the approaches required is to encourage measures regarding information exchange by the private sector through public networks. The technology architects lay the way for approaching these problems and their difficulties from a perspective of the technical-administrative eGovernment models that can be applied. The restrictions and determining factors of the developing countries and the need to encourage a world alliance for development make it an even more complicated challenge (UN, 2010).

In this sense information and communication technology (ICT) management plays a multidisciplinary role. Moreover, GCIOs should be very precise and exact in the way they approach the benefits of a pragmatic specific project policy common to all states/participating parties that is tailored to all of them.

## BACKGROUND

The effects of globalization have been closely studied from different perspectives, particularly the economic one, including the impact on the digital divide between the developed and the developing countries. However, the scientific position on information and communication technologies (ICT) is needed by governments and more so by the underdeveloped countries according to studies by United Nations experts. In this way (Al-Nasrawi & Zoughbi, 2014) and others are of the opinion that investing in the information society and making use of technology tools is a driving force to shorten the gap between the richest and poorest countries.

## The Role of the GCIO

The responsibilities of the CIO in the public sector or the GCIO of any government is crucial not only for the economy but also for a country's social and political progress.

In the literature on the role of the GCIO we must go back to what is set out in the federal regulations of the American administration, known as the Clinger-Cohen Act (CCA) of 1996. This drew up a set of competences that formed the basis for the job description of those in charge of government information systems (US Gov, 1996). These regulations delegate the development and maintenance of IT architectures to the different regions with the idea of maximizing the benefits of using information systems and setting up accounting and auditing mechanisms for costs. This is an approach towards financial decentralization to make IT policies more flexible by reducing paper and making redesign processes easier.

Likewise, in the context of the States, the heads of government in charge of information systems must take into account any possible changes of priorities or interests of their CEOs or governments as well as the peculiarities of each country, especially the developing ones. We are referring to a figure known as the GCIO, Government Chief Information Officer.

A GCIO who works in a developing region and often with limited resources (although we could say the same for all kinds of heads and contexts) must be aware of the principles that lead to adequate social sustainability. In its report (UN, 2012) on the post-2015 agenda, the United Nations Organization firstly mentioned that the major goals of the millennium must be adapted to the current challenges since the timescale for their implementation had expired (UN, 2013). This includes counteracting the effect of the inequalities in countries caused by globalization, and secondly, environmental degradation, unemployment and violence.

## The Human Team

It goes without saying that human resources, both in terms of management and qualifications, are one of the major requirements for the success of any IT challenge, The phenomenon of outsourcing has been closely studied in the technology sector as a mechanism for amplifying or substituting the efforts required to run a project. To see where we stand, the historical review in (Hatonen & Eriksson, 2009) is interesting, since the authors start out from the history prior to the last 30 years and the research in this matter. According to the literature in this matter, as in (Dibbern, Goles, hirschheim, & Jayatilaka, 2004), what is consolidated is the idea that resource management in the technology industry is a complex activity that must take account of multiple and external participation. One example of the current situation can be found in countless companies that manufacture electronic devices or provide services, where the business framework, in practice, is one of integration where the parts and resources are provided by outsourced companies.

## Critical Factors

Regarding information systems software development, it is important to evaluate the risks posed by both management and outsourcing. Some studies, such as (Smuts, Merwe, Kotzé, & Loock, 2010), state that there can be a high percentage of failures (up to 50%) if the critical success factors are not borne in mind from a development cycle point of view. Following these lines, we can focus our interest on identifying the 12 areas for grouping the key factors of a project:

- Defining needs
- Design
- Programming and code testing
- System integration and tests
- Data migration
- Starting production and technology transfer
- Integrating the business environment
- Control and management planning
- Management and leadership

- Commercial management
- Security, auditing, and risk management
- Personal relationships

Regarding research and critical factors, other works, such as (Umble, Hafl, & Umble, 2003) enumerate seven elements that theoretically must be taken into account in large ERP-type projects, although they may serve as guidelines for other complex or major projects:

- A clear understanding of the strategic goals
- The firm support of top management
- Excellent project management
- The existence of change management at a business level
- A good team for the implementation
- The quality and precision of the data
- Wide-ranging user-education and training

Other studies put the sights on sustainability, comfortability and social responsibility, with special emphasis on interoperability such as (Jiménez, Falcone, Solanas, Puyosa, Zoughbi, & González; 2015) and (Tambouris, Loutas, Peristeras, & Tarabanis; 2008).

However, if we follow the reports by Gartner (2015) on government projects, the GCIOs and IT heads in general need to bear in mind the individual culture of the organization. In the case of the Government, the following are essential: processes and bureaucratic procedures, the legacy of information systems that need to be maintained, the budget and the difficulty in finding suitable, specialized profiles for the projects and technology to be used.

## Cybersecurity and Engineering Security

Generally speaking, cybersecurity is a social concern, but it becomes particularly acute at times of economic recession, partly as a result of industry having considerable costs related to information security as cybercrime continues to rise. Preventing continuous attacks is a challenge to the standard business framework, especially in service provision and critical infrastructure businesses, such as those related to energy, defense or health. That is why the current business organization model must include risk management and control the balance of risks to be taken on. This means imposing limits when taking on risks in order to achieve profitable returns. According with (Carpio, León, Cano, & Jiménez, 2015) cybersecurity has an influence on this appetite for risk that companies accept in order to achieve their financial targets.

In government contexts security engineering is emerging as a job profile that is beginning to be standardized due to the need to administer and manage information security. For this reason, the SEO, (Security Engineer Officer), is a role with responsibilities linked to cybersecurity, engineering and information technology that is becoming highly relevant, as can be seen, for example, in the number of public vacancies in diplomatic and government agencies. Together with the heads of information systems (CIOs) and the collaboration of social partners, particularly professional associations and organizations in the areas of engineering, law or criminology, ever more persistent and complex security problems need to be tackled. Indeed, civil and military infrastructures are constantly coming under cyber-attacks. This has sounded all the alarms in the highest level of government, notoriously known in developed countries but affects all countries also developing, as such events can put world stability in jeopardy.

This is also part of the culture of cyber ethics and cybersecurity. The organizational model of not only public but also private institutions must be changed so that cyber threats are considered as part of the business model. The absence of risk management in information systems can threaten a company's continued existence and even open the gates to more flexible companies in the digital society environment.

Globalization has highlighted the behavioral changes in people in an Internet environment and in an open and easily accessible online market. If the standard system was product-based this movement has brought business closer to consumers, placing the spotlight on people. In the public sphere, citizens are questioning the effectiveness of the standard bureaucratic mechanisms, which in this case is opening the way to more participatory citizen-centered systems.

Consequently, the advances of the information and knowledge society that influence people's behavior are receiving feedback from the new demands for electronic services and new business models. In public administrations, this circular phenomenon has led to demands for greater transparency through higher quality information and a data presentation format that can be processed by the final users. In conjunction with all this, digital online service platforms, the cloud, mobile technology, social networks and Big Data form the panorama of trends that are beginning to be part of the digital trust open equation.

## International Reference Cases

Maintaining what are deemed to be essential services for society is a priority in many countries. As a result of the free market, many public service sectors that are critical, universal and of general interest are managed by private enterprise. This is the case for security strategy-related regulatory developments in many countries.

As a reference, we will take an information exchange project, set out in (Cano & Hernandez, 2013), concerning explosives, the conception, architecture, design, development and initial implementation of which was technically managed by the first author. Named as SCEPYLT (Acronym in Spanish for Explosives Control System to prevent and fight against terrorism) the European Union decided to develop a tailored system. To this end, the Project was supported as part of the European Commission's specific programme, to be exact, that of the Directorate General of Justice, Freedom and Security named under the section as "Prevention, Preparedness and Consequence Management of Terrorism and other security related risks" - CIPS).

Up to present the system has been adopted as the information exchange platform for all countries of the European Union, complementing other technology initiatives (Europol, 2011), such as the "European Bomb Data System" project, and others like the "Early Warning System" for security issues and for policing purposes under the auspices of Europol.

As can be seen, the very nature of the SCEPYLT project makes it a good example for analyzing difficulties and opportunities. However, a common technology must be chosen, highly sensitive data will have to be shared, countries and industry will be affected, and high levels of security, etc., will be required. And the benefits are shared by all the participants.

Analogous applications with similar difficulties and solutions are the control of transport and humanitarian aid. At an international policy level, even within the UN, there is a concern to promote the harmonization of Law in business areas that affect global security and also allow the interested parties to be accountable to one another and to society. Through information sharing technology strategies with trustworthy organizational criteria that are to some extent benevolent, the result can be economically viable. This means reviewing the cooperation frameworks between the private and the public sector as well as in the sectors themselves. This paradigm is a melting-pot of eGovernment ideas known as P3 or PPP (Public-Private Partnership) particularly in financial and business management areas. National, regional and local levels should promote best practices and remove barriers so as to be able to cover the needs demanded by citizens within the digital society. In the following sections, we are going to set out some of the key points of managing security-critical domains and the lessons learned regarding the development of large information projects. However, we are aware that when faced with specific situations, the peculiarities of the ecosystem of the specific project need to be considered and the appropriate adjustments made.

# ESSENTIAL ISSUES

## Managing Security-Critical Domains

With respect to technology, socio-political solutions and the gradual emergence of Open Government, the technical scene is very much tending towards innovation and is beginning to be defined. The bureaucratic procedures in eGovernment are faced with a reality where citizens are digitally more demanding. The bureaucratic paradigm must be totally revolutionised as a result of the public sector being opened up, and this includes job positions.

The access to information and the multi-channel administrative procedures are going along these lines and must be accepted as natural in the way society performs its day-to-day tasks. It is a transformation requiring leadership and the active participation of the GCIO as the coordinating element of the electronic government ecosystem. It is also a new way of doing things. As an example, we can mention a method, which if properly applied to any kind of project, and of great interest for technology projects, aims at creativity and flexibility. We are referring to Design Thinking where innovative ideas are pragmatic and user-centred. In fact, there are authors that describe it graphically, with the allegory of leaving the palace to pitch a pup tent (Vetterli, Brenner, Uebernickel, & Petrie, 2013).

The opening up of data by Governments is leading to a massive distribution and publication of datasets and the building of APIs (Application Access Interfaces) throughout the world. However, Open Data structures and technologies have yet to reach maturity, which means there is an emerging need for scientific research in this area, as can be seen in (Wimmer & Traunmuller, 2008) and in other ones such as (Ding, Peristeras, & Hausenblas, 2012).

While bearing in mind the issues related to politics and diplomacy, we understand international cooperation as a window to a solution. To build collaborative information environments it is to some extent necessary to isolate those unstable situations that do not encourage bilateral relations between the different governments involved in the problem area. In this respect, we can also take note of the manufacturing industry in the field of Collaborative Networks (CN) in order to achieve greater flexibility in the supply chains due to the changing regulations and the need for entrepreneurial flexibility (Camarinha-Matos & Afsarmanesh, 2005).

These kinds of interstate projects should be backed up or coordinated by an international body as this will help facilitate structuring the project. The UN or the EU usually take on this role. However, international technical-professional associations, like the IEEE, with a wide base or even non-governmental organisations can undertake this basic coordination and thereby serve as a starting-out element to give the project stability and generate trust. Trust is one of the first parameters to be gained by an interstate project, since the loyalty of those taking part and whether or not those who are undecided join, depends on that trust instead of finding reasons or excuses for disagreements. As political balance is sought in the building of large eGov information systems between various governments, this kind of neutral organisation can play a fundamental role for a good understanding among the participating states based on professionalism and technology.

Notwithstanding, it must be acknowledged that these kinds of projects are usually technically complex and not exempt from difficulties. Even in States with a certain economic, political and social stability undeniable disagreements can arise. This occasionally occurs when different legitimate interests clash over a matter connected with the project. Likewise, there may be internal conflicts between the different Administrations of the same state. Issues such as the technology to be used, the way to manage and share data that is especially sensitive for all the participants, and the control of the project, can all turn out to be insurmountable obstacles.

After the 9/11 terrorist attacks in New York cyberspace security has moved to the top of the list on government agendas and also affects the sphere of technology (King, 2011). The 2004 Madrid attacks and then London and Norway, followed by other countries of the international community, surprised the population by the ease with which criminal groups and organisations were able to commit these attacks.

The terrorist threat has been of constant concern for modern societies, for which reason recommendations have been made along with regulations and orders of greater or lesser importance. However, after the 11 September political and social measures took little time to appear, especially framework decisions and incentives for improving police and judicial cooperation.

The importance of sharing information among public administrations, among strategic industrial sectors and among social groups with common interests faced information engineers with a technological challenge due to the magnitude, the different political sensitivities, the protection of privacy and the national autonomy of every state. Companies are subjected to domestic legal regulations and to the competition in the economic sector in its private context. Examples of these sectors are airlines, passenger control, migratory phenomena, the control of electric power and energy transport, among others.

This chapter describes the management and technological aspects regarding the architecture and models that need to be pragmatically brought closer to critical and multifaceted security-critical domains.

## Lessons and Principles Learned

As we have already seen, the standard eGovernment service model provides electronic services that are of interest to citizens, business and Public Administrations with G2C, G2B and G2G relations. But behind the front-end of public service, electronic government consists of a substantial improvement in internal management procedures, an improvement compared to conventional customer service channels (service quality), in sum, an organizational and technical modernization (Garside, 2006). The United Nations Organization describes it as a powerful tool for human development that is essential for meeting internationally agreed development goals (Eurodac, 2010).

In line with the label of the model, public safety and anti-terrorist projects could be defined as being part of the G2G service, where business and citizens do not participate directly. However, although they do not intervene, it could be said that both business and citizens receive the fruits of this kind of government relations in an indirect way that is often difficult to measure.

One of the basic lessons we have learned is that, in practice, a G2B or G2C project cannot be dealt with in the same way as a G2G project. The way of approaching the IT development changes radically. An exclusively G2G project could be approached as if it were a question of dealing with two large companies that needed to collaborate for a common purpose.

However, we have observed that eGovernment projects involving digital services for business or citizens must be approached in the field in line with certain concerns or principles.

## Having a Clear View of the Goal

The first lesson to have in mind is to clearly set the goals and benefits for the final user in administrative terms. Therefore, a prior analysis needs to be performed of the current services, the standard procedures and the systems involved.

The first well-learned lesson is to desist if the citizen or business obtains no tangible benefit from the new electronic service. For example, this happens when the electronic procedure is more tedious than the standard procedure, and just becomes an extra load. In order to evaluate this section, either real empirical cases can be studied or a sample of them so that standard and extreme cases can be established. In the case of the transport of explosives that we use as a reference, a typical case might be a truck carrying explosives from, say, a factory in Germany to a coal mine in the United Kingdom. The standard procedures involve making an application on official stamped paper for authorization from the countries of origin and destination as well as the authorizations to pass through the countries on the route. A typical case could last 6 months before the goods could be finally transported totally legally. One tangible benefit is to offer sector companies an eGoverment service that would substantially reduce that time, to say, 2 months.

A second lesson is to question the feasibility of the project if the Public Administration does not improve its internal management or its bureaucratic complexity. This occurs when the resistance is such that there is no question of changing any part of the management system even if it is necessary to adapt to the dynamics of offering a better service. In practice, this includes bringing in new management rules and regulations for the staff who deal with the procedures so they can remove any obstacles in the procedure and offer a better service.

A third lesson is to be able to clearly visualize the common good ensuing from the project. As can be seen, the commerce of the countries offering an eGovernment service is enhanced, but also collective public safety should be enhanced through an electronic information exchange the instant it is required. This can include a detailed and automatic processing of the explosives cargo to facilitate locating, monitoring and tracing it.

## Process Redesign

One of the most significant issues is to be efficient in redesigning the processes and above all, to be creative along the lines of "Design Thinking". This means that any back-end changes must be clearly examined to evaluate the impact of each service, the work of staff and the change management.

Therefore, a well-learned lesson is that demolition is not the road to success although it may seem to be. Not to adopt the "best" process redesign technology is usually a good solution. A typical case might be the need to do away with official state paper and replace it with a certified electronic transaction. We could call this the "best" solution, but the changes required in each country might take so long that the best alternative is not a good idea. Meanwhile, as a forefront, consideration could be given to following the procedures required to give validity in advance to a simple electronic transaction that can then be checked, which does not block the expectations shown in section 1, a. above.

## Managing Empathy in Communication

If communication is to be efficiently managed, one must become aware of the importance of empathy, courtesy and a liking for the job, but without losing any effectiveness or control over the technical management. In projects where various government promoters are involved, technical management must make an effort to channel the different eGovernment sensitivities. This involves managing empathy (and a liking) as a fundamental element for the success of the project.

Therefore, development should be sufficiently versatile so as to have the flexibility to isolate service modules that can be added to the system core as an option.

In practice it is best to make the electronic procedure modules optional depending on the specific Administration being dealt with. This flexible philosophy means that while Government collaborates, the better the service provided and the higher the satisfaction of business/citizens. But the benefit is also tangible, although to a lesser extent if only a subset of administrations takes part. The software development strategy is strongly conditioned by this functional issue, for which reason this philosophy must be made clear right from the very outset of the project.

Another lesson is to communicate through empathy but properly according to the profiles of the interlocutors. Too much communication is as bad as too little, too much being understood as inappropriate in a given context. For example, if dealing with a group of experts in chemicals that are discussing the precursors of explosives, it is sometimes inappropriate to list the characteristics of the servers and the bandwidths required. In this case, it is sufficient to refer them to specialist groups or subgroups, returning (important) the feedback, but not the details themselves, to the other expert groups and those responsible.

## Take Great Care Over the Preliminary Steps

Great care in the initial stages prior to implementation is essential, which means a careful work plan, which in a very short time will lead to production. As we stated at the beginning of this chapter, it is related to terms like "cutover" and "go-live". A lesson learned is that G2B or G2C projects must speak through the mouth of the Administration and hear with the ears of an ordinary citizen.

Consequently, this highlights that change management, staff support and citizen sensitivity are all paramount. Therefore, project managers must pay close attention. For example, if a business is taking part to enhance its service quality and security in the face of possible terrorist attacks, it is logical to set up either a system for enquiries about the discovery of lost/stolen explosives for police officers and customs agents or for vehicles and drivers involved in their transport. A further projection would be online reporting by citizens of explosives finds or any irregularities observed. Thus, in some way, we all keep vigilance over our collective safety.

## The Need to Share or Have Access to Everything

The need to share is a natural and political phenomenon of countries, but also of any human group in general. However, the data that refer to or affect oneself are jealously guarded. That is why if sensitive data is to be shared in a plural or international context, it must be guaranteed beforehand that no one single person will have total control of all the information, and, therefore of everybody else.

On the contrary, the idea is that each individual controls the data they are interested in and, which, in some way, refers to them, and that the data of the whole system can only be obtained through the collaboration of all the members. This means that only sharing matters that affect others is a measure that ensures that no single party can get hold of all the information, but all the information could be obtained if all the parties agree.

## Motivation to Participate

It is advisable that citizens and/or business should take part in government projects. Using Electronic Administration techniques a considerable source of collaboration is citizens and business due to the globalization of the Internet and universal access to information. Unifying strategies provides the collaborators with a better service, society as a whole is better and the result is mutual satisfaction.

## NEW DISTRIBUTED RELATIONS FRAMEWORK

We start out from the idea that traditionally e-Government relations have been classified into three main kinds according to the participation of the subjects: Government and Citizens (G2C), Government and Business (G2B) and among governments themselves (G2G). A special kind we can take into account is the relationship between Government and government employees due to the special nature of civil servants (G2E). In our study we have not considered other kinds of relations that are inherent to electronic commerce, like B2C, where the concept of citizen is more that of a "client" or the B2B relationship between enterprises.

In addition, these relations are established by the dimension of governance: local, regional, national, supra-national and international.

A theoretical industrial relations scenario in commercial sectors that come under collective security needs to interact with the Public Administration, which may be one or more organisations depending on the business context and how the government agencies are organised. Figure 1 illustrates this scenario, where $m$ enterprises from the same business sector liaise with $n$ additional Administrations. We can attempt to measure the management of the bureaucratic procedures by calculating the number of relations that the companies of an industrial sector have to set up in a context of multiple government agencies, which is: $R_b = m + m \cdot n$ and the relations established by the public sector $R_g = 0$, since there is no requirement to collaborate.

This reflects the interoperability between governments to improve the services offered from an industry point of view and optimise companies' administrative tasks to save them costs and inconveniences. Taking the second model proposed, the

*Figure 1. MxN scenario of A2B relationships*

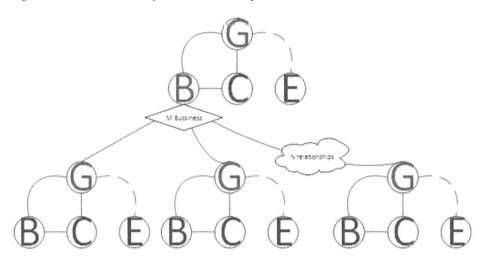

relations would be: $R_b$ = m and $R_g$ = n. Additionally, we could also mathematically quantify the bureaucratic procedures scenarios for citizens, although here we will focus on the industrial and government relations sector.

As can be seen, the administrative management procedures in the proposed model (b), means making an effort to reorganise the private and the public sector, with the latter assuming part of the responsibility. Redesigning public services means adapting jobs. From a company point of view, the complexity of the procedure $R_b$ is linear with respect to the volume of government agencies (Equation 1), while in the collaborative design it is constant (Equation 2).

$R=m(1+n)$ (1)

$R=m$ (2)

Consequently, an interoperable architecture between public administrations has a direct effect on the competitiveness of the industrial sector. But that is not the only issue that is highlighted here, but also the possibility of implementing security measures that are common to the different governments. Now, the next question is how to obtain engineering designs for public administrations that that will achieve this optimising effect in the private sector and therefore, for collective security (public and private).

Our proposal is to establish a dual-element framework: A core architecture and a set of Web-based portals. The core consists of a secure communications skeleton that implements G2G relations, and consists of designs that use information exchange with an architecture oriented to intra-administrative services and communications networks. Direct relations among governments require a point-to-point meshed communications design (p2p).

Secondly, a business service portal implementing G2B that respects any interaction between the business and its main government agency is required. Other G2B relations would be channelled using interoperability protocols by means of G2G core architecture relationships. Figure 2 shows a diagram representing the proposed conceptual model in the redesign framework.

## BASIC PRINCIPLES FOR AN INTERNATIONAL DISTRIBUTED SYSTEM

State public bodies usually have large computer systems connected to large networks. The complexity of interconnection of these systems often lies in the differences

*Figure 2. Conceptual redesign of multiple relations framework*

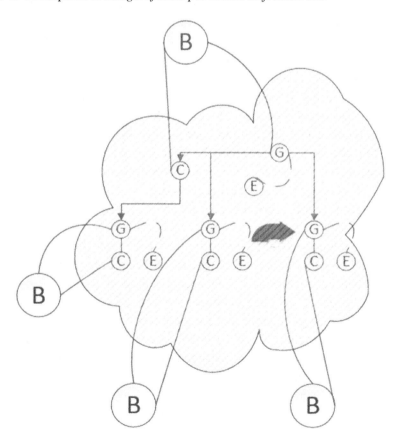

between the civil servants in charge and the way the internal network is organised. This can sometimes make it difficult to deploy applications, detect system errors and change the settings. Experience has shown us that the following basic principles may be of use for developing international distributed applications.

One of the first principles to be considered is that technology is allegorically very sovereign. We could include countries, large corporations and business. Although technology is of a universal nature each interested party often claims responsibility for the technology area. Therefore, community guidelines apart, operating the computer systems is the work of the bodies of each country. The result of this sovereign nature of the use of technology and its choice means that a transnational development project must be designed, bearing in mind whether or not each member will happily accept the solutions proposed or with reticence, because they are conditioned by a wide range of internal factors: economic, socio-cultural, organisational, political… all resulting from a diversity of interests. Admitting this approach means respecting the technology options of each party and accepting the flexibility and extra work involved.

A basic principle of group work must be underlined, which is benevolent co-operation. It must be presumed that the participants will cooperate to achieve a common goal in a loyal, constructive manner. Moreover, transparency during the development cycle means that the technical information must be accessible to the participants and a technology must be chosen that is understood by all, with well-defined deliverables and a well-organised source code. Therefore, it is recommended to use collaborative development software platforms with control over the different versions, and with free software solutions to facilitate the work.

On the other hand, communications must be made painstakingly secure. To that end, encoding and authentication must be used that are trusted by the countries. For example, widely known protocols, such as SSL/TLS, and the availability of digital certificates. Depending on the infrastructure available, it is preferable to use isolated Internet networks, shared intranets and virtual private networks (VPN) to tunnel national networks.

To expand on this, decoupling the nodes goes in the same direction. System dependency with respect to one part of the system, like a node or various nodes, should not affect the entire system. So, some of the technology options to be considered that boost availability are asynchronous communications and service oriented systems.

Finally, ontologies and internationalising the user interface and the design constitute a set of good practices that will result in successful project management and lead to a quality final product. From a practical point of view, exchanging messages between nodes requires a message exchange protocol based on a common ontology and the use of a common vocabulary that will assist system development and its subsequent maintenance.

## DATABASE-BASED DISTRIBUTED ARCHITECTURE MODELS

Distributed databases consist of a combination of various computer network nodes, physically distributed but comprising a logical unified data system: a global database. Distributed database design includes the all-important decision of choosing the type of control used to process the transactions to the other nodes forming the system. If there is one component in the distributed system that performs this function the architecture is logically known as centralised. However, if the control is shared among all the nodes the architecture is decentralised or federated, studied as a classic theme in (Papazoglou 1990). But this is not only a technical decision, since on many occasions, the actual domain of the application has to be evaluated, such as the sensation of specific proprietary data loss or the trust in security (Song & Zhang, 2011).

One of the key design points in processing the physical distribution of data in a distributed network is efficient partitioning and an optimal design of the network structure. Partitioning has a considerable influence on the performance and database administration. Vertical partitioning divides a relational entity into various subsets of columns or attributes, while horizontal partitioning obtains a set of relational fragments, each of which has a subset of rows or tuples. An interesting reference for these tasks is (Rodriguez & Xiaoou, 2011). Following are the three most relevant aspects of the architecture in line with the previously stated basic principles.

A completely decentralised distributed system means there is no coordinator node. The control of the distribution is shared equally among all the local database nodes. A centralised control design has the advantage of making the development and administration easier. However, this would mean that all the information would have the privilege of passing through one node, making it a critical infrastructure resource and entail taking measures regarding performance and security, design issues that may be discussed in some articles on the subject for years, as (Thuraisingham, Rubinovitz, Foti, & Abreu, 1993).

An alternative completely distributed decentralised system means that each node manages communication with the other system components and knows where the information is located when an enquiry is made. Moreover, it should be borne in mind that the nodes participate according to the basic principles set for an international distributed system, especially sufficiently sovereign and benevolent nodes, or a degree of compromise among them. In practice, a completely distributed system provides each member with the benefit that only what is needed for the group interest is shared. There is no database in one single place since the system is a set of distributed databases where nobody can get hold of all the information exclusively for themselves while all the nodes are equally important.

Implementing the physical network of this decentralised vision can be achieved using a meshed network topology, thus producing a distributed P2P database. However, a meshed database is more difficult to configure since each node must have an inventory of the other local nodes in the form of a configuration file.

Although there are studies, such as the work presented in (Karimi, Yousefi, Fathy, & Mazoochi, 2008) to measure the characteristics of meshed P2P files, it is usually thought that the network administration deteriorates considerably when the number of nodes is high. However, a node failure does not affect all the network, which enables a system to be designed that takes account of all the basic principles that we have presented: all nodes are equally important and none predominates over the others.

In a geographically distant environment where government networks intervene, apart from the Internet, a meshed representation of the P2P network is a logical representation that can be achieved through control software that can be monitored by means of the node connections configuration file. This does not involve any additional cost in network infrastructure or additional wiring, as can be seen in more detail in the Figure 3.

*Figure 3. More detailed representation*

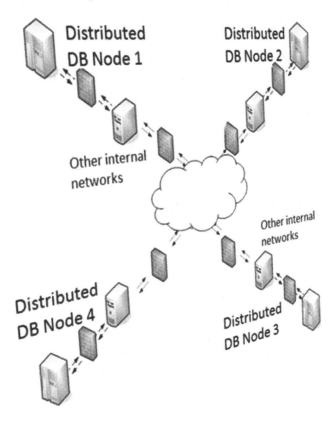

A meshed network also is more secure if one of the nodes fails: the rest contin-ues to function and there are usually no bottlenecks as all the nodes have the same role compared to the others (Tian-shi, Jiao, Gao Rong, Gang, 2010).

## DISTRIBUTED NODES OF A GLOBAL DATABASE

To design a database from a completely decentralised approach a level of control abstraction needs to be set over the local nodes of the global distributed database. This control is performed through a multilayer structure: a messaging web service layer, a common interface for everyone in the system, a business logic layer that processes the global transactions and a data persistence engine layer, as well as a database repository of local data. This architectural design is seen to be suffi-ciently independent of the technology, which means a whole range of options can be implemented.

As the Figure 4 illustrates, the control part consists of a first interface layer with the other nodes by means of XML SOAP-based messaging called "Web Services Layer", where the web services are set out that implement the specific functionally

*Figure 4. Architecture of a node*

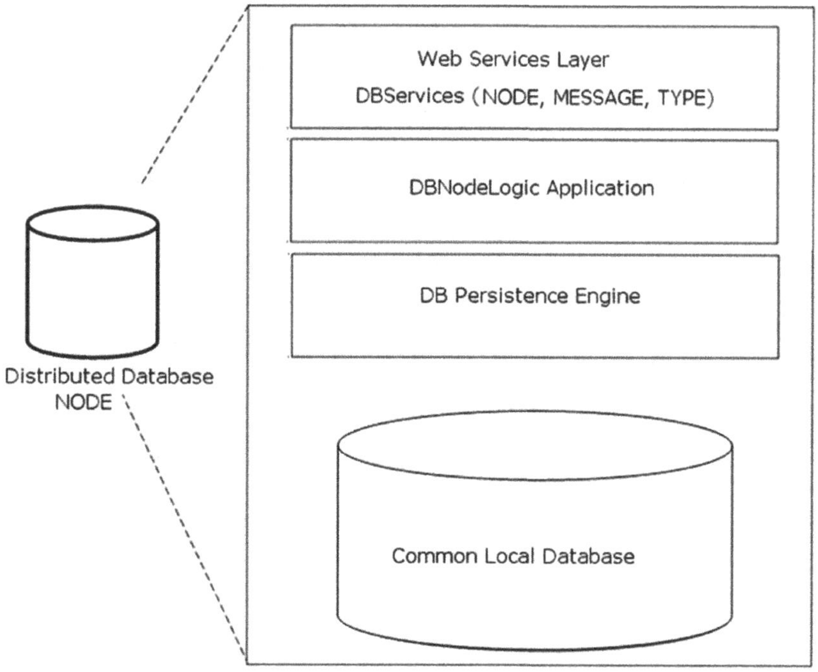

necessary global database transactions. The essential parameters are the type of transaction (TYPE), the node in which the communication is established (NODE) and the content of the transaction (MESSAGE). Completing this level of control abstraction are: the node Logic layer, where the functional operations are carried out on the database and the persistence engine layer to make the technology implementation option independent of the database management system forming the local repository.

The web service oriented approach provides a series of advantages, such as the better organisation of the functionalities that a collaborating node offers the others, the lower development costs and greater flexibility, since the service layer is the same as all the nodes. This means that any user who so wishes can use their own systems (legacy) making the adaptations necessary to comply with the services offered. In addition, it facilitates reusing the services and the code and lets higher level security layers be added, such as XML-based firewall applications.

Both the more external web service layer and the more internal persistence layer enable an architecture to be obtained that is sufficiently decoupled from the other nodes and the different technology options.

## TRANSACTIONS AND CONSULTATIONS

The purpose of the global database being partitioned horizontally is to improve the performance of the transactions and consultations. In fact, the partitioning was optimised as a result of a study of the enquiries in an appropriate set of tests.

The main design criterion chosen for our system was geographic location so that the information semantically linked to a node would be housed in its own repository. In the case of relationships whose semantics include information from two different member nodes, any consultation concerning this relationship would mean making the request via a data network. The same is true for the relationships of databases whose tuples include identification semantics from more than one member node. This network transport transfer can be extremely negative for performance.

So, as a measure, we adopted the criterion of inserting the same row in all the member nodes that are identified in a relationship, adding a horizontal redundancy to improve the enquiries in exchange for a slight increase in insertion transactions, updating and erasure. An example of this is the "itinerary" relationship where the semantics indicate geographical sections between a starting and finishing point.

However, to optimise "itineraries" enquiries each local relationship will not only have the tuples of the sections in which they are included but also the others since they are semantically related.

## ENCODED NETWORK-BASED COMMUNICATIONS

As if it were a mantra, the current trend is to make eGoverment available to all society, and as it is ideal for IT projects, this sought after tool is placed in the reach of citizens to make them part of the profit and loss account of public investment in electronic government. It is a win-win approach with a dual benefit; Public administrations meet their own management and service goals.

On the other hand, the project definition always kept very much in mind that it was in favour of technology and innovation. European institutions have designed different action plans for improving the implementation of the information society and for creating jobs. This is the case for the eEurope2005 Action Plan, now finalised, followed by the i2010 strategy, and then the "Digital Agenda for Europe" for 2020 (EU; 2015) whose aim is to create a favourable framework in the European market for private investment in information technologies, service security and universal broadband-based applications and content. The strategic European frameworks have boosted achieving a set of basic goals in the administrations of European countries. According to this plan, Europe must have:

- Modern online public services
- An electronic administration
- Electronic services for learning
- Electronic health services
- An electronic business environment that is dynamic
- Widely available broadband at competitive prices
- A secure information structure

From a technical point of view, to provide a service to the commercial explosives sector, citizens and companies can participate in the public administrations as follows:

1. Companies can provide an early warning concerning robberies, losses, transport breakdowns and incidents.
2. By identifying and making an inventory of the explosive materials transported.
3. By collaborating in meeting the requirements of electronic bureaucratic procedures.

This requires designing an "Electronic Administration Portal", independently deployed from the rest of the system, the implementation of which is organisationally optional. A specific module was designed for companies in the commercial explosives sector so they could collaborate with the Public Administration:

1. By providing alerts of incidences in their own transport;
2. By using a detailed inventory to load the consignments to be transported, computerising it and avoiding a generic or paper inventory which makes control difficult; and
3. By completing the administrative authorisations to simplify the bureaucratic procedures.

All this provides structured information that is essential for the public authorities to carry out control and investigative and preventive actions; it also results in a more flexible service for companies by improving the response times of the administrations. In sum, it improves citizen safety in general.

## FUTURE RESEARCH DIRECTIONS

The main trends highlighted in the public sector include web-based scalable architectures, which have been dealt with to a large extent in this work, and others such as Hybrid Clouds, the Internet of Things, smart city platforms, Big Data analysis and e-ID electronic identification. To this we can add data opening, multi-channel access, the recurrent digital office and interoperability, which cover a vast area of research as has been mentioned throughout this chapter. In the research to which we refer, we need to highlight the influence that the opening up of data means for society: it is estimated that in 2018 this opening up will reach 30 percent of all the information managed by electronic administration systems.

## CONCLUSION

This work proposes how to approach the difficult questions and lessons learned from a management perspective. We have aimed to show there are alternative technical-administrative models of e-Government that can be applied to the developing countries, with a flexible mindset to encourage alliances to build information and communication systems that will help reach the millennium goals and extend the idea of a driving force by taking technology as a point of support. So, we definitely propose a distributed layout to represent standard electronic service relations in a networked environment built on the paradigm of public-private collaboration and which is citizen-centred.

In this sense, the keys to international development are being adhered to, which was done through a framework of collaboration, interoperability, creative design with completely distributed architectures and decentralised databases across the commercial sector of regulated products that are potentially dangerous for people's safety.

## REFERENCES

Al-Nasrawi, S., & Zoughbi, S. (2014). Information Society, Digital Divide, and E-Governance in Developing Countries. In M. Khosrow-Pour (Ed.), Encyclopedia of Information Science and Technology (3rd ed.; pp. 6525-6533). IGI Global.

Camarinha-Matos, L. M., & Afsarmanesh, H. (2005, October). Collaborative networks: A new scientific discipline. *Journal of Intelligent Manufacturing. Springer.*, *16*(4-5), 439–452. doi:10.1007/s10845-005-1656-3

Cano, J., & Hernandez, R. (2013). SCEPYLT: An Information System for Fighting Terrorism. *IEEE Software, 30*(3), 73-79.

Carpio Cámara, M., León, A., Cano Carrillo, J., & Jiménez, C. E. (2015). *Regulación y ciberseguridad. Contribuciones al modelo de Gobernanza*. Capítulo del libro "Gobernanza de Internet en España", IGF Forum Spain. Retrieved from http://igfspain.com/doc/archivos/Gobernanza_Internet_Spain_2015.pdf

Dibbern, J., Goles, T., Hirschheim, R., & Jayatilaka, B. (2004, November). Information systems outsourcing: A survey and analysis of the literature. *SIGMIS Database*, *35*(4), 6–102. doi:10.1145/1035233.1035236

Ding, L., Peristeras, V., & Hausenblas, M. (2012). Linked Open Government Data. *IEEE Intelligent Systems, 27*(3), 11-15.

EU European Union. (2015). *Digital Agenda for Europe 2020*. Retrieved from http://ec.europa.eu/information_society/digital-agenda/index_en.htm

Eurodac Supervision Coordination Group Secretariat. (2010). *Coordinated Supervision of Eurodac Activity Report 2008-2009*. Retrieved from http://www.edps.europa.eu/EDPSWEB/edps/Supervision/Eurodac

Europol - European Police Office. (2011). *Europol Review*. General Report on Europol Activities.

Garside, A. (2006). *The political genesis and legal impact of proposals for the SIS II: what cost for data protection and security in the EU?*. Sussex Migration Working Paper no. 30. University of Sussex. Retrieved from www.sussex.ac.uk/migration/documents/mwp30.pdf

Gartner. (2015). *Highlights Top 10 Strategic Technology Trends for Government.* Retrieved from http://www.gartner.com/newsroom/id/3069117

Hatonen, J., & Eriksson, T. (2009). 30+ years of research and practice of outsourcing–Exploring the past and anticipating the future. *Journal of International Management, 15*(2), 142–155. doi:10.1016/j.intman.2008.07.002

Jiménez, C. E., Falcone, F., Solanas, A., Puyosa, H., Zoughbi, S., & González, F. (2015). Smart Government: Opportunities and Challenges in Smart Cities Development. In Ć. Dolićanin, E. Kajan, D. Randjelović, & B. Stojanović (Eds.), *Handbook of Research on Democratic Strategies and Citizen-Centered E-Government Services* (pp. 1–19). Hershey, PA: Information Science Reference; doi:10.4018/978-1-4666-7266-6.ch001

Karimi, O. B., Yousefi, S., Fathy, M., & Mazoochi, M. (2008). Availability measurement in peer to peer network management systems. *IEEE Third International Conference on Digital Information Management*, 745-750.

King, R.S. (2011). How 5 technologies fared after 9/11. *IEEE Spectrum, 48*(9), 13.

Papazoglou, M. P. (1990). Distributed database architectures. *IEEE International Conference on Databases, Parallel Architectures and Their Applications, PARBASE-90.* doi:10.1109/PARBSE.1990.77215

Rodriguez, L. & Li, X. (2011). A dynamic vertical partitioning approach for distributed database system. *IEEE International Conference on Systems, Man, and Cybernetics (SMC)*, 1853-1858.

Smuts, H., van der Merwe, A., Paula Kotzé, P., & Loock, M. (2010). Critical success factors for information systems outsourcing management: a software development lifecycle view. In *Proceedings of the 2010 Annual Research Conference of the South African Institute of Computer Scientists and Information Technologists (SAICSIT '10)*. ACM. doi:10.1145/1899503.1899537

Song, X., & Zhang, R. (2011). Research on constructing distributed large database based on J2EE. *IEEE 3rd International Conference on Communication Software and Networks (ICCSN)*, 704-707. doi:10.1109/ICCSN.2011.6014989

Talbot, E.B., Frincke, D., & Bishop, M. (2010). Demythifying Cybersecurity. *IEEE Security & Privacy, 8*(3), 56-59.

Tambouris, E., Loutas, N., Peristeras, V., & Tarabanis, K. (2008). The role of interoperability in eGovernment applications: An investigation of obstacles and implementation decisions. *Digital Information Management, 2008. ICDIM 2008. Third International Conference on*, 381-386. doi:10.1109/ICDIM.2008.4746798

Thuraisingham, B., Rubinovitz, H., Foti, D., & Abreu, A. (1993). Design and implementation of a distributed database. *IEEE COMPSAC 93 Proceedings, Seventeenth Annual International Computer Software and Applications Conference*, 152-158. doi:10.1109/CMPSAC.1993.404229

Tian-shi, L., Jiao, L,m Gao, R.-F., & Gang, M. (2010). Overview of P2P Distributed Database System. *IEEE International Conference on Web Information Systems and Mining (WISM)*, 2, 192-197.

Umble, E. J., Haft, R. R., & Umble, M. M. (2003). Enterprise resource planning: Implementation procedures and critical success factors. *European Journal of Operational Research, 146*(2), 241-257. 10.1016/S0377-2217(02)00547-7

UN United Nations. (2010). *E-Government Survey 2010: Leveraging e-government at a time of financial and economic crisis*. Retrieved from http://www2.unpan.org/egovkb/documents/2010/E_Gov_2010_Complete.pdf

UN United Nations. (2012). *The Post-2015 Agenda*. Retrieved from http://www.undp.org/content/dam/undp/library/Poverty Reduction/Realizing the future we want. pdf

UN United Nations. (2013). *Report of the UN System Task Team on the Post-2015 Development Agenda*. Retrieved from http://www.un.org/en/development/desa/policy/untaskteam_undf/report.shtml

US Government. (1996). *Summary: Information Technology Management Reform Act*. Retrieved from http://govinfo.library.unt.edu/npr/library/misc/itref.html

Vetterli, C., Brenner, W., Uebernickel, F., & Petrie, C. (2013). From Palaces to Yurts: Why Requirements Engineering Needs Design Thinking. *IEEE Internet Computing, 17*(2), 91-94.

Wimmer, M. A., & Traunmuller, R. (2008). Perspectives e-Government 2020: Results and Conclusions from the EC Roadmap 2020 Project. *Information and Communication Technologies: From Theory to Applications, 2008. ICTTA 2008. 3rd International Conference on*. doi:10.1109/ICTTA.2008.4529941

# Chapter 2
# Big Data on E-Government

**Mohd. Shahid Husain**
*Integral University, India*

**Neha Khan**
*Integral University, India*

## ABSTRACT

*All aspects of big data need to be thoroughly investigated, with emphasis on e-governance, needs, challenges and its framework. This chapters recognizes that e-governance needs big data to be reliable, fast and efficient. Another principle is that the trust of a citizen is the main concern. The extraction of meaningful data from large variety of data is a critical issue in big data hence new approaches must be developed. This chapter basically discusses the key concepts of veracity in big data on e-governance. Its main aim is to provide the comprehensive overview big data in e-governance. E-government is still struggling to move advanced level of development. Current e-government applications handle only structured data and sharing between the applications is also difficult.*

DOI: 10.4018/978-1-5225-1703-0.ch002

## INTRODUCTION

The concept of big data was firstly started by Google and yahoo. The aim of these companies is to make relevant information available for the user from the huge amount of data. According to the survey 53% (1217) of all the companies all over the world are using big data strategy. Due to the efficient result, speed and better delivery of services the public sector has also adopted big data in order to improve their services and interaction between the customers. Now a days in many fields of public sector big data plays an important role such as in development field, research field, medical field, banking etc.

In the first section of this chapter first of all the authors will discuss big data and in the other section we will give the overview of e-government then finally the role of big data in e-government. The chapter also discusses the objectives, challenges and the comparative study of both traditional and big data e-government.

## BIG DATA

Big data can be defined as data whose scale, volume and complexity is so high that it is difficult to handle data through conventional methods. To extract the value and hidden knowledge big data requires new architecture, algorithm and techniques. Big data is characterised by high volume, structured and unstructured data, uncertainty, incompleteness and high rate of changing (Rajagopalan, 2013).

Big data plays a major role in scientific computing as researchers and scientists produces huge amount of data in their experiment. Big data can be processed in many ways; every big data has different characteristics. When big data is processed and stored; data security, governance and policies plays an important role.

## CHALLENGES OF BIG DATA

The problems of big data are complex to analyze and solve. The better option for this is to classify the problem according to the data format. It is really very difficult to handle big data in every field. These challenges requires the design of new advanced architecture, algorithms, visualization techniques etc. The main challenges to handle big data are:

- Requires high computation and storage power.
- Requires new advanced algorithms.
- Requires New architecture
- Reduction in data dimension
- Scalability (Scaling up and scaling down)
- Challenge to improve performance
- How data can be secure (data security)
- Challenge in workload diversity
- Continuous availability in services and to improve cost

## CHARACTERISTICS OF BIG DATA

Big data can be categorized in terms of volume, velocity, variability and complexity.

- **Volume:** The amount of data generated is very important; this amount determines the potential of the data. Volume of data is indeed an important dimension that has influenced the data processing techniques. Telecom companies typically process from 100 million to half billion Call Details record per day. Providers also need to provide real time information to the consumer. Using traditional techniques it is indeed impossible to provide these services.
- **Variety:** This defines the different forms of data i.e. whether the data is structures unstructured or semi structured. IBM estimates that over 90% of the real time data is represented by unstructured data. Having new types of data arise new risks.
- **Velocity:** Velocity refers to the speed of the generation of the data or how fast the data is generated as well as processed. Now the data movement is real time. The high velocity of data represents Big Data.
- **Variability:** This is one of the main characteristic of big data as accuracy of the data depends on the veracity of the source data.
- **Complexity:** The management of big data is very complex process especially in the case when big amount of data comes from multiple sources. These data needs to be properly connected and correlated in order to grasp.

## E-GOVERNMENT

E-government is also known as electronic government, online government, internet government .The main purpose of e-government is the digital interaction between citizen and government, Government to government (G2G) and government to

*Figure 1. 3Vs of big data*

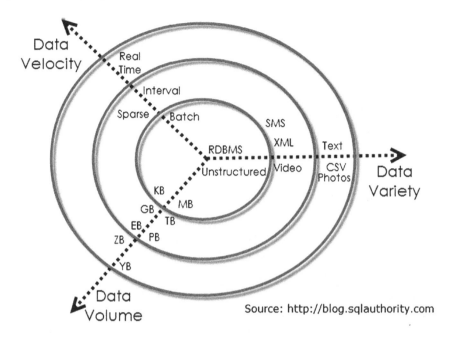

Source: http://blog.sqlauthority.com

Business (G2B). E-governance in India has evolved from computerization of government department. It plays an important role in shaping the progress of government policies and strategies of the country. The emerging e-governance allow different researchers group to work on the same data.

*E-government refers to the use of information and communication technologies to improve the efficiency, effectiveness, transparency and accountability of government.*

## Objectives of E-Governance

- The main objective of e-governance is to help the government organizations.
- To build an informed society.
- To increase government and citizen interaction.
- To encourage citizen participation.
- To bring transparency in the government processes.
- To reduce the cost of governance.
- To reduce the reaction time of the governance.
- Make government more accessible.
- To deliver online services.
- To build services around citizen's choice.

## Why E-Government?

- Used to provide improved level of services.
- Used to control fraud.
- To provide new kind of services.
- Make decisions traceable.
- Introduces transparency in data.
- Provide greater access to information through web.
- To increase citizen/customer interaction directly with government.

## BIG DATA ON E-GOVERNANCE

Delivering new and best services to the citizen is the main concern for the government, but this is quite difficult because of population and its diversity (Walker, 2014). Now a days most of the organizations have chosen big data technology for dealing big amount of data for successful business. Government whether Local, Federal or state are continuously leveraging big data to improve their services and applications which they are offering to citizen and businesses. In short big data has the potential to make government policies faster, smarter and efficient (Lobo, 2015). The huge amount of e-government policies in India are storing big amount of data into database. In Indian E-government projects, data volume per day are growing continuously due to the popularity and acceptability of the e-government applications.

Privacy is the main concern over the internet, the data which we considered private will no longer be private tomorrow. He said that securing data in a public domain is the most difficult task because the transition of electronic data is not uniform. In public policies it is really hard to understand how data is coming and from where it is coming (or not), common policies and standards should be accepted so that databases can talk to each other.

To process Citizen's idea, Indian Bhartiya Janta Party (BJP)is using Big data analytics .A large number of data analytics team is working behind the service to process main points emerging from mygov.in debates. Similarly the Telangana Government is hiring big data analytics for data collected from people across Strata.

In March 2012 the government of USA announced to use big data in research and development field in order to improve the ability to extract the hidden meaning from the huge data. Also, the Australian Government information Management office has adopted the big data approach in order to improve the delivery of new services and policies. Similarly many other countries are adopted big data strategies to improve policies and interaction between the citizens (Satpathy & Chanana, 2014):

*Figure 2*

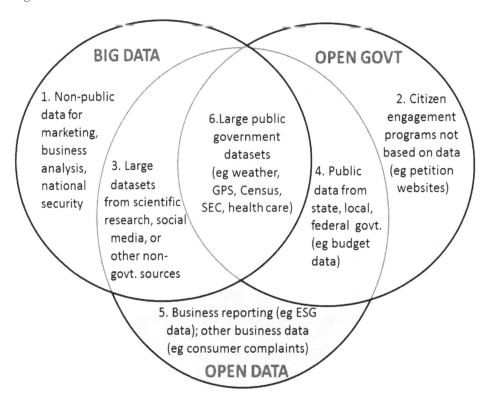

## Infrastructure Requirement to E-Governance

The infrastructure requirements to e-governance for emerging big data e-governance are:

- Requires high volume of data that should supported very long time.
- Generation of huge amount of data at high speed.
- Requires distribution and replication of multi-dimensional data.
- Support of virtual e-governance communities.
- Requires good security environment for data storage and data retrieval.
- Requires data integrity, data confidentiality and data accountability.

Basically, e-governance refers to the use of sources like internet, cell phone sets in order to improve the government policies. E-services provides good delivery of government services to citizens or businesses.

## NEED OF BIG DATA IN GOVERNMENT SECTOR

Every e-government application requires effective processes technology and data for successful implementation (Dhoot, 2014). Technical approaches are unable to handle such large amount of heterogeneous data.

1.  **Data Sharing:** Before the announcement of any social scheme, the government predict the population on the basis of health care data store hence share data with each other for further processing
2.  **Learning from Data:** On the basis of collected data from citizen, the government can improve the planning and schemes for the citizen satisfaction.
3.  **Grouping:** By analysis data from past year we can improve the data for future work. Big data provides new possibilities for grouping by granularity.
4.  **Unexplored Questions:** Traditional methods were failed to extract hidden patterns from multidimensional data, it is very complex and next to impossible to extract meaning from multi-dimensional data. Big data analysis provides high degree of meaning extraction. We can predict the weather and alert the farmers when to plant when to water, etc.

## BIG DATA FRAMEWORK

Big data framework can be divided into four main components: Resource management, Data management, data analysis and discovery of unexplored questions and the last is report.

1.  **Resource Management:** Different organizations have different framework to handle big data, all have different strength and capabilities for solving problems. Resource utilization, maintenance, performance and cost all these framework should run under common cluster.
2.  **Data Management:** This level is used to organize variety of data i.e. to organize all types of structured and unstructured data for analysis. Relational Database management system and NoSql are the data models used in third level. RDBMS is used to speed up the processing of huge data. Sqoop is used to transfer bulk data between Hadoop related systems.
3.  **Data Analysis and Discovery of Unexplored Questions:** This layer is used to analyse data and to predict unexplored questions. We can predict the future with the help of present data and can improve the working in various fields.

4. **Report:** This level is used to report the data. Tools for interactive and dynamic report and visualized output are animated. Behavioral analysis, risk analysis comparative analysis are some of the examples.

## CHALLENGES OF E-GOVERNANCE

The successful implementation of e-governance is one of the difficult tasks. Clouds provide the successful implementation of e-government policies as well as services (Accountabiulity Inmitiatiove, 2016). The e-governance can face the following challenges:

- **Scaling Data (Scaling Up and Scaling Out):** The e-government projects deal with huge amount of data, so it should support high end as well as distributed scalability. When data is too high, we scale bigger system either by scaling up and scaling out. In scaling out process we add more nodes to the system whereas in scaling up we add more resources to a single node.
- **Auditing:** Services are trace at regular interval .These services are used to control fraud in government departments. Regular auditing should be done to ensure high security. Cloud makes auditing process easier by analysing the data and detects the fraud if any.
- **Replication:** Government works at different levels therefore government applications should be presented at different level to the citizens. Cloud support the excellent architecture for replication ie the same data can be available at different level. Hence provide high availability.
- **Disaster Recovery:** Natural disaster like flood, wars, earthquakes etc makes the government services unavailable and sometimes loses the data. Cloud technologies provide back up and restoring facilities (Tiwari, Naveen, & Sharma, 2013). Therefore in the occurrence of any disaster data can easily be restored.
- **Performance:** Government technologies are required to meet the citizen's requirement. The increase in number of citizens or demand the performance should not be degraded. The e-government applications can be scaled up with the help of cloud.

## CONCLUSION

This chapter provides the overview of big data e-governance, needs, challenges and its framework. E-governance needs big data to be reliable, fast and efficient. The

*Table 1. Comparative study between traditional and big data e-government*

| Parameters | Traditional E-Government | Big Data E-Government |
|---|---|---|
| *Architecture* | *Centralized* | *Distributed* |
| Data | Structured data | Raw, unstructured and semi-structured |
| Data Size | Data in Tera bytes | Large and messy data |
| Type of analysis | Text analysis | Graph, audio and video |
| Data Model | Fixed schema | Schema less |
| Applications | Batch oriented and needs to wait jobs to complete before the hidden meaning is obtained | In real time applications |

policies should work efficiently and faster because the trust of a citizen is the main concern. The extraction of meaningful data from large variety of data is a critical issue in big data hence new approaches must be developed; therefore additional research is necessary to improve the efficiency of data in e-governance. To deal huge amount of data cloud based recovery, back up can play a complementary role in a storage strategy. Any government can change to a good government by the use of valuable raw materials. Due to this reason big data has attracted a lot of attention in government.

This chapter basically discusses the key concepts of veracity in big data on e-governance. Its main aim is to provide the comprehensive overview big data in e-governance. E-government is still struggling to move advanced level of development. Current e-government applications handles only structured data and sharing between the applications is also difficult. Recently NIC is building a platform for e-governance which can be an excellent way for big innovations in big data. There is still a lot of work to make e-government more reliable and popular.

# REFERENCES

Analytics & Modelling Division – NIC. (2015). *Business Intelligence and e-Governemnt*. National Informatic Centre, Department of Information Technology, Ministry of Communication & IT. Retrieved from http;//www.modelling.nic.in/bi-egov.doc

Dhoot, V. (2014). PMO using Big Data techniques on mygov.in to translate popular mood into government action. *The Economic Times*. Retrieved from http://articles. economictimes.indiatimes.com/2014-11-26/news/56490626_1_mygov-digital-india-modi-government

Inmitiatiove, A. (2016). *Big Data and Development*. Retrieved from http://www.accountabilityindia.in/accountabilityblog/2580-data-explosion-big-data-and-development

Lobo, S. (2015). *Government Will Adopt Big Data on a Massive Scale. Analytics Training*. Retrieved from http://analyticstraining.com/2015/jigsaw-academys-predictions-analytics-big-data-industry-2015/

Rajagopalan, M. R. (2013). Big Data Framework for National e-Governance Plan. *IEEE 2013 Eleventh International Conference on ICT and Knowledge Engineering*.

Satpathy, B. N., & Chanana, A. K. (2014). Open Data Initiative of Government of India – Fostering Innovations, Creating Opportunities. Planning Commission. Retrieved from http://www.unece.org/fileadmin/DAM/stats/documents/ece/ces/ge.50/2014/Topic_3_India.pdf

Tiwari, N., & Sharma, M.K. (2013). Cloud based Working Concept for E-Governance Citizen Charter. *International Journal of Advanced Research in Computer Science and Software Engineering, 3*(6).

Walker, A. (2014). *Trends in Big Data: A Forecast for 2014, Big Data & Analytics*. Retrieved from http://www.csc.com/big_data/publications/91710/105057-big_data_trends_2014_prediction

# Chapter 3
# Hybrid Biometrics and Watermarking Authentication

**Kareem Kamal A. Ghany**
*BeniSuef University, Egypt*

**Hossam M. Zawbaa**
*Babes-Bolyai University, Romania*

## ABSTRACT

*There are many tools and techniques that can support management in the information security field. In order to deal with any kind of security, authentication plays an important role. In biometrics, a human being needs to be identified based on some unique personal characteristics and parameters. In this book chapter, the researchers will present an automatic Face Recognition and Authentication Methodology (FRAM). The most significant contribution of this work is using three face recognition methods; the Eigenface, the Fisherface, and color histogram quantization. Finally, the researchers proposed a hybrid approach which is based on a DNA encoding process and embedding the resulting data into a face image using the discrete wavelet transform. In the reverse process, the researchers performed DNA decoding based on the data extracted from the face image.*

DOI: 10.4018/978-1-5225-1703-0.ch003

## INTRODUCTION

Biometrics identification have been a popular topic of research and study for the last decades. The number of fields that it involves makes this topic relevant through many departments and research institutions. From scientist, psychologists and many different fields of engineering and computer science has resulted in a considerable amount of knowledge. Many face analysis, face modeling, and DNA encoding techniques have progressed significantly in the last decade. However, the reliability of biometrics identification schemes still poses a great challenge to the scientific community.

Biometrics identification is an inherently difficult problem for both humans and computers. This is due to many problems and adaptations in the inputs related to the actual images of faces. The nature of human faces and fingerprint furthermore complicate this task. The spatial layout of faces being so similar makes the task somewhat challenging. This is before considering the difference in appearance of a single individual due to age, hairstyles, make-up, facial hair or glasses. Even if we could eliminate these variations of each individual, the variability of the input image due to pose, lighting and picture quality all make the process of face recognition a very complex undertaking. With all these difficulties Humans have the great ability to recognize a face in a large crowd within seconds.

DNA typing is very useful in crime detection. Since DNA requires a form of blood, tissue, or other bodily sample, it has not yet been adopted as a major biometrics method, even though it is now possible to analyze human within 10 minutes.

The DNA bases are combined in specific sequences to form base pairs which determine the physiology and anatomy of the organism. Each base pair with phosphate and sugar creates a nucleotide. Nucleotides form two long strands connected by the base pairs as a ladder and form the characteristic double helix.

Digital watermarking methods should be imperceptible in order to be effective, while at the same time robust to common image manipulations like rotation, compression, scaling, filtering, cropping, and collusion attacks through other signal processing operations. Current digital image watermarking techniques can be grouped into two main categories: spatial domain watermarking and frequency domain watermarking algorithms.

## THE PROPOSED FACE RECOGNITION AND AUTHENTICATION SYSTEM

The proposed Face Recognition and Authentication System are composed of three main phases; pre-processing, feature extraction, and classification and authentication phases. Figure 1 describes the structure of the Face Recognition and Authentication System.

## Pre-Processing Phase

By means of early vision techniques, face images are normalized and enhanced to improve the recognition performance of the system. The following pre-processing steps can be implemented in a face recognition system:

*Figure 1. The face recognition and authentication system: general structure*

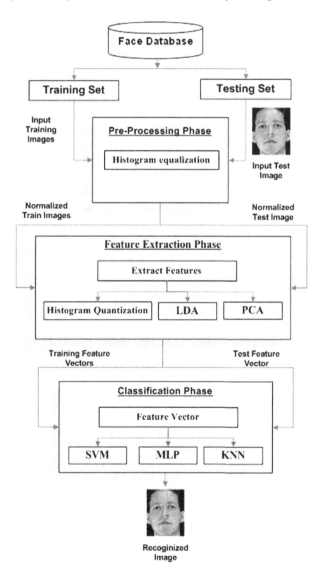

- *Image Size Normalization:* Because the Principal Components Analysis (PCA) and the Linear Discriminate Analysis (LDA) involve multiplication of arrays, it is important to normalize the size of all images. This is done by resizing all images to a default image size such as 112 x 92 pixels as in the ORL database the researchers used in this work to guarantee that information about the eyes, nose, and mouth is not lost in potentially small versions of images.

- *Illumination Normalization:* The general purpose of illumination normalization (Huang et al., 2008) is to decrease lighting effect when the observed images are captured in different lighting environments. A common approach is to adjust observed images to approximate the ones captured under a standard lighting condition.

- *Histogram Equalization:* Histogram equalization (Histogram et al., 2005) is a process of adjusting the image so that each intensity level contains an equal number of pixels such that the appearance of the image is improved by balancing light and dark areas. Histogram equalization (HE) (Histogram et al., 2005) can be used as a simple but very robust way to obtain light correction when applied to small regions such as faces. HE is to maximize the contrast of an input image, resulting in a histogram of the output image which is as close to a uniform histogram as possible. However, this does not remove the effect of a strong light source but maximizes the entropy of an image, thus reducing the effect of differences in illumination within the same "setup" of light sources. By doing so, HE makes facial recognition a somehow simpler task.

Two examples of HE of images can be seen in Figure 2.

## FEATURE EXTRACTION ALGORITHMS

A number of methods have been proposed in the last decades (Xiaoyan et al., 2006). In the field of face recognition, the dimension of the facial images is very high and

*Figure 2. Histogram equalization*

 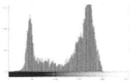  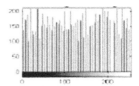

a) Before histogram Equalization              b) After histogram Equalization

require considerable amount of computing time for classification. The classification and subsequent recognition time (Huang et al., 2008) can be reduced by reducing dimension of the image data. Principal component analysis (PCA) (Xiaoyan et al., 2006) is one of the popular methods used for feature extraction and data representation. It not only reduces the dimensionality of the image, but also retains some of the variations in the image data and provides a compact representation of a face image. The key idea of the PCA method is to transform the face images into a small set of characteristics feature images, called eigenface, which are the principal components of the initial training set of the face images. PCA yields projection directions that maximize the total scatter across all classes, i.e., across all face images. In recognition process a test image is projected into the lower-dimension face space spanned by the eigenfaces and then classified either by using statistical theory or a classifier. The PCA method was developed in (Xiaoyan et al., 2006).

## Principal Component Analysis (PCA)

We implemented a face recognition system using the Principal Component Analysis (PCA) (Eleyan & Demirel, 2007) algorithm. Automatic face recognition systems try to find the identity of a given face image according to their memory. The memory of a face recognizer is generally simulated by a training set. In this chapter, our training set consists of the features extracted from known face images of different persons. Thus, the task of the face recognizer is to find the most similar feature vector among the training set to the feature vector of a given test image. Here, the researchers want to recognize the identity of a person where an image of that person (test image) is given to the system. You will use PCA as a feature extraction algorithm. The researchers had 6 steps to perform a principal component analysis on a set of data.

1.    Get face images.

$$x_i = \left[ p_i \dots p_N \right]^T, i = 1, \dots, M$$

where $X_i$ is the face image, M is the total number of images in the training set, P is the pixel color values, and T is transpose of the vector.

2.    Get the images mean.

$$m = \frac{1}{M} \sum_{i=1}^{M} x_i$$

3.    Subtract each image from mean image

$$x_i = x_i - m$$

4.    Calculate the covariance matrix.

$$\text{cov}(X,Y) = \frac{\sum_{i=1}^{n}(x_i - \bar{x})(x_i - \bar{x})^T}{(n-1)}$$

5.    Calculate the eigenvectors and eigenvalues of the covariance matrix.

$$\lambda_i = \frac{1}{M}\sum_{n=1}^{M}(e_i^T w_n)^2$$

$e^T$ is the energy of the $i^{th}$ Eigenvector, $W$ is the orthonomal "basis" for the reconstructed image space.

6.    Choosing components and forming a feature vector

Our target to select the Eigenvectors with the largest Eigenvalues, one selects the dimensions along which the face images vary the most. Since the Eigenvectors are ordered high to low by the amount of variance found between images along each Eigenvector, the last Eigenvectors find the smallest amounts of variance. The researchers set the minimum number of Eigenvectors to guarantee that energy e is greater than a threshold. A typical threshold is 0.95. If we define $e_i$ as the energy of the $i^{th}$ Eigenvector, it is the ratio of the sum of all Eigenvalues up to and including i over the sum of all the Eigenvalues.

$$e_i = \frac{\sum_{j=1}^{1}\lambda_j}{\sum_{j=1}^{k}\lambda_j} \tag{1}$$

Feature Vector = $(v_1, v_2, v_{3,} \ldots v_i)$

In the training phase (Eleyan & Demirel, 2007; Sahoolizadeh & Heidari, 2008), you should extract feature vectors for each image in the training set. Let $\Omega_A$ be a training image of person A which has a pixel resolution of M × N (M rows, N columns). In order to extract PCA features of $\Omega_A$, you will first convert the image into a pixel vector $\phi_A$ by concatenating each of the M rows into a single vector. The length (or, dimensionality) of the vector $\phi_A$ will be M ×N. In this chapter, you will use the PCA algorithm as a dimensionality reduction technique which transforms the vector $\phi A$ to a vector $\omega A$ which has a dimensionality d where d << M × N. For each training image $\Omega i$, you should calculate and store these feature vectors $\omega i$.

One of the most common problems in pattern recognition systems is the known as "curse of dimensionality". It is common to represent our data in a high dimensional space (for example an image can be represented as a point in a space with dimension the size of the image), and we could think that the high dimensionality of the data only would effect on the time and resources we will use, but there are more subjects to deal with. In summary, the problem is that as the researchers increased the number of dimensions of our feature space the volume of the space increases exponentially and for that reason, the potential complexity of the probability density functions is higher. It has been seen that, for a fixed amount of training data, the performance of the system improves when the number of features grows until a certain point when the performance decreases, as you see in Figure 3.

In the recognition phase (Sahoolizadeh & Heidari, 2008) (or, testing phase), you will be given a test image $\Omega_j$ of a known person. Let $\alpha_j$ be the identity (name) of this person. As in the training phase, you should compute the feature vector of this person using PCA and obtain $\omega_j$ . In order to identify $\Omega_j$, you should compute the similarities between $\omega_j$ and the entire feature vectors $\omega_i$'s in the training set. The similarity between feature vectors can be computed using Euclidean distance. The identity of the most similar $\omega_i$ will be the output of our face recognizer. If i = j, it means that we have correctly identified the person j, otherwise if i ≠ j, it means that we have misclassified the person j.

*Figure 3. Reducing the dimensionality of the data, we speeded up the computations, without losing too much information*

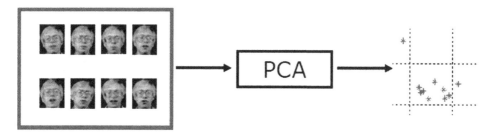

## Linear Discriminant Analysis (LDA)

In (Sahoolizadeh & Heidari, 2008), the PCA method is used for dimension reduction for linear discriminate analysis (LDA), generating a new paradigm, which called fisherface. The fisherface (Byung-Joo, 2005) approach is more insensitive to variations of lighting, illumination and facial expressions. However, this approach is more computationally expensive than the PCA approach.

In face recognition, each face is represented by a large number of pixel values. Linear discriminate analysis is primarily used here to reduce the number of features to a more manageable number before classification. Each of the new dimensions is a linear combination of pixel values, which form a template. The linear combinations obtained using LDA finds an efficient way to represent the face vector space by exploiting the class information. It differentiates individual faces but recognizes faces of the same individual. (Juwei et al., 2003). the images in the training set are divided into the corresponding classes. LDA (Juwei et al., 2003; Byung-Joo 2005) is an example of a class specific method, in the sense that it tries to "shape" the scatter in order to make it more reliable for classification. This method selects W in such a way that the ratio of the between class scatter and the within a class scatter is maximized.

Given the data images $U_i$, steps 1-4 compute the PCA eigenvectors; Step 5 computes the projected LDA (Juwei Lu et al., 2003) data on those Eigenvectors. Steps 6-8 compute the LDA directions which separate the data.

1.  Subtract the sample mean from the data:

$$y_i = U_i - \mu$$
$$i = 1, 2, ..., n$$

Where $U_i$ is the face image sample, $\mu$ is the mean face image from all samples.

2.  Compute the Covariance Matrix S:

$$s = \sum_{i=1}^{n} Y_i Y_i^T$$

3.  Compute eigenvectors $\{v1, v2 ... vk\}$ corresponding to the largest k eigenvalues of S.
4.  Let $v1, v2 ... vk$ be the columns of eigenvector matrix $A = [v1, v2 ... vk]$.
5.  The new projected LDA data are:

$$Z_i = A^T Y_i$$
$$i = 1, 2, ..., n$$

Where A is the eigenvector matrix, $Y_i$ is the face sample image.

6.  Compute the sample mean $\mu_2$ of the LDA data and the sample mean $\mu_{Zj}$ of each class.
7.  Compute the class scatter matrix $S_b$ and the within class scatter matrix $S_w$.

$$s_b = \sum_{i=1}^{c} n_i (\mu_{Zi} - \mu_Z)(\mu_{Zi} - \mu_Z)^T ; s_w = \sum_{i=1}^{c} \sum_{classK} (Z_K - \mu_{Zi})(Z_K - \mu_{Zi})^T$$

$n_i$ is the number of training samples in class i, c is the number of distinct classes, $\mu_{Zj}$ is the mean vector of samples belonging to class i and $Z_K$ represents the set of samples belonging to class k.

8.  Solve:

$$S_b w = \lambda S_w w \Rightarrow [w_1, w_2, ..., w_{c-1}]$$

## Color Histogram Quantization

In last decade; the color histogram based methods have proved simplicity and usefulness. Initially, this idea was based on Color Histogram Quantization. (Histogram et al., 2005). The researchers proposed an algorithm for computing histogram of grayscale images with 256 gray levels are used and using 24 quantization levels.

In the proposed histogram (Histogram et al., 2005; Basit et al., 2007), we got the frequency for every gray level value, so, we will have a vector nx1, where n indicates number of different gray levels in the image (as index) and its value is for the frequency of that gray level in the image. After that we quantized the gray level frequency vector into 24 quantization level with eleven gray level width (256/11= 23.3 ≈ 24 quantization level).

For training phase, Firstly, the frequency of every gray level is computed and stored in vector for further processing. Secondly, we did a quantization (Basit et al., 2007) by get the mean of consecutive eleven frequencies from the stored vectors is calculated and kept to use in testing phase. And we did the same previous processing for each testing image. So, we have a mean vector for each training images and mean vector for the test image to get its best face matching from training set. When we used the KNN classifier, it mentions on the next section in feature matching, we calculated the absolute differences among the mean of training set images and the test image mean vector, and finally, the minimum difference found identifies the matched class for the test image.

The recognition accuracy with KNN is of 100% and with SVM is 91.5% when we used 60% of faces images for training and 40% for testing, you can find all results in the experimental result section.

## FEATURE MATCHING

Feature matching (Xiaoyan et al., 2006) is the actual recognition process. The feature vector obtained from the feature extraction is matched to classes (persons) of facial images already enrolled in a database.

The choice of the classifier (Xiaoyan et al., 2006) is the next challenging stage of our system. The election of the classifier is not as dependent of the application like feature selection, and in many cases it is done by the availability of the algorithm. The researchers can find three main approaches in the design of the classifiers depending on the concept they are based on:

1.	Similarity,
2.	Geometry or
3.	Probability.

The first type of classifiers is based on similarity; that is, similar patterns should correspond to the same class. One of the possible techniques is template matching; that is, the pattern to be recognized is matched against the stored templates and then a similarity measure like a correlation is estimated. Another option is the use of a minimum distance classifier, where we should select a metric (e.g. Euclidean) and a prototype for the class, for example the mean of the samples of every class. Then the class with a minimum distance between the sample and the prototype is chosen.

The second type is based on geometry. These classifiers try to estimate the decision boundaries; that is, the hyper planes that separates the classes, directly by optimizing some error criteria. Examples of this approach are support vector machines (SVM).

Finally, we have the probabilistic approach, Depending on the available information. If we do not have any information, we can only make a decision based on the a priori class probability, obtained from a large enough number of random samples, and then choose the class with the higher probability.

# CLASSIFICATION

The choice of the classifier is the next challenging stage of our system. As we have commented previously, the election of the classifier is not as dependent of the application like feature selection, and in many cases it is done by the availability of the algorithm.

Now the problem is how to classify the feature vectors in different classes to help us on the recognition of the faces. One of the first ideas about this problem is the one commented in (Xiaoyan et al., 2006). This simple method consists in finding the face class $k$ that minimizes the Euclidian distance between the vector $x$ and the vector $xk$ which describes the $k$th class. The vectors $xk$ are calculated by averaging the feature vectors of the training faces of the same person. So, for each new face to be identified, the vector $x$ is calculated and also the distances to each known class. If the minimum distance is lower than a fixed threshold, we could classify the face to that class, and if it is greater, it may be classified as unknown and optionally used to begin a new face class. Finally, the eigenfaces are recalculated to add the new faces classified as known to the model. We will focus on two classifiers the: $k$-NN and SVM.

## K-Nearest-Neighbor Algorithm (K-NN)

The first classifier we will take about, the $k$-NN ($k$-nearest neighbor) (Chiriacescu, 2009) is one of the simplest classification techniques, it is based on similarity and it is based also on the idea of finding the classes of the $k$-nearest neighbor vectors. Then the most represented class on those $k$ neighbors is found and it is assigned to the test sample.

In this algorithm the classification of a new object is based on attributes and training samples, the result of new instance query is classified based on majority of K-nearest neighbor category (K is predefined integer), given a query point, the algorithm find K number of objects or training points closest to the query point. Simply it works based on minimum distance from the searching query to the training one to determine the K-nearest neighbors, after we gathered K-nearest neighbors we take simple majority of these K-nearest neighbors to be the prediction of the query instance.

We can compute the distance between query instance and each training data using some distance function d(x,y), *where* x,y are the *s*amples composed of N features, such that

$x=\{x1,x2,...,x_N\}, y=\{y_1,y2,...,y_N\}$

We used Euclidean distance measuring as distance function.

$$d(x,y) = \sum_{i=1}^{N} \sqrt{x_i^2 - y_i^2} \qquad (2)$$

1. **Advantages of K-Nearest Neighbors:** Robust to noisy training data especially in Inverse Square of weighted distance and effective if the training data is large.
2. **Disadvantages of KNN:** Need to determine value of parameter K (number of nearest neighbors), distance based learning is not clear which type of distance to use and which attribute to use to produce the best results, and computation cost is quite high because we need to compute distance of each query instance to all training samples.

## Support Vector Machines (SVM)

The second classifier we will take about is the Support vector machines; SVM (Zhifeng & Tang, 2004) is a binary classification method it is based on geometry. (SVMs) give us a supervised learning method for classifying both facial features and individuals based upon these. After a decent amount of training, an SVM (Zhifeng & Tang, 2004) can predict whether an input falls into one of two categories. This is done by first constructing a hyper plane in a high dimensional space and then mapping input to points in this space. The input is determined to be in one category or the other by measuring its distance from the hyper plane. The strength of the category correspondence is then given by the magnitude of this distance.

## Basic Theory of Support Vector Machine

The basic idea of SVM (Du et al., 2002) is to map the linear non-separable input vectors into some higher dimensional space such that a more suitable hyper plane can be found with minimal classification errors.

We started with training data,

$$D = \{(x_i, y_i)\}_{i=1}^{1} \qquad (3)$$

where $x_i$ is the input vector, $y_i$ is the target output and $y_i \in \{-1,1\}, x_i \in R^N$

Then map the training data into some other inner product space F via a nonlinear map,

$$\phi : R^N \to F \tag{4}$$

The separating hyper plane in the space F must satisfy the following constraints,

$$y_i(w^T z_i + b) \geq 1, z_i \in F, i = 1, 2, ..., 1 \tag{5}$$

Where w is normal to the hyper plane, T is the transpose of the vector, $z_i$ is the input vector, b / ‖w‖ is the perpendicular distance from the hyper plane to the origin, the hyper plane capable of performing a linear separation of the training data and the optimal hyper plane H is $w_D^T z + b_D = 0$.

We can constrain the hyper plane is to observe that on either side of the hyper plane, we may have $\mathbf{w}^T\mathbf{x}+b>=0$ or $\mathbf{w}^T\mathbf{x}+b<0$. Thus, if we placed the hyper plane midway between the two closest points to the hyper plane, the distance between the closest vectors to the hyper plane H is,

$$p(w,b) = \min_{\{x \mid y = 1\}} \frac{z^T w}{\| w \|} - \max_{\{x \mid y = -1\}} \frac{z^T w}{\| w \|} \tag{6}$$

With its maximum,

$$p(w_0, b_0) = \frac{2}{\| w_0 \|} = \frac{2}{\sqrt{w_0^T w_0}} \tag{7}$$

where $x_{y=1}$ and $x_{y=-1}$ are two points on opposite sides of the hyper plane, Where $w_0$ is the maximum normal to the hyper plane, T is the transpose of the vector, $z_i$ is the input vector, $b_0$ / ‖$w_0$‖ is the maximum perpendicular distance from the hyper plane to the origin, the canonical hyper plane is found by maximizing the margin, and the minimum distance between two classes is at least [2/(‖$\mathbf{w}$‖)]

So, the optimal separating hyper plane is determined by the vector w, which minimizes the functional.

$$\phi(w) = \frac{1}{2}(w^T w) \tag{8}$$

Subject to $y_i(w^T z_i + b) \geq 1, i = 1, 2, ..., 1$ where $\phi(w)$ is the optimal separating hyperplane.

It's modified for the non-separable case to,

$$\phi(w) = \frac{1}{2} w^T w + \gamma \sum_{i=1}^{1} \xi_i \tag{9}$$

where the $\xi_i$ are measure of the misclassification error. In terms of Lagrange multipliers, $w_0$ can be written as

$$w_0 = \sum_{i=1}^{1} \lambda_i y_i z_i \tag{10}$$

so the decision function,

$$f = \text{sgn}\left[\sum_{i=1}^{1} \lambda_i y_i (z^T z_i) + b\right] \tag{11}$$

In order to impose the equality constraint we introduced an additional Lagrange multiplier $\lambda$, $\lambda \in [0, 1]$, The theorem of functional analysis shows that a positive semi definite symmetrical function K(u, v) can solely define a Hilbert space $H_k$, K is the reproducing kernel of feature space $H_k$,

$$K(u, v) = \sum_{k} \alpha_k \varphi_k(u) \varphi_k(v) \tag{12}$$

where $\alpha_k$ are clearly positive or zero (in fact the $\alpha_k$ will only be zero if all training points have the same class), $\varphi_k$ is input vector in the feature space, K (u,v) is The kernel matrix, which represents a inner product in the feature space.

$$z_i^T z = \phi(x_i)^T \phi(x) = K(x_i, x) \tag{13}$$

where $\varphi$ is a function on $R^N$ with range $\{\pm 1, 0\}$, $\varphi(x_i) \in \{\pm 1\} \, \forall \, x_i$.

So, we will convince you that the corresponding Φ can map two vectors that are linearly dependent in L onto two vectors that are linearly independent in H.

The decision function can thus be written as

$$f = \text{sgn} \left[ \sum_{i=1}^{1} \lambda_i y_i K(x_i, x) + b \right] \tag{14}$$

The K[th] classifier will be trained to classify the training data of class k against all other training data. The decision function for each of the classifier will be combined to give the final classification decision on the K-class classification problem.

## SVM in Multi-Class Classification

The formulation of SVM (Zhifeng & Tang, 2007) in previous section was based on a two-class problem; hence SVM is basically a binary classifier. Several different schemes can be applied to the basic SVM algorithm to handle the K-class pattern classification problem. The schemes which have been proposed in (Histogram et al., 2005) for solving the multi-class problem are as listed below:

Using k one-to-rest classifiers is the simplest scheme, and it does give reasonable results. K classifiers will be constructed, one for each class. The K[th] classifier will be trained to classify the training data of class k against all other training data. The decision function for each of the classifier will be combined to give the final classification decision on the K-class classification problem,

$$f(x) = \frac{\arg \max}{k} \sum_{i=1}^{1} \lambda_i^k y_i K^k(x_i, x) + b^k \tag{15}$$

Using k (k-1)/2 pair wise classifiers with majority voting or pair wise coupling as the voting scheme. The schemes require a binary classifier for each possible pair of classes. The decision function of the SVM classifier for K[i] -to-K[j] and K[j] -to-K[i] has reflection symmetry in the zero planes. Hence only one of these pairs of classifier is needed. The total number of classifiers for a K-class problem will then be K (K-1)/2. The training data for each classifier is a subset of the available training data, and it will only contain the data for the two involved classes. The data will be reliable accordingly, i.e. one will be labeled as +1 whiles the other as -1. These classifiers will then be combined with some voting scheme to give the final classification results, such as majority voting or pair wise coupling.

# THE PROPOSED DNA RECOGNITION AND AUTHENTICATION SYSTEM

The proposed hybrid two ways approach based on DNA encoding process and embedding it into the face template by using Discrete Wavelet Transform (DWT) and Inverse Discrete Wavelet Transform (IDWT) then we applied the enrollment process applied in (Ghany et al., 2013) as shown in Figure 4. Also we applied the DNA decoding process and extracting it from the face template by using (DWT) after applying the authentication process applied in (Ghany et al., 2013) as shown in Figure 5.

## DNA Encoding and Decoding

A DNA sequence contains four nucleic acid bases (Zhang et al., 2010) A. adenine, C .cytosine, G .guanine, T .thymine, where A and T are complementary, and G and C are complementary. In the binary, 0 and 1 are complementary, so 00 and 11 are complementary, 01 and 10 are also complementary. In this chapter, we used C, A, T, G to denote 00, 01, 10, 11, respectively.

*Figure 4. Enroll face image with DNA encoding*

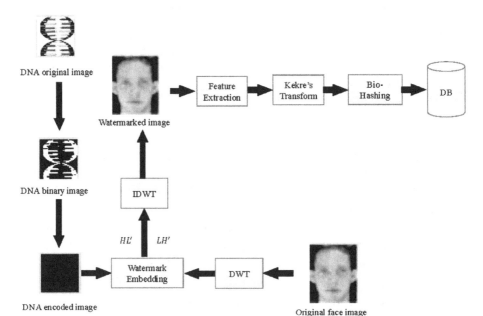

*Figure 5. Authenticate face image with DNA decoding*

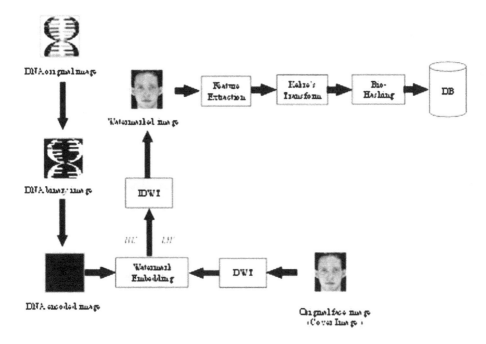

For 8 bit grey images, each pixel can be expressed a DNA sequence whose length is 4. For example: If the first pixel value of the original image is 173, convert it into a binary stream as T10101101U, by using the above DNA encoding rule to encode the stream, we can get a DNA sequence TTTGAU. Whereas using 00, 01, 10, 11 to denote C, A, T, G, respectively, to decode the above DNA sequence, we can get a binary sequence T10101101U.

DNA Encoding process is applied using the following steps:

1. Convert Binary sequence to DNA sequence as (00='A', 01='T', 10='C' and 11='G').
2. Apply Complementary Rule to DNA sequence as ((A) C), (C) G), (G) T), (T) A)).
3. Extract the index of each couple nucleotides in DNA reference sequence as the DNA Reference Sequence (Balsaminaceae).
4. Convert index to binary sequence again for the final representation of DNA image (W).

## Watermarking Embedding Using DWT

The proposed approach uses discrete wavelet transform for embedding the watermark into the detail wavelet coefficients of the original image using algorithm (2). In this process firstly we tacked the gray scale original fingerprint image and the 3-level DWT is applied to the image which decomposes image into low frequency and high frequency components. At the same time, the 3-level DWT is also applied to the watermark DNA image which is to be embedded in the fingerprint template.

We used the alpha blending technique (Sharma & Swami, 2013) for inserting the watermark. In this technique the decomposed components of the host image and the watermark are multiplied by a scaling factor and are added.

The Watermarking Embedding technique is applied using the following steps:

1. Apply the 3-level DWT to cover image (CI) to generate the its wavelet coefficients (LL1, LH1, HL1, and HH1).
2. HL0 = HL + ($\alpha$ * W), where HL is the high frequency components and $\alpha$ is a scaling factor.
3. LH0 = LH + ($\alpha$ * W), where LH is the low frequency components.
4. Apply the 3-level IDWT to obtain watermarked image (Iw).

## Watermark Extraction Using DWT

In this process firstly we applied the 3-level DWT to the watermarked image and the cover image which decomposed the image in sub-bands. After that we recovered the DNA image from the watermarked image by using the alpha blending technique. After the extraction process is done, we applied the 3-level Inverse discrete wavelet transform to the watermark image coefficient to generate the final watermark extracted image.

The watermark extraction technique using DWT is applied using the following steps:

1. Apply the 3-level DWT to CI to generate the its wavelet coefficients (LL1, LH1, HL1, and HH1).
2. W= (LH0 - LH) / $\alpha$.
3. Convert each eight binary bits to decimal numbers to get the index.
4. Get the corresponding nucleotides using index from the DNA reference sequence to represent DNA sequence.
5. Apply Complementary Rule to DNA sequence as ((A → C), (C → G), (G → T), (T → A)).

6.  Convert DNA sequence to Binary sequence as ('A'=00, 'T'=01, 'C'=10 and 'G'=11).
7.  Reshape the binary sequence to represent the final DNA image.

## EXPERIMENTAL RESULTS

The ORL faces database is used in the experiments. The ORL faces database contains have 40 persons with 10 face images for each person with large illumination variation. We used a varying number of images as a training set and testing set, see Table 1.

The recognition rates for PCA with KNN ranges from 91.3% to 95%, and with SVM ranges from 85% to 93.8%, for different training and test percentage. The recognition rates for LDA with KNN ranges from 92.5% to 95.8%, and with SVM ranges from 77% to 92.5%, for different training and test percentage. The recognition rates for Histogram Quantization method with KNN ranges from 99.4% to 100%, and with SVM ranges from 88% to 95%, for different training and test percentage.

The experimental results for the proposed approach have been evaluated using the following measures:

1.  Structural Similarity Index Measure (SSIM): SSIM is a paradigm metric designed to improve on traditional methods like peak signal-to-noise ratio (PSNR) and mean square error (MSE) for quality assessment. It is based on the hypothesis that Human Visual System (HVS) is highly adapted for extracting structural information. The measure of structural similarity compares local patterns of pixel intensities that have been normalized for luminance and contrast. In practice a single overall index is sufficient enough to evaluate the overall image quality. SSIM is defined as in Equation 16:

$$SSIM(x,y) = \frac{(2\mu_x \mu_y + C_1)(2\sigma_x y + C_1)}{(\mu_x^2 + \mu_y^2 + C_1)(\sigma_x^2 + \sigma_y^2 + C_1)} \quad (16)$$

2.  Peak Signal to Noise Ratio (PSNR): Signal-to-noise ratio (SNR) is a mathematical measure of image quality based on the pixel difference between two images. The SNR measure is an estimate of quality of reconstructed image compared with original image. PSNR is defined as in Equation 17:

*Table 1. Experimental results of face recognition and authentication system*

| Total Classes | Training Percentage | Testing Percentage | Feature Extraction | Classifier | Total Correct | Total False | Accuracy |
|---|---|---|---|---|---|---|---|
| 40 | 60% | 40% | PCA | KNN | 146/160 | 14/160 | 91.25% |
| 40 | 70% | 30% | PCA | KNN | 112/120 | 8/120 | 93.3% |
| 40 | 80% | 20% | PCA | KNN | 75/80 | 5/80 | 93.75% |
| 40 | 90% | 10% | PCA | KNN | 38/40 | 2/40 | 95% |
| 40 | 60% | 40% | PCA | SVM | 136/160 | 24/160 | 85% |
| 40 | 70% | 30% | PCA | SVM | 105/120 | 15/120 | 87.5% |
| 40 | 80% | 20% | PCA | SVM | 75/80 | 5/80 | 93.75% |
| 40 | 90% | 10% | PCA | SVM | 37/40 | 3/40 | 92.5% |
| 40 | 60% | 40% | LDA | KNN | 151/160 | 9/160 | 94.4% |
| 40 | 70% | 30% | LDA | KNN | 115/120 | 5/120 | 95.8% |
| 40 | 80% | 20% | LDA | KNN | 76/80 | 4/80 | 95% |
| 40 | 90% | 10% | LDA | KNN | 37/40 | 3/40 | 92.5% |
| 40 | 60% | 40% | LDA | SVM | 123/160 | 37/160 | 77% |
| 40 | 70% | 30% | LDA | SVM | 99/120 | 21/120 | 82.5% |
| 40 | 80% | 20% | LDA | SVM | 70/80 | 10/80 | 87.5% |
| 40 | 90% | 10% | LDA | SVM | 37/40 | 3/40 | 92.5% |
| 40 | 60% | 40% | Histogram Quant. | KNN | 159/160 | 1/160 | 99.4% |
| 40 | 70% | 30% | Histogram Quant. | KNN | 120/120 | 0/120 | 100% |
| 40 | 80% | 20% | Histogram Quant. | KNN | 80/80 | 0/80 | 100% |
| 40 | 90% | 10% | Histogram Quant. | KNN | 40/40 | 0/40 | 100% |
| 40 | 60% | 40% | Histogram Quant. | SVM | 141/160 | 19/160 | 88.13% |
| 40 | 70% | 30% | Histogram Quant. | SVM | 111/120 | 9/120 | 92.5% |
| 40 | 80% | 20% | Histogram Quant. | SVM | 74/80 | 6/80 | 92.5% |
| 40 | 90% | 10% | Histogram Quant. | SVM | 38/40 | 2/40 | 95% |

$$PSNR = 10\log_{10} \frac{\max^2}{MSE} \tag{17}$$

where max = 255 for an 8-bit image, MSE is the Mean Square Error, and the PSNR is basically the SNR when all pixel values are equal to the maximum possible value.

3.    Mean Square Error (MSE): MSE is computed by averaging the squared intensity of the original (input) image and the watermarked (output) image pixels as given in Equation 18:

$$MSE = \frac{1}{\min} \sum_{x=0}^{m-1} \sum_{y-1}^{n-1} (1(x,y) - W(x,y))^2 \qquad (18)$$

where *I* and *W* are the original and the watermarked images having a resolution of (m * n)

The result of the evaluation measures is shown in Table 2.

The target histogram must ensure that the watermarked image is most likely or identical to the original image, and we proved that with the resulted histograms as shown in Figure 6.

Also to compare the similarity of the two images mathematically we used the correlation equation shown in Equation 19:

$$r = \frac{n\sum xy - (\sum x)(\sum y)}{\sqrt{(n\sum x^2 - (\sum x)^2)(n\sum y^2 - (\sum y)^2)}} \qquad (19)$$

The correlation coefficient always takes a value between -1 and 1, and if the value is 1 or -1 this indicates perfect correlation, when we applied the previous equation on all embedding factors we found that the embedding factor equal to ten gives almost the perfect correlation between the original image and the watermarked image.

*Table 2. Experimental results of DNA recognition and authentication system*

| Embedding Factor (k) | SSIM | PSNR | MSE |
|---|---|---|---|
| 10 | 0.0712 | 26.8133 | 135.4416 |
| 30 | 0.0705 | 26.8007 | 135.8337 |
| 50 | 0.0694 | 26.7817 | 136.4306 |
| 70 | 0.0681 | 26.7705 | 136.7836 |
| 90 | 0.066 | 26.786 | 136.8432 |
| 110 | 0.0653 | 26.7691 | 136.8254 |
| 130 | 0.0640 | 26.7698 | 136.8057 |

*Figure 6. Authenticate face image with DNA decoding*

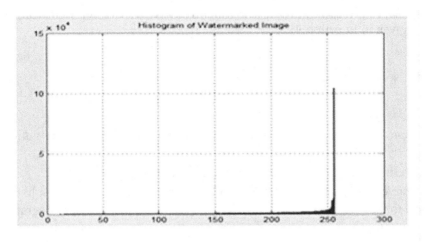

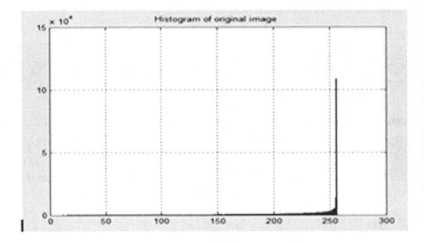

## CONCLUSION

In this chapter the researchers used a multimodal biometric approach combining the face image and the DNA to increase the security of the authentication system. The researchers used DWT to hide the DNA sequence into a face template, then The researchers used the approach proposed in Zhao, Chellappa, Phillips, and Rosenfeld (2003) to enroll the face template into the DB. On the other hand we succeeded in applying the inverse process to extract signature image from the watermarked image, then we used the approach proposed in Zhao, Chellappa, Phillips, and Rosenfeld (2003) to check the matching of the face template.

Our work focused on applying PCA, LDA and Histogram Quantization for feature extraction algorithms using the ORL (Olivetti Research Laboratories) database, it's made up of 400 images of 40 individuals, 10 of each person with various illuminations, expression and pose. Its grayscale image and the resolution is $112 \times 92$. The researchers have presented the face recognition experiment using the PCA and LDA methods were investigated and compared. The comparative experiment showed that the LDA (Fisherface) method outperformed the PCA (Eigenface) method. The usefulness of the Fisherface method under varying illumination was verified. The color histogram quantization method gets the best result more than PCA and LDA methods. And KNN classifier gets higher recognition rates than SVM classifier.

Also we evaluated our approach by using PSNR, SSIM and MSE, and we clearly found that the watermarks generated with the proposed approach are invisible and the quality of the watermarked image and the recovered image are improved.

In our future work, The ORL database is limited, so, we will try other data sets to check its results with methodology. Another improvement to our work may involve applying some other algorithms for face recognition and compare them with PCA, LDA and Histogram Quantization methods algorithms such as Neural Networks (feed forward, feed backward, Radial Basis Functions (RBF)). Also we will try to apply the proposed approach with another type of biometric such as human ear.

## ACKNOWLEDGMENT

This work was partially supported by the IPROCOM Marie Curie initial training network, funded through the People Programme (Marie Curie Actions) of the European Union's Seventh Framework Programme FP7/2007-2013/ under REA grant agreement No. 316555. This fund only applies to one author (Hossam M. Zawbaa).

## REFERENCES

Basit, F. E., Javed, Y., & Qayyum, U. (2007). Face Recognition using processed histogram and phase only correlation. *3rd IEEE International Conference on Emerging Technology*, 238-242.

Byung-Joo, O. (2005). Face Recognition using Radial Basis Function Network based on LDA. World Academy of Science, Engineering and Technology.

Chiriacescu, I. (2009). *Automatic Emotion Analysis Based on Speech* (MSc Thesis). Faculty of Eng, Mathematics and CS, Delft University of Technology.

Du, P., Zhang, Y., & Liu, C. (2002). *Face Recognition using Multi-class SVM*. The 5th Asian Conference on Computer Vision, Melbourne, Australia.

Eleyan, A., & Demirel, H. (2007). PCA and LDA based neural networks for human face recognition. I-Tech Education and Publishing.

Ghany, K. K. A., Hefny, H. A., Hassanien, A. E., & Tolba, M. F. (2013). *Kekres Transform for Protecting Fingerprint Template*. The 13th International Conference on Hybrid Intelligent Systems (HIS13), Tunisia.

Haddadnia, J., Ahmadi, M., & Raahemifar, K. (2003). An effective feature extraction methods for face recognition. *ICIP 2003*.

Huang, G. B., Narayana, M., & Miller, E. (2008). Towards unconstrained face recognition. *Proc. of IEEE Computer Society Workshop on Perceptual Organization in Computer Vision IEEE CVPR*.

Juwei, L., & Kostantinos, N. (2003, January). Face Recognition Using LDA Based Algorithms. *IEEE Transactions on Neural Networks*, *14*(1), 195–200. doi:10.1109/TNN.2002.806647

Kishore, K., Krishna, & Varma, G. (2010). Hybrid Face Recognition System using Multi Feature Neural Network. *Journal of Computing*, *2*(7).

Mandal, T., Jonathan, Q. M., & Yuan, Y. (2009). Curvelet based face recognition via dimension reduction. Elsevier.

Sahoolizadeh, A. H., & Heidari, B. Z. (2008). A New Face Recognition Method using PCA,LDA and Neural Network, World Academy of Science. *Engineering and Technology*, *41*, 7–12.

Sharma, P., & Swami, S. (2013). Digital Image Watermarking Using 3 level Discrete Wavelet Transform. *Conference on Advances in Communication and Control Systems* (CAC2S2013), 129-133.

Villegas, M., & Paredes, R. (2005). Comparison of illumination normalization methods for face recognition. In *Third COST 275 Workshop - Biometrics on the Internet*. University of Hertfordshire.

Xiaoyan, M., Watta, P., & Hassoun, M. H. (2006). A Weighted Voting and Sequential Combination of Classifiers Scheme for Human Face Recognition. *IEEE Conferences, Neural Networks*, 3929 – 3935.

Yang, J., Frangi, A. F., Yang, J., Zhang, D., & Jin, Z. (2005, February). KPCA Plus LDA: A Complete Kernel Fisher Discriminant Framework for Feature Extraction and Recognition. *IEEE Transactions on Pattern Analysis and Machine Intelligence*, *27*(2), 230–244. doi:10.1109/TPAMI.2005.33 PMID:15688560

Zhang, Q., Guo, L., & Wei, X. (2010). Image encryption using DNA addition combining with chaotic maps. *Mathematical and Computer Modelling*, *52*(11-12), 2028–2035. doi:10.1016/j.mcm.2010.06.005

Zhao, W., Chellappa, R., Phillips, J., & Rosenfeld, A. (2003, December). Face Recognition in Still and Video Images: A Literature Survey. *ACM Computing Surveys*, *35*(4), 399–458. doi:10.1145/954339.954342

Zhifeng, L., & Tang, X. (2004). Bayesian Face Recognition Using Support Vector Machine and Face Clustering. *IEEE Computer Society Conference on Computer Vision and Pattern Recognition* (CVPR'04).

Zhifeng, L., & Tang, X. (2007). *Using Support Vector Machines to Enhance the Performance of Bayesian Face Recognition. IEEE Transactions on Information Forensics And Security, 2*, 174–180.

Chapter 4

# An Empirical Investigation of M–Government Acceptance in Developing Countries:
## A Case of Kenya

**Gilbert Bundi Mwirigi**
*Ministry of Interior and Coordination
of National Government, South Korea*

**Jae Jeung Rho**
*Korea Advanced Institute of Science
and Technology, South Korea*

**Hangjung Zo**
*Korea Advanced Institute of Science
and Technology, South Korea*

**Min Jae Park**
*Korea Advanced Institute of Science
and Technology, South Korea*

## ABSTRACT

*Technological development in the past decade has motivated governments in developing countries to focus on leveraging new technologies for efficient and effective public service delivery. M-government has been singled out as one of the fundamental aspect for socio-economic growth in developing countries. Therefore, this study aims at investigating the factors that influence individuals in adoption of new technology, specifically m-government in the context of developing countries. Precisely, this study was to present and empirically validate a research model based on user behavior that examine m-government acceptance in developing countries and inspect the moderating role of facilitating conditions on m-government adoption. The*

DOI: 10.4018/978-1-5225-1703-0.ch004

*research model was tested using data from 248 respondents from Kenya, surveyed between August and September 2011. The results indicated that the proposed model explained a variance of 60.5 percent of behavior intention to use m-government. In addition, facilitating conditions were found to be a crucial spur to m-government acceptance in developing countries.*

## INTRODUCTION

In the quest to catch-up with the developed countries, governments in developing countries have been investing heavily on information technology in order to have an infrastructure that provides extensive and proactive services to their citizenry. However, these efforts are thwarted by low levels of acceptance of information technology. It is indisputable that m-government is an essential element for socio-economic improvement in developing countries; yet, little is known about factors and conditions surrounding its acceptance in developing countries.

Consequently, policy makers in developing countries are faced with a dilemma of determining the success levels of m-government projects before the actual introduction. Thus, unless there is a clear understanding of perspectives and factors related to how developing countries perceive and accept m-government (Avgerou, 2002), this essential technology will remain speculative, and therefore, alien to the populace in developing countries.

Prior, to the advent of the Internet, governments provided services manually through multiple service locations countrywide, for example, provincial, district, and location government administrative offices. In contrast, e-government which is predecessor to m-government, paved way for provision of services online. Recently, growth in mobile technologies, particularly the introduction of smart phones, ipads, and mobile phones that have access to the Internet and wireless networks, a new channel to deliver government services to the citizens in a more effective and economical way has been created (Du Preez, 2009; Yoojung Kim et al., 2004). These developments have advanced a new avenue known as m-government, which brings government services closer to the people. According to Ostberg (2003), m-government is the use of mobile wireless telecommunication technology within the public administration, to deliver services and information to citizens and businesses.

Currently, many governments in developing countries are directing their efforts towards efficient public service delivery through e-government projects (Ishmatova & Obi, 2009). However, advancement in mobile technology together with high mobile device penetration, which has by far exceeded personal computer adoption

(Al-Khamayseh et al., 2006) in many developing countries, has influenced many governments to consider m-government in public service delivery as it offers better personalization and easier accessibility to government services due to its mobility features. Ishmatova and Obi (2009) underscored the strength of "anywhere any time" ubiquitous access provided by mobile device technology, thereby promoting convenience to access government services without having to walk into Internet cafes or Internet community centers.

## OVERVIEW OF THE COUNTRY PROFILE

Kenya is relatively a large country covering about 581, 313 sq. km. with a population of 38.6 million people (Kenya National Bureau of Statistics, 2014). The population is not evenly distributed around the country in addition to the country having mountainous regions and vast areas of arid and semi-arid regions. Also, influencing the demographics is the socio-cultural behavior of communities, particularly the pastoralists who are known to move from one place to another in search of fodder for their animals. In this regard therefore, it poses a challenge to provide government services using e-government to these communities as they are always on the move. Furthermore, statistics from the telecommunication regulator Communications Authority of Kenya (CAK) indicated that mobile penetration has reached 80.5% of the total population in Kenya, with mobile networks covering over 90% of the total population and 45% of the land mass. This fact serves as a motivation to study the deployment of m-government as a supplement to e-government in areas that are not served by e-government due to lack of fixed telecommunication infrastructure.

## PURPOSE OF THE STUDY

While attempting to model the way in which government services can be channeled to reach every citizen in all corners of the country through the use of new technology such as m-government, the researchers appreciate the challenge of addressing the implication of individuals' adoption and use of technology, recognizing that adoption is not just about convincing people of the benefits of technology (selling the technology) but rather, training, teaching, and encouraging individuals to ensure they have the requisite skills and confidence (self-efficacy) so as to be successful in the use of technology. To this end therefore, the resolve of this study is to investigate the factors that influence individuals in adoption of new technology, specifically m-government in the context of developing world.

## LITERATURE REVIEW

In the past few years, developing countries have witnessed a rapid diffusion of mobile telephone and services which make m-government an inevitable technology (Kushchu & Kuscu, 2003). In addition, m-government exemplifies unique features and attributes such as mobility, ubiquity, convenience, localization, personalization, and device optimization (Serenko & Bontis, 2004) that enable government services to reach more people in remote and underserved areas.

Mobile government initiatives in developing countries are in their early stages, nevertheless, there is an increasing interest and acknowledgement that m-government has a potential to overcome the shortcomings of e-government such as mobility and convenience and therefore, it is poised to provide public services in a more efficient and effective way. However, like any other innovation, and despite the proclaimed benefits, m-government has not been widely accepted, and therefore, it has remained a "potential technology" only to be marveled at, while its actual implementation in developing countries remains a mirage. Consequently, unless m-government technology commands broad acceptance in developing countries, the asserted benefits will not be realized.

It is imperative to note that most of the previous studies that empirically verified factors that determine adoption and usage of information systems (e.g. Davis, 1989; Mathieson, 1991; Venkatesh & Davis, 2000) focused on usage behavior after the systems had already been implemented (Karahanna & Straub, 1999). According to Lu et al. (2005), the beliefs and motivation identified by those studies are mostly suitable for studying continued-use behavior.

Few studies have addressed the subject of behavior intention that encompasses pre-adoption criteria of information systems which remains a critical issue in information systems research (Lu et al., 2005). In the context of this study, pre-adoption criteria are an important aspect for acceptance of m-government in developing countries, which is still in its infant stages of implementation. In addition, Hung et al. (2006) highlighted two reasons contributing to failure of m-government to garner sufficient understanding. First, they noted that past studies on information system acceptance and adoption focused on businesses and profitable organizations with few studying government organizations. Second, much of the studies that have already been conducted and aimed at improving m-government services have not been empirically validated.

Consequently, this study was aimed at providing a useful instrument to policy makers in developing countries, which exemplifies possible drivers of acceptance of m-government that can be used as a basis for assessing the likelihood of success of m-government projects prior to implementation. Moreover, such knowledge can assist policy makers to proactively devise mechanisms aimed at stemming possible resistance to m-government. Specifically, this study was to:

1.  Present and empirically validate a research model based on user behavior that examines m-government acceptance in developing countries anchored on Social Cognitive Theory;
2.  Validate the model with data collected from a developing country; and
3.  Examine the moderating role of facilitating conditions on m-government acceptance in developing countries.

## THEORETICAL FRAMEWORK

Prior information systems research has proposed several theoretical models in an effort to conceptualize the complex behavioral and social process (Agarwal & Prasad, 1998) by which individuals accept new information technologies. Social Cognitive Theory (SCT)empirically validated a model for understanding and predicting an individual's behavior (Bandura, 1977, 1986). The theory is based on a model of causation involving triadic reciprocal determinism, where, behavior, cognitive and other personal factors, and environmental influences all operate as interacting determinants that influence each other bi-directionally (Bandura, 1977).

Behavior in a given situation is affected by environmental and cognitive factors (Compeau & Higgins, 1995b; Wu et al., 2010); as a result, people decide the surroundings in which they want to exist, in addition to being influenced by those surroundings. Environmental factors comprise social and physical environment that can influence an individual's behavior, while cognitive factors describe personal cognition, affect and biological events (Wu et al., 2010).

*Figure 1. Triadic reciprocality*
*Source: Adapted from Compeau & Higgins, 1995b*

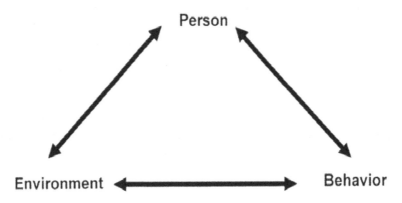

Like other theories in information system, SCT has many dimensions that have facilitated researchers in understanding and predicting both individual and group behavior. Furthermore, SCT has demonstrated its usefulness in identifying methods in which behavior can be adapted or changed. Many researchers have previously investigated people's behavior towards adoption and use of information technology in the field of information system through various theoretical perspectives (Compeau et al., 1999). Nevertheless, most theories perceive behavior as a result of a set of beliefs about technology and a set of affective responses to behavior; thus focusing almost entirely on beliefs about the technology and the outcomes of using it (Compeau et al., 1999). In contrast, SCT, embrace other beliefs such as self-efficacy that might influence behavior, independent of perceived outcome.

Building on Compeau and Higgins (1995b), SCT focuses principally on two constructs as the cognitive forces that influence behavior. The first construct is the outcome expectation, which perceives individuals as more likely to perform behaviors they believe will result in a positive outcome than those they perceive to have negative results.

The second is self-efficacy which is a belief about an individual's ability to perform a specific behavior (Bandura, 1977). Moreover, Compeau and Higgins (1995b) noted that self-efficacy influences choice on behaviors to be performed, how much effort will be expended, and how long it will be sustained in the face of difficulty in the performance of those behaviors, and consequently definitive mastery of the behavior.

The capacity of SCT in providing a practical theoretical framework for understanding and predicting acceptance of new information technologies has been empirically demonstrated by previous studies (such as Bandura, 1977, 1986; Compeau & Higgins, 1995a, 1995b; Compeau et al., 1999). Therefore, this provides sufficient evidence that signifies the effectiveness of SCT in explaining individuals behavior intention to adopt new information technologies such as m-government.

## RESEARCH MODEL AND HYPOTHESIS

The research model and hypotheses in this study draws reference from SCT that serves as the prime theoretical perspective for behavior towards acceptance of technology. Furthermore, other extant literatures pertaining to information systems research were reviewed prior to development of this model. The model has seven constructs which integrates the three forces of triadic reciprocal determinism as shown in Figure 2.

*Figure 2. Research model*

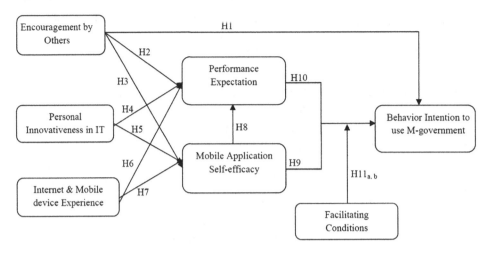

# ENCOURAGEMENT BY OTHERS

Encouragement by others is defined as the degree to which individuals perceive how other people, they consider important, feel about their adoption of the new system (Venkatesh et al., 2003). Consistent with Datta (2011), perceptions of members of a reference group happen to be significant to adopters who may not have enough experience with the system and looks upon others for opinions and guidance.

SCT argue that it is possible to persuade people through encouragement and suggestions into believing they possess potential to handle even intricate situations (Bandura, 1977). Compeau and Higgins (1995b) found encouragement by others within an individual's reference group to have an impact on both self-efficacy and performance expectation. They noted that individuals regard opinions of others as a basis of obtaining guidance on behavior, which they use in forming judgments about their own abilities.

According to Hassan and Jafar (2004), among the main sources of information individuals use to form perceptions of self-efficacy is encouragement from others. Similarly, past studies (Bandura, 1986; Compeau & Higgins, 1995b) found encouragement by others had influence on self-efficacy provided the source of encouragement was perceived as dependable. Furthermore, if others in the reference group encourage the use of a technology, the individual's judgment about the likely outcome of the behavior will be affected, thereby influencing the intention to use (Compeau & Higgins, 1995b; Venkatesh et al., 2003). Thus, the following hypotheses are proposed:

- **H1:** Encouragement of use by members of an individual's reference group will positively influence the individual's behavior intention to use m-government.
- **H2:** Encouragement of use by members of an individual's reference group will positively influence the individual's performance expectation.
- **H3:** Encouragement of use by members of an individual's reference group will positively influence the individual's mobile application self-efficacy.

## PERSONAL INNOVATIVENESS IN IT

Agarwal and Prasad (1998) defined personal innovativeness in information technology (PIIT) as the willingness of an individual to try out any new information technology. They depicted personal innovativeness to signify the risk-taking tendency that exists in certain people but not in others. PIIT is attributed to individuals' change acceptance (Hurt et al., 1977), and is thought to be the reason behind risk tolerance (Bommer & Jalajas, 1999).

According to Thatcher and Perrewe (2002), highly innovative individuals are known to seek out new, mentally or sensually stimulating experiences more often, and thus, they tend to demonstrate higher levels of self-confidence about performing new tasks. Similarly, Lu et al. (2005) alluded that most individuals do not have much knowledge and experience to assist them in forming clear perception beliefs when faced with decisions of adopting information systems innovation, and therefore, sheer boldness and curiosity in their characters have a strong influence in their perception of both potential usefulness and confidence in their capabilities to handle the technology being adopted. Thus, the authors propose the following hypotheses.

- **H4:** Personal innovativeness in IT will have a direct positive relationship with performance expectation.
- **H5:** Personal innovativeness in IT will have a direct positive relationship with mobile application self-efficacy.

## INTERNET AND MOBILE DEVICE EXPERIENCE

According to Hassan and Jafar (2004), prior experience in a specific domain provides the most dependable and accurate source of efficacy. Moreover, when users are increasingly using their mobile devices and the Internet, they are also increasing self-efficacy towards mobile applications and the Internet. In addition, an individual's performance on a task is a function of that individual's ability and motivation to perform successfully (Hassan & Jafar, 2004).

Similarly, experience has been found to be the most influential determinant of self-efficacy (Liaw, 2002, 2007). For example, a study of user perception on World Wide Web environments by Liaw (2002), confirmed that respondents who used computers and the Internet more, demonstrated higher self-efficacy than those who did not. Hackbarth et al. (2003) shares the same view that as individuals get more experience about the system and learn the necessary skills, they are likely to develop more favorable perception, thereby increasing their efficacy and performance expectation. Consequently, the researchers propose the following hypotheses.

- **H6:** The Internet and mobile device experience will have a positive impact on an individual's performance expectation.
- **H7:** The Internet and mobile device experience will have a positive impact on an individual's mobile application self-efficacy.

## MOBILE APPLICATION SELF-EFFICACY

Self-efficacy is an individual's judgment of their capabilities to perform an action that requires some specific performance outcome (Bandura, 1986). The concept recognizes the futility of our expectation of positive outcome of a behavior if we doubt our capability to successfully accomplish the behavior (Bandura, 1997; Compeau et al., 1999). Consequently, if severe uncertainties in self-efficacy concerning performance of a task are present, then self-efficacy would not influence behavior (Liaw, 2007). The major concern of self-efficacy is the judgment of the extent to which the skills possessed by an individual can be exercised rather than what skills one possesses (Bandura, 1986).

Compeau and Higgins (1995b) noted that self-efficacy is not concerned with past performance outcomes, but rather with judgment of what could be done in the future. Previous research has confirmed a strong link between self-efficacy and individual's choice of task and diligence in achieving the task (Fagan et al., 2003). Similarly, there is evidence of a relationship between self-efficacy and individual's reaction towards acceptance and use of diverse technologically advanced products (Burkhardt et al., 1990; Compeau & Higgins, 1995b; Compeau et al., 1999; Hill et al., 1987; Taylor & Todd 1995).

Kinzie et al. (1994) defined self-efficacy in terms of individual's capability to perform a behavior, noting the relevance of an individual's confidence in performing that behavior which would lead to specific outcomes and is considered to directly impact performance expectation. Thus, the researchers hypothesize as follows:

- **H8:** Mobile application self-efficacy will have a positive influence on performance expectation.
- **H9:** Mobile application self-efficacy will positively affect behavior intention to use m-government.

## PERFORMANCE EXPECTATION

Performance expectation is the degree to which users believe that using the system will help them attain gains in job performance (Venkatesh et al., 2003). According to SCT, a prospect on the outcome of a behavior has a strong influence in guiding an individual's actions towards that behavior. Compeau and Higgins (1995b) conceives that people are likely to perform behaviors they trust will result in favorable outcomes than those perceived to have adverse results.

Correspondingly, performance expectation is the outcome associated with situation performance (i.e. efficiency and effectiveness) that is derived from use of technology (Compeau et al., 1999). For example, individuals who expect positive results from using m-government would be probable to be highly aggravated than those who do not expect positive rewards. Moreover, perceived usefulness, which is a similar construct to performance expectation (Compeau & Higgins, 1995a; Venkatesh et al., 2003; Wu et al., 2010) was found to have a positive effect on behavior intention (Compeau & Higgins, 1995b; Compeau et al., 1999; Igbaria 1993; Liaw, 2007; Venkatesh et al., 2003). Thus, the authors propose the following hypothesis.

- **H10:** Performance expectation will have a positive influence on behavior intention to use m-government.

## FACILITATING CONDITIONS

Facilitating conditions are a measure of the degree to which an individual believes that enabling factors exist to support adoption and use of a new technology (Venkatesh et al., 2003). They include aspects of technological and/or organizational environment that are intended to eliminate barriers to use (Venkatesh et al., 2003).

According to Datta (2011), conduciveness of the macro-level climate is a critical factor in adoption of a technology, independent of user-level perceptions. He noted that facilitating conditions emphasize user perceptions of the macro-level socio-economic situation that depicts the overall adoption climate that is independent of the individual user opinion. Furthermore, in an effort to expound more on the enabling factors, Datta (2011) highlighted four dimensions that comprise facilitating conditions:

1. Policy,
2. Societal aspects,
3. Access, and
4. Economic facilitation.

Facilitating conditions are independent of individual attributes and therefore, they draw their foundation from the national climate (Datta, 2011). In essence, this means, despite users being sensationalized by the idea of a new technology like m-government, rarity of technology support or networking infrastructure will diminish their hopes of adopting the technology. Consequently, the authors argue that facilitating conditions play a moderating role between user perceptions of m-government and the user's intention to use m-government technology. Thus, the following hypotheses were proposed.

- **H11a:** Facilitating conditions will positively moderate the relationship between performance expectation and intention to use m-government.
- **H11b:** Facilitating conditions will positively moderate the relationship between mobile application self-efficacy and intention to use m-government.

## RESEARCH METHODOLOGY

The study utilized questionnaire-based field survey method for collecting data that was used to test the proposed model and the associated hypotheses. The respondents, who consisted of Kenyan citizens were surveyed online and offline during the months of August and September 2011. Furthermore, they were informed of the importance of the survey and were invited to respond honestly. In addition, respondents were chosen such that they had literacy in the Internet and mobile devices with the capacity to make adoption decisions.

The survey instrument development process ensured that survey items were carefully assessed for content validity (Kerlinger, 1986). Basically, measurement items were adopted from previous research. However, in view of the fact that considerable modifications were made to the items in order to align with the context of this study, it was deemed necessary to subject the items into a Q-Sort analysis (McKeown & Thomas, 1998; Nahm et al., 2002). Table 1 summarizes the constructs in the model and the sources from where survey items they were adopted.

*Table 1. Primary sources of survey items*

| Constructs | Source |
|---|---|
| Behaivor intention to use m-government | Venkatesh et al. (2003); Hu et al. (2003); Hung et al. (2006). |
| Facilitating conditions | Venkatesh et al (2003); Hung et al. (2006); Datta (2011). |
| Performance expectation | Compeau & Higgins (1995b); Hu et al. (2003); Venkatesh et al. (2003); Hung et al. (2006); Datta (2011). |
| Mobile application self-efficacy | Compeau & Higgins (1995b); Thatcher & Perrewe (2002); Hu et al. (2003); Venkatesh et al. (2003); Hung et al. (2006). |
| Encouragement by others | Compeau & Higgins (1995); Venkatesh et al. (2003); Lu et al. (2005); Hung et al. (2006); Datta (2011). |
| Personal innovativeness in IT | Agarwal & Prasad (1998); Thatcher & Perrewe (2002); Lu et al. (2005); Hung et al. (2006). |
| Internet & mobile device experience | Hackbarth et al., (2003); Hassan & Jafar (2004); Fagan et al. (2003); Liaw (2002, 2007). |

Subsequent to the development of survey items, 389 questionnaires were sent to potential respondents, and 257 completed questionnaires were returned. However, nine were partly completed, and therefore were not included in the analysis, leaving a total of 248 questionnaires that represented a response rate of 64 percent; a rate that falls within the acceptable norm of between 40 and 80 percent response rate for academic studies involving convectional population (Baruch, 1999). Survey items were measured on a five-point Likert scale ranging from "strongly disagree" to "strongly agree".

## DATA ANALYSIS

This study utilized Structural Equation Modeling (SEM) for testing the hypothesis. Consistent with Hair et al. (1998), SEM demonstrated two major benefits. First, it offered a simplified means for managing multiple relationships simultaneously, while at the same time providing statistical efficiency. Second, SEM was useful for evaluating relationships expansively while providing a changeover from tentative to confirmatory analysis. Moreover, our study was confirmatory in nature and therefore, SEM was found to be the most appropriate method for testing the proposed model.

Partial Least Squares (PLS), which is an SEM technique was chosen for analyzing the research model. This was informed by the fact that PLS utilizes a principal component-based assessment that is practical for model testing (Datta, 2011); in addition to placing fewer demands on sample size or residual distributions (Chin et al., 2003; Datta, 2011). PLS follows a two-stage approach in data analysis. First, the measurement model is assessed for validity and reliability. This aims at demonstrating the validity and reliability of data, internal consistency, convergent validity, and discriminant validity. Second, the structural model is tested for the purpose of establishing the validity of the hypotheses.

## RESULTS

Both the results of the reliability analysis for the measurement model and the inter-correlation of latent variables in the structural model are reported in this section.

## Demographic Profile of the Respondents

Out of the 248 usable respondents analyzed (Table 2); the results indicated no big difference between the male and female respondents (56% male, 44% female). On the age distribution, respondents aged between 26 and 35 years were the dominant

*Table 2. Demographic profile of respondents*

| Variable | | Count | Percentage |
|---|---|---|---|
| Gender | Male | 139 | 56 |
| | Female | 109 | 44 |
| Age | 18-25 | 25 | 10.1 |
| | 26-35 | 113 | 45.6 |
| | 36-45 | 71 | 28.6 |
| | 46-55 | 27 | 10.9 |
| | >55 | 12 | 4.8 |
| Education | Basic (primary & high school) | 18 | 7 |
| | Degree/diploma | 183 | 74 |
| | Post graduate | 47 | 19 |
| Income per month (KES) | <1000 | 14 | 5.6 |
| | 1000-10000 | 33 | 13.3 |
| | 10001-20000 | 29 | 11.7 |
| | 20001-30000 | 48 | 19.4 |
| | 30001-40000 | 53 | 21.4 |
| | 40001-50000 | 29 | 11.7 |
| | >50000 | 42 | 16.9 |

group, representing a tally of 45.6%. Regarding the highest level of education attained; respondents who had a college degree or a diploma prevailed at 74%. Monthly income levels of the respondents did not influence much on the number of respondents, meaning, respondents were evenly distributed at all levels of income. Therefore, based on these findings, the researchers conclude that people aged between 26 and 35 years, with a college degree or diploma have the highest intention to use m-government services irrespective of their gender or income levels.

## The Measurement Model

Reliability was assessed through internal consistency reliability scores as indicated by composite reliability and Chronbach's alpha values. As illustrated in Table 3, composite reliability scores ranged from 0.86 to 0.92 and the Chronbach's alpha coefficients ranged from 0.79 to 0.88. This satisfied the minimum acceptable reliability score of 0.70 for social science research (Nunnally, 1978). Furthermore, the average variance extracted for each measure ought to be greater than 0.50, in addition to being higher than its correlations with other constructs (Chin, 1998; Fornell & Larcker, 1981). This requirement was achieved for measures in this study.

Convergent and discriminant validity, was verified by ensuring that indicator loadings on the hypothesized factor were greater than their cross loadings on some other factor. Consistent with Fornell and Larcker (1981), and as shown in Table 4, the square roots of AVE for all constructs (diagonal values) were computed to a score higher than 0.70 and higher than their correlations with other constructs (off-diagonal values). This demonstrated both internal consistency, and convergent and discriminant validity of our measures.

*Table 3. Reliability analysis*

| Constructs | AVE | Composite Reliability | Chronbach's Alpha |
|---|---|---|---|
| Behavior Intention to use M-government | 0.7431 | 0.9201 | 0.8829 |
| Encouragement by Others | 0.7168 | 0.9093 | 0.8640 |
| Facilitating conditions | 0.6489 | 0.8806 | 0.8366 |
| Internet & Mobile device Experience | 0.6672 | 0.8886 | 0.8365 |
| Mobile Application Self-efficacy | 0.6260 | 0.8700 | 0.8019 |
| Performance Expectation | 0.6140 | 0.8638 | 0.7905 |
| Personal Innovativeness in IT | 0.7596 | 0.9036 | 0.8351 |

*Table 4. Convergent and discriminant validity of constructs*

|  | BI | EO | FC | IME | MSE | PE | PIIT |
|---|---|---|---|---|---|---|---|
| **BI** | **0.862** | | | | | | |
| **EO** | 0.3721 | **0.8466** | | | | | |
| **FC** | 0.6146 | 0.3385 | **0.8055** | | | | |
| **IME** | 0.4744 | 0.239 | 0.5187 | **0.8168** | | | |
| **MSE** | 0.6869 | 0.2776 | 0.5666 | 0.5913 | **0.7912** | | |
| **PE** | 0.6938 | 0.4338 | 0.5966 | 0.5869 | 0.6684 | **0.7836** | |
| **PIIT** | 0.4176 | 0.2053 | 0.45 | 0.4622 | 0.5223 | 0.4877 | **0.8715** |

## The Structural Model

Phase two of the analysis involved structural model to confirm hypotheses relationships among the constructs in the model. A bootstrapping method was used to approximate the significance of the path coefficients (Chin, 1998). Consistent with recommendations of Löhmoeller (1984) for estimating significance of path coefficients and indicator loadings, the parameter vector estimates was used to calculate parameter means, standard errors, significance of path coefficients, indicator loadings, and indicator weights. Furthermore, this approach has been used by previous studies in information systems (Chin & Gopal, 1995; Wu et al., 2010).

To evaluate the entire model, the significance of each hypothesized path plus the variance explained –$R^2$ values (Barclay et al., 1995) for mobile application self-efficacy, performance expectation, and behavior intention to use m-government were computed. Figure 3 presents the standardized PLS path coefficient results of structural model analysis.

According to Wu et al. (2010), statistical significance of weights has the capability of verifying the relative magnitude of the indicators in forming a latent construct. Most of the path coefficients in our research model were significant. The results indicated that latent factors explained 60.5% of the intention to use m-government. Equally, a variance of 44.1% of mobile application self-efficacy, and 56.9% of performance expectation were explained by associated predecessor constructs. Overall, the results provided support for our research model. The summary of the results of direct, indirect, and total effects of the analysis are provided in Table 5.

As projected, most of the hypotheses were supported. Mobile application self-efficacy and performance expectation, which are presumed as the principal predictors of behavior in SCT (Compeau & Higgins, 1995b) had direct and significant influence on behavior intention to use m-government. Furthermore, the relationship between mobile application self-efficacy and performance expectation was also

*Figure 3. Standardized PLS path coefficient results*

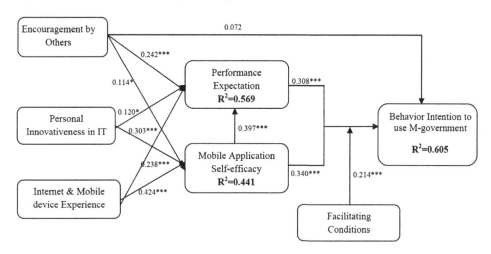

\* denotes significance at p<0.05
\*\* denotes significance at p<0.01
\*\*\* denotes significance at p<0.001

*Table 5. Standardized casual effects of PLS analysis*

| Dependent Latent Variables | Independent Latent Variables | Standardized Casual Effects | | |
|---|---|---|---|---|
| | | Direct | Indirect | Total |
| Performance expectation | Encouragement by others | 0.242 | 0.045 | 0.287 |
| | Personal innovativeness in IT | 0.12 | 0.12 | 0.24 |
| | Internet and mobile device experience | 0.238 | 0.168 | 0.406 |
| | Mobile application self-efficacy | 0.397 | n/a | 0.397 |
| Mobile application self-efficacy | Encouragement by others | 0.114 | n/a | 0.114 |
| | Personal innovativeness in IT | 0.303 | n/a | 0.303 |
| | Internet and mobile device experience | 0.424 | n/a | 0.424 |
| Behavior Intention to use m-government | Encouragement by others | 0.072 | 0.127 | 0.199 |
| | Personal innovativeness in IT | n/a | 0.177 | 0.177 |
| | Internet and mobile device experience | n/a | 0.269 | 0.269 |
| | Performance expectation | 0.308 | n/a | 0.308 |
| | Mobile application self-efficacy | 0.34 | n/a | 0.34 |
| | Facilitating conditions | 0.214 | n/a | 0.214 |

significant. However, contrary to our expectation, encouragement by others which was hypothesized to have a positive and direct influence on behavior intention to use m-government was not supported. Nevertheless, its interaction with performance expectation and mobile application self-efficacy was positive and significant.

Similarly, the results provide support for hypotheses H4 and H5, as well as H6 and H7 drawn from personal innovativeness in IT and Internet and mobile device experience, to performance expectation and mobile application self-efficacy respectively. Overall, facilitating conditions significantly moderated both performance expectation and mobile application self-efficacy, a finding that highlights the significant role played by facilitating conditions in cultivating a favorable environment for m-government acceptance, which in turn heightens users' intention to use m-government in developing countries. Table 6 summarizes the results of hypotheses testing.

*Table 6. Results of hypothesis testing*

| Hypotheses | Hypothesized Direction | T-Statistics | Findings |
|---|---|---|---|
| H1: Encouragement by others → Behavior intention (BI) | + | 1.716 | Not supported |
| H2: Encouragement by others → Performance expectation | + | 3.992*** | Supported |
| H3: Encouragement by others → Mobile application SE | + | 2.142* | Supported |
| H4: Personal innovativeness in IT→ Performance expectation | + | 2.145* | Supported |
| H5: Personal innovativeness in IT→ Mobile application SE | + | 6.161*** | Supported |
| H6: Internet & Mobile Experience → Performance expectation | + | 4.444*** | Supported |
| H7: Internet & Mobile Experience → Mobile application SE | + | 7.334*** | Supported |
| H8: Mobile application SE→ Performance expectation | + | 5.757*** | Supported |
| H9: Mobile application SE→ Behavior intention | + | 6.290*** | Supported |
| H10: Performance expectation→ Behavior intention | + | 4.965*** | Supported |
| H11a: Performance expectation* Facilitating conditions → BI | + | 2.773** | Supported |
| H11b: Mobile application SE* Facilitating conditions → BI | + | 2.327* | Supported |

## DISCUSSION

This study examined factors that explain behavior intention to accept m-government in developing countries by means of a theoretical model based on SCT. In general, the results provide support for our research model and offer a strong empirical explanation of behavior intention to use m-government in developing countries. The estimates of the variance explained of 56.9% for performance expectation, provides ample support for the hypothesized impact of encouragement by others, personal innovativeness in IT, Internet and mobile device experience, as well as mobile application self-efficacy on dependent variable performance expectation. Likewise, the variance of 44.1% on mobile application self-efficacy offers credence to the hypothesized impact of encouragement by others, personal innovativeness in IT, and Internet and mobile device experience on mobile application self-efficacy.

On the whole, the variance of 60.5% of behavior intention to use m-government was explained by both direct and indirect mediation of performance expectation and mobile application self-efficacy. This demonstrated a strong support for the research model, and affords a high explicatory capacity for behavior intention to use m-government in developing countries. The results compares with previous studies such as Mathieson (1991) whose variance explained was 62 percent, Taylor and Todd (1995), whose model accounted for 60 percent, and Lu et al. (2005), which returned a variance of 57 percent.

Contrary to our prospect, hypothesis 1 in which encouragement by others was envisaged to have a positive influence on intention to use m-government, failed to return significant results. The authors feel this finding might have been caused by low literacy levels, particularly computer literacy in developing countries. The finding contradicts previous research such as Venkatesh et al. (2003) that found social influence; a similar construct to encouragement by others to have had significant influence on behavior intention to technology acceptance. However, it is imperative to acknowledge that Venkatesh model was tested in the context of organizations in developed countries where literacy levels required for using new information technologies is not a big issue. Also, consistent with Compeau et al. (1999) observation that acceptance of information technology is not just about convincing people of the benefits of the technology, but rather, ensuring that individuals have the necessary skills and confidence for successful use, makes skills required for utilizing new information systems a precedence in developing countries.

Additionally, it is evident that there is a great disparity between developed and developing countries in terms of computer skills (Allen et al., 2001; Chen et al., 2006; Ndou, 2004). Thus, mere encouragement of usage of new information technologies in developing countries where acute shortage of computer skills is a dominant phenomenon (Baliamoune-Lutz, 2003; Chen et al., 2006; Kiiski & Pohjola, 2002), would not produce the desired behavioral orientation.

The significance of Hypothesis 2, in form of encouragement by others on performance expectation $p<0.001$, is an indication of the influence others have on individuals' perception of performance expectation. The finding echoes previous studies (e.g. Compeau & Higgins, 1995b; Gefen & Keil, 1998; Lu et al., 2005; Venkatesh & Davis, 2000) that comprise similar suggestions. The support for Hypothesis 3, encouragement by others on mobile application self-efficacy, $p<0.05$, supports Compeau and Higgins (1995b) proposition that encouragement by others influence behavior indirectly through self-efficacy. Furthermore, personal innovativeness in IT demonstrated a positive relationship with performance expectation and mobile application self-efficacy as hypothesized on H4, $p<0.05$ and H5, $p<0.001$.

This finding was consistent with previous research by Agarwal and Prasad (1998), Lewis et al. (2003), and Lu et al. (2005) who found similar results of PIIT on perceived usefulness which is a similar construct to performance expectation (Venkatesh et al., 2003). In addition, the strong positive correlation between PIIT and mobile application self-efficacy supported the findings of Agarwal et al. (2000) and Thatcher and Perrewe (2002).

Also, supported was Hypothesis 6, $p<0.001$ and Hypothesis 7, $p<0.001$, which demonstrated a positive impact of the Internet and mobile device experience on both performance expectation and mobile application self-efficacy. As predicted, prior experience on Internet and mobile devices positively influenced individuals' self-efficacy; the finding was consistent with past studies (e.g. Agarwal et al., 2000; Fagan et al., 2003; Hassan & Jafar, 2004; Liaw, 2002, 2007) that found prior experience to have a direct impact on self-efficacy and consequent indirect influence on behavior intention. Furthermore, studies by Harrison and Rainer (1992), and Hassan and Jafar (2004) found positive relationship between experience and performance expectation. As predicted, Hypothesis 8 confirmed the theorized relationship between mobile application self-efficacy and performance expectation, $p<0.001$. This finding is in line with previous studies (Compeau & Higgins, 1995b; Hassan & Jafar, 2004; Kinzie et al., 1994; Liaw, 2002, 2007) that envisage self-efficacy as the force that propel individuals' confidence in performing certain behaviors necessary to produce certain results.

Both mobile application self-efficacy (H9, $p<0.001$) and performance expectation (H10, $p<0.001$) had significant direct impact on behavior intention to use m-government. The two findings suggest that individuals with confidence in their ability to use a mobile application in addition to exhibiting higher performance expectation on m-government technology are likely to demonstrate intention to use m-government.

Moreover, the results indicated that performance expectation and mobile application self-efficacy are the two principal determinants of behavior intention to use m-government in developing countries, while encouragement by others, personal innovativeness in IT, and Internet and mobile device experience provide indirect influence on behavior intention to use m-government through the two.

Consequently, the significance of mobile application self-efficacy, supports Compeau and Higgins (1995b) suggestion that self-efficacy plays a key role in influencing individuals' behavior towards acceptance of information technology; in addition to supporting previous studies such as Gefen and Straub (1997); Liaw (2002, 2007); and Szajna (1996).Similarly, the impact of performance expectation on behavior intention draws support from previous studies such as Compeau and Higgins (1995b); Davis (1989); Davis et al. (1989); Keil et al. (1995); Liaw (2002, 2007); and Lu et al. (2005).

Another remarkable finding was the crucial role of facilitating conditions as a spur to behavior intention to use m-government. Facilitating conditions significantly moderated performance expectation and mobile application self-efficacies, an outcome that demonstrated the importance of facilitating conditions as an enabler that creates conducive environment for embracing m-government in developing countries. The finding was consistent with Datta (2011), whose findings suggest that facilitating conditions serve as enabler to acceptance of information systems innovations in developing countries. Datta (2011) emphasized the importance of facilitating conditions, noting that unfavorable conditions in this regard would impede individual's propensity to exploit emerging technologies thereby failing to inspire intention and consequently actual usage.

Overall, these findings provide preliminary insights into the factors that are possible drivers of acceptance of m-government, and that can be used to assist policy makers in developing countries to plan and proactively devise interventions aimed at alleviating resistance from users who might be less willing to accept m-government.

## Implications for Research and Practice

This study proposes implications for both academic and managerial government policy makers. From a research perspective, this study made two important contributions: first, the study proposed and validated a comprehensive theoretical framework that explicates determinants of behavior intention to use m-government in developing countries. This is a contribution towards advancing technology acceptance research in developing countries.

Second, the fact that encouragement by others had no direct significant influence on behavior intention to use m-government, demonstrated the differences in technological adoption behaviors in developed and developing countries. Consequently, contextual settings of research studies need to be recognized when generalizing results and researchers should refrain from assuming that technology adoption behaviors are similar for developed and developing countries.

Also, implications to policy makers responsible for development and implementation of strategies for rolling out m-government services in developing countries were provided by this study. First, the results of this study confirmed that individuals with high performance expectation and confidence in their ability to accomplish a task using a mobile application are probable to exhibit behavior intention to use m-government. Therefore, policy makers should devise proactive measures such as training and awareness campaigns to increase users' confidence and perceived usefulness of m-government.

Second, this study provides policy makers with six significant factors that are responsible for acceptance of m-government in developing countries. Thus, to successfully implement m-government given the limitations of resources in developing countries, government policy makers can prioritize based on these factors.

Third, the findings provide evidence that literacy and particularly computer literacy plays a key role on users' confidence in making adoption decisions. Thus, policy makers should devise long term plans such as planning school curriculums that are geared towards enhancing computer literacy and other incentives to boost confidence of users prior to implementing m-government.

Finally, facilitating conditions played a key role as an enabler to m-government acceptance; users had every intention of using m-government services provided facilitating conditions were present. This finding presents an important implication for policy makers in developing countries to improve strategic planning for m-government services through investment that avail the necessary facilitating conditions (e.g. policy, infrastructure, training, hardware and software) that will create a more conducive environment for embracing m-government.

## LIMITATIONS AND FUTURE RESEARCH DIRECTIONS

Despite the general support for the research model, this study had some limitations. First, the research model was validated by data collected from one country and thus, caution should be exercised when generalizing these results. Therefore, future research should be undertaken to collect data from different developing countries that will provide a more representative sample to validate the findings of this study.

In addition, given the diversity and complexity of technology adoption in developing countries (Datta, 2011; Donner, 2008), a research that explores other dimensions of m-government acceptance such as communities, culture, religion, and other contexts merit attention in future studies. Second, the data used to validate our model was self-reported and therefore, the typical limitations related to self-reported measures need to be acknowledged when interpreting the results of this study.

Essentially, this study sets the stage for future study on factors behind acceptance of m-government in developing countries. Therefore, a longitudinal study can be conducted with a view of scrutinizing the interaction among the identified variables, and thus, may serve to extend this study. Lastly, the findings of this study cannot be exhaustive, and therefore, more studies should be undertaken to find out additional determinants of m-government acceptance in developing countries.

## CONCLUSION

Regardless of the universal consensus from policy makers, scholars, and practitioners that technologies such as m-government are fundamental for socio-economic growth in developing countries (Avgerou, 2002), their benefits will not be realized unless they receive wide acceptance among the people in developing countries.

This study has demonstrated the need for clear understanding of perspectives and factors related to how developing countries perceive and accept information technology (Avgerou, 2002), particularly m-government, if successful deployment is to be achieved. Overall, the findings provide preliminary insights into the factors that are possible drivers of acceptance of m-government in developing countries, and that can be used as a basis for assessing the likelihood of success of m-government.

By way of understanding users' behavior, policy makers in developing countries can plan and proactively devise interventions aimed at persuading populations of users that may be less willing to accept m-government. There is confidence that this study is a step in the right direction and serves to progress the research on technology acceptance in developing countries.

## REFERENCES

Agarwal, R., & Prasad, J. (1998). A conceptual and operational definition of personal innovativeness in the domain of information technology. *Information Systems Research*, 9(2), 204–215. doi:10.1287/isre.9.2.204

Agarwal, R., Sambamurthy, V., & Stair, R. M. (2000). The evolving relationship between general and specific computer self-efficacy–An empirical assessment. *Information Systems Research*, 11(4), 418–430. doi:10.1287/isre.11.4.418.11876

Allen, A. B., Juillet, L., Paquet, G., & Roy, J. (2001). E-governance and government online in Canada: Partnerships, people and prospects. *Government Information Quarterly*, *18*(2), 93–104. doi:10.1016/S0740-624X(01)00063-6

Avgerou, C. (2002). *Information Systems and Global Diversity*. New York, NY: Oxford University Press.

Baliamoune-Lutz, M. (2003). An analysis of the determinants and effects of ICT diffusion in developing countries. *Information Technology for Development*, *10*(3), 151–169. doi:10.1002/itdj.1590100303

Bandura, A. (1977). Self-efficacy: Toward a unifying theory of behavioral change. *Psychological Review*, *84*(2), 191–215. doi:10.1037/0033-295X.84.2.191 PMID:847061

Bandura, A. (1986). *Social foundations of thought and action*. Englewood Cliffs, NJ: Prentice Hall.

Bandura, A. (1997). *Self-efficacy: The exercise of control*. New York: W.H. Freeman &Co.

Barclay, D., Thompson, R., & Higgins, C. (1995). The partial least squares (PLS) approach to causal modeling: Personal computer adoption and use as an illustration. *Technology Studies*, *2*(2), 285–309.

Bommer, M., & Jalajas, D. S. (1999). The threat of organizational downsizing on the innovative propensity of R&D professionals. *R & D Management*, *29*(1), 27–34. doi:10.1111/1467-9310.00114

Burkhardt, M. E., & Brass, D. J. (1990). Changing patterns or patterns of change: The effects of a change in technology on social network structure and power. *Administrative Science Quarterly*, *35*(1), 104–127. doi:10.2307/2393552

Chen, Y. N., Chen, H. M., Huang, W., & Ching, R. K. H. (2006). E-Government strategies in developed and developing countries: An implementation framework and case study. *Journal of Global Information Management*, *14*(1), 23–46. doi:10.4018/jgim.2006010102

Chin, W. W. (Ed.). (1998). *The partial least squares approach for structural equation modeling: Modern methods for business research*. Hillsdale, NJ: Lawrence Erlbaum Associates.

Chin, W. W., & Gopal, A. (1995). Adoption intention in GSS: Relative importance of beliefs. *The Data Base for Advances in Information Systems*, *26*(2), 42–63. doi:10.1145/217278.217285

Chin, W. W., Marcolin, B. L., & Newsted, P. R. (2003). A partial least squares latent variable modeling approach for measuring interactions effects: Results from a Monte Carlo simulation study and electronic-mail emotion/adoption study. *Information Systems Research, 14*(2), 189–217. doi:10.1287/isre.14.2.189.16018

Compeau, D. R., & Higgins, C. A. (1995a). Application of social cognitive theory to training for computer skills. *Information Systems Research, 6*(2), 118–143. doi:10.1287/isre.6.2.118

Compeau, D. R., & Higgins, C. A. (1995b). Computer self-efficacy: Development of a measure and initial test. *Management Information Systems Quarterly, 19*(2), 189–211. doi:10.2307/249688

Compeau, D. R., Higgins, C. A., & Huff, S. (1999). Social cognitive theory and individual reactions to computing technology: A longitudinal study. *Management Information Systems Quarterly, 23*(2), 145–158. doi:10.2307/249749

Datta, P. (2011). A preliminary study of ecommerce adoption in developing countries. *Information Systems Journal, 21*(1), 2–32. doi:10.1111/j.1365-2575.2009.00344.x

Davis, F. D. (1989). Perceived usefulness, perceived ease of use, and user acceptance of information technology. *Management Information Systems Quarterly, 13*(3), 319–340. doi:10.2307/249008

Davis, F. D., Bagozzi, R. P., & Warshaw, P. R. (1989). User acceptance of computer technology: A comparison of two theoretical models. *Management Science, 35*(8), 982–1003. doi:10.1287/mnsc.35.8.982

Du Preez, J. (2009). *Assessing the m-government readiness within the provincial government Western Cape* (Unpublished master's thesis). University of Stellenbosch, Cape Town, South Africa.

Fagan, M. H., Stern, N., & Wooldridge, B. R. (2003). An empirical investigation into the relationship between computer self-efficacy, anxiety, experience, support, and usage. *Journal of Computer Information Systems, 44*(2), 95–104.

Fornell, C., & Larcker, V. F. (1981). Evaluating structural equation models with unobservable variables and measurement error. *JMR, Journal of Marketing Research, 18*(1), 39–50. doi:10.2307/3151312

Gefen, D., & Keil, M. (1998). The impact of developer responsiveness on perceptions of usefulness and ease of use: An extension of the technology acceptance model. *The Data Base for Advances in Information Systems, 29*(2), 35–49. doi:10.1145/298752.298757

Gefen, D., & Straub, D. W. (1997). Gender differences in the perception and use of e-mail: An extension to the technology acceptance model. *Management Information Systems Quarterly*, *21*(4), 389–400. doi:10.2307/249720

Hackbarth, G., Grover, V., & Yi, M. Y. (2003). Computer playfulness and anxiety: Positive and negative mediators of the system experience effect on perceived ease of use. *Information & Management*, *40*(3), 221–232. doi:10.1016/S0378-7206(02)00006-X

Hair, J. F., Tatham, R. L., Anderson, R. E., & Black, W. (1998). *Multivariate data analysis*. New York, NY: McMillan Publishing Company.

Harrison, A., & Rainer, K. Jr. (1992). The influence of individual differences on skills in end-user computing. *Journal of Management Information Systems*, *9*(1), 93–111. doi:10.1080/07421222.1992.11517949

Hassan, B., & Jafar, M. H. (2004). An Empirical Examination of a Model of Computer Learning Performance. *Journal of Computer Information Systems*.

Hill, T., Smith, N. D., & Mann, M. F. (1987). Role efficacy expectations in predicting the decision to use advanced technologies: The case of computers. *The Journal of Applied Psychology*, *72*(2), 307–313. doi:10.1037/0021-9010.72.2.307

Hu, P. J. H., Clark, T. H. K., & Ma, W. W. (2003). Examining technology acceptance by school teachers: A longitudinal study. *Information & Management*, *41*(2), 227–241. doi:10.1016/S0378-7206(03)00050-8

Hung, S. Y., Chia-Ming, C., & Yu, T. J. (2006). Determinants of user acceptance of the e-government services: The case of online tax filing and payment system. *Government Information Quarterly*, *23*(1), 97–122. doi:10.1016/j.giq.2005.11.005

Hurt, H. T., Joseph, K., & Cooed, C. D. (1977). Scales for the measurement of innovativeness. *Human Communication Research*, *4*(1), 58–65. doi:10.1111/j.1468-2958.1977.tb00597.x

Igbaria, M. (1993). User acceptance of microcomputer technology: An empirical test. *OMEGA International Journal of Management Science*, *21*(1), 73–90. doi:10.1016/0305-0483(93)90040-R

Ishmatova, D., & Obi, T. (2009). M-government services: User needs and value. *I-Ways Journal of E-Government Policy and Regulation*, *32*(1), 39–46.

Karahanna, E., Straub, D. W., & Chervany, N. L. (1999). Information technology adoption across time: A cross-sectional comparison of pre-adoption and post-adoption beliefs. *Management Information Systems Quarterly*, *23*(2), 183–214. doi:10.2307/249751

Keil, M., Beranek, P. M., & Konsynski, B. R. (1995). Usefulness and ease of use: Field study evidence regarding task considerations. *Decision Support Systems*, *13*(1), 75–91. doi:10.1016/0167-9236(94)E0032-M

Kenya National Bureau of Statistics. (2014). *Statistical Abstract 2014*. Nairobi, Kenya: Government Press.

Kerlinger, F. N. (1986). *Foundations of Behavioral Research*. Fort Worth, TX: Holt, Rinehart &Winston Inc.

Kiiski, C., & Matti, P. (2002). Cross country diffusion of the internet. *Information Economics and Policy*, *14*(2), 297–310. doi:10.1016/S0167-6245(01)00071-3

Kinzie, M. B., Delcourt, M. A. B., & Powers, S. M. (1994). Computer technologies: Attitudes and self-efficacy across undergraduate disciplines. *Research in Higher Education*, *35*(6), 745–768. doi:10.1007/BF02497085

Kushchu, I., & Kuscu, H. M. (2003). From e-government to m-government: Facing the inevitable. In *Proceeding of European Conference on E-Government (ECEG)*. Trinity College.

Lewis, W., Agarwal, R., & Sambamurthy, V. (2003). Sources of influence on beliefs about information technology use: An empirical study of knowledge workers. *Management Information Systems Quarterly*, *27*(4), 657–679.

Liaw, S. S. (2002). Understanding user perceptions of World-Wide Web environments. *Journal of Computer Assisted Learning*, *18*(2), 137–148. doi:10.1046/j.0266-4909.2001.00221.x

Liaw, S. S. (2007). Computers and the Internet as a job assisted tool: Based on the three-tier use model approach. *Computers in Human Behavior*, *23*(1), 399–414. doi:10.1016/j.chb.2004.10.018

Löhmoeller, J. B. (1984). *LVPS 1.6 program manual: Latent variable path analysis with partial least squares estimation*. Universitaetzu Koehn, Zentralarchivfuer EmpirischeSozialforschung.

Lu, J., Yao, J. E., & Yu, C. S. (2005). Personal innovativeness, social influences and adoption of wireless internet services via mobile technology. *The Journal of Strategic Information Systems, 14*(3), 245–268. doi:10.1016/j.jsis.2005.07.003

Mathieson, K. (1991). Predicting user intention: Comparing the technology acceptance model with theory of planned behavior. *Information Systems Research, 2*(3), 173–191. doi:10.1287/isre.2.3.173

McKeown, B., & Thomas, D. (1988). *Q Methodology*. Newbury Park, CA: Sage Publications, Inc. doi:10.4135/9781412985512

Nahm, A. Y., Solis-Galvan, L. E., & Rao, S. S. (2002). The Q-Sort method: Assessing reliability and construct validity of questionnaire items at a pre-testing stage. *Journal of Modern Applied Statistical Methods; JMASM, 1*(1), 114–125. doi:10.22237/jmasm/1020255360

Ndou, V. (2004). E-government for developing countries: Opportunities and challenges. *Electronic Journal on Information Systems in Developing Countries, 18*(1), 1–24.

Nunnally, J. C. (1978). *Psychometric Theory*. New York: McGraw-Hill.

Ostberg, O. (2003). A Swedish view on 'mobile government'. *Proceedings of International Symposium on E- & M-Government*.

Serenko, A., & Bontis, N. (2004). A model of user adoption of mobile portals. *Quarterly Journal of Electronic Commerce, 4*(1), 64–98.

Szajna, B. (1996). Empirical evaluation of the revised technology acceptance model. *Management Science, 42*(1), 85–92. doi:10.1287/mnsc.42.1.85

Taylor, S., & Todd, P. A. (1995). Assessing IT usage: The role of prior experience. *Management Information Systems Quarterly, 19*(4), 561–570. doi:10.2307/249633

Thatcher, J. B., & Perrewé, P. L. (2002). An empirical examination of individual traits as antecedents to computer anxiety and computer self-efficacy. *Management Information Systems Quarterly, 26*(4), 381–396. doi:10.2307/4132314

Venkatesh, V., & Davis, F. D. (2000). A theoretical extension of the technology acceptance model: Four longitudinal field studies. *Management Science, 46*(2), 186–204. doi:10.1287/mnsc.46.2.186.11926

Venkatesh, V., Morris, M. G., Davis, G. B., & Davis, F. D. (2003). User acceptance of information technology: Toward a unified view. *Management Information Systems Quarterly*, *27*(3), 425–478.

Wu, J. H., Tennyson, R. D., & Hsia, T. L. (2010). A study of student satisfaction in a blended e-learning system environment. *Computers & Education*, *55*(1), 155–164. doi:10.1016/j.compedu.2009.12.012

Chapter 5

# A Smart Government Framework for Mobile Application Services in Mongolia

**Tumennast Erdenebold**
*Global Information Telecommunications Technology Program, South Korea*

## ABSTRACT

*The Smart Government is the advanced e-Government which has been indicated as an emerging global trend in public service delivery. The utilization of Smart Government mobile service is having various numbers of challenges including complexity of different technologies, and reducing duplication among existing and new systems in the application field. In order to get over these challenges, an integrated, an innovative and common system architecture is required to design for the mobile services of Smart Government. Hence, this study designed and proposed "A Smart Government framework for mobile application services" to integrate common parts of the application service. The research covered mobile application service components, and centered on mobile G2C and C2G interactions in the front-office application domain. In addition, the Federal Enterprise Architecture Framework is used, and designed architecture followed up recommendations are proposed for decision makers, government officials, researchers who related to ICT and e-Government.*

DOI: 10.4018/978-1-5225-1703-0.ch005

## INTRODUCTION

According to the emerging technologies such as smart devices, social media, cloud computing, big data and open data, life style of people and paradigm are changing and moving gradually into smarter usages. The demand of smart usage is pushing the electronic services on whole of e-Government area has become more advanced, improved and smarter than previous ones.

Therefore, now developing and developed countries around the world are more concerned and pay attention on the Smart government, and a number of countries have already started to implement the initiatives on Smart Government. For instance, Korea has developed its plan called "Smart Government Implementation Plan 2011-2015", Dubai has started implementing "Smart Government" in United Arabian Emiratis, and India has started its "Smart Governance" national initiative, etc.

## THE RESEARCH

### Research Motivations

There are numerous important reasons for motivating on this research named "A Smart Government framework for Mobile Application Services in Mongolia". Firstly, Information Communications Technology (ICT) strategy and policy of Mongolia are towards to the seamless e-Government. Secondly, the global trend of mobile and smart device growth is skyrocketing. Third, a mobile usage penetration is higher than a fixed internet in Mongolia. And finally, mobile services have key benefits and opportunities including advanced transactions of available data, information from everywhere and anytime access.

### Purpose and Objectives of the Research

The focal point of this study is to design and to propose a valuable research for Smart Government EA framework for mobile application services which dedicated for support policy and decision makers, Government CIOs, ICT and e-Government related officials, researchers, organizations and institutions in Mongolia, and to make contribution on development of the new service architecture based on the EA, and cloud computing, and to fill the gap non existing Smart Government framework for mobile services delivery in Mongolia.

The explicit objectives of the study are offering a new framework for mobile public services Government to Citizen (G2C), and provide participation from Citizen to Government (C2G) in Mongolia, including:

1.  Study and propose a suitable EA framework for Smart Government in Mongolia;
2.  Literature review, and case studies from developed and developing countries; and
3.  Design high-level smart Government framework for mobile application service to citizens.

## Research Method and Scope

The methodology of this study is based on literature review, and case studies on developed (Korea) and developing countries (India) related to the study context, and proposed to Smart Government framework for mobile application services, and Federal Enterprise Architecture Framework (FEAF) with application architecture (AA) is used as a main research framework. This research scope covered mobile service delivery by Smart Government, and centered on G2C and C2G perspectives.

## Literature Review

This part consists of the studies that defining the research scope, and including different types of Government terminologies, interactions of mobile service, and mobile application for the Smart government concept, and theoretical background of the research framework.

## Overview of Government Variety

*The Conventional or Traditional Government is defined as an organization that has the influence to make and enforce the laws and regulations for a certain terrain. In traditional Government, the communication among a government and a citizen or a business is occurring in the public service delivery office (Mengistu & Jeoung, 2009)*

*Electronic Government (e-Government) is an improved public service delivery using information and communications technology (ICT) (Heeks, 2003)*

Mobile Government (m-Government) is a strategic approach to the use of various types of mobile and wireless technology, devices, applications and services aimed at enhancing supports to electronic Government participants among citizens, businesses, and government institutions (Kushchu & Kuscu, 2003)

Smart Government is a concept of advanced government that citizen can avail themselves of including services, participation, and communication anytime, anywhere and with any device made possible through the convergence and integration of smart IT and government services (MoPAS & NIA of Korea, 2011-2015),

## Details of Smart Government Mobile Service

M-Government is part of e-Government which focused on mobile and portable devices (mobile phone, smart phone, tablet, PDA, etc.) that connected to a wireless network, and used to deliver mobile e-services (Lallan, 2008). Therefore, Smart Government Mobile service is involved in M-Government concepts, so that the author can apply m-Government concept to our study with similar perception.

Four types of relation domains in Mobile government are m-Government to citizen (mG2C), m-Government to business (mG2B), m-Government to employee (mG2E), m-overnment to government (mG2G(Kumar, Hanumanthappa & Reddy, 2008), (Chiristos, Georgiadis, & Stiakakis, 2010)

According to Ntaliani most developed type of m-Government interaction is mG2C (Ntaliani, 2007), therefore within this study scope narrowed down to mG2C interaction that enables C2G, G2C services with anywhere, and at any time.

There are M-Government front-office and back-office applications are existing, and described by (Desta, 2010). Back-office applications group is centered on utilization of mobile devices inside the inter government institutions and officials (G2E, G2G) to increase government communication efficiency and reduction of cost. Whereas, front-office applications group centered on utilization of mobile devices to provide public e-services for citizens and business (G2C, G2B) commonly through mobile phones. In this study, since the author already adjusted to G2C and C2G, the author narrowed down and focused to front-office application.

Electronic services (e-service) is any type of traditional government services can be delivered electronically integrating with ICT solutions in order to operate online process to deliver to users. M-Service refers to delivering public e-service to users through portable and mobile devices such as mobile phone, PDA, tablet, smart phone and handset.

## Research Framework

The Enterprise Architecture (EA) is implemented through the use of the research framework. Numerous different frameworks exist; out of the lot some are considered general purpose and others are highly specialized. And many companies have implemented the existing framework to meet their needs (Urbaczewski & Mrdalj, 2006).

## CHOOSING ENTERPRISE ARCHITECTURE

### Background

Firstly, the initial e-Government master plan framework "Mongolian ICT Development e-Government Framework Project Report" (ICTA, KOICA, 2006) of Mongolia, is followed by the Federal Enterprise Architecture Framework (FEAF) guide, and all the e-Government nationwide project's foundations, and interoperability is based on FEAF standard. Therefore, Smart Government is an advanced e-Government; so it should be comply with existing EAF basis.

Secondly, Odongo done analysis among the most commonly used EAFs including "Zachman-Framework", "The Open-Group Architecture-Framework" (TOGAF), the US "Federal Enterprise-Architecture-Framework" (FEAF), the "Department of Defense Architecture-Framework" (DoDAF), and the "Treasury Enterprise-Architecture-Framework" (TEAF), and the study found that FEAF is the second most popular EA Framework, closely behind the DoDAF (Odongo & Agnes, 2009).

Therefore, in this study FEAF standard is used as the core framework for designing a Smart Government EA framework for mobile application services in Mongolia.

### Overview of FEAF

It is initially introduced in 1999 by U.S Federal Government, and it affords holistic common approach for the integration of strategic planning, technology and management perspectives as part of institutions' performance and design improvement. And FEAF consists of four architectural models with business, data, application, and technology areas that assist as a reference guide for the effective information flow, shared business process, and technology across Federal Agencies of the US Government (FEAF, 1999).

This research is focused on application architecture of FEAF to design a Smart Government Mobile Service architecture framework in Mongolia. The reason why application architecture is that it presents the services in a way the IT officials and policy makers may easily understand and most widely used part (Desta, 2010) in EA.

### Application Architecture (AA)

FEAF exhibit models defined application architecture from the perspectives of designer as "A model of automatic or manual logical-system operation which supports the organizations' business process. The model can specify the mechanism and control addition with input/output to the logical-system illustrations of the process, and system roles" (Desta, 2010). FEAF has an Application Reference Model (ARM) which consists of an interface, application components and system main three parts (Desta, 2010).

In this research, the author used above parts to our architecture main three domains such as interfaces, application components, and systems, and adopted to design and to construct the components as core domains.

## Cloud Computing System

Cloud computing is a latest technological model for the service providers to enable their computing resource pool as visualized and shared, and to become more convenient on-demand network-access based, and can assist with less management effort (NIST, 2011). The Deloitte consulting company announced that the "cloud makes the EA more important, not less" (Deloitte, 2014). In the cloud computing system, there are different key service models exist including "Software as A-service" (SaaS), "Platform as A-Service" (PaaS) and "Infrastructure as A-Service" (IaaS) (de la Criuz, vmartinezdelacruz.com, 2016).

Business Wire Company the year 2013 survey result of the cloud computing highlighted that "SaaS service model remains the most widely used in cloud computing services, and the model is used by 63 percent of organizations".

Thus, on this study is more focused and used in the SaaS model of the cloud computing solution in order to establish new mobile application service on it, and to support EA with one of the latest technology trend.

## Research Methodology

The study methodology of this research is based on the literature review including:

- Smart Government;
- Mobile applications;
- Mobile services;
- Cloud computing and EA systems;
- Case studies from developed and developing countries; and
- Construct main data components of architecture; and
- Design and build Smart Government service architecture in Mongolia by using a chosen research framework with EA reference models.

## CASE STUDIES

The case study is analysis of key institutions and systems that can use with a method of holistic study by Thomas (2011), type of research approach among data capturing methodological and technique's paradigms by Lamnek (2005).

### Country Case: The Republic of Korea

Mobile e-Government Service Support Center (MGSSC) plays the key role in managing mobile infrastructure system to prevent the duplicative development of mobile services, and operating common channel through which administrative services can be safely and efficiently delivered (MoPAS, 2013).

M-Government Service platform consist of a mobile messaging center, mobile payment, mobile Public Key Infrastructure (PKI), Mobile Location Based System (LBS), and messaging platform (Bae, 2011) as shown in Figure 1.

In addition, the Korean "Common Infrastructure for the mobile government" was established since 2012, and its expansion m-Government service architecture has built to provide consistent and systematic mobile services at the national level by developing and distributing common components. By using common components the all governments and public organizations can develop mobile public services easily, shorten development period, save budget by preventing overlapping investments and enhance user's satisfaction by providing safe and reliable mobile public services (MoPAS, 2013).

*Figure 1. M-Gov service platform of Korea*
Source: Bae & Kyoung Yul, 2011

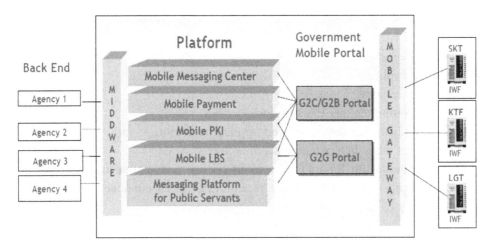

## Country Case: India

India has "Mobile Seva" system, and it is owned by the Department of Electronics and Information Technology (Deity, deity.gov.in/content/msdg, 2016) and (Mobile Seva: deity.gov.in/content/msdg, 2014), Government of India.

The Mobile Service Delivery Gateway (MSDG) delivers Government services over mobile devices using mobile applications. MSDG is a centralized, cloud-based and integrated system, and it has developed based on "Interoperability Interface Protocol / Interoperability Interface Specifications" standards of government of India, it provides an integrated whole-of-government platform for all Government departments and agencies in the country for delivery of public services to citizens and businesses over mobile devices using SMS, USSD, IVRS, LBS, and mobile applications installed on mobile phones. The diagram shown in Figure 2 illustrates the numerous components of Mobile Seva system (Mobile Seva: deity.gov.in/content/msdg, 2014).

*Figure 2. Mobile Seva system*
*Source: Deity,* deity.gov.in/content/msdg, *2016 of India*

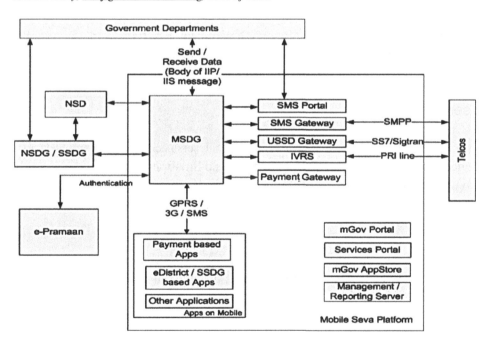

## RESULT AND RECOMMENDATIONS

This part consists of designed and offered To-Be architecture of Smart Government Enterprise Architecture Framework for mobile application services in Mongolia, and its conceptual high-level models, and architecture follow up recommendations.

### To-Be Architecture Design

Based on Application Reference Model of FEAF, our main category components including Interfaces, Application components, and Systems are built. Then, based on literature review, and the case study of mobile service framework architecture of Korea and India, main and detailed system components are constructed and listed, as shown in Table 1.

### Conceptual Framework Design

In order to present and to more view the components of entities and their relationship, structure used conceptual model for the designed framework. The view of the designed framework of Smart Government Enterprise Architecture Framework for mobile application services in Mongolia are as shown in Figure 3.

In the conceptual model of Smart Government EA framework for mobile application service, the author added three entity domains including user related access part user interface, carries, and National Data Center.

### User Interface

User access to the system through user interface. Users need to have terminal access devices such as mobile phone, PDA, tablets, and Smartphones with a mobile web browser or installed mobile application to access the Smart m-Government system.

### Carriers (Mobile Network Operators)

This entity domain includes existing mobile telecommunications service providers, and wireless (Wifi, WiMax) internet network operators in Mongolia.

### National Datacenter

In this entity domain includes National Data Center as main integrated warehouse for all m-Service application resource pool within its existing cloud computing service architecture with communication security, user authentication, encryption,

*Table 1. Constructed components for mobile service architecture of smart government*

| Components Category Domains | Main Components | Components of Detailed Systems |
|---|---|---|
| Interfaces | Mobile Internet Web browser component | Mobile Web-browser (Bae, 2011), (Deity.gov.in, 2014), (Mobile Seva. 2014), (Yoojung Jongsoo Yoon, Seungbong, Jeamin, 2004), Mobile application (Deity. gov.in, 2014), (Mobile Seva. 2014), (MoPAS 2013) |
| | Mobile web-browser representation | Mobile web page format (Yoojung Jongsoo Yoon, Seungbong, Jeamin, 2004),, Client-Side script language (Yoojung Jongsoo Yoon, Seungbong, Jeamin, 2004), |
| Application Components | Mobile Gateway (G/W) | Wireless Internet G/W (Yoojung Jongsoo Yoon, Seungbong, Jeamin, 2004),, Messaging G/W (Yoojung Jongsoo Yoon, Seungbong, Jeamin, 2004), (Bae,2013), Location Based Service (LBS) G/W (Yoojung Jongsoo Yoon, Seungbong, Jeamin, 2004), (Bae,2013),, Unstructured Supplementary Service Data (USSD) (Deity.gov.in, 2014), (Mobile Seva. 2014),, Interactive Voice Response System (IVRS) (Deity.gov.in, 2014), (Mobile Seva. 2014), Mobile Payment G/W (Bae, 2011), (Deity.gov.in, 2014), (Mobile Seva. 2014), (Yoojung Jongsoo Yoon, Seungbong, Jeamin, 2004) |
| | Mobile system integration | Data exchange format (Yoojung Jongsoo Yoon, Seungbong, Jeamin, 2004), Communications linkage format (Yoojung Jongsoo Yoon, Seungbong, Jeamin, 2004) |
| Systems | m-Service applications | Mobile applications (Bae, 2011), (Deity.gov.in, 2014), (Mobile Seva. 2014), (Yoojung Jongsoo Yoon, Seungbong, Jeamin, 2004) |
| | Service Platform | (mGov Portal, Payment Portal, mGov AppStore) (Bae, 2011), (Deity.gov.in, 2014), (Mobile Seva. 2014), (Yoojung Jongsoo Yoon, Seungbong, Jeamin, 2004) |
| | Service Access Management System | (App Modification Prevention System, Screen Capture Prevention System, Message Push System) (Bae, 2011), (Yoojung Jongsoo Yoon, Seungbong, Jeamin, 2004) |
| | Security | (Telecommunications security, Encryption, User authentication) (Bae, 2011), (Deity.gov.in, 2014), (Mobile Seva. 2014), (Yoojung Jongsoo Yoon, Seungbong, Jeamin, 2004) |

and protection systems. The data center resource pool consists of on SaaS, Paas, IaaS and Security parts of the centralized cloud solution.

## Recommendations

The recommendations are categorized under the Technology, Organization, and Environment (TOE) framework, and following up with newly designed "Smart

*Figure 3. Designed smart government architecture for mobile application services*

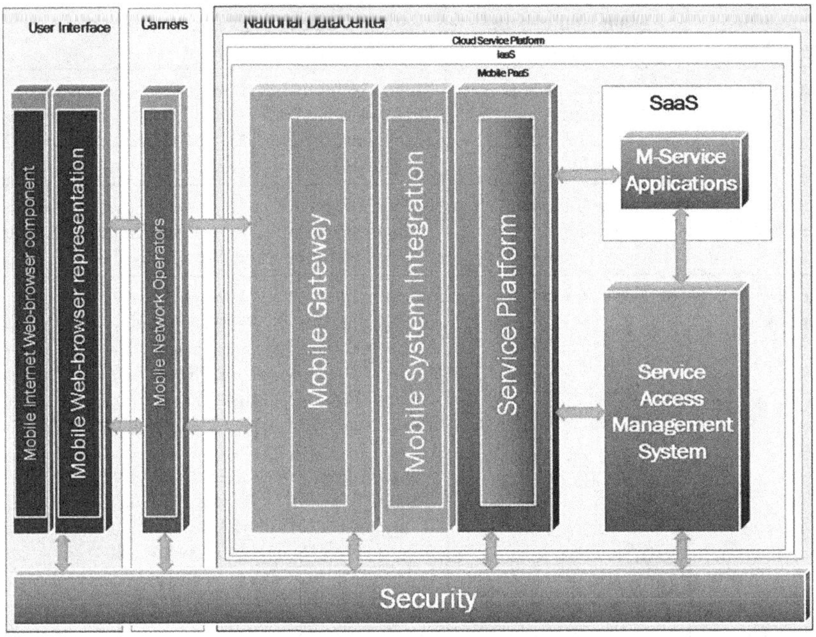

Government Enterprise Architecture framework for mobile application services". And the recommendations are dedicated for policy makers, ICT officials, Government CIOs, e-Government relevant researchers and institutions of Mongolia.

## Recommendations on Environment

Should develop a new and specific policy and regulatory documents such as a national strategy, standards, guidelines for the Smart Government initiative, which is to define clearly about usage of newly designed EA, and mobile service architecture. Additionally, that should include centralized, inter-operable common platform for mobile services to build at National Data Center of Mongolia, to apply to among all the government agencies, and to follow the guideline for the establishment of their new mobile application Services

## Recommendations on Organization

For ITPTA should initiate, lead, and define a comprehensive strategy, policy, implementation and action plan for Smart Government's mobile application services.

Furthermore, ITPTA implement, support and coordinate the projects related to Smart Government's mobile application service initiatives at National level.

For Mongolian National Data Center should establish Smart Government mobile service center within itself, and take responsibility for the service and maintenance. And should host and operate a common infrastructure of Smart government's mobile application services on the SaaS service model solution in cloud computing. Finally, should provide technological support, training, and instruct guidelines for the all stakeholders.

## Recommendations on Technology

Firstly, should use FEAF including with its BA, DA, AA, TA architectural models in whole of Smart Government. Second, should host mobile application service platform for centralized cloud computing in the National Data Center. Provide m-Government service portal and mobile app store with one-stop-shop for all services, and access through a single sign-on. Finally, should protect all components of the mobile service application framework with security technologies.

## CONCLUSION

This study generally has investigated delivering mobile application service in Smart government. The main goal of this study was to design Smart Government EA framework for mobile application services, and to offer it for policy makers, ICT officials, Government CIOs, e-Government relevant researchers and institutions of Mongolia.

The contributions of the study are that the novel framework for mobile application service in Smart Government is designed, and the recommendations related to the newly designed framework are offered for government organizations.

The emphasizes of the offering framework are:

1.    The designed framework is constructed from Korea and India case studies, as well as current international best practice frameworks in advanced e-Government at global level;
2.    Smart Government concept, and latest innovative technologies in ICT and e-Government are involved, such as cloud computing, and enhanced security functions on mobile.

The limitation of the study is dedicated for one country, and focused on only application architecture of the Federal Enterprise Architecture Framework. Moreover, the study covered in mobile service G2C interactions with front office parts.

Therefore future studies should be conducted on business architecture, data architecture, and technical architecture of the Federal Enterprise Architecture Framework. In addition, remaining mobile service G2G, G2B, G2E interactions with back office application parts should be designed.

# REFERENCES

Chiristos, Georgiadis, & Stiakakis. (2010). *Extending electronic Government service Measurement Framework to mobile Government.* Academic Press.

Deity. (n.d.). *MSDG.* Retrieved 17 May 2014, from weblink: http://deity.gov.in/content/msdg

Deloitte. (n.d.). *Cloud computing debate.* Retrieved from http://www.deloitte.com

Desta. (2010). *M-Government System Service Architecture Using Enterprise Architecture Framework.* Academic Press.

FEAF. (2009). *Federal Enterprise Architecture Framework guide by U.S CIO council.* Academic Press.

Heeks, R. (2003). *Most e-Gov for development projects fail how risks can be reduced.* Academic Press.

Kim, Y., Yoon, J., Park, S., & Han, J. (2004). *Architecture for Implementing the Mobile Government Services in Korea.* doi:10.1007/978-3-540-30466-1_55

Koica, S. K. (2006). *Mongolian ICT Development e-Gov Framework Project Report.* Academic Press.

Kumar, Hanumanthappa, & Reddy. (2008). *Security issues in m-government.* Academic Press.

Kushchu. (2003). *From e-Government to m-Government Facing the Inevitable.* Academic Press.

Lallan, E. (2003). *e-Government for development, m-Government definitions and models.* Retrieved from http://www.egov4dev.org/mgovernment/index.shtml

Martinez de la Cruz, V. (n.d.). *Something about clouds*. Retrieved from http://vmartinezdelacruz.com

Mengistu, H., & Rho, J. (2009). *M-Government opportunities and Challenges to Deliver Mobile Government Services in Developing Countries*. Academic Press.

MoPAS. NIA of Korea. (2013). m-Government of Korea. Author.

MoPAS & NIA of Korea. (2011). *Smart Government Implementation Plan*. Retrieved from http://www.mospa.go.kr/

NIST. (2011). *Cloud computing definition publication*. NIST.

Ntaliani, M. (2006). *M-Government challenges for agriculture*. Academic Press.

Odongo, A. O. (2009). *Electronic Government system architecture design directed by an e-Government development process*. Academic Press.

Seva, M. (2014). *What is Mobile Seva*. Retrieved from https://mgov.gov.in/msdpbasic.jsp

Urbaczewski & Mrdalj. (2007). *A comparison of EAFs*. Academic Press.

# Chapter 6
# Cloud Computing in E-Governance:
## Indian Perspective

**Mohd. Shahid Husain**
*Integral University, India*

**M. Akheela Khanum**
*Integral University, India*

## ABSTRACT

CLOUD COMPUTING IS BECOMING A RAPIDLY ACCEPTED AND DEPLOYED PARADIGM BOTH BY INDIVIDUALS AND ORGANIZATIONS ALIKE. THE GOVERNMENT OF VARIOUS COUNTRIES IS ALSO MOVING ITS SERVICES TO CLOUD TO OFFER BETTER AND JUST IN TIME SERVICES TO THE USERS. THIS CHAPTER EXPLORES THE BASIC CONCEPTS OF CLOUD COMPUTING, WHICH INCLUDES THE MAIN FEATURES OF CLOUD COMPUTING, THE CLOUD DEPLOYMENT MODELS, THE SERVICES OFFERED BY THE CLOUD, MOTIVATIONS BEHIND ADOPTION OF CLOUD BY ORGANIZATIONS, IN GENERAL AND BY THE GOVERNMENT, IN PARTICULAR. WE ALSO LAY AN INSIGHT INTO THE VARIOUS CLOUD COMPUTING INITIATIVES TAKEN BY THE GOVERNMENT OF INDIA TO FACILITATE ITS CITIZENS WITH EASY ACCESS TO INFORMATION/SERVICES.

DOI: 10.4018/978-1-5225-1703-0.ch006

## INTRODUCTION

Cloud Computing is becoming a rapidly accepted and deployed paradigm both by individuals and organizations alike. The government of various countries is also moving its services to cloud to offer better and just in time services to the users.

This chapter explores the basic concepts of Cloud Computing, which includes the main features of Cloud Computing, the cloud deployment models, the services offered by the cloud, motivations behind adoption of cloud by organizations, in general and by the Government, in particular. We also lay an insight into the various Cloud Computing initiatives taken by the Government of India to facilitate its citizens with easy access to information/services.

## CLOUD COMPUTING

The term Cloud Computing is becoming a common buzzword in the field of IT. Basically, Cloud is a collection of shared software, hardware and network resources. Cloud Computing involves sharing of various IT resources including the IT infrastructure and IT services over the internet. Many organizations are now breaking their nutshell and moving towards a vast collection of resources that are available to them on demand through the Cloud.

Cloud Computing has been defined differently by different researchers. Some of the definitions are as follows:

*Cloud Computing has been coined as an umbrella term to describe a category of sophisticated on-demand computing services initially offered by commercial providers, such as Amazon, Google, and Microsoft. It denotes a model on which a computing infrastructure is viewed as a "cloud," from which businesses and individuals access applications from anywhere in the world on demand (Buyya, Yeo, Venugopal, Broberg, & Brandic, 2009).*

Buyya et al. (2009) have defined Cloud Computing as a "parallel and distributed computing system consisting of a collection of inter-connected and virtualized computers that are dynamically provisioned and presented as one or more unified computing resources based on service-level agreements (SLA) established through negotiation between the service provider and consumers."

Vaquero et al. (2009) have stated "clouds are a large pool of easily usable and accessible virtualized resources (such as hardware, development platforms and/or services). These resources can be dynamically reconfigured to adjust to a variable load (scale), allowing also for an optimum resource utilization.

This pool of resources is typically exploited by a pay-per-use model in which guarantees are offered by the Infrastructure Provider by means of customized Service Level Agreements."

Cloud Computing is aimed at allowing users with on demand access to large amount of computing power in a fully virtualized manner, by aggregating resources and offering a single system view.

Cloud Computing involves a service oriented architecture, reduced information technology overhead for the end-user, greater flexibility, reduced total cost of ownership, on demand services and many other things.

The basis of Cloud Computing is virtualization of resources.

The idea of virtualizing a computer system's resources, including processors, memory, and I/O devices, has been well established for decades, aiming at improving sharing and utilization of computer systems. Hardware virtualization allows running multiple operating systems and software stacks on a single physical platform. Figure 1 depicts the concept of virtualization. a software layer, the virtual machine monitor (VMM), also called a hypervisor, mediates access to the physical hardware presenting to each guest operating system a virtual machine (VM), which is a set of virtual platform interfaces.

*Figure 1. Virtualization*

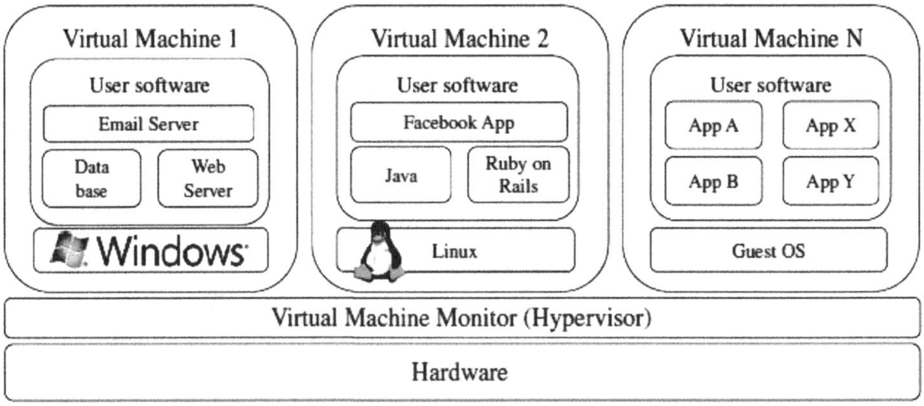

# MOTIVATION FOR CLOUD COMPUTING

Cloud Computing has characteristic features which makes it more suitable & adoptable computing by consumers. Some of them are listed below:

- **On Demand Service:** Consumers of Cloud Computing services expect on-demand, nearly instant access to resources. To support this expectation, clouds must allow self-service access so that customers can request, customize, pay, and use services without intervention of human operators (Mell & Grance, 2009).
- **Elasticity:** Cloud Computing gives every user the illusion of infinite computing resources available on demand. Therefore users expect clouds to provide resources in any quantity as and when needed. When an application load increases, it is expected that the added resources should be provisioned automatically (Scaling up), and when the load decreases the resources should be released (scaling down).
- **Measured Services:** Users must pay for what they have used, just like electricity bill. Services must be priced on a short-term basis (e.g., by the hour), so that users can release the resources as soon as they are not needed. So, the clouds must have features like pricing of services (metering depends on the type of service like storage, infrastructure etc.), billing and accounting.
- **Multi-Tenancy:** The multi-tenancy aspect of clouds requires multiple customers with different requirements to be served by a single hardware infrastructure. This is achieved by the concept of virtualization. Virtualized resources (CPUs, memory, etc.) can be sized and resized with certain flexibility. These features make hardware virtualization, the ideal technology to create a virtual infrastructure that partitions a data center among multiple tenants.
- **Performance:** With the help of virtualization concept workload isolation is achieved since all program instructions are fully confined inside a VM, due to which better performance control is attained since execution of one VM should not affect the performance of another VM.
- **Productivity:** ICT (Information and Communication Technology) is now a critical success factor. It significantly influences competitiveness. The impact of fluctuations in the quality of ICT services (for example, availability) is felt immediately. The demands are also increasing when it comes to teamwork and collaboration. Solutions not only have to deliver speed plus ease of use, they also have to support simultaneous work on the same documents, conduct team meetings with participants on different continents, and provide

the necessary infrastructure (anywhere access, avoidance of data redundancy, etc.). That is no easy task in today's environment.

By availing services through cloud (for example data center), organizations don't have to worry about the maintenance of the infrastructure and can focus on the productivity and customer satisfaction.

- **Reliability:** Virtualization also helps to achieve reliability because software failures inside one VM do not affect others.
- **Scalability:** In the Cloud Computing domain, distributed storage technologies have emerged, which seek to be robust and highly scalable, at the expense of relational structure and convenient query languages.

## CLOUD DEVELOPMENT MODELS

A cloud can be deployed in different ways (as shown in Figure 2), depending on the group of users for whom the cloud services are available.

- **Public Cloud:** In public cloud model, the cloud services are open for public in general. Anyone can use the cloud services as per need and pay according to the usage to the service provider. Amazon Elastic Compute Cloud (EC2), IBM's Blue Cloud, Sun Cloud, Google AppEngine and Windows Azure Services Platform are some examples of public clouds.
- **Private Cloud:** The private cloud provides all the facilities of a public cloud to restricted users. The users of a private cloud are from a particular organization. Eucalyptus, Elastra, VMware, Microsoft Azure are some examples of private cloud.
- **Community Cloud:** Community cloud is shared by several organizations of a particular community (having same objectives).
- **Hybrid Cloud:** Temporary renting capacity from public cloud to handle sudden peak in load (Cloud-Bursting) by a private cloud forms a hybrid cloud.

## CLOUD SERVICES

Cloud Computing facilitates its users with various types of cloud services (as shown in Figure 3) which includes:

*Figure 2. Cloud deployment models*
Source: leadconsultant.com/2010

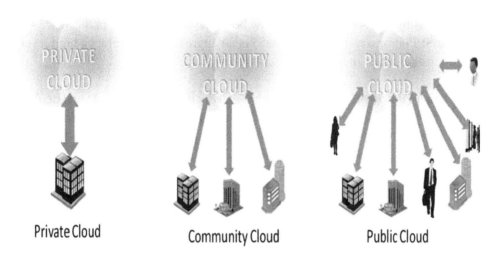

*Figure 3. Cloud services*
Source: www.valuesaas.com, 2016

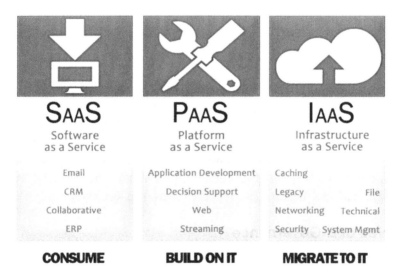

- **SaaS:** This model of delivering applications, known as Software as a Service (SaaS), alleviates the burden of software maintenance for customers and simplifies development and testing for providers. Applications reside on the top of the cloud stack. Services provided by this layer can be accessed by end users through Web portals. Therefore, consumers are increasingly shifting from locally installed computer programs to on-line software services that offer the same functionally. Traditional desktop applications such as word processing and spreadsheet can now be accessed as a service in the Web.

- **PaaS:** Platform as a Service (PaaS) is an approach which offers a high level of abstraction to make a cloud easily programmable.

A cloud platform offers an environment on which developers create and deploy applications and do not necessarily need to know how many processors or how much memory that applications will be using. In addition, multiple programming models and specialized services (e.g., data access, authentication, and payments) are offered as building blocks to new applications

- **IaaS:** Infrastructure as a Service (IaaS) offers virtualized resources (computation, storage, and communication) on demand.

A cloud infrastructure enables on-demand provisioning of servers running several choices of operating systems and a customized software stack. Infrastructure services are considered to be the bottom layer of Cloud Computing systems.

## E-GOVERNMENT

E-governance is now a reality and a necessary part of governance. E-governance can transform citizen services, provide access to information to empower citizens, enable their participation in government and enhance citizen economic and social opportunities. According to the World Bank's definition "E-Government" refers to the use by government agencies of information technologies (such as Wide Area Networks, the Internet, and mobile computing) that have the ability to transform relations with citizens, businesses, and other arms of government.

### Objectives of E-Governance

The main objective of e-governance is to help the government organizations:

- To build an informed society;
- To increase government and citizen interaction;
- To encourage citizen participation;
- To bring transparency in the government processes;
- To reduce the cost of governance;
- To reduce the reaction time of the governance;

- Make government more accessible;
- To deliver online services;
- To build services around citizen's choice.

## Why E-Government?

- Used to provide improved level of services;
- Used to control fraud;
- To provide new kind of services;
- To increase citizen/customer interaction directly with government.

## CLOUD INITIATIVES BY THE GOVERNMENT OF INDIA

## E-Governance in India

The National e-Governance Plan (NeGP) of Indian Government was approved on May 18, 2006 with the aim of providing all the government services to the citizens of India via electronic media. NeGP has been formulated by the Department of Electronics and Information Technology (DeitY) and Department of Administrative Reforms and Public Grievances (DARPG).

The main thrust for e-Governance was provided by the launching of NICNET in 1987 – the national satellite-based computer network. This was followed by the launch of the District Information System of the National Informatics Centre (DISNIC) programme to computerize all district offices in the country. NICNET was extended via the State capitals to all district headquarters by 1990. In the ensuing years, with ongoing computerization, tele-connectivity and internet connectivity established a large number of e-Governance initiatives, both at the Central and State levels. The formulation of National e-Governance Plan (NeGP) in 2006 has boosted the e-Governance process. Several initiatives has been taken by Indian govt. to promote e-governance like National e-Governance Plan (NeGP), National e-Governance Division (NeGD), e-Governance Infrastructure, Citizens Services, Business Services, Government Services, R&D in e-Governance.

## Cloud Initiatives by Indian Government

The Government of India has launched the National Cloud, "MeghRaj", formerly known as "GI Cloud" in order to make use of the benefits of Cloud Computing in governance. "MeghRaj" initiative will ensure improved development and deployment of eGov applications.

The main objectives of "MeghRaj" are as follows: Optimum utilization of existing infrastructure, speeding up the development and deployment of eGov applications, Easy replication of successful applications across States to avoid duplication of effort and cost in development of similar applications, Availability of certified applications following common standards at one place

The "MeghRaj" consist of multiple National and State Clouds. The agencies responsible for operating and managing the National and State Clouds may engage Managed Service Providers (MSPs) for managing the respective Cloud Computing environments (see Figure 4).

National Clouds provides infrastructure services (like compute, storage and network), platform services, backup and recovery, application development, migration and hosting etc. in future, clouds at the national level will also provide infrastructure scaling and remote infrastructure management for the State Clouds.

*Figure 4. "MeghRaj": network of national and state clouds*
*Source: deity.gov.in, 2016*

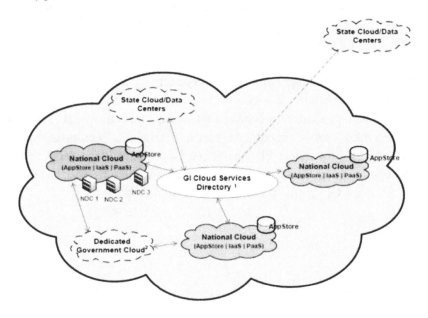

*Table 1. Current status of GI-cloud*

| S. No. | Initiative | Status |
|---|---|---|
| 1 | Cloud Computing platforms at National & State levels | Various states are under bid process management to implement cloud. National Cloud phase-I: implementation completed by NIC, which is ready for launch |
| 2 | Common platform to host and run applications – eGov AppStore | Prototype version is launched in May' 2013 and available at http://apps.gov.in |
| 3 | GI Cloud services directory | To be initiated |
| 4 | Set of Protocols, guidelines & standards for GI Cloud | AMU (Architecture Management Unit) is yet to be initiated |
| 5 | Centre of Excellence | Establishment of CoE is under process |

## Projects To Be Implemented Under "MeghRaj" Initiative

The various projects to be implemented in diffirent phases as a part of "MeghRaj" initiative are: setting up of National & State Clouds, AppStore (e-RAAS: Reusable Application Availability Store), GI Cloud Services Directory, Common set of guidelines and standards for National & State Clouds, define mechanism to operate and manage the GI Cloud environment, working as a Centre, for awareness building, best practices creation, providing advisory services to the departments on cloud adoption, showcasing the cloud technologies, international collaboration and research and development.

## Challenges

In India, most of the states are willing to adopt the e-Governance model to offer government services online up to last level, some major barriers are: unavailability of required infrastructure, unavailability of e-Governance application, unavailability of trained workforce in IT and unavailability of required funds. However, States like Jammu and Kashmir (J&K) is the first to adopt Cloud Computing for its e-governance services. Madhya Pradesh is providing e-governance services such as issuing of trade licenses through the cloud.

## FUTURE DIRECTIONS

Cloud Computing is a rapidly growing concept that offers a good number of benefits to its users. However, it also possesses some security issues which may become a concern. An understanding into the various vulnerabilities that exists in the Cloud will help organizations to make the shift towards the Cloud. Even though Cloud Computing provides a flexible, and cost-effective platform for delivering business or consumer IT services over the Internet, it presents an additional level of risk. The risk is due to the fact that the services are often outsourced to a different party, which may make data security and privacy a cause of concern. As it has been found that every new technology comes with its challenges, and cloud is no exception. Cloud computing services offered by third party providers may be looked as security vulnerability. However, cloud deployment by the Government to provide various services in the field of education, healthcare and social upliftment of the citizens can be viewed as easier, dependable and viable IT solution in future.

## REFERENCES

Buyya, Yeo, Venugopal, Broberg, & Brandic. (2009). Cloud Computing and emerging IT platforms: Vision, hype, and reality for delivering computing as the 5th utility. *Future Generation Computer Systems, 25*, 599-616.

Megh, R. (2015). *GI Cloud– A Cloud Computing Initiative of MeitY*. Ministry of Electronics and Information Technology, India. Retrieved from http://deity.gov.in/content/e-governance

Mell, P., & Grance, T. (2009). The NIST Definition of Cloud Computing, National Institute of Standards and Technology, Information Technology Laboratory. *Technical Report Version, 15*, 2009.

Ministry of Electronics and Information Technology. (2015). *National e-Governance Plan of India*. Retrieved from http://deity.gov.in/content/national-e-governance-plan

NIC Data Centers. (2014). *Core of e-Governance Infrastructure of India*. Retrieved from http://datacentres.nic.in/ndcshastripark.html

Vaquero, L.M., Rodero-Merino, L., Caceres, J., & Lindner, M. (2009). A break in the clouds: Towards a cloud definition. *SIGCOMM Computer Communications Review, 39*, 50-55.

Chapter 7

# Major Issues Affecting Government Data and Information in Developing Countries

**Saleem Zoughbi**
*Bethlehem University, Palestine*

## ABSTRACT

*The ever-developing technology is multifaceted, not only in technical specifications, but also in mode, type and characteristics. New technologies are designed and produced, new ways of using these technologies also are being suggested, tested and adopted. Telecommunications and digital technology provide today remarkable smart technologies that enable people to capture, process, maintain, disseminate and store efficiently all kinds of information at very fast speed, with high degree of efficiency and correctness. Much of government data collected are continuously affected by the development in such technology. Recent trends of technology currently and for 2017 and beyond have shown that the impact of such trends will enhance the impact on the way governments handle data. This chapter presents an overview of such trends. However, a common strategy for government data should be developed in a concise way that will guide the process of dealing with the trends of modern technologies. Therefore government data platform will adopt new technologies, new hardware and software but essentially the way government data is kept and managed still remain the same, just new tools have been adopted.*

DOI: 10.4018/978-1-5225-1703-0.ch007

## INTRODUCTION

Dimensions of government data refer to the aspect or scope of an issue. The 2015-launched sustainable development goals of the United Nations (SDGFs) are quintessential for development plans, which in turn require, use, generate and maintain government data. Building and maintaining government data is so vital to the success and maintenance of good government data such that architecting it is as important as using it.

In this chapter an overview of certain relevant issues affecting government data is presented. The issues presented are observed in many developing countries, with focus on two regions: South East Asian countries and Middle East countries, however these are valid in general for any country with different degrees of alarm and relevance.

## PRIMARY DIMENSIONS OF GOVERNMENT DATA

Secure government data require essential criteria to be met. There are many, however the following four are of primary significance.

### Leadership

A Very basic criterion for secure government data is having the proper effective leadership. Government data programs often face resistance both from bureaucratic forces within government with a culture of secrecy, and by actors inside and outside government who have benefitted from privileged access to data. Strong, sustained, political leadership is therefore important in overcoming resistance and giving cover to political and other risks from opening up government information.

### Policy/Legal Framework

Every government should have a legal framework that governs its data, security of data, cyber legislation and laws (Headayetullah & Pradhan, 2010). Therefore government data programs should wherever possible work within and leverage existing legal codes and policies. In particular it is important to do this when data is being restructured or designed. Many developing countries may not have such legislation, but that does not exclude the significance of having a framework that is as legal as possible, even if developed by policy experts adopted informally until the government decides otherwise. Examples of such legislation may include reuse of public sector information, government copyright and freedom of information. This will help government and independent organizations responsible for these policies became strong partners and supporters of the initiative (Fokoue, Srivatsa, Rohatgi, Wrobel, & Yesberg, 2009).

## Government Data Ecosystem

When government data is shared with the public, part of it is classified as open data. Experience through many government initiatives about data has demonstrated that open data initiatives are more sustainable and high-impact when such efforts use an ecosystem approach. This will result in governments to invest not only in providing data but also addressing the policy/legal framework, institutional readiness, capacity building (for government and users), citizen engagement, innovation financing and technology infrastructure.

## National Technology and Skills Infrastructure

One other significant factor is certainly the ICT resources and the infrastructure of the government. Practically it is impossible to implement, maintain and secure a government data and information initiative if there is a poor infrastructure, in terms of technology platforms and ICT skills among officials, users and the general public. The adequacy of infrastructure capabilities would be easily tested through widespread access to the Internet through broadband and mobile devices, with access everywhere. Human resources and skills are necessary, not only within large companies and government organizations, but small businesses that will be able to build data-driven applications. Government web portals should be mature enough to allow e-government applications to run and deliver e-services efficiently to citizens using the government data.

## Financing

Financing government data is a very critical process, since to achieve success and results it has to adopt a framework and regulation that permits financing both the "supply side" and "demand side". In other words financing should be provided so as government data operations and architecture is fully operative in a feasible, efficient and practical way, and at the same time, financing should exists on demand side, that is for users of data and benefiting from it, cost is provided somehow. This kind of financial actions would provide an indicator of the return on investment (ROI). The modality and success of such balancing between supply and demand financing would be a critical factor that has to be well addressed. This dimension is so important and directly connected to all other dimensions.

# SUSTAINABLE DEVELOPMENT WORK

## Sustainable Development Goals

Developing countries have been the focus of international development for a long time. Following the Millennium Development Goals (MDG's of 2000-2015) a new set has been developed at high expert level and a new World Agenda has been adopted by the World Leaders (September 2015), for the purpose of achieving sustainable development over a period of 15 years. In as much as the Millennium development Goals was useful for world development during the period of 2001 to 2015, this new Agenda is a plan of action for people, planet and prosperity (UN Secretary-General's Expert Advisory Group on Data Revolution, 2014). It also seeks to strengthen universal peace in larger freedom. The World Leaders promised: "As we embark on this collective journey, we pledge that no one will be left behind". A set of seventeen development goals are adopted, and referred to as the United Nations Sustainable Development Goals (Thomson, 2015).

It directly addresses governments' national plans and development. In this regard, government data, especially for developing countries, is perhaps one of the most important driving engines for such development.

It is essential that a closer look should be taken at government data and how to make sure it facilitates and enables sustainable development on the national level be examined.

Congruent to the sustainable development goals (SDGs) (UN General Assembly, 2014), developing countries would find that their government data should be both a product and a resource to all SDG-related development actions. In developing countries, their government data is subject to several conditions which may make them incomplete, unstable, and at some time vulnerable. Assuming that the government provides enough secure measures, the type and content of such data can be classified into three categories that fit best the priorities of developing countries. These are as follows:

1.  **Category "A" Goals.** These are the goals that are rich with the possibility of training and capacity building needs. This includes virtual training, expert group meetings and modalities of its Engaged Learning and related education scope of work. These include goals 4 (Quality education), 5 (Gender equality) and 17 (partnerships for the goals). Data related to these actions are and should be part of government data, open to as many stakeholders as possible for better understanding the community and society and wider planning for projects.

*Table 1. Category A of priority SDGs*

| No | Title | Description | Logo |
|---|---|---|---|
| 4 | Quality Education | Ensure inclusive and equitable quality education and promote lifelong learning opportunities for all | |
| 5 | Gender Equality | Achieve gender equality and empower all women and girls | |
| 17 | Partner-ships for the Goals | Strengthen the means of implementation and revitalize the global partnership for sustainable development | |

2. **Category "B" Goals.** The sustainable development addresses in addition to education two other very essential scopes of concerns: health support and economic development. Promoting the well-being for all at all ages require efficient government staff that would be able to employ information and communication technologies (ICTs) in a way to support health-related projects and services properly delivered by respective development agencies, be through government, private or international agents. Electronic governance, e-government platforms and e-services are instrumental in such support. This is not true only for health. It is also true for economic development and employment. These are goals 3 (good health), 8 (good jobs and economic growth) and 10 (reduced in equalities). Table 2 summarizes them.

3. **Category "C" Goals.** There are three developing sectors of development globally, and to a more relevance to Asia and the Pacific. These are in many ways not new, but it is well acknowledged by United Nations and other international development organizations worldwide:

   ○ **Sustainable Cities and Communities:** Using smart technologies in cities and in local e-government platforms particularly provide a great opportunity for sustainable development. Using new trends in

*Table 2. Category B of priority SDGs*

| NO | Title | Description | Logo |
|---|---|---|---|
| 3 | Good Health | Ensure healthy lives and promote well-being for all at all ages | |
| 8 | Good Jobs and Economic Growth | Promote sustained, inclusive and sustainable economic growth, full and productive employment and decent work for all | |
| 10 | Reduced Inequalities | Reduce inequality within and among countries | |

ICT is paramount to any society development in city dwellings and communities, even in rural and poor areas.

○ **Life Below Water:** There are many countries that have a large percentage of their borders costal. Pacific islands are also among these countries. The wise use oceans, seas and marine resources involve certainly practices of economic development, needed training on managing these resources, in much the same way as managing rural areas.

○ **Peace and Justice:** Another essential topic is how to harness information and communication technologies to serve the very sensitive issue of development to serve peace and justice. There is an ever increasing need for proper training, capacity building and substantive support work for enabling governments and societies to work for peace, realize justice for all. The huge growth of refugees in 2014 and till present (2016), with the region of South East Asia, central Asia and not only the Middle East are a clear indication of "Man-made disasters". Government data should be well prepared to handle data related such disaster risk management and Information Security and Privacy.

Therefore, three other goals are selected in this category. They are 11 (Life below Water), 14 (Sustainable cities and communities) and 16 (Peace and justice). Table 3 shows a summary.

## Open Government Data

Data owned by the government is one way to define government data. However, obligations to this data ownership extend from identifying, generating, maintaining, processing and sharing as needed and approved by the government, would be a more conclusive definition. If this data is made in part or in full free to access by all citizens, then we identify an open government data (World Bank, 2014).

In fact, many governmental agencies produce and collect a wide range of data. Making this data open will enable sharing these data on a public platform, which allows private businesses, academia, citizens, and civic organizations to get informed and reuse data for valuable and different purposes (The Register, 2010).

There are reasons that make Open Government Data necessary to achieve sustainable development goals (SDGs). Current challenges that prevent open government data to be used effectively in solving development issues are many, but can be controllable, hence increasing the chances of benefiting from such data.

In examining the kind of data that are generated and/or used by actions trying to implement these goals government of developing countries have the opportunity to enrich their government data with important data sets. In many of these cases such data can be public, with upholding personal information and producing only statistics-like data that can be of great help for decision making applications.

This enormous potential that open government data has to facilitate implementation of SDGs is not easy it as it may sound. In fact, there are technical and organizational challenges which hinders progress before open government data are well established and utilized fully.

## Sustainability of Government Data

Sustainability of government data is completely different from government data for sustainable development. Naturally the data generated and used for sustainable development as specified by the SDGs should be sustainable in the sense that it is continuously updated, maintained, enriched, processed and supported (World Bank, 2014).

Two additional aspects are worth taking note of here: the first is that this sustainability is not limited to data that can be used for projects aiming at implementing SDGs, rather it is making sure that such data owned by the government is continuously valid and maintained, and accessed (according to government

*Table 3. Category C priority SDGs*

| No | Title | Description | Logo |
|---|---|---|---|
| 11 | Sustainable cities and communities | Make cities and human settlements inclusive, safe, resilient and sustainable | |
| 14 | Life Below Water | Conserve and sustainably use the oceans, seas and marine resources for sustainable development | |
| 16 | Peace and Justice | Promote peaceful and inclusive societies for sustainable development, provide access to justice for all and build effective, accountable and inclusive institutions at all levels | |

regulations) anytime and from anywhere (almost, as infrastructures difficulties do exists always in developing countries) for whatever reason it sis used as indicated by the government. The second issue is that citizens and the public sector have a stake in using the open part of government data. This empowerment will enhance participation of government and other stakeholders, making new architectures and policies of securing government data.

The World Bank has a set basic principles that protects the existence of government data in form essential information and knowledge resource for the implementation of projects on sustainable development goals implementation. They in fact refer to them as the *Basic Principles of Data Revolution for SDGs*. They are outlined as follows:

1.  **Data Quality and Integrity:** Open Data exposes data to public view in a way that allows for crowdsourced review and quality control.
2.  **Data Disaggregation:** Open Data has many elements of being disaggregated and being highly accessible to many or even any party that wishes to use it.
3.  **Data Timeliness:** Open Data allows for private-sector and citizen contributions to open datasets that can make data more timely and relevant.
4.  **Data Transparency and Openness:** This principle can be directly linked to Open Data and its promotion of transparency and tightened feedback loops between data users and data suppliers (namely government).
5.  **Data Usability and Curation:** Through Open Data Roundtables and similar events, data users can provide feedback on open datasets that makes them more accessible and useful.
6.  **Data Protection and Privacy:** The challenge of opening datasets while anonymizing sensitive information on health, finance, or other PII sets a high bar for developing data privacy safeguards.
7.  **Data Governance and Independence:** The Open Data Charter, Open Government Partnership, and other international efforts are beginning to provide a governance structure for Open Data.
8.  **Data Resources and Capacity:** This is directly in line with the recommendation for "new resources for capacity building". Open Data assessments and the implementation of Open Data Initiatives help client countries develop their ability to produce "high-quality statistics in line with global standards," and to consequently disseminate this data to the private sector/non-profit sector.
9.  **Data Rights:** The entire concept of Open Data is based on, and reinforces, the fundamental right for the public to have access to key datasets.

With these principles, and dimensions mentioned above, government data can be safely and clearly identified not only for secure government operations and usage, but also for the public and stakeholders at all levels. This can be in such a way that facilitates the implementation of SDGs yielding opportunities for actual implementation of priority goals for each country as seen by its government.

Examples of specific applications can be found (Chongthammakun & Jackson, 2012; Headayetullah & Pradhan, 2010).

## ARCHITECTING GOVERNMENT DATA

As the ongoing accelerated technological advances and rapid diffusion of information and communication technologies (ICTs) has brought in all countries to adopting technologies, one could easily identify three major phenomena that is widely observed:

1. Transformation of people's everyday life to the extent that many people are now dependent on ICTs when carrying out daily activities.
2. Exponential increase in the wealth of knowledge, information and data. It is estimated that 90 per cent of the data stored worldwide has been generated in the last two years!
3. Pervasion of ICTs in all sectors, and a general agreement that ICTs are essential for social and economic development.

As a result, a disciplined approach to the management of those systems and data has developed. It adopts a holistic approach to systems architecture that includes data content design, management and storage. This approach is called enterprise architecture. Rightly so, government data as huge may be, would benefit greatly from applying techniques to architect data in a more suitable, efficient and secure way, yet maintaining low cost.

Since then, this discipline became known as enterprise architecture. The main goal of adopting it is to reverse the situation in an enterprise (i.e., company, organization, entity, etc.) from more cost, less value to less cost, more value. This is known as increasing the return on investment (ROI). Government data is strictly government structure, and achieving this reverse goal will be very much wanted, particularly in developing countries.

In architecting government data structures four major principles are to be addressed. They form a protective life cycle where each action empowers the next action, and ensures the effectiveness of the development and implementation process. These principles have a well-defined strategy that guides the architecting process as follows:

Through essential aspects of the enterprise, reduce costs and optimize ICT adoption in such a way to maximize the ROI.

This can be presented in a simpler way by outlining the following four principles:

1. **Align:** Data sets, components and attributes are to be clearly linked to each other, and be central in usage and significance (not necessarily physical location) to all parts of the government data stakeholders. direct links to essential and critical sections of the enterprise.
2. **Optimize:** As growing data is a living entity that can go out of bounds, it is important to produce more and do more with available resources, thus optimizing the resources required by integrated government data structures is a necessary task for government data care takers.
3. **Externalize:** The ICT environment in which government data is nourished, maintained and housed can be a decisive factor in the sustainability of this

data, and hence external support has to be programmed, planned and relied on as needed. This can be for example achieved through moving some of its assets outside of the government data operating environment, if they do not add value or can be replaced in another way at less cost and more efficient operation.

4. **Consolidate:** The huge volume of data in all its versatile types and characteristics would provide opportunities for redundancy of data and unnecessary content. It is important to view such possibilities in order to reduce unnecessary redundancies.

This kind of "architecting procedure is not a one-time task. In fact it has to be scheduled periodically, depending on the changing characteristics of government data, such as the rate of growth, data usage, stakeholders' operations, etc. Good documentation and reasoning should be well retained, not only historically, but that will help observe and learn on the growth and usage of government data, which will help in better planning for the ongoing development in data operations and performance, this will result in retaining a high value to the goals of government data.

## REGIONAL THREATS: ECONOMIC, POLITICAL AND OTHERS

A word has to be said on an issue that may look trivial or minor. However in developing countries this issue could pause a fateful situation on their government data.

There are many risks of interruptions, weakening, or even failure of government data environments. These risks which are of technical or financial nature are the easiest to handle, in the sense that the required action to mitigate such risks are identifiable easily and thus the question remains simply of availability of technical or financial resources or not.

However there are other threats that are not so simple, and yet are not "impossible" to happen. In particular, in developing countries there are quite serious internal political unrest that reflects directly on technical achievements of various government actors. Needless to say that this is targeted to data environment offices and caretakers. Data is used and shared under of course priority regulations among different authorities, that could be cities and local governments, or neighboring countries which share common governance agreements and require data exchange and sharing across political borders. The presence of central versus local government data protocols and exchange framework, as well as regional ones, pose a serious threat to the viability and robustness of government data.

## REFERENCES

Chongthammakun, R., & Jackson, S. J. (2012). Boundary Objects, Agents, and Organizations: Lessons from E-Document Systems Development in Thailand. *Proceedings of 2012 45th Hawaii International Conference on Systems Sciences.* doi:10.1109/HICSS.2012.133

Fokoue, A., Srivatsa, M., Rohatgi, P., Wrobel, P., & Yesberg, J. (2009). A Decision Support System for Secure Information Sharing. *Proceedings of the 14th ACM Symposium on Access Control Models and Technologies*, 105-114. doi:10.1145/1542207.1542226

Headayetullah, M., & Pradhan, G. K. (2010). Efficient and Secure Information Sharing For Security Personnels: A Role and Cooperation Based Approach. *International Journal on Computer Science and Engineering*, 2(3), 2010.

The Earth Institute Columbia University. (2016). *ICT and the SDGs: How Information and Communications Technology Can Achieve The Sustainable Development Goals.* Retrieved from: https://www.ericsson.com/res/docs/2015/ict-and-sdg-interim-report.pdf

The Register. (2010). *Citizens rail against government data sharing.* Retrieved from: http://www.theregister.co.uk/2010/02/23/public_data_shari ng_poll/

Thomson, S. (2015). *What are the Sustainable Development Goals? From World Economic Forum.* Retrieved from: https://www.weforum.org/agenda/2015/09/what-are-the-sustainable-development-goals/

UN General Assmebly. (2014). *Report of the Open Working Group of the General Assembly on Sustainable Development Goals* (A/68/970). Retrieved from: http://www.un.org/ga/search/view_doc.asp?symbol=A/68/970&Lang=E

UN Secretary-General's Expert Advisory Group on Data Revolution. (2014). *Ref: 2 "A World That Counts".* Retrieved from: http://www.unglobalpulse.org/IEAG-Data-Revolution-Report-A-World-That-Counts

World Bank. (2014). *Open data for Sustainable Development.* Retrieved from http://pubdocs.worldbank.org/en/741081441230716917/Open-Data-for-Sustainable-development-PN-FINAL-ONLINE-September1.pdf

# Chapter 8
# Major Technology Trends Affecting Government Data in Developing Countries

**Saleem Zoughbi**
*Bethlehem University, Palestine*

## ABSTRACT

*The success of government data platforms and systems do not depend only on technology. There are other issues that affect this progress. Some of these are very essential to the continuity and not only the implementation, such as leadership. Other issues are the absence of a clear well adopted policy and legal framework that governs its data, security of data, cyber legislation and laws. The government-provided ICT resources and the infrastructure would also be an important issue that would affect government data. Financing is also another critical issue. For developing countries, sustainability of development is a necessity for best impact of development projects. As it is adopted by the United Nations, sustainable development goals (SDG's for the agenda of 2030) have substantial dependency on information and communications technology. All goals practically require government data in one way or another, and hence sustainable development is directly related to government data should successful development is sought. Other issues include open data, open government. This chapter discusses such issues and sheds light on ways of handing them.*

DOI: 10.4018/978-1-5225-1703-0.ch008

## INTRODUCTION

We witness this decade an ever going, and increasing, growth of technology development. This has resulted in a greater opportunities providing the world with very efficient means of technology for social and economic development, be that software or hardware. Telecommunications and digital technology provides today remarkable smart technologies that enable people to capture, process, maintain, disseminate and store efficiently all kinds of information at very fast speed, with high degree of efficiency and correctness. Much of government data collected are continuously affected by the development in such technology.

Recent trends of technology currently and for 2017 (Gartner Group, 2016) and beyond have shown that the impact of such trends will enhance the impact on the way governments handle data. This chapter present an overview of such trends. However, a common strategy for government data should be developed in a concise way that will guide the process of dealing with the trends of modern technologies.

## GOVERNMENT DATA STRATEGY

Any part of the government operating in an information technology environment should have already been consulted regarding the national ICT strategy and the long-term plan for development sector needs to optimize the value of its ICT investments. The scope of that plan and the need for alignment with plans of other parts of the government have been already addressed. A sub-strategy of this ICT strategy has become necessary to distinctly identify, that is the government data strategy. This suggestion for a government data strategy could include the following pillars.

- Develop different models based on ways using and needs for government data. Government data solutions must be appropriate to the context in which they are used and easily adapted to changes in that context if they are to have long-term value.
- Align strategy of government data with the broader ICT national strategy. Consideration should not be only the ways in which the government data platform currently operates, but necessary changes to meet its strategic goals and contribute to achievement of good governance.
- Invest in a technology portfolio of field-tested technologies - a platform of plug-and-play components - that addresses common data needs and can be quickly adapted and extended to address local variations as needed. This will reduce the time, cost and risk of embedding new technologies.

- Develop strategic partnerships with stakeholders of government dat. These partnerships should evolve, scale and sustain policies and regulations of government data.

## FUTURE TRENDS AFFECTING GOVERNMENT DATA

The word "Future" has much reference to the present in his title. Many of these trends are already clear and if not implemented, they are being developed for presentation to the consumers and users in the very near future. In looking at future trends, we should keep in mind the current technology development and the areas where the most impact is observed (McKinsey & Company, 2015). These include many areas, like Cloud Computing, Smart Systems, Mobile Devices, Analytics, 3D Printing, Connectivity, Social Media, Internet of Things and Digital Services.

### Overview of Trends

In determining the path along which technology is being developed, one should not consider the very technical and specific content and possibilities that may exist for taking this technology further. Instead we should focus on the philosophic concept of what new technology is possible. In other words, we let the details come later, and think of brave and ambitious trends of development in technologies, and let the engineers and industries work them out.

Gartner research and reports adopted a realistic vision, yet ambitious in details, in order to look at future trends. It foresees three major paths along which technology development is nourished and encouraged. These are the following:

1.  Working out to bridge the gap between the real world and the virtual world. Through developing technologies we could enhance the exchange of data and process it in a combination of these two worlds!
2.  No matter what development happens in infrastructure, the development of software is crucial element. Intelligent software should be continuously the main trend of future.
3.  The new reality of using technology is another important trend. It is developing existing technology in reality and have them used in a more effective and challenging ways.

## Computing Power Development

Highlights of ICT Technology of the Future Today include unbelievable possibilities. Some of them seem like dreams or science fiction, but nobody contests the huge potentials of the industry and technology, powered by funding and string research worldwide (Satell, 2013). Under the term "computing power" one can include the advances in technology in eth following areas:

- **Processors Hardware Power:** The increasing deigns of processors that provide very fast and reliable computation has led to better design of efficient computing machines.
- **Networking Capabilities and Devices:** Tools and methods of networking different kinds of devices have been well developed. They are able to handle interoperability properly and making the networking a seamless environment for exchange of data and information across all networked devices.
- **Telecommunications Channels:** Multi channels communication has been effectively developed, and networking these days can spread over different kinds of channels, without being tied to specifics of each channel. Protocols and devices were able to provide such wealth of channel networking.
- **Data Managements and Processing Techniques:** The ever-developing science and technology in enhancing data management in intelligent ways have been also a major trend in technology development.
- **Next Generation Operating Systems:** This is an ongoing research as well, but perhaps has been slower relative to other trends.
- **Real Time Systems and Data Acquisition Devices:** A major push towards smart sensors and real time data acquisition has led to a "revolution" in the ways data is captured, processed and maintained, apart from the ongoing discussion on defining what is government or what is public and what is private data.

## Guiding Principles of Modern Technology Development

These trends have been characterized by three major principles in developing related technologies (European Commission, 2014).

1. **Transformation:** Improving service delivery, empowering the user, linking governments and service providers.
2. **Connectivity:** Affordable access to broadband, Attention to gender and special needs, technology for remote and rural areas.

3.  **Innovation:** Developing competitive IT-based service industries, fostering ICT innovation across the economy.

## Strategic Trends in New Technologies

As an overall summary, strategies in developing new technologies as guided by the previous principles, have focused on three strategic areas in current years.

1.  **Merging the Real World and the Virtual World:** Pervasive computing, Internet of Things, smart sensors and real time systems, 3D printing;
2.  **Intelligent Technology:** Advanced data means and methods for analytics, smart machines, artificial intelligence applications;
3.  **New Information Technologies:** Cloud/client computing, software-defined applications and infrastructures, web-oriented architecture, risk and security applications.

## Computing Everywhere

At the dawn of computing, mainframe computers were characterized, and until today, by the fact that each computer serves many people, or in other words, many persons share one computer. When personal computers appeared, it was meant that one person uses one computer. As the internet grew, it was evident that many people use many computers and in a very dynamic nature. As we move along into ubiquitous computing, and sometimes referred to as computing everywhere, it develops into "many computers share one person"!

Computing everywhere is based on the idea that having many computing devices in a physical environment. In fact they focus not only on enhancing computing use by having many electronic devices or services available through the physical environment (networked efficiently) but also on making them effectively invisible to the user.

Computing everywhere has become also a necessity when it comes to devices that are embedded, wearable, handheld devices communicate transparently to provide different services and data to the users. In addition, devices that utilize multiple on-board sensors are used to gather information about surrounding environments, hence capturing data, transmitting it and so on. This is of ultimate importance to government data for not only planning socio-economic development, but also maintaining awareness and governance.

## The Internet of Things

In most organizations, similar to government data centers, information travels along familiar routes. Such information is generated inside or outside the government data environment. Information also originates externally, gathered from public sources, harvested from the Internet, or purchased from information suppliers.

The physical world itself is becoming a type of information system. We use the term "Internet of Things", sensors and actuators embedded in physical objects are linked through wired and wireless networks, often using the same Internet Protocol (IP) that connects the Internet. These networks exchange huge volumes of data that flow to computers for analysis. The data legislation and regulations adopted by the government will enable us to classify which part of this huge data belongs to the government data, and whether it is public or not, and who may use it (McKinsey Global Institute, 2015).

There is a lot to discuss and study about the Internet of Things, however minor role it has now in relation to government data, this role is going to grow in an increasing way. Hence future trends in government data should consider the IoT role.

## The New IT Reality

As the reality of new technology become clear and well introduced, a different reality of dealing with information technology becomes the omnipotent factor in setting up high level policies regarding government information. As these technologies would introduce new ways of dealing with information, government data and information can easily be integrated into this new technology environment, hence achieving the value-added advantages of using new technologies without having to change user policies and operation regulations. Examples of such technologies are the following:

1. **Cloud/Client Computing:** Institutionalize the computing platform to deal with cloud systems, would affect the data itself in the sense of providing higher speeds, more availability everywhere, providing excellent data verification.
2. **Software-Defined Applications and Infrastructure:** The future is software defined! This is a statement that may roughly summarized the future trend indicated by this. The development of networking, storage, security, and real-time infrastructure, service oriented and model-driven architecture are all examples of how programming is becoming the future trend for data development given cloud and technology is progressing as observed (Verizon, 2015).
3. **Web-Scale IT:** This is perhaps the most controversial aspect of future trends of technology: should it be Web-based in large scale and specialized features?

The trend is to use open source for example to promote web-based IT platforms that has the following focus technology areas:

a.  Industrially designed data centers
b.  Risk-embracing culture
c.  Collaborative aligned organizations
d.  Velocity-focused processes
e.  Infrastructure as a code
f.  Web-oriented architecture

4.  **Risk-Based Security and Self-Protection:** This trend in fact is not new (Global Security, 2016). It is always there, always evolving and always present in different ways. However the future trend here is to enable applications to "protect themselves". This is a process that spreads over applications' run time. From dynamic interaction to providing high-assurance security vulnerabilities, the trend is based on two principles:

a.  The application code should be designed with security awareness in mind, and
b.  Provide some mechanism of runtime application self-protection.

## FUTURE TECHNOLOGIES FOR GOVERNMENT DATA

Over the last two decades alone, many advances in information and communication technologies have revolutionized how governments interact with their citizens, societies, companies and organizations. These technologies such as mobile communications, digital connectivity, and others provide unparalleled opportunities to deliver social impact and economic returns to millions of people in developing countries. There are countless examples of how enhanced access to government data, information and services can empower citizens and open new windows for delivering more effective and better living conditions.

## CONCLUSION

The new trends in information and communication technology development are quite challenging, versatile and imply a major change in eth way we deal with ICT processes, projects, life as we know it. However this will provide a great opportunity to government data platforms in order to progress confidently to a status where these new technologies are embedded somehow. In fact three possibilities exists:

*Figure 1.*

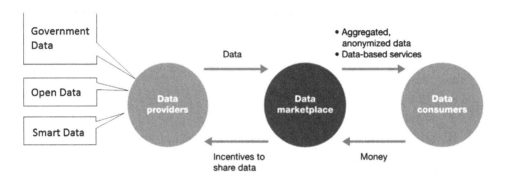

1.  The government data platform will adopt new technologies, new hardware and software but essentially the way government data is kept and managed still remain the same, just new tools have been adopted.
2.  The platform designers in the government will adopt an enterprise architecture (EA) that is more suited, and hence embark on a recreation of the government data as the new trends of technology imply, so such technology can be best and most efficiently integrated in the government data platform.
3.  Finally, the last option is a combination of both possibilities: Just update part of the government data platform with new technologies keeping the same operational and characteristics, and just redesign and integrate new technologies in another part of the existing government data platform. This heterogeneous structure can be practical and reasonable once the resources are considered.

In all cases, it is reasonable to assume the new ICT reality in the sense of including business part of the overall government data platform. This is done by viewing government data as a data marketplace from which data providers and data consumers have to deal in businesslike operations with the marketplace. This is originally suggested by McKinsey and associates (see Figure 1).

## REFERENCES

European Commission. (2014). *DG Enterprise & Industry: ICT TRENDS 2020 Main Trends for Information and Communication Technologies (ICT) and their Implications for e-Leadership Skills.* Retrieved from http://eskills-lead.eu/fileadmin/ lead/reports/lead_-_technology_trends_-_august_2014_rev_sep1.pdf

Gartner Group. (2016). *Top 10 Strategic Technology Trends for 2017*. Retrieved from http://www.gartner.com/newsroom/id/3482617

Global Security. (2016). *Voice verification*. Retrieved from http://www.globalsecurity. org/security/systems/biometrics-voice.htm

McKinsey & Company (2015). *The Internet of Things: Mapping the Value behind the Hype*. Author.

McKinsey Global Institute. (2015). *Unlocking the potential of the Internet of Things*. Retrieved from http://www.mckinsey.com/business-functions/digital-mckinsey/our-insights/the-internet-of-things-the-value-of-digitizing-the-physical-world

Satell, G. (2013). 5 Trends That Will Drive the Future of Technology. *Forbes*. Retrieved from http://www.forbes.com/sites/gregsatell/2013/03/12/5-trends-that-will-drive-the-future-of-technology/#12af5e1a4cf5

Verizon. (2015). *State of the Market: Internet of Things 2016: Accelerating innovation, productivity and value*. Retrieved from http://www.verizon.com/about/sites/default/files/state-of-the-internet-of-things-market-report-2016.pdf

# Related References

To continue our tradition of advancing information science and technology research, we have compiled a list of recommended IGI Global readings. These references will provide additional information and guidance to further enrich your knowledge and assist you with your own research and future publications.

Acharjya, D. P., & Mary, A. G. (2014). Privacy preservation in information system. In B. Tripathy & D. Acharjya (Eds.), *Advances in secure computing, internet services, and applications* (pp. 49–72). Hershey, PA: IGI Global. doi:10.4018/978-1-4666-4940-8.ch003

Adeyemo, O. (2013). The nationwide health information network: A biometric approach to prevent medical identity theft. In *User-driven healthcare: Concepts, methodologies, tools, and applications* (pp. 1636–1649). Hershey, PA: IGI Global. doi:10.4018/978-1-4666-2770-3.ch081

Adler, M., & Henman, P. (2009). Justice beyond the courts: The implications of computerisation for procedural justice in social security. In A. Martínez & P. Abat (Eds.), *E-justice: Using information communication technologies in the court system* (pp. 65–86). Hershey, PA: IGI Global. doi:10.4018/978-1-59904-998-4.ch005

Aflalo, E., & Gabay, E. (2013). An information system for coping with student dropout. In L. Tomei (Ed.), *Learning tools and teaching approaches through ICT advancements* (pp. 176–187). Hershey, PA: IGI Global. doi:10.4018/978-1-4666-2017-9.ch016

Agamba, J., & Keengwe, J. (2012). Pre-service teachers perceptions of information assurance and cyber security. *International Journal of Information and Communication Technology Education*, *8*(2), 94–101. doi:10.4018/jicte.2012040108

**Related References**

Aggarwal, R. (2013). Dispute settlement for cyber crimes in India: An analysis. In R. Khurana & R. Aggarwal (Eds.), *Interdisciplinary perspectives on business convergence, computing, and legality* (pp. 160–171). Hershey, PA: IGI Global. doi:10.4018/978-1-4666-4209-6.ch015

Agwu, E. (2013). Cyber criminals on the internet super highways: A technical investigation of different shades and colours within the Nigerian cyber space. *International Journal of Online Marketing*, *3*(2), 56–74. doi:10.4018/ijom.2013040104

Ahmad, A. (2012). Security assessment of networks. In *Wireless technologies: Concepts, methodologies, tools and applications* (pp. 208–224). Hershey, PA: IGI Global. doi:10.4018/978-1-61350-101-6.ch111

Ahmed, M. A., Janssen, M., & van den Hoven, J. (2012). Value sensitive transfer (VST) of systems among countries: Towards a framework. *International Journal of Electronic Government Research*, *8*(1), 26–42. doi:10.4018/jegr.2012010102

Ahmed, N., & Jensen, C. D. (2012). Security of dependable systems. In L. Petre, K. Sere, & E. Troubitsyna (Eds.), *Dependability and computer engineering: Concepts for software-intensive systems* (pp. 230–264). Hershey, PA: IGI Global. doi:10.4018/978-1-60960-747-0.ch011

Aikins, S. K. (2008). Issues and trends in internet-based citizen participation. In G. Garson & M. Khosrow-Pour (Eds.), *Handbook of research on public information technology* (pp. 31–40). Hershey, PA: IGI Global. doi:10.4018/978-1-59904-857-4.ch004

Aikins, S. K. (2009). A comparative study of municipal adoption of internet-based citizen participation. In C. Reddick (Ed.), *Handbook of research on strategies for local e-government adoption and implementation: Comparative studies* (pp. 206–230). Hershey, PA: IGI Global. doi:10.4018/978-1-60566-282-4.ch011

Aikins, S. K. (2012). Improving e-government project management: Best practices and critical success factors. In *Digital democracy: Concepts, methodologies, tools, and applications* (pp. 1314–1332). Hershey, PA: IGI Global. doi:10.4018/978-1-4666-1740-7.ch065

Akabawi, M. S. (2011). Ghabbour group ERP deployment: Learning from past technology failures. In E. Business Research and Case Center (Ed.), Cases on business and management in the MENA region: New trends and opportunities (pp. 177-203). Hershey, PA: IGI Global. doi:10.4018/978-1-60960-583-4.ch012

Akabawi, M. S. (2013). Ghabbour group ERP deployment: Learning from past technology failures. In *Industrial engineering: Concepts, methodologies, tools, and applications* (pp. 933–958). Hershey, PA: IGI Global. doi:10.4018/978-1-4666-1945-6.ch051

Akbulut, A. Y., & Motwani, J. (2008). Integration and information sharing in e-government. In G. Putnik & M. Cruz-Cunha (Eds.), *Encyclopedia of networked and virtual organizations* (pp. 729–734). Hershey, PA: IGI Global. doi:10.4018/978-1-59904-885-7.ch096

Akers, E. J. (2008). Technology diffusion in public administration. In G. Garson & M. Khosrow-Pour (Eds.), *Handbook of research on public information technology* (pp. 339–348). Hershey, PA: IGI Global. doi:10.4018/978-1-59904-857-4.ch033

Al, M., & Yoshigoe, K. (2012). Security and attacks in wireless sensor networks. In *Wireless technologies: Concepts, methodologies, tools and applications* (pp. 1811–1846). Hershey, PA: IGI Global. doi:10.4018/978-1-61350-101-6.ch706

Al-Ahmad, W. (2011). Building secure software using XP. *International Journal of Secure Software Engineering*, 2(3), 63–76. doi:10.4018/jsse.2011070104

Al-Bayatti, A. H., & Al-Bayatti, H. M. (2012). Security management and simulation of mobile ad hoc networks (MANET). In H. Al-Bahadili (Ed.), *Simulation in computer network design and modeling: Use and analysis* (pp. 297–314). Hershey, PA: IGI Global. doi:10.4018/978-1-4666-0191-8.ch014

Al-Bayatti, A. H., Zedan, H., Cau, A., & Siewe, F. (2012). Security management for mobile ad hoc network of networks (MANoN). In I. Khalil & E. Weippl (Eds.), *Advancing the next-generation of mobile computing: Emerging technologies* (pp. 1–18). Hershey, PA: IGI Global. doi:10.4018/978-1-4666-0119-2.ch001

Al-Hamdani, W. A. (2011). Three models to measure information security compliance. In H. Nemati (Ed.), *Security and privacy assurance in advancing technologies: New developments* (pp. 351–373). Hershey, PA: IGI Global. doi:10.4018/978-1-60960-200-0.ch022

Al-Hamdani, W. A. (2014). Secure e-learning and cryptography. In K. Sullivan, P. Czigler, & J. Sullivan Hellgren (Eds.), *Cases on professional distance education degree programs and practices: Successes, challenges, and issues* (pp. 331–369). Hershey, PA: IGI Global. doi:10.4018/978-1-4666-4486-1.ch012

*Related References*

Al-Jaljouli, R., & Abawajy, J. H. (2012). Security framework for mobile agents-based applications. In A. Kumar & H. Rahman (Eds.), *Mobile computing techniques in emerging markets: Systems, applications and services* (pp. 242–269). Hershey, PA: IGI Global. doi:10.4018/978-1-4666-0080-5.ch009

Al-Jaljouli, R., & Abawajy, J. H. (2014). Mobile agents security protocols. In *Crisis management: Concepts, methodologies, tools and applications* (pp. 166–202). Hershey, PA: IGI Global. doi:10.4018/978-1-4666-4707-7.ch007

Al-Shafi, S. (2008). Free wireless internet park services: An investigation of technology adoption in Qatar from a citizens perspective. *Journal of Cases on Information Technology*, *10*(3), 21–34. doi:10.4018/jcit.2008070103

Al-Shafi, S., & Weerakkody, V. (2009). Implementing free wi-fi in public parks: An empirical study in Qatar. *International Journal of Electronic Government Research*, *5*(3), 21–35. doi:10.4018/jegr.2009070102

Al-Suqri, M. N., & Akomolafe-Fatuyi, E. (2012). Security and privacy in digital libraries: Challenges, opportunities and prospects. *International Journal of Digital Library Systems*, *3*(4), 54–61. doi:10.4018/ijdls.2012100103

Aladwani, A. M. (2002). Organizational actions, computer attitudes and end-user satisfaction in public organizations: An empirical study. In C. Snodgrass & E. Szewczak (Eds.), *Human factors in information systems* (pp. 153–168). Hershey, PA: IGI Global. doi:10.4018/978-1-931777-10-0.ch012

Aladwani, A. M. (2002). Organizational actions, computer attitudes, and end-user satisfaction in public organizations: An empirical study. *Journal of Organizational and End User Computing*, *14*(1), 42–49. doi:10.4018/joeuc.2002010104

Alavi, R., Islam, S., Jahankhani, H., & Al-Nemrat, A. (2013). Analyzing human factors for an effective information security management system. *International Journal of Secure Software Engineering*, *4*(1), 50–74. doi:10.4018/jsse.2013010104

Alazab, A., Abawajy, J. H., & Hobbs, M. (2013). Web malware that targets web applications. In L. Caviglione, M. Coccoli, & A. Merlo (Eds.), *Social network engineering for secure web data and services* (pp. 248–264). Hershey, PA: IGI Global. doi:10.4018/978-1-4666-3926-3.ch012

Alazab, A., Hobbs, M., Abawajy, J., & Khraisat, A. (2013). Malware detection and prevention system based on multi-stage rules. *International Journal of Information Security and Privacy*, *7*(2), 29–43. doi:10.4018/jisp.2013040102

Alazab, M., Venkatraman, S., Watters, P., & Alazab, M. (2013). Information security governance: The art of detecting hidden malware. In D. Mellado, L. Enrique Sánchez, E. Fernández-Medina, & M. Piattini (Eds.), *IT security governance innovations: Theory and research* (pp. 293–315). Hershey, PA: IGI Global. doi:10.4018/978-1-4666-2083-4.ch011

Alhaj, A., Aljawarneh, S., Masadeh, S., & Abu-Taieh, E. (2013). A secure data transmission mechanism for cloud outsourced data. *International Journal of Cloud Applications and Computing*, *3*(1), 34–43. doi:10.4018/ijcac.2013010104

Ali, M., & Jawandhiya, P. (2012). Security aware routing protocols for mobile ad hoc networks. In K. Lakhtaria (Ed.), *Technological advancements and applications in mobile ad-hoc networks: Research trends* (pp. 264–289). Hershey, PA: IGI Global. doi:10.4018/978-1-4666-0321-9.ch016

Ali, S. (2012). Practical web application security audit following industry standards and compliance. In J. Zubairi & A. Mahboob (Eds.), *Cyber security standards, practices and industrial applications: Systems and methodologies* (pp. 259–279). Hershey, PA: IGI Global. doi:10.4018/978-1-60960-851-4.ch013

Aljawarneh, S. (2013). Cloud security engineering: Avoiding security threats the right way. In S. Aljawarneh (Ed.), *Cloud computing advancements in design, implementation, and technologies* (pp. 147–153). Hershey, PA: IGI Global. doi:10.4018/978-1-4666-1879-4.ch010

Allen, B., Juillet, L., Paquet, G., & Roy, J. (2005). E-government and private-public partnerships: Relational challenges and strategic directions. In M. Khosrow-Pour (Ed.), *Practicing e-government: A global perspective* (pp. 364–382). Hershey, PA: IGI Global. doi:10.4018/978-1-59140-637-2.ch016

Alshaer, H., Muhaidat, S., Shubair, R., & Shayegannia, M. (2014). Security and connectivity analysis in vehicular communication networks. In D. Rawat, B. Bista, & G. Yan (Eds.), *Security, privacy, trust, and resource management in mobile and wireless communications* (pp. 83–107). Hershey, PA: IGI Global. doi:10.4018/978-1-4666-4691-9.ch005

Alshawaf, A., & Knalil, O. E. (2008). IS success factors and IS organizational impact: Does ownership type matter in Kuwait? *International Journal of Enterprise Information Systems*, *4*(2), 13–33. doi:10.4018/jeis.2008040102

Alzamil, Z. A. (2012). Information security awareness at Saudi Arabians organizations: An information technology employees perspective. *International Journal of Information Security and Privacy*, *6*(3), 38–55. doi:10.4018/jisp.2012070102

## Related References

Ambali, A. R. (2009). Digital divide and its implication on Malaysian e-government: Policy initiatives. In H. Rahman (Ed.), *Social and political implications of data mining: Knowledge management in e-government* (pp. 267–287). Hershey, PA: IGI Global. doi:10.4018/978-1-60566-230-5.ch016

Amoretti, F. (2007). Digital international governance. In A. Anttiroiko & M. Malkia (Eds.), *Encyclopedia of digital government* (pp. 365–370). Hershey, PA: IGI Global. doi:10.4018/978-1-59140-789-8.ch056

Amoretti, F. (2008). Digital international governance. In A. Anttiroiko (Ed.), *Electronic government: Concepts, methodologies, tools, and applications* (pp. 688–696). Hershey, PA: IGI Global. doi:10.4018/978-1-59904-947-2.ch058

Amoretti, F. (2008). E-government at supranational level in the European Union. In A. Anttiroiko (Ed.), *Electronic government: Concepts, methodologies, tools, and applications* (pp. 1047–1055). Hershey, PA: IGI Global. doi:10.4018/978-1-59904-947-2.ch079

Amoretti, F. (2008). E-government regimes. In A. Anttiroiko (Ed.), *Electronic government: Concepts, methodologies, tools, and applications* (pp. 3846–3856). Hershey, PA: IGI Global. doi:10.4018/978-1-59904-947-2.ch280

Amoretti, F. (2009). Electronic constitution: A Braudelian perspective. In F. Amoretti (Ed.), *Electronic constitution: Social, cultural, and political implications* (pp. 1–19). Hershey, PA: IGI Global. doi:10.4018/978-1-60566-254-1.ch001

Amoretti, F., & Musella, F. (2009). Institutional isomorphism and new technologies. In M. Khosrow-Pour (Ed.), *Encyclopedia of information science and technology* (2nd ed.; pp. 2066–2071). Hershey, PA: IGI Global. doi:10.4018/978-1-60566-026-4.ch325

Andersen, K. V., & Henriksen, H. Z. (2007). E-government research: Capabilities, interaction, orientation, and values. In D. Norris (Ed.), *Current issues and trends in e-government research* (pp. 269–288). Hershey, PA: IGI Global. doi:10.4018/978-1-59904-283-1.ch013

Anderson, K. V., & Henriksen, H. Z. (2005). The first leg of e-government research: Domains and application areas 19982003. *International Journal of Electronic Government Research*, *1*(4), 26–44. doi:10.4018/jegr.2005100102

Anttiroiko, A. (2009). Democratic e-governance. In M. Khosrow-Pour (Ed.), *Encyclopedia of information science and technology* (2nd ed.; pp. 990–995). Hershey, PA: IGI Global. doi:10.4018/978-1-60566-026-4.ch158

Anyiwo, D., & Sharma, S. (2011). Web services and e-business technologies: Security issues. In O. Bak & N. Stair (Eds.), *Impact of e-business technologies on public and private organizations: Industry comparisons and perspectives* (pp. 249–261). Hershey, PA: IGI Global. doi:10.4018/978-1-60960-501-8.ch015

Apostolakis, I., Chryssanthou, A., & Varlamis, I. (2011). A holistic perspective of security in health related virtual communities. In *Virtual communities: Concepts, methodologies, tools and applications* (pp. 1190–1204). Hershey, PA: IGI Global. doi:10.4018/978-1-60960-100-3.ch406

Arnett, K. P., Templeton, G. F., & Vance, D. A. (2011). Information security by words alone: The case for strong security policies. In H. Nemati (Ed.), *Security and privacy assurance in advancing technologies: New developments* (pp. 154–159). Hershey, PA: IGI Global. doi:10.4018/978-1-60960-200-0.ch011

Arogundade, O. T., Akinwale, A. T., Jin, Z., & Yang, X. G. (2011). A unified use-misuse case model for capturing and analysing safety and security requirements. *International Journal of Information Security and Privacy*, 5(4), 8–30. doi:10.4018/jisp.2011100102

Arshad, J., Townend, P., Xu, J., & Jie, W. (2012). Cloud computing security: Opportunities and pitfalls. *International Journal of Grid and High Performance Computing*, 4(1), 52–66. doi:10.4018/jghpc.2012010104

Asim, M., & Petkovic, M. (2012). Fundamental building blocks for security interoperability in e-business. In E. Kajan, F. Dorloff, & I. Bedini (Eds.), *Handbook of research on e-business standards and protocols: Documents, data and advanced web technologies* (pp. 269–292). Hershey, PA: IGI Global. doi:10.4018/978-1-4666-0146-8.ch013

Askary, S., Goodwin, D., & Lanis, R. (2012). Improvements in audit risks related to information technology frauds. *International Journal of Enterprise Information Systems*, 8(2), 52–63. doi:10.4018/jeis.2012040104

Aurigemma, S. (2013). A composite framework for behavioral compliance with information security policies. *Journal of Organizational and End User Computing*, 25(3), 32–51. doi:10.4018/joeuc.2013070103

Avalle, M., Pironti, A., Pozza, D., & Sisto, R. (2011). JavaSPI: A framework for security protocol implementation. *International Journal of Secure Software Engineering*, 2(4), 34–48. doi:10.4018/jsse.2011100103

## Related References

Axelrod, C. W. (2012). A dynamic cyber security economic model: incorporating value functions for all involved parties. In M. Gupta, J. Walp, & R. Sharman (Eds.), *Threats, countermeasures, and advances in applied information security* (pp. 462–477). Hershey, PA: IGI Global. doi:10.4018/978-1-4666-0978-5.ch024

Ayanso, A., & Herath, T. (2012). Law and technology at crossroads in cyberspace: Where do we go from here? In A. Dudley, J. Braman, & G. Vincenti (Eds.), *Investigating cyber law and cyber ethics: Issues, impacts and practices* (pp. 57–77). Hershey, PA: IGI Global. doi:10.4018/978-1-61350-132-0.ch004

Baars, T., & Spruit, M. (2012). Designing a secure cloud architecture: The SeCA model. *International Journal of Information Security and Privacy*, 6(1), 14–32. doi:10.4018/jisp.2012010102

Bachmann, M. (2011). Deciphering the hacker underground: First quantitative insights. In T. Holt & B. Schell (Eds.), *Corporate hacking and technology-driven crime: Social dynamics and implications* (pp. 105–126). Hershey, PA: IGI Global. doi:10.4018/978-1-61692-805-6.ch006

Bachmann, M., & Smith, B. (2012). Internet fraud. In Z. Yan (Ed.), *Encyclopedia of cyber behavior* (pp. 931–943). Hershey, PA: IGI Global. doi:10.4018/978-1-4666-0315-8.ch077

Bai, Y., & Khan, K. M. (2011). Ell secure information system using modal logic technique. *International Journal of Secure Software Engineering*, 2(2), 65–76. doi:10.4018/jsse.2011040104

Baker, P. M., Bell, A., & Moon, N. W. (2009). Accessibility issues in municipal wireless networks. In C. Reddick (Ed.), *Handbook of research on strategies for local e-government adoption and implementation: Comparative studies* (pp. 569–588). Hershey, PA: IGI Global. doi:10.4018/978-1-60566-282-4.ch030

Bandeira, G. S. (2014). Criminal liability of organizations, corporations, legal persons, and similar entities on law of portuguese cybercrime: A brief discussion on the issue of crimes of "false information," the "damage on other programs or computer data," the "computer-software sabotage," the "illegitimate access," the "unlawful interception," and "illegitimate reproduction of the protected program". In I. Portela & F. Almeida (Eds.), *Organizational, legal, and technological dimensions of information system administration* (pp. 96–107). Hershey, PA: IGI Global. doi:10.4018/978-1-4666-4526-4.ch006

Barjis, J. (2012). Software engineering security based on business process modeling. In K. Khan (Ed.), *Security-aware systems applications and software development methods* (pp. 52–68). Hershey, PA: IGI Global. doi:10.4018/978-1-4666-1580-9. ch004

Becker, S. A., Keimer, R., & Muth, T. (2010). A case on university and community collaboration: The sci-tech entrepreneurial training services (ETS) program. In S. Becker & R. Niebuhr (Eds.), *Cases on technology innovation: Entrepreneurial successes and pitfalls* (pp. 68–90). Hershey, PA: IGI Global. doi:10.4018/978-1-61520-609-4.ch003

Becker, S. A., Keimer, R., & Muth, T. (2012). A case on university and community collaboration: The sci-tech entrepreneurial training services (ETS) program. In Regional development: Concepts, methodologies, tools, and applications (pp. 947-969). Hershey, PA: IGI Global. doi:10.4018/978-1-4666-0882-5.ch507

Bedi, P., Gandotra, V., & Singhal, A. (2013). Innovative strategies for secure software development. In H. Singh & K. Kaur (Eds.), *Designing, engineering, and analyzing reliable and efficient software* (pp. 217–237). Hershey, PA: IGI Global. doi:10.4018/978-1-4666-2958-5.ch013

Belsis, P., Skourlas, C., & Gritzalis, S. (2011). Secure electronic healthcare records management in wireless environments. *Journal of Information Technology Research*, *4*(4), 1–17. doi:10.4018/jitr.2011100101

Bernardi, R. (2012). Information technology and resistance to public sector reforms: A case study in Kenya. In T. Papadopoulos & P. Kanellis (Eds.), *Public sector reform using information technologies: Transforming policy into practice* (pp. 59–78). Hershey, PA: IGI Global. doi:10.4018/978-1-60960-839-2.ch004

Bernardi, R. (2013). Information technology and resistance to public sector reforms: A case study in Kenya. In *User-driven healthcare: Concepts, methodologies, tools, and applications* (pp. 14–33). Hershey, PA: Medical IGI Global. doi:10.4018/978-1-4666-2770-3.ch002

Bernik, I. (2012). Internet study: Cyber threats and cybercrime awareness and fear. *International Journal of Cyber Warfare & Terrorism*, *2*(3), 1–11. doi:10.4018/ijcwt.2012070101

Bhatia, M. S. (2011). World war III: The cyber war. *International Journal of Cyber Warfare & Terrorism*, *1*(3), 59–69. doi:10.4018/ijcwt.2011070104

*Related References*

Blanco, C., Rosado, D., Gutiérrez, C., Rodríguez, A., Mellado, D., Fernández-Medina, E., & Piattini, M. et al. (2011). Security over the information systems development cycle. In H. Mouratidis (Ed.), *Software engineering for secure systems: Industrial and research perspectives* (pp. 113–154). Hershey, PA: IGI Global. doi:10.4018/978-1-61520-837-1.ch005

Bobbert, Y., & Mulder, H. (2012). A research journey into maturing the business information security of mid market organizations. In W. Van Grembergen & S. De Haes (Eds.), *Business strategy and applications in enterprise IT governance* (pp. 236–259). Hershey, PA: IGI Global. doi:10.4018/978-1-4666-1779-7.ch014

Boddington, R. (2011). Digital evidence. In D. Kerr, J. Gammack, & K. Bryant (Eds.), *Digital business security development: Management technologies* (pp. 37–72). Hershey, PA: IGI Global. doi:10.4018/978-1-60566-806-2.ch002

Bolívar, M. P., Pérez, M. D., & Hernández, A. M. (2012). Municipal e-government services in emerging economies: The Latin-American and Caribbean experiences. In Y. Chen & P. Chu (Eds.), *Electronic governance and cross-boundary collaboration: Innovations and advancing tools* (pp. 198–226). Hershey, PA: IGI Global. doi:10.4018/978-1-60960-753-1.ch011

Borycki, E. M., & Kushniruk, A. W. (2010). Use of clinical simulations to evaluate the impact of health information systems and ubiquitous computing devices upon health professional work. In S. Mohammed & J. Fiaidhi (Eds.), *Ubiquitous health and medical informatics: The ubiquity 2.0 trend and beyond* (pp. 552–573). Hershey, PA: Medical IGI Global. doi:10.4018/978-1-61520-777-0.ch026

Borycki, E. M., & Kushniruk, A. W. (2011). Use of clinical simulations to evaluate the impact of health information systems and ubiquitous computing devices upon health professional work. In *Clinical technologies: Concepts, methodologies, tools and applications* (pp. 532–553). Hershey, PA: Medical IGI Global. doi:10.4018/978-1-60960-561-2.ch220

Bossler, A. M., & Burruss, G. W. (2011). The general theory of crime and computer hacking: Low self-control hackers? In T. Holt & B. Schell (Eds.), *Corporate hacking and technology-driven crime: Social dynamics and implications* (pp. 38–67). Hershey, PA: IGI Global. doi:10.4018/978-1-61692-805-6.ch003

Bouras, C., & Stamos, K. (2011). Security issues for multi-domain resource reservation. In D. Kar & M. Syed (Eds.), *Network security, administration and management: Advancing technology and practice* (pp. 38–50). Hershey, PA: IGI Global. doi:10.4018/978-1-60960-777-7.ch003

Bracci, F., Corradi, A., & Foschini, L. (2014). Cloud standards: Security and interoperability issues. In H. Mouftah & B. Kantarci (Eds.), *Communication infrastructures for cloud computing* (pp. 465–495). Hershey, PA: IGI Global. doi:10.4018/978-1-4666-4522-6.ch020

Brodsky, J., & Radvanovsky, R. (2011). Control systems security. In T. Holt & B. Schell (Eds.), *Corporate hacking and technology-driven crime: Social dynamics and implications* (pp. 187–204). Hershey, PA: IGI Global. doi:10.4018/978-1-61692-805-6.ch010

Brooks, D. (2013). Security threats and risks of intelligent building systems: Protecting facilities from current and emerging vulnerabilities. In C. Laing, A. Badii, & P. Vickers (Eds.), *Securing critical infrastructures and critical control systems: Approaches for threat protection* (pp. 1–16). Hershey, PA: IGI Global. doi:10.4018/978-1-4666-2659-1.ch001

Buchan, J. (2011). Developing a dynamic and responsive online learning environment: A case study of a large Australian university. In B. Czerkawski (Ed.), *Free and open source software for e-learning: Issues, successes and challenges* (pp. 92–109). Hershey, PA: IGI Global. doi:10.4018/978-1-61520-917-0.ch006

Buenger, A. W. (2008). Digital convergence and cybersecurity policy. In G. Garson & M. Khosrow-Pour (Eds.), *Handbook of research on public information technology* (pp. 395–405). Hershey, PA: IGI Global. doi:10.4018/978-1-59904-857-4.ch038

Bülow, W., & Wester, M. (2012). The right to privacy and the protection of personal data in a digital era and the age of information. In C. Akrivopoulou & N. Garipidis (Eds.), *Human rights and risks in the digital era: Globalization and the effects of information technologies* (pp. 34–45). Hershey, PA: IGI Global. doi:10.4018/978-1-4666-0891-7.ch004

Burn, J. M., & Loch, K. D. (2002). The societal impact of world wide web - Key challenges for the 21st century. In A. Salehnia (Ed.), *Ethical issues of information systems* (pp. 88–106). Hershey, PA: IGI Global. doi:10.4018/978-1-931777-15-5.ch007

Burn, J. M., & Loch, K. D. (2003). The societal impact of the world wide web-Key challenges for the 21st century. In M. Khosrow-Pour (Ed.), *Advanced topics in information resources management* (Vol. 2, pp. 32–51). Hershey, PA: IGI Global. doi:10.4018/978-1-59140-062-2.ch002

## Related References

Bwalya, K. J., Du Plessis, T., & Rensleigh, C. (2012). The "quicksilver initiatives" as a framework for e-government strategy design in developing economies. In K. Bwalya & S. Zulu (Eds.), *Handbook of research on e-government in emerging economies: Adoption, e-participation, and legal frameworks* (pp. 605–623). Hershey, PA: IGI Global. doi:10.4018/978-1-4666-0324-0.ch031

Cabotaje, C. E., & Alampay, E. A. (2013). Social media and citizen engagement: Two cases from the Philippines. In S. Saeed & C. Reddick (Eds.), *Human-centered system design for electronic governance* (pp. 225–238). Hershey, PA: IGI Global. doi:10.4018/978-1-4666-3640-8.ch013

Camillo, A., Di Pietro, L., Di Virgilio, F., & Franco, M. (2013). Work-groups conflict at PetroTech-Italy, S.R.L.: The influence of culture on conflict dynamics. In B. Christiansen, E. Turkina, & N. Williams (Eds.), *Cultural and technological influences on global business* (pp. 272–289). Hershey, PA: IGI Global. doi:10.4018/978-1-4666-3966-9.ch015

Canongia, C., & Mandarino, R. (2014). Cybersecurity: The new challenge of the information society. In Crisis management: Concepts, methodologies, tools and applications (pp. 60-80). Hershey, PA: IGI Global. doi:10.4018/978-1-4666-4707-7.ch003

Cao, X., & Lu, Y. (2011). The social network structure of a computer hacker community. In H. Nemati (Ed.), *Security and privacy assurance in advancing technologies: New developments* (pp. 160–173). Hershey, PA: IGI Global. doi:10.4018/978-1-60960-200-0.ch012

Capra, E., Francalanci, C., & Marinoni, C. (2008). Soft success factors for m-government. In A. Anttiroiko (Ed.), *Electronic government: Concepts, methodologies, tools, and applications* (pp. 1213–1233). Hershey, PA: IGI Global. doi:10.4018/978-1-59904-947-2.ch089

Cardholm, L. (2014). Identifying the business value of information security. In T. Tsiakis, T. Kargidis, & P. Katsaros (Eds.), *Approaches and processes for managing the economics of information systems* (pp. 157–180). Hershey, PA: IGI Global. doi:10.4018/978-1-4666-4983-5.ch010

Cardoso, R. C., & Gomes, A. (2012). Security issues in massively multiplayer online games. In M. Cruz-Cunha (Ed.), *Handbook of research on serious games as educational, business and research tools* (pp. 290–314). Hershey, PA: IGI Global. doi:10.4018/978-1-4666-0149-9.ch016

Carpen-Amarie, A., Costan, A., Leordeanu, C., Basescu, C., & Antoniu, G. (2012). Towards a generic security framework for cloud data management environments. *International Journal of Distributed Systems and Technologies*, *3*(1), 17–34. doi:10.4018/jdst.2012010102

Cartelli, A. (2009). The implementation of practices with ICT as a new teaching-learning paradigm. In A. Cartelli & M. Palma (Eds.), *Encyclopedia of information communication technology* (pp. 413–417). Hershey, PA: IGI Global. doi:10.4018/978-1-59904-845-1.ch055

Caushaj, E., Fu, H., Sethi, I., Badih, H., Watson, D., Zhu, Y., & Leng, S. (2013). Theoretical analysis and experimental study: Monitoring data privacy in smartphone communications. *International Journal of Interdisciplinary Telecommunications and Networking*, *5*(2), 66–82. doi:10.4018/jitn.2013040106

Cepheli, Ö., & Kurt, G. K. (2014). Physical layer security in wireless communication networks. In D. Rawat, B. Bista, & G. Yan (Eds.), *Security, privacy, trust, and resource management in mobile and wireless communications* (pp. 61–81). Hershey, PA: IGI Global. doi:10.4018/978-1-4666-4691-9.ch004

Chakraborty, P., & Raghuraman, K. (2013). Trends in information security. In K. Buragga & N. Zaman (Eds.), *Software development techniques for constructive information systems design* (pp. 354–376). Hershey, PA: IGI Global. doi:10.4018/978-1-4666-3679-8.ch020

Chandrakumar, T., & Parthasarathy, S. (2012). Enhancing data security in ERP projects using XML. *International Journal of Enterprise Information Systems*, *8*(1), 51–65. doi:10.4018/jeis.2012010104

Chapple, M. J., Striegel, A., & Crowell, C. R. (2011). Firewall rulebase management: Tools and techniques. In M. Quigley (Ed.), *ICT ethics and security in the 21st century: New developments and applications* (pp. 254–276). Hershey, PA: IGI Global. doi:10.4018/978-1-60960-573-5.ch013

Charalabidis, Y., Lampathaki, F., & Askounis, D. (2010). Investigating the landscape in national interoperability frameworks. *International Journal of E-Services and Mobile Applications*, *2*(4), 28–41. doi:10.4018/jesma.2010100103

Charalabidis, Y., Lampathaki, F., & Askounis, D. (2012). Investigating the landscape in national interoperability frameworks. In A. Scupola (Ed.), *Innovative mobile platform developments for electronic services design and delivery* (pp. 218–231). Hershey, PA: IGI Global. doi:10.4018/978-1-4666-1568-7.ch013

### Related References

Chen, I. (2005). Distance education associations. In C. Howard, J. Boettcher, L. Justice, K. Schenk, P. Rogers, & G. Berg (Eds.), *Encyclopedia of distance learning* (pp. 599–612). Hershey, PA: IGI Global. doi:10.4018/978-1-59140-555-9.ch087

Chen, I. (2008). Distance education associations. In L. Tomei (Ed.), *Online and distance learning: Concepts, methodologies, tools, and applications* (pp. 562–579). Hershey, PA: IGI Global. doi:10.4018/978-1-59904-935-9.ch048

Chen, L., Hu, W., Yang, M., & Zhang, L. (2011). Security and privacy issues in secure e-mail standards and services. In H. Nemati (Ed.), *Security and privacy assurance in advancing technologies: new developments* (pp. 174–185). Hershey, PA: IGI Global. doi:10.4018/978-1-60960-200-0.ch013

Chen, L., Varol, C., Liu, Q., & Zhou, B. (2014). Security in wireless metropolitan area networks: WiMAX and LTE. In D. Rawat, B. Bista, & G. Yan (Eds.), *Security, privacy, trust, and resource management in mobile and wireless communications* (pp. 11–27). Hershey, PA: IGI Global. doi:10.4018/978-1-4666-4691-9.ch002

Chen, Y. (2008). Managing IT outsourcing for digital government. In A. Anttiroiko (Ed.), *Electronic government: Concepts, methodologies, tools, and applications* (pp. 3107–3114). Hershey, PA: IGI Global. doi:10.4018/978-1-59904-947-2.ch229

Chen, Y., & Dimitrova, D. V. (2006). Electronic government and online engagement: Citizen interaction with government via web portals. *International Journal of Electronic Government Research*, 2(1), 54–76. doi:10.4018/jegr.2006010104

Chen, Y., & Knepper, R. (2005). Digital government development strategies: Lessons for policy makers from a comparative perspective. In W. Huang, K. Siau, & K. Wei (Eds.), *Electronic government strategies and implementation* (pp. 394–420). Hershey, PA: IGI Global. doi:10.4018/978-1-59140-348-7.ch017

Chen, Y., & Knepper, R. (2008). Digital government development strategies: Lessons for policy makers from a comparative perspective. In H. Rahman (Ed.), *Developing successful ICT strategies: Competitive advantages in a global knowledge-driven society* (pp. 334–356). Hershey, PA: IGI Global. doi:10.4018/978-1-59904-654-9.ch017

Cherdantseva, Y., & Hilton, J. (2014). Information security and information assurance: Discussion about the meaning, scope, and goals. In I. Portela & F. Almeida (Eds.), *Organizational, legal, and technological dimensions of information system administration* (pp. 167–198). Hershey, PA: IGI Global. doi:10.4018/978-1-4666-4526-4.ch010

Cherdantseva, Y., & Hilton, J. (2014). The 2011 survey of information security and information assurance professionals: Findings. In I. Portela & F. Almeida (Eds.), *Organizational, legal, and technological dimensions of information system administration* (pp. 243–256). Hershey, PA: IGI Global. doi:10.4018/978-1-4666-4526-4.ch013

Cherian, E. J., & Ryan, T. W. (2014). Incongruent needs: Why differences in the iron-triangle of priorities make health information technology adoption and use difficult. In C. El Morr (Ed.), *Research perspectives on the role of informatics in health policy and management* (pp. 209–221). Hershey, PA: Medical IGI Global. doi:10.4018/978-1-4666-4321-5.ch012

Cho, H. J., & Hwang, S. (2010). Government 2.0 in Korea: Focusing on e-participation services. In C. Reddick (Ed.), *Politics, democracy and e-government: Participation and service delivery* (pp. 94–114). Hershey, PA: IGI Global. doi:10.4018/978-1-61520-933-0.ch006

Chorus, C., & Timmermans, H. (2010). Ubiquitous travel environments and travel control strategies: Prospects and challenges. In M. Wachowicz (Ed.), *Movement-aware applications for sustainable mobility: Technologies and approaches* (pp. 30–51). Hershey, PA: IGI Global. doi:10.4018/978-1-61520-769-5.ch003

Chowdhury, M. U., & Ray, B. R. (2013). Security risks/vulnerability in a RFID system and possible defenses. In N. Karmakar (Ed.), *Advanced RFID systems, security, and applications* (pp. 1–15). Hershey, PA: IGI Global. doi:10.4018/978-1-4666-2080-3.ch001

Chuanshen, R. (2007). E-government construction and China's administrative litigation act. In A. Anttiroiko & M. Malkia (Eds.), *Encyclopedia of digital government* (pp. 507–510). Hershey, PA: IGI Global. doi:10.4018/978-1-59140-789-8.ch077

Ciaghi, A., & Villafiorita, A. (2012). Law modeling and BPR for public administration improvement. In K. Bwalya & S. Zulu (Eds.), *Handbook of research on e-government in emerging economies: Adoption, e-participation, and legal frameworks* (pp. 391–410). Hershey, PA: IGI Global. doi:10.4018/978-1-4666-0324-0.ch019

Ciaramitaro, B. L., & Skrocki, M. (2012). mHealth: Mobile healthcare. In B. Ciaramitaro (Ed.), Mobile technology consumption: Opportunities and challenges (pp. 99-109). Hershey, PA: IGI Global. doi:10.4018/978-1-61350-150-4.ch007

Cofta, P., Lacohée, H., & Hodgson, P. (2011). Incorporating social trust into design practices for secure systems. In H. Mouratidis (Ed.), *Software engineering for secure systems: Industrial and research perspectives* (pp. 260–284). Hershey, PA: IGI Global. doi:10.4018/978-1-61520-837-1.ch010

## Related References

Comite, U. (2012). Innovative processes and managerial effectiveness of e-procurement in healthcare. In A. Manoharan & M. Holzer (Eds.), *Active citizen participation in e-government: A global perspective* (pp. 206–229). Hershey, PA: IGI Global. doi:10.4018/978-1-4666-0116-1.ch011

Conway, M. (2012). What is cyberterrorism and how real is the threat? A review of the academic literature, 1996 – 2009. In P. Reich & E. Gelbstein (Eds.), *Law, policy, and technology: Cyberterrorism, information warfare, and internet immobilization* (pp. 279–307). Hershey, PA: IGI Global. doi:10.4018/978-1-61520-831-9.ch011

Cordella, A. (2013). E-government success: How to account for ICT, administrative rationalization, and institutional change. In J. Gil-Garcia (Ed.), *E-government success factors and measures: Theories, concepts, and methodologies* (pp. 40–51). Hershey, PA: IGI Global. doi:10.4018/978-1-4666-4058-0.ch003

Corser, G. P., Arslanturk, S., Oluoch, J., Fu, H., & Corser, G. E. (2013). Knowing the enemy at the gates: Measuring attacker motivation. *International Journal of Interdisciplinary Telecommunications and Networking*, *5*(2), 83–95. doi:10.4018/jitn.2013040107

Cropf, R. A. (2009). ICT and e-democracy. In M. Khosrow-Pour (Ed.), *Encyclopedia of information science and technology* (2nd ed.; pp. 1789–1793). Hershey, PA: IGI Global. doi:10.4018/978-1-60566-026-4.ch281

Cropf, R. A. (2009). The virtual public sphere. In M. Pagani (Ed.), *Encyclopedia of multimedia technology and networking* (2nd ed.; pp. 1525–1530). Hershey, PA: IGI Global. doi:10.4018/978-1-60566-014-1.ch206

Crosbie, M. (2013). Hack the cloud: Ethical hacking and cloud forensics. In K. Ruan (Ed.), *Cybercrime and cloud forensics: Applications for investigation processes* (pp. 42–58). Hershey, PA: IGI Global. doi:10.4018/978-1-4666-2662-1.ch002

Curran, K., Carlin, S., & Adams, M. (2012). Security issues in cloud computing. In L. Chao (Ed.), *Cloud computing for teaching and learning: Strategies for design and implementation* (pp. 200–208). Hershey, PA: IGI Global. doi:10.4018/978-1-4666-0957-0.ch014

Czosseck, C., Ottis, R., & Talihärm, A. (2011). Estonia after the 2007 cyber attacks: Legal, strategic and organisational changes in cyber security. *International Journal of Cyber Warfare & Terrorism*, *1*(1), 24–34. doi:10.4018/ijcwt.2011010103

Czosseck, C., & Podins, K. (2012). A vulnerability-based model of cyber weapons and its implications for cyber conflict. *International Journal of Cyber Warfare & Terrorism*, *2*(1), 14–26. doi:10.4018/ijcwt.2012010102

D'Abundo, M. L. (2013). Electronic health record implementation in the United States healthcare industry: Making the process of change manageable. In V. Wang (Ed.), *Handbook of research on technologies for improving the 21st century workforce: Tools for lifelong learning* (pp. 272–286). Hershey, PA: IGI Global. doi:10.4018/978-1-4666-2181-7.ch018

da Silva, F. A., Moura, D. F., & Galdino, J. F. (2012). Classes of attacks for tactical software defined radios. *International Journal of Embedded and Real-Time Communication Systems, 3*(4), 57–82. doi:10.4018/jertcs.2012100104

Dabcevic, K., Marcenaro, L., & Regazzoni, C. S. (2013). Security in cognitive radio networks. In T. Lagkas, P. Sarigiannidis, M. Louta, & P. Chatzimisios (Eds.), *Evolution of cognitive networks and self-adaptive communication systems* (pp. 301–335). Hershey, PA: IGI Global. doi:10.4018/978-1-4666-4189-1.ch013

Dahbur, K., Mohammad, B., & Tarakji, A. B. (2013). Security issues in cloud computing: A survey of risks, threats and vulnerabilities. In S. Aljawarneh (Ed.), *Cloud computing advancements in design, implementation, and technologies* (pp. 154–165). Hershey, PA: IGI Global. doi:10.4018/978-1-4666-1879-4.ch011

Damurski, L. (2012). E-participation in urban planning: Online tools for citizen engagement in Poland and in Germany. *International Journal of E-Planning Research, 1*(3), 40–67. doi:10.4018/ijepr.2012070103

Dark, M. (2011). Data breach disclosure: A policy analysis. In M. Dark (Ed.), *Information assurance and security ethics in complex systems: Interdisciplinary perspectives* (pp. 226–252). Hershey, PA: IGI Global. doi:10.4018/978-1-61692-245-0.ch011

Das, S., Mukhopadhyay, A., & Bhasker, B. (2013). Todays action is better than tomorrows cure - Evaluating information security at a premier indian business school. *Journal of Cases on Information Technology, 15*(3), 1–23. doi:10.4018/jcit.2013070101

Dasgupta, D., & Naseem, D. (2014). A framework for compliance and security coverage estimation for cloud services: A cloud insurance model. In S. Srinivasan (Ed.), *Security, trust, and regulatory aspects of cloud computing in business environments* (pp. 91–114). Hershey, PA: IGI Global. doi:10.4018/978-1-4666-5788-5.ch005

de Almeida, M. O. (2007). E-government strategy in Brazil: Increasing transparency and efficiency through e-government procurement. In M. Gascó-Hernandez (Ed.), *Latin America online: Cases, successes and pitfalls* (pp. 34–82). Hershey, PA: IGI Global. doi:10.4018/978-1-59140-974-8.ch002

**Related References**

De Fuentes, J. M., González-Tablas, A. I., & Ribagorda, A. (2011). Overview of security issues in vehicular ad-hoc networks. In M. Cruz-Cunha & F. Moreira (Eds.), *Handbook of research on mobility and computing: Evolving technologies and ubiquitous impacts* (pp. 894–911). Hershey, PA: IGI Global. doi:10.4018/978-1-60960-042-6.ch056

De Groef, W., Devriese, D., Reynaert, T., & Piessens, F. (2013). Security and privacy of online social network applications. In L. Caviglione, M. Coccoli, & A. Merlo (Eds.), *Social network engineering for secure web data and services* (pp. 206–221). Hershey, PA: IGI Global. doi:10.4018/978-1-4666-3926-3.ch010

de Juana Espinosa, S. (2008). Empirical study of the municipalitites' motivations for adopting online presence. In A. Anttiroiko (Ed.), *Electronic government: Concepts, methodologies, tools, and applications* (pp. 3593–3608). Hershey, PA: IGI Global. doi:10.4018/978-1-59904-947-2.ch262

de Souza Dias, D. (2002). Motivation for using information technology. In C. Snodgrass & E. Szewczak (Eds.), *Human factors in information systems* (pp. 55–60). Hershey, PA: IGI Global. doi:10.4018/978-1-931777-10-0.ch005

Demediuk, P. (2006). Government procurement ICT's impact on the sustainability of SMEs and regional communities. In S. Marshall, W. Taylor, & X. Yu (Eds.), *Encyclopedia of developing regional communities with information and communication technology* (pp. 321–324). Hershey, PA: IGI Global. doi:10.4018/978-1-59140-575-7.ch056

Denning, D. E. (2011). Cyber conflict as an emergent social phenomenon. In T. Holt & B. Schell (Eds.), *Corporate hacking and technology-driven crime: Social dynamics and implications* (pp. 170–186). Hershey, PA: IGI Global. doi:10.4018/978-1-61692-805-6.ch009

Desai, A. M., & Mock, K. (2013). Security in cloud computing. In A. Bento & A. Aggarwal (Eds.), *Cloud computing service and deployment models: Layers and management* (pp. 208–221). Hershey, PA: IGI Global. doi:10.4018/978-1-4666-2187-9.ch011

Devonshire, E., Forsyth, H., Reid, S., & Simpson, J. M. (2013). The challenges and opportunities of online postgraduate coursework programs in a traditional university context. In B. Tynan, J. Willems, & R. James (Eds.), *Outlooks and opportunities in blended and distance learning* (pp. 353–368). Hershey, PA: IGI Global. doi:10.4018/978-1-4666-4205-8.ch026

Di Cerbo, F., Scotto, M., Sillitti, A., Succi, G., & Vernazza, T. (2007). Toward a GNU/Linux distribution for corporate environments. In S. Sowe, I. Stamelos, & I. Samoladas (Eds.), *Emerging free and open source software practices* (pp. 215–236). Hershey, PA: IGI Global. doi:10.4018/978-1-59904-210-7.ch010

Diesner, J., & Carley, K. M. (2005). Revealing social structure from texts: Meta-matrix text analysis as a novel method for network text analysis. In V. Narayanan & D. Armstrong (Eds.), *Causal mapping for research in information technology* (pp. 81–108). Hershey, PA: IGI Global. doi:10.4018/978-1-59140-396-8.ch004

Dionysiou, I., & Ktoridou, D. (2012). Enhancing dynamic-content courses with student-oriented learning strategies: The case of computer security course. *International Journal of Cyber Ethics in Education*, 2(2), 24–33. doi:10.4018/ijcee.2012040103

Disterer, G. (2012). Attacks on IT systems: Categories of motives. In T. Chou (Ed.), *Information assurance and security technologies for risk assessment and threat management: Advances* (pp. 1–16). Hershey, PA: IGI Global. doi:10.4018/978-1-61350-507-6.ch001

Dologite, D. G., Mockler, R. J., Bai, Q., & Viszhanyo, P. F. (2006). IS change agents in practice in a US-Chinese joint venture. In M. Hunter & F. Tan (Eds.), *Advanced topics in global information management* (Vol. 5, pp. 331–352). Hershey, PA: IGI Global. doi:10.4018/978-1-59140-923-6.ch015

Dougan, T., & Curran, K. (2012). Man in the browser attacks. *International Journal of Ambient Computing and Intelligence*, 4(1), 29–39. doi:10.4018/jaci.2012010103

Drnevich, P., Brush, T. H., & Luckock, G. T. (2011). Process and structural implications for IT-enabled outsourcing. *International Journal of Strategic Information Technology and Applications*, 2(4), 30–43. doi:10.4018/jsita.2011100103

Dubey, R., Sharma, S., & Chouhan, L. (2013). Security for cognitive radio networks. In M. Ku & J. Lin (Eds.), *Cognitive radio and interference management: Technology and strategy* (pp. 238–256). Hershey, PA: IGI Global. doi:10.4018/978-1-4666-2005-6.ch013

Dunkels, E., Frånberg, G., & Hällgren, C. (2011). Young people and online risk. In E. Dunkels, G. Franberg, & C. Hallgren (Eds.), *Youth culture and net culture: Online social practices* (pp. 1–16). Hershey, PA: IGI Global. doi:10.4018/978-1-60960-209-3.ch001

*Related References*

Dunkerley, K., & Tejay, G. (2012). The development of a model for information systems security success. In Z. Belkhamza & S. Azizi Wafa (Eds.), *Measuring organizational information systems success: New technologies and practices* (pp. 341–366). Hershey, PA: IGI Global. doi:10.4018/978-1-4666-0170-3.ch017

Dunkerley, K., & Tejay, G. (2012). Theorizing information security success: Towards secure e-government. In V. Weerakkody (Ed.), *Technology enabled transformation of the public sector: Advances in e-government* (pp. 224–235). Hershey, PA: IGI Global. doi:10.4018/978-1-4666-1776-6.ch014

Dwivedi, A. N. (2009). Handbook of research on information technology management and clinical data administration in healthcare (Vols. 1–2). Hershey, PA: IGI Global. doi:10.4018/978-1-60566-356-2

Eisenga, A., Jones, T. L., & Rodriguez, W. (2012). Investing in IT security: How to determine the maximum threshold. *International Journal of Information Security and Privacy*, *6*(3), 75–87. doi:10.4018/jisp.2012070104

Elbeltagi, I., McBride, N., & Hardaker, G. (2006). Evaluating the factors affecting DSS usage by senior managers in local authorities in Egypt. In M. Hunter & F. Tan (Eds.), *Advanced topics in global information management* (Vol. 5, pp. 283–307). Hershey, PA: IGI Global. doi:10.4018/978-1-59140-923-6.ch013

Eom, S., & Fountain, J. E. (2013). Enhancing information services through public-private partnerships: Information technology knowledge transfer underlying structures to develop shared services in the U.S. and Korea. In J. Gil-Garcia (Ed.), *E-government success around the world: Cases, empirical studies, and practical recommendations* (pp. 15–40). Hershey, PA: IGI Global. doi:10.4018/978-1-4666-4173-0.ch002

Esteves, T., Leuenberger, D., & Van Leuven, N. (2012). Reaching citizen 2.0: How government uses social media to send public messages during times of calm and times of crisis. In K. Kloby & M. D'Agostino (Eds.), *Citizen 2.0: Public and governmental interaction through web 2.0 technologies* (pp. 250–268). Hershey, PA: IGI Global. doi:10.4018/978-1-4666-0318-9.ch013

Estevez, E., Fillottrani, P., Janowski, T., & Ojo, A. (2012). Government information sharing: A framework for policy formulation. In Y. Chen & P. Chu (Eds.), *Electronic governance and cross-boundary collaboration: Innovations and advancing tools* (pp. 23–55). Hershey, PA: IGI Global. doi:10.4018/978-1-60960-753-1.ch002

Eyitemi, M. (2012). Regulation of cybercafés in Nigeria. In *Cyber crime: Concepts, methodologies, tools and applications* (pp. 1305–1313). Hershey, PA: IGI Global. doi:10.4018/978-1-61350-323-2.ch606

Ezumah, B., & Adekunle, S. O. (2012). A review of privacy, internet security threat, and legislation in Africa: A case study of Nigeria, South Africa, Egypt, and Kenya. In J. Abawajy, M. Pathan, M. Rahman, A. Pathan, & M. Deris (Eds.), *Internet and distributed computing advancements: Theoretical frameworks and practical applications* (pp. 115–136). Hershey, PA: IGI Global. doi:10.4018/978-1-4666-0161-1.ch005

Ezz, I. E. (2008). E-governement emerging trends: Organizational challenges. In A. Anttiroiko (Ed.), *Electronic government: Concepts, methodologies, tools, and applications* (pp. 3721–3737). Hershey, PA: IGI Global. doi:10.4018/978-1-59904-947-2.ch269

Fabri, M. (2009). The Italian style of e-justice in a comparative perspective. In A. Martínez & P. Abat (Eds.), *E-justice: Using information communication technologies in the court system* (pp. 1–19). Hershey, PA: IGI Global. doi:10.4018/978-1-59904-998-4.ch001

Fagbe, T., & Adekola, O. D. (2010). Workplace safety and personnel well-being: The impact of information technology. *International Journal of Green Computing*, *1*(1), 28–33. doi:10.4018/jgc.2010010103

Fagbe, T., & Adekola, O. D. (2011). Workplace safety and personnel well-being: The impact of information technology. In *Global business: Concepts, methodologies, tools and applications* (pp. 1438–1444). Hershey, PA: IGI Global. doi:10.4018/978-1-60960-587-2.ch509

Farmer, L. (2008). Affective collaborative instruction with librarians. In S. Kelsey & K. St.Amant (Eds.), *Handbook of research on computer mediated communication* (pp. 15–24). Hershey, PA: IGI Global. doi:10.4018/978-1-59904-863-5.ch002

Farooq-i-Azam, M., & Ayyaz, M. N. (2014). Embedded systems security. In *Software design and development: Concepts, methodologies, tools, and applications* (pp. 980–998). Hershey, PA: IGI Global. doi:10.4018/978-1-4666-4301-7.ch047

Fauzi, A. H., & Taylor, H. (2013). Secure community trust stores for peer-to-peer e-commerce applications using cloud services. *International Journal of E-Entrepreneurship and Innovation*, *4*(1), 1–15. doi:10.4018/jeei.2013010101

Favier, L., & Mekhantar, J. (2007). Use of OSS by local e-administration: The French situation. In K. St.Amant & B. Still (Eds.), *Handbook of research on open source software: Technological, economic, and social perspectives* (pp. 428–444). Hershey, PA: IGI Global. doi:10.4018/978-1-59140-999-1.ch033

### Related References

Fenz, S. (2011). E-business and information security risk management: Challenges and potential solutions. In E. Kajan (Ed.), *Electronic business interoperability: Concepts, opportunities and challenges* (pp. 596–614). Hershey, PA: IGI Global. doi:10.4018/978-1-60960-485-1.ch024

Fernandez, E. B., Yoshioka, N., Washizaki, H., Jurjens, J., VanHilst, M., & Pernu, G. (2011). Using security patterns to develop secure systems. In H. Mouratidis (Ed.), *Software engineering for secure systems: Industrial and research perspectives* (pp. 16–31). Hershey, PA: IGI Global. doi:10.4018/978-1-61520-837-1.ch002

Fernando, S. (2009). Issues of e-learning in third world countries. In M. Khosrow-Pour (Ed.), *Encyclopedia of information science and technology* (2nd ed.; pp. 2273–2277). Hershey, PA: IGI Global. doi:10.4018/978-1-60566-026-4.ch360

Filho, J. R., & dos Santos Junior, J. R. (2009). Local e-government in Brazil: Poor interaction and local politics as usual. In C. Reddick (Ed.), *Handbook of research on strategies for local e-government adoption and implementation: Comparative studies* (pp. 863–878). Hershey, PA: IGI Global. doi:10.4018/978-1-60566-282-4.ch045

Fletcher, P. D. (2004). Portals and policy: Implications of electronic access to U.S. federal government information services. In A. Pavlichev & G. Garson (Eds.), *Digital government: Principles and best practices* (pp. 52–62). Hershey, PA: IGI Global. doi:10.4018/978-1-59140-122-3.ch004

Fletcher, P. D. (2008). Portals and policy: Implications of electronic access to U.S. federal government information services. In A. Anttiroiko (Ed.), *Electronic government: Concepts, methodologies, tools, and applications* (pp. 3970–3979). Hershey, PA: IGI Global. doi:10.4018/978-1-59904-947-2.ch289

Flores, A. E., Win, K. T., & Susilo, W. (2011). Secure exchange of electronic health records. In A. Chryssanthou, I. Apostolakis, & I. Varlamis (Eds.), *Certification and security in health-related web applications: Concepts and solutions* (pp. 1–22). Hershey, PA: Medical IGI Global. doi:10.4018/978-1-61692-895-7.ch001

Fonseca, J., & Vieira, M. (2014). A survey on secure software development lifecycles. In *Software design and development: Concepts, methodologies, tools, and applications* (pp. 17–33). Hershey, PA: IGI Global. doi:10.4018/978-1-4666-4301-7.ch002

Forlano, L. (2004). The emergence of digital government: International perspectives. In A. Pavlichev & G. Garson (Eds.), *Digital government: Principles and best practices* (pp. 34–51). Hershey, PA: IGI Global. doi:10.4018/978-1-59140-122-3.ch003

Fournaris, A. P., Kitsos, P., & Sklavos, N. (2013). Security and cryptographic engineering in embedded systems. In M. Khalgui, O. Mosbahi, & A. Valentini (Eds.), *Embedded computing systems: Applications, optimization, and advanced design* (pp. 420–438). Hershey, PA: IGI Global. doi:10.4018/978-1-4666-3922-5.ch021

Franqueira, V. N., van Cleeff, A., van Eck, P., & Wieringa, R. J. (2013). Engineering security agreements against external insider threat. *Information Resources Management Journal*, *26*(4), 66–91. doi:10.4018/irmj.2013100104

Franzel, J. M., & Coursey, D. H. (2004). Government web portals: Management issues and the approaches of five states. In A. Pavlichev & G. Garson (Eds.), *Digital government: Principles and best practices* (pp. 63–77). Hershey, PA: IGI Global. doi:10.4018/978-1-59140-122-3.ch005

French, T., Bessis, N., Maple, C., & Asimakopoulou, E. (2012). Trust issues on crowd-sourcing methods for urban environmental monitoring. *International Journal of Distributed Systems and Technologies*, *3*(1), 35–47. doi:10.4018/jdst.2012010103

Fu, Y., Kulick, J., Yan, L. K., & Drager, S. (2013). Formal modeling and verification of security property in Handel C program. *International Journal of Secure Software Engineering*, *3*(3), 50–65. doi:10.4018/jsse.2012070103

Furnell, S., von Solms, R., & Phippen, A. (2011). Preventative actions for enhancing online protection and privacy. *International Journal of Information Technologies and Systems Approach*, *4*(2), 1–11. doi:10.4018/jitsa.2011070101

Gaivéo, J. (2011). SMEs e-business security issues. In M. Cruz-Cunha & J. Varajão (Eds.), *Innovations in SMEs and conducting e-business: Technologies, trends and solutions* (pp. 317–337). Hershey, PA: IGI Global. doi:10.4018/978-1-60960-765-4.ch018

Gaivéo, J. M. (2013). Security of ICTs supporting healthcare activities. In M. Cruz-Cunha, I. Miranda, & P. Gonçalves (Eds.), *Handbook of research on ICTs for human-centered healthcare and social care services* (pp. 208–228). Hershey, PA: IGI Global. doi:10.4018/978-1-4666-3986-7.ch011

Garson, G. D. (1999). *Information technology and computer applications in public administration: Issues and trends*. Hershey, PA: IGI Global. doi:10.4018/978-1-87828-952-0

Garson, G. D. (2003). Toward an information technology research agenda for public administration. In G. Garson (Ed.), *Public information technology: Policy and management issues* (pp. 331–357). Hershey, PA: IGI Global. doi:10.4018/978-1-59140-060-8.ch014

*Related References*

Garson, G. D. (2004). The promise of digital government. In A. Pavlichev & G. Garson (Eds.), *Digital government: Principles and best practices* (pp. 2–15). Hershey, PA: IGI Global. doi:10.4018/978-1-59140-122-3.ch001

Garson, G. D. (2007). An information technology research agenda for public administration. In G. Garson (Ed.), *Modern public information technology systems: Issues and challenges* (pp. 365–392). Hershey, PA: IGI Global. doi:10.4018/978-1-59904-051-6.ch018

Gasco, M. (2007). Civil servants' resistance towards e-government development. In A. Anttiroiko & M. Malkia (Eds.), *Encyclopedia of digital government* (pp. 190–195). Hershey, PA: IGI Global. doi:10.4018/978-1-59140-789-8.ch028

Gasco, M. (2008). Civil servants' resistance towards e-government development. In A. Anttiroiko (Ed.), *Electronic government: Concepts, methodologies, tools, and applications* (pp. 2580–2588). Hershey, PA: IGI Global. doi:10.4018/978-1-59904-947-2.ch190

Gelbstein, E. E. (2013). Designing a security audit plan for a critical information infrastructure (CII). In C. Laing, A. Badii, & P. Vickers (Eds.), *Securing critical infrastructures and critical control systems: Approaches for threat protection* (pp. 262–285). Hershey, PA: IGI Global. doi:10.4018/978-1-4666-2659-1.ch011

Ghere, R. K. (2010). Accountability and information technology enactment: Implications for social empowerment. In E. Ferro, Y. Dwivedi, J. Gil-Garcia, & M. Williams (Eds.), *Handbook of research on overcoming digital divides: Constructing an equitable and competitive information society* (pp. 515–532). Hershey, PA: IGI Global. doi:10.4018/978-1-60566-699-0.ch028

Gibson, I. W. (2012). Simulation modeling of healthcare delivery. In A. Kolker & P. Story (Eds.), *Management engineering for effective healthcare delivery: Principles and applications* (pp. 69–89). Hershey, PA: IGI Global. doi:10.4018/978-1-60960-872-9.ch003

Gil-Garcia, J. R. (2007). Exploring e-government benefits and success factors. In A. Anttiroiko & M. Malkia (Eds.), *Encyclopedia of digital government* (pp. 803–811). Hershey, PA: IGI Global. doi:10.4018/978-1-59140-789-8.ch122

Gil-Garcia, J. R., & González Miranda, F. (2010). E-government and opportunities for participation: The case of the Mexican state web portals. In C. Reddick (Ed.), *Politics, democracy and e-government: Participation and service delivery* (pp. 56–74). Hershey, PA: IGI Global. doi:10.4018/978-1-61520-933-0.ch004

Gódor, G., & Imre, S. (2012). Security aspects in radio frequency identification systems. In D. Saha & V. Sridhar (Eds.), *Next generation data communication technologies: Emerging trends* (pp. 187–223). Hershey, PA: IGI Global. doi:10.4018/978-1-61350-477-2.ch009

Gogolin, G. (2011). Security and privacy concerns of virtual worlds. In B. Ciaramitaro (Ed.), *Virtual worlds and e-commerce: Technologies and applications for building customer relationships* (pp. 244–256). Hershey, PA: IGI Global. doi:10.4018/978-1-61692-808-7.ch014

Gogoulos, F. I., Antonakopoulou, A., Lioudakis, G. V., Kaklamani, D. I., & Venieris, I. S. (2014). Trust in an enterprise world: A survey. In M. Cruz-Cunha, F. Moreira, & J. Varajão (Eds.), *Handbook of research on enterprise 2.0: Technological, social, and organizational dimensions* (pp. 199–219). Hershey, PA: IGI Global. doi:10.4018/978-1-4666-4373-4.ch011

Goldfinch, S. (2012). Public trust in government, trust in e-government, and use of e-government. In Z. Yan (Ed.), *Encyclopedia of cyber behavior* (pp. 987–995). Hershey, PA: IGI Global. doi:10.4018/978-1-4666-0315-8.ch081

Goldman, J. E., & Ahuja, S. (2011). Integration of COBIT, balanced scorecard and SSE-CMM as an organizational & strategic information security management (ISM) framework. In M. Quigley (Ed.), *ICT ethics and security in the 21st century: New developments and applications* (pp. 277–309). Hershey, PA: IGI Global. doi:10.4018/978-1-60960-573-5.ch014

Goldschmidt, C., Dark, M., & Chaudhry, H. (2011). Responsibility for the harm and risk of software security flaws. In M. Dark (Ed.), *Information assurance and security ethics in complex systems: Interdisciplinary perspectives* (pp. 104–131). Hershey, PA: IGI Global. doi:10.4018/978-1-61692-245-0.ch006

Goodyear, M. (2012). Organizational change contributions to e-government project transitions. In S. Aikins (Ed.), *Managing e-government projects: Concepts, issues, and best practices* (pp. 1–21). Hershey, PA: IGI Global. doi:10.4018/978-1-4666-0086-7.ch001

Gordon, S., & Mulligan, P. (2003). Strategic models for the delivery of personal financial services: The role of infocracy. In S. Gordon (Ed.), *Computing information technology: The human side* (pp. 220–232). Hershey, PA: IGI Global. doi:10.4018/978-1-93177-752-0.ch014

Gordon, T. F. (2007). Legal knowledge systems. In A. Anttiroiko & M. Malkia (Eds.), *Encyclopedia of digital government* (pp. 1161–1166). Hershey, PA: IGI Global. doi:10.4018/978-1-59140-789-8.ch175

*Related References*

Graham, J. E., & Semich, G. W. (2008). Integrating technology to transform pedagogy: Revisiting the progress of the three phase TUI model for faculty development. In L. Tomei (Ed.), *Adapting information and communication technologies for effective education* (pp. 1–12). Hershey, PA: IGI Global. doi:10.4018/978-1-59904-922-9.ch001

Grahn, K., Karlsson, J., & Pulkkis, G. (2011). Secure routing and mobility in future IP networks. In M. Cruz-Cunha & F. Moreira (Eds.), *Handbook of research on mobility and computing: Evolving technologies and ubiquitous impacts* (pp. 952–972). Hershey, PA: IGI Global. doi:10.4018/978-1-60960-042-6.ch059

Grandinetti, L., & Pisacane, O. (2012). Web services for healthcare management. In D. Prakash Vidyarthi (Ed.), *Technologies and protocols for the future of internet design: Reinventing the web* (pp. 60–94). Hershey, PA: IGI Global. doi:10.4018/978-1-4666-0203-8.ch004

Greitzer, F. L., Frincke, D., & Zabriskie, M. (2011). Social/ethical issues in predictive insider threat monitoring. In M. Dark (Ed.), *Information assurance and security ethics in complex systems: Interdisciplinary perspectives* (pp. 132–161). Hershey, PA: IGI Global. doi:10.4018/978-1-61692-245-0.ch007

Grobler, M. (2012). The need for digital evidence standardisation. *International Journal of Digital Crime and Forensics*, *4*(2), 1–12. doi:10.4018/jdcf.2012040101

Groenewegen, P., & Wagenaar, F. P. (2008). VO as an alternative to hierarchy in the Dutch police sector. In G. Putnik & M. Cruz-Cunha (Eds.), *Encyclopedia of networked and virtual organizations* (pp. 1851–1857). Hershey, PA: IGI Global. doi:10.4018/978-1-59904-885-7.ch245

Gronlund, A. (2001). Building an infrastructure to manage electronic services. In S. Dasgupta (Ed.), *Managing internet and intranet technologies in organizations: Challenges and opportunities* (pp. 71–103). Hershey, PA: IGI Global. doi:10.4018/978-1-878289-95-7.ch006

Gronlund, A. (2002). Introduction to electronic government: Design, applications and management. In Å. Grönlund (Ed.), *Electronic government: Design, applications and management* (pp. 1–21). Hershey, PA: IGI Global. doi:10.4018/978-1-930708-19-8.ch001

Guo, J., Marshall, A., & Zhou, B. (2014). A multi-parameter trust framework for mobile ad hoc networks. In D. Rawat, B. Bista, & G. Yan (Eds.), *Security, privacy, trust, and resource management in mobile and wireless communications* (pp. 245–277). Hershey, PA: IGI Global. doi:10.4018/978-1-4666-4691-9.ch011

Gupta, A., Woosley, R., Crk, I., & Sarnikar, S. (2009). An information technology architecture for drug effectiveness reporting and post-marketing surveillance. In J. Tan (Ed.), *Medical Informatics: Concepts, methodologies, tools, and applications* (pp. 631–646). Hershey, PA: Medical IGI Global. doi:10.4018/978-1-60566-050-9.ch047

Gururajan, R., & Hafeez-Baig, A. (2011). Wireless handheld device and LAN security issues: A case study. In D. Kerr, J. Gammack, & K. Bryant (Eds.), *Digital business security development: Management technologies* (pp. 129–151). Hershey, PA: IGI Global. doi:10.4018/978-1-60566-806-2.ch006

Ha, H. (2012). Online security and consumer protection in ecommerce an Australian case. In K. Mohammed Rezaul (Ed.), *Strategic and pragmatic e-business: Implications for future business practices* (pp. 217–243). Hershey, PA: IGI Global. doi:10.4018/978-1-4666-1619-6.ch010

Hagen, J. M. (2012). The contributions of information security culture and human relations to the improvement of situational awareness. In C. Onwubiko & T. Owens (Eds.), *Situational awareness in computer network defense: Principles, methods and applications* (pp. 10–28). Hershey, PA: IGI Global. doi:10.4018/978-1-4666-0104-8.ch002

Hai-Jew, S. (2011). The social design of 3D interactive spaces for security in higher education: A preliminary view. In A. Rea (Ed.), *Security in virtual worlds, 3D webs, and immersive environments: Models for development, interaction, and management* (pp. 72–96). Hershey, PA: IGI Global. doi:10.4018/978-1-61520-891-3.ch005

Halder, D., & Jaishankar, K. (2012). Cyber crime against women and regulations in Australia. In *Cyber crime: Concepts, methodologies, tools and applications* (pp. 757–764). Hershey, PA: IGI Global. doi:10.4018/978-1-61350-323-2.ch404

Halder, D., & Jaishankar, K. (2012). Cyber victimization of women and cyber laws in India. In *Cyber crime: Concepts, methodologies, tools and applications* (pp. 742–756). Hershey, PA: IGI Global. doi:10.4018/978-1-61350-323-2.ch403

Halder, D., & Jaishankar, K. (2012). Definition, typology and patterns of victimization. In *Cyber crime: Concepts, methodologies, tools and applications* (pp. 1016–1042). Hershey, PA: IGI Global. doi:10.4018/978-1-61350-323-2.ch502

Hallin, A., & Lundevall, K. (2007). mCity: User focused development of mobile services within the city of Stockholm. In I. Kushchu (Ed.), Mobile government: An emerging direction in e-government (pp. 12-29). Hershey, PA: IGI Global. doi:10.4018/978-1-59140-884-0.ch002

### Related References

Hallin, A., & Lundevall, K. (2009). mCity: User focused development of mobile services within the city of Stockholm. In S. Clarke (Ed.), Evolutionary concepts in end user productivity and performance: Applications for organizational progress (pp. 268-280). Hershey, PA: IGI Global. doi:10.4018/978-1-60566-136-0.ch017

Hallin, A., & Lundevall, K. (2009). mCity: User focused development of mobile services within the city of Stockholm. In D. Taniar (Ed.), Mobile computing: Concepts, methodologies, tools, and applications (pp. 3455-3467). Hershey, PA: IGI Global. doi:10.4018/978-1-60566-054-7.ch253

Hamlen, K., Kantarcioglu, M., Khan, L., & Thuraisingham, B. (2012). Security issues for cloud computing. In H. Nemati (Ed.), *Optimizing information security and advancing privacy assurance: New technologies* (pp. 150–162). Hershey, PA: IGI Global. doi:10.4018/978-1-4666-0026-3.ch008

Hanson, A. (2005). Overcoming barriers in the planning of a virtual library. In M. Khosrow-Pour (Ed.), *Encyclopedia of information science and technology* (pp. 2255–2259). Hershey, PA: IGI Global. doi:10.4018/978-1-59140-553-5.ch397

Haque, A. (2008). Information technology and surveillance: Implications for public administration in a new word order. In T. Loendorf & G. Garson (Eds.), *Patriotic information systems* (pp. 177–185). Hershey, PA: IGI Global. doi:10.4018/978-1-59904-594-8.ch008

Harnesk, D. (2011). Convergence of information security in B2B networks. In E. Kajan (Ed.), *Electronic business interoperability: Concepts, opportunities and challenges* (pp. 571–595). Hershey, PA: IGI Global. doi:10.4018/978-1-60960-485-1.ch023

Harnesk, D., & Hartikainen, H. (2011). Multi-layers of information security in emergency response. *International Journal of Information Systems for Crisis Response and Management*, *3*(2), 1–17. doi:10.4018/jiscrm.2011040101

Hauck, R. V., Thatcher, S. M., & Weisband, S. P. (2012). Temporal aspects of information technology use: Increasing shift work effectiveness. In J. Wang (Ed.), *Advancing the service sector with evolving technologies: Techniques and principles* (pp. 87–104). Hershey, PA: IGI Global. doi:10.4018/978-1-4666-0044-7.ch006

Hawk, S., & Witt, T. (2006). Telecommunications courses in information systems programs. *International Journal of Information and Communication Technology Education*, *2*(1), 79–92. doi:10.4018/jicte.2006010107

Hawrylak, P. J., Hale, J., & Papa, M. (2013). Security issues for ISO 18000-6 type C RFID: Identification and solutions. In *Supply chain management: Concepts, methodologies, tools, and applications* (pp. 1565–1581). Hershey, PA: IGI Global. doi:10.4018/978-1-4666-2625-6.ch093

He, B., Tran, T. T., & Xie, B. (2014). Authentication and identity management for secure cloud businesses and services. In S. Srinivasan (Ed.), *Security, trust, and regulatory aspects of cloud computing in business environments* (pp. 180–201). Hershey, PA: IGI Global. doi:10.4018/978-1-4666-5788-5.ch011

Helms, M. M., Moore, R., & Ahmadi, M. (2009). Information technology (IT) and the healthcare industry: A SWOT analysis. In J. Tan (Ed.), *Medical informatics: Concepts, methodologies, tools, and applications* (pp. 134–152). Hershey, PA: IGI Global. doi:10.4018/978-1-60566-050-9.ch012

Hendrickson, S. M., & Young, M. E. (2014). Electronic records management at a federally funded research and development center. In J. Krueger (Ed.), *Cases on electronic records and resource management implementation in diverse environments* (pp. 334–350). Hershey, PA: IGI Global. doi:10.4018/978-1-4666-4466-3.ch020

Henman, P. (2010). Social policy and information communication technologies. In J. Martin & L. Hawkins (Eds.), *Information communication technologies for human services education and delivery: Concepts and cases* (pp. 215–229). Hershey, PA: IGI Global. doi:10.4018/978-1-60566-735-5.ch014

Henrie, M. (2012). Cyber security in liquid petroleum pipelines. In J. Zubairi & A. Mahboob (Eds.), *Cyber security standards, practices and industrial applications: Systems and methodologies* (pp. 200–222). Hershey, PA: IGI Global. doi:10.4018/978-1-60960-851-4.ch011

Herath, T., Rao, H. R., & Upadhyaya, S. (2012). Internet crime: How vulnerable are you? Do gender, social influence and education play a role in vulnerability? In *Cyber crime: Concepts, methodologies, tools and applications* (pp. 1–13). Hershey, PA: IGI Global. doi:10.4018/978-1-61350-323-2.ch101

Hilmi, M. F., Pawanchik, S., Mustapha, Y., & Ali, H. M. (2013). Information security perspective of a learning management system: An exploratory study. *International Journal of Knowledge Society Research*, *4*(2), 9–18. doi:10.4018/jksr.2013040102

Hismanoglu, M. (2011). Important issues in online education: E-pedagogy and marketing. In U. Demiray & S. Sever (Eds.), *Marketing online education programs: Frameworks for promotion and communication* (pp. 184–209). Hershey, PA: IGI Global. doi:10.4018/978-1-60960-074-7.ch012

*Related References*

Ho, K. K. (2008). The e-government development, IT strategies, and portals of the Hong Kong SAR government. In A. Anttiroiko (Ed.), *Electronic government: Concepts, methodologies, tools, and applications* (pp. 715–733). Hershey, PA: IGI Global. doi:10.4018/978-1-59904-947-2.ch060

Holden, S. H. (2003). The evolution of information technology management at the federal level: Implications for public administration. In G. Garson (Ed.), *Public information technology: Policy and management issues* (pp. 53–73). Hershey, PA: IGI Global. doi:10.4018/978-1-59140-060-8.ch003

Holden, S. H. (2007). The evolution of federal information technology management literature: Does IT finally matter? In G. Garson (Ed.), *Modern public information technology systems: Issues and challenges* (pp. 17–34). Hershey, PA: IGI Global. doi:10.4018/978-1-59904-051-6.ch002

Holland, J. W. (2009). Automation of American criminal justice. In M. Khosrow-Pour (Ed.), *Encyclopedia of information science and technology* (2nd ed.; pp. 300–302). Hershey, PA: IGI Global. doi:10.4018/978-1-60566-026-4.ch051

Holloway, K. (2013). Fair use, copyright, and academic integrity in an online academic environment. In *Digital rights management: Concepts, methodologies, tools, and applications* (pp. 917–928). Hershey, PA: IGI Global. doi:10.4018/978-1-4666-2136-7.ch044

Hommel, W. (2012). Security and privacy management for learning management systems. In *Virtual learning environments: Concepts, methodologies, tools and applications* (pp. 1151–1170). Hershey, PA: IGI Global. doi:10.4018/978-1-4666-0011-9.ch602

Hoops, D. S. (2012). Lost in cyberspace: Navigating the legal issues of e-commerce. *Journal of Electronic Commerce in Organizations*, *10*(1), 33–51. doi:10.4018/jeco.2012010103

Horiuchi, C. (2005). E-government databases. In L. Rivero, J. Doorn, & V. Ferraggine (Eds.), *Encyclopedia of database technologies and applications* (pp. 206–210). Hershey, PA: IGI Global. doi:10.4018/978-1-59140-560-3.ch035

Horiuchi, C. (2006). Creating IS quality in government settings. In E. Duggan & J. Reichgelt (Eds.), *Measuring information systems delivery quality* (pp. 311–327). Hershey, PA: IGI Global. doi:10.4018/978-1-59140-857-4.ch014

Houmb, S., Georg, G., Petriu, D., Bordbar, B., Ray, I., Anastasakis, K., & France, R. (2011). Balancing security and performance properties during system architectural design. In H. Mouratidis (Ed.), *Software engineering for secure systems: Industrial and research perspectives* (pp. 155–191). Hershey, PA: IGI Global. doi:10.4018/978-1-61520-837-1.ch006

Hsiao, N., Chu, P., & Lee, C. (2012). Impact of e-governance on businesses: Model development and case study. In *Digital democracy: Concepts, methodologies, tools, and applications* (pp. 1407–1425). Hershey, PA: IGI Global. doi:10.4018/978-1-4666-1740-7.ch070

Huang, E., & Cheng, F. (2012). Online security cues and e-payment continuance intention. *International Journal of E-Entrepreneurship and Innovation*, *3*(1), 42–58. doi:10.4018/jeei.2012010104

Huang, T., & Lee, C. (2010). Evaluating the impact of e-government on citizens: Cost-benefit analysis. In C. Reddick (Ed.), *Citizens and e-government: Evaluating policy and management* (pp. 37–52). Hershey, PA: IGI Global. doi:10.4018/978-1-61520-931-6.ch003

Hunter, M. G., Diochon, M., Pugsley, D., & Wright, B. (2002). Unique challenges for small business adoption of information technology: The case of the Nova Scotia ten. In S. Burgess (Ed.), *Managing information technology in small business: Challenges and solutions* (pp. 98–117). Hershey, PA: IGI Global. doi:10.4018/978-1-930708-35-8.ch006

Hurskainen, J. (2003). Integration of business systems and applications in merger and alliance: Case metso automation. In T. Reponen (Ed.), *Information technology enabled global customer service* (pp. 207–225). Hershey, PA: IGI Global. doi:10.4018/978-1-59140-048-6.ch012

Iazzolino, G., & Pietrantonio, R. (2011). The soveria.it project: A best practice of e-government in southern Italy. In D. Piaggesi, K. Sund, & W. Castelnovo (Eds.), *Global strategy and practice of e-governance: Examples from around the world* (pp. 34–56). Hershey, PA: IGI Global. doi:10.4018/978-1-60960-489-9.ch003

Ifinedo, P. (2011). Relationships between information security concerns and national cultural dimensions: Findings in the global financial services industry. In H. Nemati (Ed.), *Security and privacy assurance in advancing technologies: New developments* (pp. 134–153). Hershey, PA: IGI Global. doi:10.4018/978-1-60960-200-0.ch010

### Related References

Imran, A., & Gregor, S. (2012). A process model for successful e-government adoption in the least developed countries: A case of Bangladesh. In F. Tan (Ed.), *International comparisons of information communication technologies: Advancing applications* (pp. 321–350). Hershey, PA: IGI Global. doi:10.4018/978-1-61350-480-2.ch014

Inden, U., Lioudakis, G., & Rückemann, C. (2013). Awareness-based security management for complex and internet-based operations management systems. In C. Rückemann (Ed.), *Integrated information and computing systems for natural, spatial, and social sciences* (pp. 43–73). Hershey, PA: IGI Global. doi:10.4018/978-1-4666-2190-9.ch003

Inoue, Y., & Bell, S. T. (2005). Electronic/digital government innovation, and publishing trends with IT. In M. Khosrow-Pour (Ed.), *Encyclopedia of information science and technology* (pp. 1018–1023). Hershey, PA: IGI Global. doi:10.4018/978-1-59140-553-5.ch180

Islam, M. M., & Ehsan, M. (2013). Understanding e-governance: A theoretical approach. In M. Islam & M. Ehsan (Eds.), *From government to e-governance: Public administration in the digital age* (pp. 38–49). Hershey, PA: IGI Global. doi:10.4018/978-1-4666-1909-8.ch003

Islam, S., Mouratidis, H., Kalloniatis, C., Hudic, A., & Zechner, L. (2013). Model based process to support security and privacy requirements engineering. *International Journal of Secure Software Engineering*, *3*(3), 1–22. doi:10.4018/jsse.2012070101

Itani, W., Kayssi, A., & Chehab, A. (2012). Security and privacy in body sensor networks: Challenges, solutions, and research directions. In M. Watfa (Ed.), *E-healthcare systems and wireless communications: Current and future challenges* (pp. 100–127). Hershey, PA: Medical IGI Global. doi:10.4018/978-1-61350-123-8.ch005

Jaeger, B. (2009). E-government and e-democracy in the making. In M. Khosrow-Pour (Ed.), *Encyclopedia of information science and technology* (2nd ed.; pp. 1318–1322). Hershey, PA: IGI Global. doi:10.4018/978-1-60566-026-4.ch208

Jain, R. B. (2007). Revamping the administrative structure and processes in India for online diplomacy. In A. Anttiroiko & M. Malkia (Eds.), *Encyclopedia of digital government* (pp. 1418–1423). Hershey, PA: IGI Global. doi:10.4018/978-1-59140-789-8.ch217

Jain, R. B. (2008). Revamping the administrative structure and processes in India for online diplomacy. In A. Anttiroiko (Ed.), *Electronic government: Concepts, methodologies, tools, and applications* (pp. 3142–3149). Hershey, PA: IGI Global. doi:10.4018/978-1-59904-947-2.ch233

Jansen van Vuuren, J., Grobler, M., & Zaaiman, J. (2012). Cyber security awareness as critical driver to national security. *International Journal of Cyber Warfare & Terrorism, 2*(1), 27–38. doi:10.4018/ijcwt.2012010103

Jansen van Vuuren, J., Leenen, L., Phahlamohlaka, J., & Zaaiman, J. (2012). An approach to governance of CyberSecurity in South Africa. *International Journal of Cyber Warfare & Terrorism, 2*(4), 13–27. doi:10.4018/ijcwt.2012100102

Jauhiainen, J. S., & Inkinen, T. (2009). E-governance and the information society in periphery. In C. Reddick (Ed.), *Handbook of research on strategies for local e-government adoption and implementation: Comparative studies* (pp. 497–514). Hershey, PA: IGI Global. doi:10.4018/978-1-60566-282-4.ch026

Jensen, J., & Groep, D. L. (2012). Security and trust in a global research infrastructure. In J. Leng & W. Sharrock (Eds.), *Handbook of research on computational science and engineering: Theory and practice* (pp. 539–566). Hershey, PA: IGI Global. doi:10.4018/978-1-61350-116-0.ch022

Jensen, M. J. (2009). Electronic democracy and citizen influence in government. In C. Reddick (Ed.), *Handbook of research on strategies for local e-government adoption and implementation: Comparative studies* (pp. 288–305). Hershey, PA: IGI Global. doi:10.4018/978-1-60566-282-4.ch015

Jiao, Y., Hurson, A. R., Potok, T. E., & Beckerman, B. G. (2009). Integrating mobile-based systems with healthcare databases. In J. Erickson (Ed.), *Database technologies: Concepts, methodologies, tools, and applications* (pp. 484–504). Hershey, PA: IGI Global. doi:10.4018/978-1-60566-058-5.ch031

Johnsen, S. O. (2014). Safety and security in SCADA systems must be improved through resilience based risk management. In *Crisis management: Concepts, methodologies, tools and applications* (pp. 1422–1436). Hershey, PA: IGI Global. doi:10.4018/978-1-4666-4707-7.ch071

Johnston, A. C., Wech, B., & Jack, E. (2012). Engaging remote employees: The moderating role of remote status in determining employee information security policy awareness. *Journal of Organizational and End User Computing, 25*(1), 1–23. doi:10.4018/joeuc.2013010101

Joia, L. A. (2002). A systematic model to integrate information technology into metabusinesses: A case study in the engineering realms. In F. Tan (Ed.), *Advanced topics in global information management* (Vol. 1, pp. 250–267). Hershey, PA: IGI Global. doi:10.4018/978-1-930708-43-3.ch016

*Related References*

Jones, T. H., & Song, I. (2000). Binary equivalents of ternary relationships in entity-relationship modeling: A logical decomposition approach. *Journal of Database Management*, *11*(2), 12–19. doi:10.4018/jdm.2000040102

Juana-Espinosa, S. D. (2007). Empirical study of the municipalitites' motivations for adopting online presence. In L. Al-Hakim (Ed.), *Global e-government: Theory, applications and benchmarking* (pp. 261–279). Hershey, PA: IGI Global. doi:10.4018/978-1-59904-027-1.ch015

Jun, K., & Weare, C. (2012). Bridging from e-government practice to e-government research: Past trends and future directions. In K. Bwalya & S. Zulu (Eds.), *Handbook of research on e-government in emerging economies: Adoption, e-participation, and legal frameworks* (pp. 263–289). Hershey, PA: IGI Global. doi:10.4018/978-1-4666-0324-0.ch013

Jung, C., Rudolph, M., & Schwarz, R. (2013). Security evaluation of service-oriented systems using the SiSOA method. In K. Khan (Ed.), *Developing and evaluating security-aware software systems* (pp. 20–35). Hershey, PA: IGI Global. doi:10.4018/978-1-4666-2482-5.ch002

Junqueira, A., Diniz, E. H., & Fernandez, M. (2010). Electronic government implementation projects with multiple agencies: Analysis of the electronic invoice project under PMBOK framework. In J. Cordoba-Pachon & A. Ochoa-Arias (Eds.), *Systems thinking and e-participation: ICT in the governance of society* (pp. 135–153). Hershey, PA: IGI Global. doi:10.4018/978-1-60566-860-4.ch009

Juntunen, A. (2009). Joint service development with the local authorities. In C. Reddick (Ed.), *Handbook of research on strategies for local e-government adoption and implementation: Comparative studies* (pp. 902–920). Hershey, PA: IGI Global. doi:10.4018/978-1-60566-282-4.ch047

Kaiya, H., Sakai, J., Ogata, S., & Kaijiri, K. (2013). Eliciting security requirements for an information system using asset flows and processor deployment. *International Journal of Secure Software Engineering*, *4*(3), 42–63. doi:10.4018/jsse.2013070103

Kalloniatis, C., Kavakli, E., & Gritzalis, S. (2011). Designing privacy aware information systems. In H. Mouratidis (Ed.), *Software engineering for secure systems: Industrial and research perspectives* (pp. 212–231). Hershey, PA: IGI Global. doi:10.4018/978-1-61520-837-1.ch008

Kamel, S. (2001). *Using DSS for crisis management*. Hershey, PA: IGI Global. doi:10.4018/978-1-87828-961-2.ch020

Kamel, S. (2006). DSS for strategic decision making. In M. Khosrow-Pour (Ed.), *Cases on information technology and organizational politics & culture* (pp. 230–246). Hershey, PA: IGI Global. doi:10.4018/978-1-59904-411-8.ch013

Kamel, S. (2009). The software industry in Egypt as a potential contributor to economic growth. In M. Khosrow-Pour (Ed.), *Encyclopedia of information science and technology* (2nd ed.; pp. 3531–3537). Hershey, PA: IGI Global. doi:10.4018/978-1-60566-026-4.ch562

Kamel, S., & Hussein, M. (2008). Xceed: Pioneering the contact center industry in Egypt. *Journal of Cases on Information Technology*, *10*(1), 67–91. doi:10.4018/jcit.2008010105

Kamel, S., & Wahba, K. (2003). The use of a hybrid model in web-based education: "The Global campus project. In A. Aggarwal (Ed.), *Web-based education: Learning from experience* (pp. 331–346). Hershey, PA: IGI Global. doi:10.4018/978-1-59140-102-5.ch020

Kamoun, F., & Halaweh, M. (2012). User interface design and e-commerce security perception: An empirical study. *International Journal of E-Business Research*, *8*(2), 15–32. doi:10.4018/jebr.2012040102

Kamruzzaman, J., Azad, A. K., Karmakar, N. C., Karmakar, G., & Srinivasan, B. (2013). Security and privacy in RFID systems. In N. Karmakar (Ed.), *Advanced RFID systems, security, and applications* (pp. 16–40). Hershey, PA: IGI Global. doi:10.4018/978-1-4666-2080-3.ch002

Kaosar, M. G., & Yi, X. (2011). Privacy preserving data gathering in wireless sensor network. In D. Kar & M. Syed (Eds.), *Network security, administration and management: Advancing technology and practice* (pp. 237–251). Hershey, PA: IGI Global. doi:10.4018/978-1-60960-777-7.ch012

Kar, D. C., Ngo, H. L., Mulkey, C. J., & Sanapala, G. (2011). Advances in security and privacy in wireless sensor networks. In H. Nemati (Ed.), *Security and privacy assurance in advancing technologies: New developments* (pp. 186–213). Hershey, PA: IGI Global. doi:10.4018/978-1-60960-200-0.ch014

Karadsheh, L., & Alhawari, S. (2011). Applying security policies in small business utilizing cloud computing technologies. *International Journal of Cloud Applications and Computing*, *1*(2), 29–40. doi:10.4018/ijcac.2011040103

*Related References*

Kardaras, D. K., & Papathanassiou, E. A. (2008). An exploratory study of the e-government services in Greece. In G. Garson & M. Khosrow-Pour (Eds.), *Handbook of research on public information technology* (pp. 162–174). Hershey, PA: IGI Global. doi:10.4018/978-1-59904-857-4.ch016

Karokola, G., Yngström, L., & Kowalski, S. (2012). Secure e-government services: A comparative analysis of e-government maturity models for the developing regions–The need for security services. *International Journal of Electronic Government Research*, 8(1), 1–25. doi:10.4018/jegr.2012010101

Kassahun, A. E., Molla, A., & Sarkar, P. (2012). Government process reengineering: What we know and what we need to know. In *Digital democracy: Concepts, methodologies, tools, and applications* (pp. 1730–1752). Hershey, PA: IGI Global. doi:10.4018/978-1-4666-1740-7.ch086

Kassim, N. M., & Ramayah, T. (2013). Security policy issues in internet banking in Malaysia. In *IT policy and ethics: Concepts, methodologies, tools, and applications* (pp. 1274–1293). Hershey, PA: IGI Global. doi:10.4018/978-1-4666-2919-6.ch057

Kayem, A. V. (2013). Security in service oriented architectures: Standards and challenges. In *Digital rights management: Concepts, methodologies, tools, and applications* (pp. 50–73). Hershey, PA: IGI Global. doi:10.4018/978-1-4666-2136-7.ch004

Kelarev, A. V., Brown, S., Watters, P., Wu, X., & Dazeley, R. (2011). Establishing reasoning communities of security experts for internet commerce security. In J. Yearwood & A. Stranieri (Eds.), *Technologies for supporting reasoning communities and collaborative decision making: Cooperative approaches* (pp. 380–396). Hershey, PA: IGI Global. doi:10.4018/978-1-60960-091-4.ch020

Kerr, D., Gammack, J. G., & Boddington, R. (2011). Overview of digital business security issues. In D. Kerr, J. Gammack, & K. Bryant (Eds.), *Digital business security development: Management technologies* (pp. 1–36). Hershey, PA: IGI Global. doi:10.4018/978-1-60566-806-2.ch001

Khan, B. (2005). Technological issues. In B. Khan (Ed.), *Managing e-learning strategies: Design, delivery, implementation and evaluation* (pp. 154–180). Hershey, PA: IGI Global. doi:10.4018/978-1-59140-634-1.ch004

Khan, K. M. (2011). A decision support system for selecting secure web services. In *Enterprise information systems: Concepts, methodologies, tools and applications* (pp. 1113–1120). Hershey, PA: IGI Global. doi:10.4018/978-1-61692-852-0.ch415

Khan, K. M. (2012). Software security engineering: Design and applications. *International Journal of Secure Software Engineering*, *3*(1), 62–63. doi:10.4018/Jsse.2012010104

Khasawneh, A., Bsoul, M., Obeidat, I., & Al Azzam, I. (2012). Technology fears: A study of e-commerce loyalty perception by Jordanian customers. In J. Wang (Ed.), *Advancing the service sector with evolving technologies: Techniques and principles* (pp. 158–165). Hershey, PA: IGI Global. doi:10.4018/978-1-4666-0044-7.ch010

Khatibi, V., & Montazer, G. A. (2012). E-research methodology. In A. Juan, T. Daradoumis, M. Roca, S. Grasman, & J. Faulin (Eds.), *Collaborative and distributed e-research: Innovations in technologies, strategies and applications* (pp. 62–81). Hershey, PA: IGI Global. doi:10.4018/978-1-4666-0125-3.ch003

Kidd, T. (2011). The dragon in the school's backyard: A review of literature on the uses of technology in urban schools. In L. Tomei (Ed.), *Online courses and ICT in education: Emerging practices and applications* (pp. 242–257). Hershey, PA: IGI Global. doi:10.4018/978-1-60960-150-8.ch019

Kidd, T. T. (2010). My experience tells the story: Exploring technology adoption from a qualitative perspective - A pilot study. In H. Song & T. Kidd (Eds.), *Handbook of research on human performance and instructional technology* (pp. 247–262). Hershey, PA: IGI Global. doi:10.4018/978-1-60566-782-9.ch015

Kieley, B., Lane, G., Paquet, G., & Roy, J. (2002). e-Government in Canada: Services online or public service renewal? In Å. Grönlund (Ed.), Electronic government: Design, applications and management (pp. 340-355). Hershey, PA: IGI Global. doi:10.4018/978-1-930708-19-8.ch016

Kilger, M. (2011). Social dynamics and the future of technology-driven crime. In T. Holt & B. Schell (Eds.), *Corporate hacking and technology-driven crime: Social dynamics and implications* (pp. 205–227). Hershey, PA: IGI Global. doi:10.4018/978-1-61692-805-6.ch011

Kim, P. (2012). "Stay out of the way! My kid is video blogging through a phone!": A lesson learned from math tutoring social media for children in underserved communities. In *Wireless technologies: Concepts, methodologies, tools and applications* (pp. 1415–1428). Hershey, PA: IGI Global. doi:10.4018/978-1-61350-101-6.ch517

Kirlidog, M. (2010). Financial aspects of national ICT strategies. In S. Kamel (Ed.), *E-strategies for technological diffusion and adoption: National ICT approaches for socioeconomic development* (pp. 277–292). Hershey, PA: IGI Global. doi:10.4018/978-1-60566-388-3.ch016

*Related References*

Kirwan, G., & Power, A. (2012). Hacking: Legal and ethical aspects of an ambiguous activity. In A. Dudley, J. Braman, & G. Vincenti (Eds.), *Investigating cyber law and cyber ethics: Issues, impacts and practices* (pp. 21–36). Hershey, PA: IGI Global. doi:10.4018/978-1-61350-132-0.ch002

Kisielnicki, J. (2006). Transfer of information and knowledge in the project management. In E. Coakes & S. Clarke (Eds.), *Encyclopedia of communities of practice in information and knowledge management* (pp. 544–551). Hershey, PA: IGI Global. doi:10.4018/978-1-59140-556-6.ch091

Kittner, M., & Van Slyke, C. (2006). Reorganizing information technology services in an academic environment. In M. Khosrow-Pour (Ed.), *Cases on the human side of information technology* (pp. 49–66). Hershey, PA: IGI Global. doi:10.4018/978-1-59904-405-7.ch004

Kline, D. M., He, L., & Yaylacicegi, U. (2011). User perceptions of security technologies. *International Journal of Information Security and Privacy*, 5(2), 1–12. doi:10.4018/jisp.2011040101

Knoell, H. D. (2008). Semi virtual workplaces in German financial service enterprises. In P. Zemliansky & K. St.Amant (Eds.), *Handbook of research on virtual workplaces and the new nature of business practices* (pp. 570–581). Hershey, PA: IGI Global. doi:10.4018/978-1-59904-893-2.ch041

Koh, S. L., & Maguire, S. (2009). Competing in the age of information technology in a developing economy: Experiences of an Indian bank. In S. Koh & S. Maguire (Eds.), *Information and communication technologies management in turbulent business environments* (pp. 326–350). Hershey, PA: IGI Global. doi:10.4018/978-1-60566-424-8.ch018

Kolkowska, E., Hedström, K., & Karlsson, F. (2012). Analyzing information security goals. In M. Gupta, J. Walp, & R. Sharman (Eds.), *Threats, countermeasures, and advances in applied information security* (pp. 91–110). Hershey, PA: IGI Global. doi:10.4018/978-1-4666-0978-5.ch005

Kollmann, T., & Häsel, M. (2009). Competence of information technology professionals in internet-based ventures. In I. Lee (Ed.), *Electronic business: Concepts, methodologies, tools, and applications* (pp. 1905–1919). Hershey, PA: IGI Global. doi:10.4018/978-1-60566-056-1.ch118

Kollmann, T., & Häsel, M. (2009). Competence of information technology professionals in internet-based ventures. In A. Cater-Steel (Ed.), *Information technology governance and service management: Frameworks and adaptations* (pp. 239–253). Hershey, PA: IGI Global. doi:10.4018/978-1-60566-008-0.ch013

Kollmann, T., & Häsel, M. (2010). Competence of information technology professionals in internet-based ventures. In *Electronic services: Concepts, methodologies, tools and applications* (pp. 1551–1565). Hershey, PA: IGI Global. doi:10.4018/978-1-61520-967-5.ch094

Korhonen, J. J., Hiekkanen, K., & Mykkänen, J. (2012). Information security governance. In M. Gupta, J. Walp, & R. Sharman (Eds.), *Strategic and practical approaches for information security governance: Technologies and applied solutions* (pp. 53–66). Hershey, PA: IGI Global. doi:10.4018/978-1-4666-0197-0.ch004

Korovessis, P. (2011). Information security awareness in academia. *International Journal of Knowledge Society Research*, 2(4), 1–17. doi:10.4018/jksr.2011100101

Koskosas, I., & Sariannidis, N. (2011). Project commitment in the context of information security. *International Journal of Information Technology Project Management*, 2(3), 17–29. doi:10.4018/jitpm.2011070102

Kotsonis, E., & Eliakis, S. (2013). Information security standards for health information systems: The implementer's approach. In *User-driven healthcare: Concepts, methodologies, tools, and applications* (pp. 225–257). Hershey, PA: Medical IGI Global. doi:10.4018/978-1-4666-2770-3.ch013

Kraemer, K., & King, J. L. (2006). Information technology and administrative reform: Will e-government be different? *International Journal of Electronic Government Research*, 2(1), 1–20. doi:10.4018/jegr.2006010101

Kraemer, K., & King, J. L. (2008). Information technology and administrative reform: Will e-government be different? In D. Norris (Ed.), *E-government research: Policy and management* (pp. 1–20). Hershey, PA: IGI Global. doi:10.4018/978-1-59904-913-7.ch001

Krishna, A. V. (2014). A randomized cloud library security environment. In S. Dhamdhere (Ed.), *Cloud computing and virtualization technologies in libraries* (pp. 278–296). Hershey, PA: IGI Global. doi:10.4018/978-1-4666-4631-5.ch016

Kruck, S. E., & Teer, F. P. (2011). Computer security practices and perceptions of the next generation of corporate computer users. In H. Nemati (Ed.), *Pervasive information security and privacy developments: Trends and advancements* (pp. 255–265). Hershey, PA: IGI Global. doi:10.4018/978-1-61692-000-5.ch017

Kumar, M., Sareen, M., & Chhabra, S. (2011). Technology related trust issues in SME B2B E-Commerce. *International Journal of Information Communication Technologies and Human Development*, 3(4), 31–46. doi:10.4018/jicthd.2011100103

*Related References*

Kumar, P., & Mittal, S. (2012). The perpetration and prevention of cyber crime: An analysis of cyber terrorism in India. *International Journal of Technoethics*, *3*(1), 43–52. doi:10.4018/jte.2012010104

Kumar, P. S., Ashok, M. S., & Subramanian, R. (2012). A publicly verifiable dynamic secret sharing protocol for secure and dependable data storage in cloud computing. *International Journal of Cloud Applications and Computing*, *2*(3), 1–25. doi:10.4018/ijcac.2012070101

Kumar, S., & Dutta, K. (2014). Security issues in mobile ad hoc networks: A survey. In D. Rawat, B. Bista, & G. Yan (Eds.), *Security, privacy, trust, and resource management in mobile and wireless communications* (pp. 176–221). Hershey, PA: IGI Global. doi:10.4018/978-1-4666-4691-9.ch009

Lampathaki, F., Tsiakaliaris, C., Stasis, A., & Charalabidis, Y. (2011). National interoperability frameworks: The way forward. In Y. Charalabidis (Ed.), *Interoperability in digital public services and administration: Bridging e-government and e-business* (pp. 1–24). Hershey, PA: IGI Global. doi:10.4018/978-1-61520-887-6.ch001

Lan, Z., & Scott, C. R. (1996). The relative importance of computer-mediated information versus conventional non-computer-mediated information in public managerial decision making. *Information Resources Management Journal*, *9*(1), 27–0. doi:10.4018/irmj.1996010103

Law, W. (2004). *Public sector data management in a developing economy*. Hershey, PA: IGI Global. doi:10.4018/978-1-59140-259-6.ch034

Law, W. K. (2005). Information resources development challenges in a cross-cultural environment. In M. Khosrow-Pour (Ed.), *Encyclopedia of information science and technology* (pp. 1476–1481). Hershey, PA: IGI Global. doi:10.4018/978-1-59140-553-5.ch259

Law, W. K. (2009). Cross-cultural challenges for information resources management. In M. Khosrow-Pour (Ed.), *Encyclopedia of information science and technology* (2nd ed.; pp. 840–846). Hershey, PA: IGI Global. doi:10.4018/978-1-60566-026-4.ch136

Law, W. K. (2011). Cross-cultural challenges for information resources management. In *Global business: Concepts, methodologies, tools and applications* (pp. 1924–1932). Hershey, PA: IGI Global. doi:10.4018/978-1-60960-587-2.ch704

Lawson, S. (2013). Motivating cybersecurity: Assessing the status of critical infrastructure as an object of cyber threats. In C. Laing, A. Badii, & P. Vickers (Eds.), *Securing critical infrastructures and critical control systems: Approaches for threat protection* (pp. 168–189). Hershey, PA: IGI Global. doi:10.4018/978-1-4666-2659-1.ch007

Leitch, S., & Warren, M. (2011). The ethics of security of personal information upon Facebook. In M. Quigley (Ed.), *ICT ethics and security in the 21st century: New developments and applications* (pp. 46–65). Hershey, PA: IGI Global. doi:10.4018/978-1-60960-573-5.ch003

Li, M. (2013). Security terminology. In A. Miri (Ed.), *Advanced security and privacy for RFID technologies* (pp. 1–13). Hershey, PA: IGI Global. doi:10.4018/978-1-4666-3685-9.ch001

Ligaarden, O. S., Refsdal, A., & Stølen, K. (2013). Using indicators to monitor security risk in systems of systems: How to capture and measure the impact of service dependencies on the security of provided services. In D. Mellado, L. Enrique Sánchez, E. Fernández-Medina, & M. Piattini (Eds.), *IT security governance innovations: Theory and research* (pp. 256–292). Hershey, PA: IGI Global. doi:10.4018/978-1-4666-2083-4.ch010

Lim, J. S., Chang, S., Ahmad, A., & Maynard, S. (2012). Towards an organizational culture framework for information security practices. In M. Gupta, J. Walp, & R. Sharman (Eds.), *Strategic and practical approaches for information security governance: Technologies and applied solutions* (pp. 296–315). Hershey, PA: IGI Global. doi:10.4018/978-1-4666-0197-0.ch017

Lin, X., & Luppicini, R. (2011). Socio-technical influences of cyber espionage: A case study of the GhostNet system. *International Journal of Technoethics*, 2(2), 65–77. doi:10.4018/jte.2011040105

Lindström, J., & Hanken, C. (2012). Security challenges and selected legal aspects for wearable computing. *Journal of Information Technology Research*, 5(1), 68–87. doi:10.4018/jitr.2012010104

Maheshwari, H., Hyman, H., & Agrawal, M. (2012). A comparison of cyber-crime definitions in India and the United States. In *Cyber crime: Concepts, methodologies, tools and applications* (pp. 714–726). Hershey, PA: IGI Global. doi:10.4018/978-1-61350-323-2.ch401

## Related References

Malcolmson, J. (2014). The role of security culture. In I. Portela & F. Almeida (Eds.), *Organizational, legal, and technological dimensions of information system administration* (pp. 225–242). Hershey, PA: IGI Global. doi:10.4018/978-1-4666-4526-4.ch012

Malkia, M., & Savolainen, R. (2004). eTransformation in government, politics and society: Conceptual framework and introduction. In M. Malkia, A. Anttiroiko, & R. Savolainen (Eds.), eTransformation in governance: New directions in government and politics (pp. 1-21). Hershey, PA: IGI Global. doi:10.4018/978-1-59140-130-8.ch001

Mandujano, S. (2011). Network manageability security. In D. Kar & M. Syed (Eds.), *Network security, administration and management: Advancing technology and practice* (pp. 158–181). Hershey, PA: IGI Global. doi:10.4018/978-1-60960-777-7.ch009

Mantas, G., Lymberopoulos, D., & Komninos, N. (2011). Security in smart home environment. In A. Lazakidou, K. Siassiakos, & K. Ioannou (Eds.), *Wireless technologies for ambient assisted living and healthcare: Systems and applications* (pp. 170–191). Hershey, PA: Medical IGI Global. doi:10.4018/978-1-61520-805-0.ch010

Maple, C., Short, E., Brown, A., Bryden, C., & Salter, M. (2012). Cyberstalking in the UK: Analysis and recommendations. *International Journal of Distributed Systems and Technologies*, *3*(4), 34–51. doi:10.4018/jdst.2012100104

Maqousi, A., & Balikhina, T. (2011). Building security awareness culture to serve e-government initiative. In A. Al Ajeeli & Y. Al-Bastaki (Eds.), *Handbook of research on e-services in the public sector: E-government strategies and advancements* (pp. 304–311). Hershey, PA: IGI Global. doi:10.4018/978-1-61520-789-3.ch024

Marich, M. J., Schooley, B. L., & Horan, T. A. (2012). A normative enterprise architecture for guiding end-to-end emergency response decision support. In M. Jennex (Ed.), *Managing crises and disasters with emerging technologies: Advancements* (pp. 71–87). Hershey, PA: IGI Global. doi:10.4018/978-1-4666-0167-3.ch006

Markov, R., & Okujava, S. (2008). Costs, benefits, and risks of e-government portals. In G. Putnik & M. Cruz-Cunha (Eds.), *Encyclopedia of networked and virtual organizations* (pp. 354–363). Hershey, PA: IGI Global. doi:10.4018/978-1-59904-885-7.ch047

Martin, N., & Rice, J. (2013). Spearing high net wealth individuals: The case of online fraud and mature age internet users. *International Journal of Information Security and Privacy*, *7*(1), 1–15. doi:10.4018/jisp.2013010101

Martin, N., & Rice, J. (2013). Evaluating and designing electronic government for the future: Observations and insights from Australia. In V. Weerakkody (Ed.), *E-government services design, adoption, and evaluation* (pp. 238–258). Hershey, PA: IGI Global. doi:10.4018/978-1-4666-2458-0.ch014

i.    Martinez, A. C. (2008). Accessing administration's information via internet in Spain. In F. Tan (Ed.), *Global information technologies: Concepts, methodologies, tools, and applications* (pp. 2558–2573). Hershey, PA: IGI Global. doi:10.4018/978-1-59904-939-7.ch186

Martino, L., & Bertino, E. (2012). Security for web services: Standards and research issues. In L. Jie-Zhang (Ed.), *Innovations, standards and practices of web services: Emerging research topics* (pp. 336–362). Hershey, PA: IGI Global. doi:10.4018/978-1-61350-104-7.ch015

Massonet, P., Michot, A., Naqvi, S., Villari, M., & Latanicki, J. (2013). Securing the external interfaces of a federated infrastructure cloud. In *IT policy and ethics: Concepts, methodologies, tools, and applications* (pp. 1876–1903). Hershey, PA: IGI Global. doi:10.4018/978-1-4666-2919-6.ch082

Maumbe, B., & Owei, V. T. (2013). Understanding the information security landscape in South Africa: Implications for strategic collaboration and policy development. In B. Maumbe & C. Patrikakis (Eds.), *E-agriculture and rural development: Global innovations and future prospects* (pp. 90–102). Hershey, PA: IGI Global. doi:10.4018/978-1-4666-2655-3.ch009

Mazumdar, C. (2011). Enterprise information system security: A life-cycle approach. In *Enterprise information systems: Concepts, methodologies, tools and applications* (pp. 154–168). Hershey, PA: IGI Global. doi:10.4018/978-1-61692-852-0.ch111

Mbarika, V. W., Meso, P. N., & Musa, P. F. (2006). A disconnect in stakeholders' perceptions from emerging realities of teledensity growth in Africa's least developed countries. In M. Hunter & F. Tan (Eds.), *Advanced topics in global information management* (Vol. 5, pp. 263–282). Hershey, PA: IGI Global. doi:10.4018/978-1-59140-923-6.ch012

Mbarika, V. W., Meso, P. N., & Musa, P. F. (2008). A disconnect in stakeholders' perceptions from emerging realities of teledensity growth in Africa's least developed countries. In F. Tan (Ed.), *Global information technologies: Concepts, methodologies, tools, and applications* (pp. 2948–2962). Hershey, PA: IGI Global. doi:10.4018/978-1-59904-939-7.ch209

*Related References*

McCune, J., & Haworth, D. A. (2012). Securing America against cyber war. *International Journal of Cyber Warfare & Terrorism*, 2(1), 39–49. doi:10.4018/ijcwt.2012010104

Means, T., Olson, E., & Spooner, J. (2013). Discovering ways that don't work on the road to success: Strengths and weaknesses revealed by an active learning studio classroom project. In A. Benson, J. Moore, & S. Williams van Rooij (Eds.), *Cases on educational technology planning, design, and implementation: A project management perspective* (pp. 94–113). Hershey, PA: IGI Global. doi:10.4018/978-1-4666-4237-9.ch006

Melitski, J., Holzer, M., Kim, S., Kim, C., & Rho, S. (2008). Digital government worldwide: An e-government assessment of municipal web sites. In G. Garson & M. Khosrow-Pour (Eds.), *Handbook of research on public information technology* (pp. 790–804). Hershey, PA: IGI Global. doi:10.4018/978-1-59904-857-4.ch069

Melvin, A. O., & Ayotunde, T. (2011). Spirituality in cybercrime (Yahoo Yahoo) activities among youths in south west Nigeria. In E. Dunkels, G. Franberg, & C. Hallgren (Eds.), *Youth culture and net culture: Online social practices* (pp. 357–380). Hershey, PA: IGI Global. doi:10.4018/978-1-60960-209-3.ch020

Memmola, M., Palumbo, G., & Rossini, M. (2009). Web & RFID technology: New frontiers in costing and process management for rehabilitation medicine. In L. Al-Hakim & M. Memmola (Eds.), *Business web strategy: Design, alignment, and application* (pp. 145–169). Hershey, PA: IGI Global. doi:10.4018/978-1-60566-024-0.ch008

Meng, Z., Fahong, Z., & Lei, L. (2008). Information technology and environment. In Y. Kurihara, S. Takaya, H. Harui, & H. Kamae (Eds.), *Information technology and economic development* (pp. 201–212). Hershey, PA: IGI Global. doi:10.4018/978-1-59904-579-5.ch014

Mentzingen de Moraes, A. J., Ferneda, E., Costa, I., & Spinola, M. D. (2011). Practical approach for implementation of governance process in IT: Information technology areas. In N. Shi & G. Silvius (Eds.), *Enterprise IT governance, business value and performance measurement* (pp. 19–40). Hershey, PA: IGI Global. doi:10.4018/978-1-60566-346-3.ch002

Merwin, G. A. Jr, McDonald, J. S., & Odera, L. C. (2008). Economic development: Government's cutting edge in IT. In M. Raisinghani (Ed.), *Handbook of research on global information technology management in the digital economy* (pp. 1–37). Hershey, PA: IGI Global. doi:10.4018/978-1-59904-875-8.ch001

Meso, P., & Duncan, N. (2002). Can national information infrastructures enhance social development in the least developed countries? An empirical investigation. In M. Dadashzadeh (Ed.), *Information technology management in developing countries* (pp. 23–51). Hershey, PA: IGI Global. doi:10.4018/978-1-931777-03-2.ch002

Meso, P. N., & Duncan, N. B. (2002). Can national information infrastructures enhance social development in the least developed countries? In F. Tan (Ed.), *Advanced topics in global information management* (Vol. 1, pp. 207–226). Hershey, PA: IGI Global. doi:10.4018/978-1-930708-43-3.ch014

Middleton, M. (2008). Evaluation of e-government web sites. In G. Garson & M. Khosrow-Pour (Eds.), *Handbook of research on public information technology* (pp. 699–710). Hershey, PA: IGI Global. doi:10.4018/978-1-59904-857-4.ch063

Miller, J. M., Higgins, G. E., & Lopez, K. M. (2013). Considering the role of e-government in cybercrime awareness and prevention: Toward a theoretical research program for the 21st century. In *Digital rights management: Concepts, methodologies, tools, and applications* (pp. 789–800). Hershey, PA: IGI Global. doi:10.4018/978-1-4666-2136-7.ch036

Millman, C., Whitty, M., Winder, B., & Griffiths, M. D. (2012). Perceived criminality of cyber-harassing behaviors among undergraduate students in the United Kingdom. *International Journal of Cyber Behavior, Psychology and Learning, 2*(4), 49–59. doi:10.4018/ijcbpl.2012100104

Minami, N. A. (2012). Employing dynamic models to enhance corporate IT security policy. *International Journal of Agent Technologies and Systems, 4*(2), 42–59. doi:10.4018/jats.2012040103

Mingers, J. (2010). Pluralism, realism, and truth: The keys to knowledge in information systems research. In D. Paradice (Ed.), *Emerging systems approaches in information technologies: Concepts, theories, and applications* (pp. 86–98). Hershey, PA: IGI Global. doi:10.4018/978-1-60566-976-2.ch006

Mirante, D. P., & Ammari, H. M. (2014). Wireless sensor network security attacks: A survey. In *Crisis management: Concepts, methodologies, tools and applications* (pp. 25–59). Hershey, PA: IGI Global. doi:10.4018/978-1-4666-4707-7.ch002

Mishra, A., & Mishra, D. (2013). Cyber stalking: A challenge for web security. In J. Bishop (Ed.), *Examining the concepts, issues, and implications of internet trolling* (pp. 32–42). Hershey, PA: IGI Global. doi:10.4018/978-1-4666-2803-8.ch004

Mishra, S. (2011). Wireless sensor networks: Emerging applications and security solutions. In D. Kar & M. Syed (Eds.), *Network security, administration and management: Advancing technology and practice* (pp. 217–236). Hershey, PA: IGI Global. doi:10.4018/978-1-60960-777-7.ch011

Mital, K. M. (2012). ICT, unique identity and inclusive growth: An Indian perspective. In A. Manoharan & M. Holzer (Eds.), *E-governance and civic engagement: Factors and determinants of e-democracy* (pp. 584–612). Hershey, PA: IGI Global. doi:10.4018/978-1-61350-083-5.ch029

Mitra, S., & Padman, R. (2012). Privacy and security concerns in adopting social media for personal health management: A health plan case study. *Journal of Cases on Information Technology*, *14*(4), 12–26. doi:10.4018/jcit.2012100102

Mizell, A. P. (2008). Helping close the digital divide for financially disadvantaged seniors. In F. Tan (Ed.), *Global information technologies: Concepts, methodologies, tools, and applications* (pp. 2396–2402). Hershey, PA: IGI Global. doi:10.4018/978-1-59904-939-7.ch173

Modares, H., Lloret, J., Moravejosharieh, A., & Salleh, R. (2014). Security in mobile cloud computing. In J. Rodrigues, K. Lin, & J. Lloret (Eds.), *Mobile networks and cloud computing convergence for progressive services and applications* (pp. 79–91). Hershey, PA: IGI Global. doi:10.4018/978-1-4666-4781-7.ch005

Mohammadi, S., Golara, S., & Mousavi, N. (2012). Selecting adequate security mechanisms in e-business processes using fuzzy TOPSIS. *International Journal of Fuzzy System Applications*, *2*(1), 35–53. doi:10.4018/ijfsa.2012010103

Mohammed, L. A. (2012). ICT security policy: Challenges and potential remedies. In *Cyber crime: Concepts, methodologies, tools and applications* (pp. 999–1015). Hershey, PA: IGI Global. doi:10.4018/978-1-61350-323-2.ch501

Molinari, F., Wills, C., Koumpis, A., & Moumtzi, V. (2011). A citizen-centric platform to support networking in the area of e-democracy. In H. Rahman (Ed.), *Cases on adoption, diffusion and evaluation of global e-governance systems: Impact at the grass roots* (pp. 282–302). Hershey, PA: IGI Global. doi:10.4018/978-1-61692-814-8.ch014

Molinari, F., Wills, C., Koumpis, A., & Moumtzi, V. (2013). A citizen-centric platform to support networking in the area of e-democracy. In H. Rahman (Ed.), *Cases on progressions and challenges in ICT utilization for citizen-centric governance* (pp. 265–297). Hershey, PA: IGI Global. doi:10.4018/978-1-4666-2071-1.ch013

Molok, N. N., Ahmad, A., & Chang, S. (2012). Online social networking: A source of intelligence for advanced persistent threats. *International Journal of Cyber Warfare & Terrorism, 2*(1), 1–13. doi:10.4018/ijcwt.2012010101

Monteleone, S. (2011). Ambient intelligence: Legal challenges and possible directions for privacy protection. In C. Akrivopoulou & A. Psygkas (Eds.), *Personal data privacy and protection in a surveillance era: Technologies and practices* (pp. 201–221). Hershey, PA: IGI Global. doi:10.4018/978-1-60960-083-9.ch012

Monteverde, F. (2010). The process of e-government public policy inclusion in the governmental agenda: A framework for assessment and case study. In J. Cordoba-Pachon & A. Ochoa-Arias (Eds.), *Systems thinking and e-participation: ICT in the governance of society* (pp. 233–245). Hershey, PA: IGI Global. doi:10.4018/978-1-60566-860-4.ch015

Moodley, S. (2008). Deconstructing the South African government's ICT for development discourse. In A. Anttiroiko (Ed.), *Electronic government: Concepts, methodologies, tools, and applications* (pp. 622–631). Hershey, PA: IGI Global. doi:10.4018/978-1-59904-947-2.ch053

Moodley, S. (2008). Deconstructing the South African government's ICT for development discourse. In C. Van Slyke (Ed.), *Information communication technologies: Concepts, methodologies, tools, and applications* (pp. 816–825). Hershey, PA: IGI Global. doi:10.4018/978-1-59904-949-6.ch052

Mora, M., Cervantes-Perez, F., Gelman-Muravchik, O., Forgionne, G. A., & Mejia-Olvera, M. (2003). DMSS implementation research: A conceptual analysis of the contributions and limitations of the factor-based and stage-based streams. In G. Forgionne, J. Gupta, & M. Mora (Eds.), *Decision-making support systems: Achievements and challenges for the new decade* (pp. 331–356). Hershey, PA: IGI Global. doi:10.4018/978-1-59140-045-5.ch020

Moralis, A., Pouli, V., Grammatikou, M., Kalogeras, D., & Maglaris, V. (2012). Security standards and issues for grid computing. In N. Preve (Ed.), *Computational and data grids: Principles, applications and design* (pp. 248–264). Hershey, PA: IGI Global. doi:10.4018/978-1-61350-113-9.ch010

Mörtberg, C., & Elovaara, P. (2010). Attaching people and technology: Between e and government. In S. Booth, S. Goodman, & G. Kirkup (Eds.), *Gender issues in learning and working with information technology: Social constructs and cultural contexts* (pp. 83–98). Hershey, PA: IGI Global. doi:10.4018/978-1-61520-813-5.ch005

**Related References**

Mouratidis, H., & Kang, M. (2011). Secure by design: Developing secure software systems from the ground up. *International Journal of Secure Software Engineering, 2*(3), 23–41. doi:10.4018/jsse.2011070102

Murphy, J., Harper, E., Devine, E. C., Burke, L. J., & Hook, M. L. (2011). Case study: Lessons learned when embedding evidence-based knowledge in a nurse care planning and documentation system. In A. Cashin & R. Cook (Eds.), *Evidence-based practice in nursing informatics: Concepts and applications* (pp. 174–190). Hershey, PA: IGI Global. doi:10.4018/978-1-60960-034-1.ch014

Murthy, A. S., Nagadevara, V., & De', R. (2012). Predictive models in cybercrime investigation: An application of data mining techniques. In J. Wang (Ed.), *Advancing the service sector with evolving technologies: Techniques and principles* (pp. 166–177). Hershey, PA: IGI Global. doi:10.4018/978-1-4666-0044-7.ch011

Mutula, S. M. (2013). E-government's role in poverty alleviation: Case study of South Africa. In H. Rahman (Ed.), *Cases on progressions and challenges in ICT utilization for citizen-centric governance* (pp. 44–68). Hershey, PA: IGI Global. doi:10.4018/978-1-4666-2071-1.ch003

Nabi, S. I., Al-Ghmlas, G. S., & Alghathbar, K. (2012). Enterprise information security policies, standards, and procedures: A survey of available standards and guidelines. In M. Gupta, J. Walp, & R. Sharman (Eds.), *Strategic and practical approaches for information security governance: Technologies and applied solutions* (pp. 67–89). Hershey, PA: IGI Global. doi:10.4018/978-1-4666-0197-0.ch005

Nachtigal, S. (2011). E-business and security. In O. Bak & N. Stair (Eds.), *Impact of e-business technologies on public and private organizations: Industry comparisons and perspectives* (pp. 262–277). Hershey, PA: IGI Global. doi:10.4018/978-1-60960-501-8.ch016

Namal, S., & Gurtov, A. (2012). Security and mobility aspects of femtocell networks. In R. Saeed, B. Chaudhari, & R. Mokhtar (Eds.), *Femtocell communications and technologies: Business opportunities and deployment challenges* (pp. 124–156). Hershey, PA: IGI Global. doi:10.4018/978-1-4666-0092-8.ch008

Naqvi, D. E. (2011). Designing efficient security services infrastructure for virtualization oriented architectures. In H. Nemati (Ed.), *Pervasive information security and privacy developments: Trends and advancements* (pp. 149–171). Hershey, PA: IGI Global. doi:10.4018/978-1-61692-000-5.ch011

Nath, R., & Angeles, R. (2005). Relationships between supply characteristics and buyer-supplier coupling in e-procurement: An empirical analysis. *International Journal of E-Business Research, 1*(2), 40–55. doi:10.4018/jebr.2005040103

Neto, A. A., & Vieira, M. (2011). Security gaps in databases: A comparison of alternative software products for web applications support. *International Journal of Secure Software Engineering*, 2(3), 42–62. doi:10.4018/jsse.2011070103

Ngugi, B., Mana, J., & Segal, L. (2011). Evaluating the quality and usefulness of data breach information systems. *International Journal of Information Security and Privacy*, 5(4), 31–46. doi:10.4018/jisp.2011100103

Nhlabatsi, A., Bandara, A., Hayashi, S., Haley, C., Jurjens, J., & Kaiya, H. ... Yu, Y. (2011). Security patterns: Comparing modeling approaches. In H. Mouratidis (Ed.), *Software engineering for secure systems: Industrial and research perspectives* (pp. 75-111). Hershey, PA: IGI Global. doi:10.4018/978-1-61520-837-1.ch004

Nicho, M. (2013). An information governance model for information security management. In D. Mellado, L. Enrique Sánchez, E. Fernández-Medina, & M. Piattini (Eds.), *IT security governance innovations: Theory and research* (pp. 155–189). Hershey, PA: IGI Global. doi:10.4018/978-1-4666-2083-4.ch007

Nicho, M., Fakhry, H., & Haiber, C. (2011). An integrated security governance framework for effective PCI DSS implementation. *International Journal of Information Security and Privacy*, 5(3), 50–67. doi:10.4018/jisp.2011070104

Nissen, M. E. (2006). Application cases in government. In M. Nissen (Ed.), *Harnessing knowledge dynamics: Principled organizational knowing & learning* (pp. 152–181). Hershey, PA: IGI Global. doi:10.4018/978-1-59140-773-7.ch008

Nobelis, N., Boudaoud, K., Delettre, C., & Riveill, M. (2012). Designing security properties-centric communication protocols using a component-based approach. *International Journal of Distributed Systems and Technologies*, 3(1), 1–16. doi:10.4018/jdst.2012010101

Norris, D. F. (2003). Leading-edge information technologies and American local governments. In G. Garson (Ed.), *Public information technology: Policy and management issues* (pp. 139–169). Hershey, PA: IGI Global. doi:10.4018/978-1-59140-060-8.ch007

Norris, D. F. (2008). Information technology among U.S. local governments. In G. Garson & M. Khosrow-Pour (Eds.), *Handbook of research on public information technology* (pp. 132–144). Hershey, PA: IGI Global. doi:10.4018/978-1-59904-857-4.ch013

### Related References

Northrop, A. (1999). The challenge of teaching information technology in public administration graduate programs. In G. Garson (Ed.), *Information technology and computer applications in public administration: Issues and trends* (pp. 1–22). Hershey, PA: IGI Global. doi:10.4018/978-1-87828-952-0.ch001

Northrop, A. (2003). Information technology and public administration: The view from the profession. In G. Garson (Ed.), *Public information technology: Policy and management issues* (pp. 1–19). Hershey, PA: IGI Global. doi:10.4018/978-1-59140-060-8.ch001

Northrop, A. (2007). Lip service? How PA journals and textbooks view information technology. In G. Garson (Ed.), *Modern public information technology systems: Issues and challenges* (pp. 1–16). Hershey, PA: IGI Global. doi:10.4018/978-1-59904-051-6.ch001

Null, E. (2013). Legal and political barriers to municipal networks in the United States. In A. Abdelaal (Ed.), *Social and economic effects of community wireless networks and infrastructures* (pp. 27–56). Hershey, PA: IGI Global. doi:10.4018/978-1-4666-2997-4.ch003

Ohashi, M., & Hori, M. (2011). Security management services based on authentication roaming between different certificate authorities. In M. Cruz-Cunha & J. Varajao (Eds.), *Enterprise information systems design, implementation and management: Organizational applications* (pp. 72–84). Hershey, PA: IGI Global. doi:10.4018/978-1-61692-020-3.ch005

Okubo, T., Kaiya, H., & Yoshioka, N. (2012). Analyzing impacts on software enhancement caused by security design alternatives with patterns. *International Journal of Secure Software Engineering*, *3*(1), 37–61. doi:10.4018/jsse.2012010103

Okunoye, A., Frolick, M., & Crable, E. (2006). ERP implementation in higher education: An account of pre-implementation and implementation phases. *Journal of Cases on Information Technology*, *8*(2), 110–132. doi:10.4018/jcit.2006040106

Olasina, G. (2012). A review of egovernment services in Nigeria. In A. Tella & A. Issa (Eds.), *Library and information science in developing countries: Contemporary issues* (pp. 205–221). Hershey, PA: IGI Global. doi:10.4018/978-1-61350-335-5.ch015

Oost, D., & Chew, E. K. (2012). Investigating the concept of information security culture. In M. Gupta, J. Walp, & R. Sharman (Eds.), *Strategic and practical approaches for information security governance: Technologies and applied solutions* (pp. 1–12). Hershey, PA: IGI Global. doi:10.4018/978-1-4666-0197-0.ch001

Orgeron, C. P. (2008). A model for reengineering IT job classes in state government. In G. Garson & M. Khosrow-Pour (Eds.), *Handbook of research on public information technology* (pp. 135–146). Hershey, PA: IGI Global. doi:10.4018/978-1-59904-857-4.ch066

Otero, A. R., Ejnioui, A., Otero, C. E., & Tejay, G. (2013). Evaluation of information security controls in organizations by grey relational analysis. *International Journal of Dependable and Trustworthy Information Systems*, 2(3), 36–54. doi:10.4018/jdtis.2011070103

Ouedraogo, M., Mouratidis, H., Dubois, E., & Khadraoui, D. (2011). Security assurance evaluation and IT systems context of use security criticality. *International Journal of Handheld Computing Research*, 2(4), 59–81. doi:10.4018/jhcr.2011100104

Owsinski, J. W., & Pielak, A. M. (2011). Local authority websites in rural areas: Measuring quality and functionality, and assessing the role. In Z. Andreopoulou, B. Manos, N. Polman, & D. Viaggi (Eds.), *Agricultural and environmental informatics, governance and management: Emerging research applications* (pp. 39–60). Hershey, PA: IGI Global. doi:10.4018/978-1-60960-621-3.ch003

Owsiński, J. W., Pielak, A. M., Sęp, K., & Stańczak, J. (2014). Local web-based networks in rural municipalities: Extension, density, and meaning. In Z. Andreopoulou, V. Samathrakis, S. Louca, & M. Vlachopoulou (Eds.), *E-innovation for sustainable development of rural resources during global economic crisis* (pp. 126–151). Hershey, PA: IGI Global. doi:10.4018/978-1-4666-4550-9.ch011

Pagani, M., & Pasinetti, C. (2008). Technical and functional quality in the development of t-government services. In A. Anttiroiko (Ed.), *Electronic government: Concepts, methodologies, tools, and applications* (pp. 2943–2965). Hershey, PA: IGI Global. doi:10.4018/978-1-59904-947-2.ch220

Pal, S. (2013). Cloud computing: Security concerns and issues. In A. Bento & A. Aggarwal (Eds.), *Cloud computing service and deployment models: Layers and management* (pp. 191–207). Hershey, PA: IGI Global. doi:10.4018/978-1-4666-2187-9.ch010

Palanisamy, R., & Mukerji, B. (2012). Security and privacy issues in e-government. In M. Shareef, N. Archer, & S. Dutta (Eds.), *E-government service maturity and development: Cultural, organizational and technological perspectives* (pp. 236–248). Hershey, PA: IGI Global. doi:10.4018/978-1-60960-848-4.ch013

Pan, Y., Yuan, B., & Mishra, S. (2011). Network security auditing. In D. Kar & M. Syed (Eds.), *Network security, administration and management: Advancing technology and practice* (pp. 131–157). Hershey, PA: IGI Global. doi:10.4018/978-1-60960-777-7.ch008

Pani, A. K., & Agrahari, A. (2005). On e-markets in emerging economy: An Indian experience. In M. Khosrow-Pour (Ed.), *Advanced topics in electronic commerce* (Vol. 1, pp. 287–299). Hershey, PA: IGI Global. doi:10.4018/978-1-59140-819-2.ch015

Papadopoulos, T., Angelopoulos, S., & Kitsios, F. (2011). A strategic approach to e-health interoperability using e-government frameworks. In A. Lazakidou, K. Siassiakos, & K. Ioannou (Eds.), *Wireless technologies for ambient assisted living and healthcare: Systems and applications* (pp. 213–229). Hershey, PA: IGI Global. doi:10.4018/978-1-61520-805-0.ch012

Papadopoulos, T., Angelopoulos, S., & Kitsios, F. (2013). A strategic approach to e-health interoperability using e-government frameworks. In *User-driven healthcare: Concepts, methodologies, tools, and applications* (pp. 791–807). Hershey, PA: IGI Global. doi:10.4018/978-1-4666-2770-3.ch039

Papaleo, G., Chiarella, D., Aiello, M., & Caviglione, L. (2012). Analysis, development and deployment of statistical anomaly detection techniques for real e-mail traffic. In T. Chou (Ed.), *Information assurance and security technologies for risk assessment and threat management: Advances* (pp. 47–71). Hershey, PA: IGI Global. doi:10.4018/978-1-61350-507-6.ch003

Papp, R. (2003). Information technology & FDA compliance in the pharmaceutical industry. In M. Khosrow-Pour (Ed.), *Annals of cases on information technology* (Vol. 5, pp. 262–273). Hershey, PA: IGI Global. doi:10.4018/978-1-59140-061-5.ch017

Parsons, T. W. (2007). Developing a knowledge management portal. In A. Tatnall (Ed.), *Encyclopedia of portal technologies and applications* (pp. 223–227). Hershey, PA: IGI Global. doi:10.4018/978-1-59140-989-2.ch039

Passaris, C. E. (2007). Immigration and digital government. In A. Anttiroiko & M. Malkia (Eds.), *Encyclopedia of digital government* (pp. 988–994). Hershey, PA: IGI Global. doi:10.4018/978-1-59140-789-8.ch148

Patel, A., Taghavi, M., Júnior, J. C., Latih, R., & Zin, A. M. (2012). Safety measures for social computing in wiki learning environment. *International Journal of Information Security and Privacy*, 6(2), 1–15. doi:10.4018/jisp.2012040101

Pathan, A. K. (2012). Security management in heterogeneous distributed sensor networks. In S. Bagchi (Ed.), *Ubiquitous multimedia and mobile agents: Models and implementations* (pp. 274–294). Hershey, PA: IGI Global. doi:10.4018/978-1-61350-107-8.ch012

Paul, C., & Porche, I. R. (2011). Toward a U.S. army cyber security culture. *International Journal of Cyber Warfare & Terrorism*, *1*(3), 70–80. doi:10.4018/ijcwt.2011070105

Pavlichev, A. (2004). The e-government challenge for public administration. In A. Pavlichev & G. Garson (Eds.), *Digital government: Principles and best practices* (pp. 276–290). Hershey, PA: IGI Global. doi:10.4018/978-1-59140-122-3.ch018

Pavlidis, M., Mouratidis, H., & Islam, S. (2012). Modelling security using trust based concepts. *International Journal of Secure Software Engineering*, *3*(2), 36–53. doi:10.4018/jsse.2012040102

Pendegraft, N., Rounds, M., & Stone, R. W. (2012). Factors influencing college students' use of computer security. In H. Nemati (Ed.), *Optimizing information security and advancing privacy assurance: New technologies* (pp. 225–234). Hershey, PA: IGI Global. doi:10.4018/978-1-4666-0026-3.ch013

Penrod, J. I., & Harbor, A. F. (2000). Designing and implementing a learning organization-oriented information technology planning and management process. In L. Petrides (Ed.), *Case studies on information technology in higher education: Implications for policy and practice* (pp. 7–19). Hershey, PA: IGI Global. doi:10.4018/978-1-878289-74-2.ch001

Petkovic, M., & Ibraimi, L. (2011). Privacy and security in e-health applications. In C. Röcker & M. Ziefle (Eds.), *E-health, assistive technologies and applications for assisted living: Challenges and solutions* (pp. 23–48). Hershey, PA: IGI Global. doi:10.4018/978-1-60960-469-1.ch002

Picazo-Sanchez, P., Ortiz-Martin, L., Peris-Lopez, P., & Hernandez-Castro, J. C. (2013). Security of EPC class-1. In P. Lopez, J. Hernandez-Castro, & T. Li (Eds.), *Security and trends in wireless identification and sensing platform tags: Advancements in RFID* (pp. 34–63). Hershey, PA: IGI Global. doi:10.4018/978-1-4666-1990-6.ch002

Pieters, W., Probst, C. W., Lukszo, Z., & Montoya, L. (2014). Cost-effectiveness of security measures: A model-based framework. In T. Tsiakis, T. Kargidis, & P. Katsaros (Eds.), *Approaches and processes for managing the economics of information systems* (pp. 139–156). Hershey, PA: IGI Global. doi:10.4018/978-1-4666-4983-5.ch009

*Related References*

Pirim, T., James, T., Boswell, K., Reithel, B., & Barkhi, R. (2011). Examining an individual's perceived need for privacy and security: Construct and scale development. In H. Nemati (Ed.), *Pervasive information security and privacy developments: Trends and advancements* (pp. 1–13). Hershey, PA: IGI Global. doi:10.4018/978-1-61692-000-5.ch001

Planas-Silva, M. D., & Joseph, R. C. (2011). Perspectives on the adoption of electronic resources for use in clinical trials. In M. Guah (Ed.), *Healthcare delivery reform and new technologies: Organizational initiatives* (pp. 19–28). Hershey, PA: IGI Global. doi:10.4018/978-1-60960-183-6.ch002

Podhradsky, A., Casey, C., & Ceretti, P. (2012). The bluetooth honeypot project: Measuring and managing bluetooth risks in the workplace. *International Journal of Interdisciplinary Telecommunications and Networking, 4*(3), 1–22. doi:10.4018/jitn.2012070101

Pomazalová, N., & Rejman, S. (2013). The rationale behind implementation of new electronic tools for electronic public procurement. In N. Pomazalová (Ed.), *Public sector transformation processes and internet public procurement: Decision support systems* (pp. 85–117). Hershey, PA: IGI Global. doi:10.4018/978-1-4666-2665-2.ch006

Pomponiu, V. (2011). Security in e-health applications. In C. Röcker & M. Ziefle (Eds.), *E-health, assistive technologies and applications for assisted living: Challenges and solutions* (pp. 94–118). Hershey, PA: IGI Global. doi:10.4018/978-1-60960-469-1.ch005

Pomponiu, V. (2014). Securing wireless ad hoc networks: State of the art and challenges. In *Crisis management: Concepts, methodologies, tools and applications* (pp. 81–101). Hershey, PA: IGI Global. doi:10.4018/978-1-4666-4707-7.ch004

Pope, M. B., Warkentin, M., & Luo, X. R. (2012). Evolutionary malware: Mobile malware, botnets, and malware toolkits. *International Journal of Wireless Networks and Broadband Technologies, 2*(3), 52–60. doi:10.4018/ijwnbt.2012070105

Postorino, M. N. (2012). City competitiveness and airport: Information science perspective. In M. Bulu (Ed.), *City competitiveness and improving urban subsystems: Technologies and applications* (pp. 61–83). Hershey, PA: IGI Global. doi:10.4018/978-1-61350-174-0.ch004

Poupa, C. (2002). Electronic government in Switzerland: Priorities for 2001-2005 - Electronic voting and federal portal. In Å. Grönlund (Ed.), *Electronic government: Design, applications and management* (pp. 356–369). Hershey, PA: IGI Global. doi:10.4018/978-1-930708-19-8.ch017

Powell, S. R. (2010). Interdisciplinarity in telecommunications and networking. In *Networking and telecommunications: Concepts, methodologies, tools and applications* (pp. 33–40). Hershey, PA: IGI Global. doi.10.4018/978-1-60566-986-1.ch004

Prakash, S., Vaish, A., Coul, N. G. S., Srinidhi, T., & Botsa, J. (2013). Child security in cyberspace through moral cognition. *International Journal of Information Security and Privacy*, *7*(1), 16–29. doi:10.4018/jisp.2013010102

Priya, P. S., & Mathiyalagan, N. (2011). A study of the implementation status of two e-governance projects in land revenue administration in India. In M. Shareef, V. Kumar, U. Kumar, & Y. Dwivedi (Eds.), *Stakeholder adoption of e-government services: Driving and resisting factors* (pp. 214–230). Hershey, PA: IGI Global. doi:10.4018/978-1-60960-601-5.ch011

Prysby, C., & Prysby, N. (2000). Electronic mail, employee privacy and the workplace. In L. Janczewski (Ed.), *Internet and intranet security management: Risks and solutions* (pp. 251–270). Hershey, PA: IGI Global. doi:10.4018/978-1-878289-71-1.ch009

Prysby, C. L., & Prysby, N. D. (2003). Electronic mail in the public workplace: Issues of privacy and public disclosure. In G. Garson (Ed.), *Public information technology: Policy and management issues* (pp. 271–298). Hershey, PA: IGI Global. doi:10.4018/978-1-59140-060-8.ch012

Prysby, C. L., & Prysby, N. D. (2007). You have mail, but who is reading it? Issues of e-mail in the public workplace. In G. Garson (Ed.), *Modern public information technology systems: Issues and challenges* (pp. 312–336). Hershey, PA: IGI Global. doi:10.4018/978-1-59904-051-6.ch016

Pye, G. (2011). Critical infrastructure systems: Security analysis and modelling approach. *International Journal of Cyber Warfare & Terrorism*, *1*(3), 37–58. doi:10.4018/ijcwt.2011070103

Radl, A., & Chen, Y. (2005). Computer security in electronic government: A state-local education information system. *International Journal of Electronic Government Research*, *1*(1), 79–99. doi:10.4018/jegr.2005010105

Rahman, H. (2008). Information dynamics in developing countries. In C. Van Slyke (Ed.), *Information communication technologies: Concepts, methodologies, tools, and applications* (pp. 104–114). Hershey, PA: IGI Global. doi:10.4018/978-1-59904-949-6.ch008

**Related References**

Rahman, M. M., & Rezaul, K. M. (2012). Information security management: Awareness of threats in e-commerce. In M. Gupta, J. Walp, & R. Sharman (Eds.), *Threats, countermeasures, and advances in applied information security* (pp. 66–90). Hershey, PA: IGI Global. doi:10.4018/978-1-4666-0978-5.ch004

Rak, M., Ficco, M., Luna, J., Ghani, H., Suri, N., Panica, S., & Petcu, D. (2012). Security issues in cloud federations. In M. Villari, I. Brandic, & F. Tusa (Eds.), *Achieving federated and self-manageable cloud infrastructures: Theory and practice* (pp. 176–194). Hershey, PA: IGI Global. doi:10.4018/978-1-4666-1631-8.ch010

Ramachandran, M., & Mahmood, Z. (2011). A framework for internet security assessment and improvement process. In M. Ramachandran (Ed.), *Knowledge engineering for software development life cycles: Support technologies and applications* (pp. 244–255). Hershey, PA: IGI Global. doi:10.4018/978-1-60960-509-4.ch013

Ramachandran, S., Mundada, R., Bhattacharjee, A., Murthy, C., & Sharma, R. (2011). Classifying host anomalies: Using ontology in information security monitoring. In R. Santanam, M. Sethumadhavan, & M. Virendra (Eds.), *Cyber security, cyber crime and cyber forensics: Applications and perspectives* (pp. 70–86). Hershey, PA: IGI Global. doi:10.4018/978-1-60960-123-2.ch006

Ramamurthy, B. (2014). Securing business IT on the cloud. In S. Srinivasan (Ed.), *Security, trust, and regulatory aspects of cloud computing in business environments* (pp. 115–125). Hershey, PA: IGI Global. doi:10.4018/978-1-4666-5788-5.ch006

Ramanathan, J. (2009). Adaptive IT architecture as a catalyst for network capability in government. In P. Saha (Ed.), *Advances in government enterprise architecture* (pp. 149–172). Hershey, PA: IGI Global. doi:10.4018/978-1-60566-068-4.ch007

Ramos, I., & Berry, D. M. (2006). Social construction of information technology supporting work. In M. Khosrow-Pour (Ed.), *Cases on information technology: Lessons learned* (Vol. 7, pp. 36–52). Hershey, PA: IGI Global. doi:10.4018/978-1-59140-673-0.ch003

Raspotnig, C., & Opdahl, A. L. (2012). Improving security and safety modelling with failure sequence diagrams. *International Journal of Secure Software Engineering*, *3*(1), 20–36. doi:10.4018/jsse.2012010102

Ray, D., Gulla, U., Gupta, M. P., & Dash, S. S. (2009). Interoperability and constituents of interoperable systems in public sector. In V. Weerakkody, M. Janssen, & Y. Dwivedi (Eds.), *Handbook of research on ICT-enabled transformational government: A global perspective* (pp. 175–195). Hershey, PA: IGI Global. doi:10.4018/978-1-60566-390-6.ch010

Reddick, C. G. (2007). E-government and creating a citizen-centric government: A study of federal government CIOs. In G. Garson (Ed.), *Modern public information technology systems: Issues and challenges* (pp. 143–165). Hershey, PA: IGI Global. doi:10.4018/978-1-59904-051-6.ch008

Reddick, C. G. (2010). Citizen-centric e-government. In C. Reddick (Ed.), *Homeland security preparedness and information systems: Strategies for managing public policy* (pp. 45–75). Hershey, PA: IGI Global. doi:10.4018/978-1-60566-834-5.ch002

Reddick, C. G. (2010). E-government and creating a citizen-centric government: A study of federal government CIOs. In C. Reddick (Ed.), *Homeland security preparedness and information systems: Strategies for managing public policy* (pp. 230–250). Hershey, PA: IGI Global. doi:10.4018/978-1-60566-834-5.ch012

Reddick, C. G. (2010). Perceived effectiveness of e-government and its usage in city governments: Survey evidence from information technology directors. In C. Reddick (Ed.), *Homeland security preparedness and information systems: Strategies for managing public policy* (pp. 213–229). Hershey, PA: IGI Global. doi:10.4018/978-1-60566-834-5.ch011

Reddick, C. G. (2012). Customer relationship management adoption in local governments in the United States. In S. Chhabra & M. Kumar (Eds.), *Strategic enterprise resource planning models for e-government: Applications and methodologies* (pp. 111–124). Hershey, PA: IGI Global. doi:10.4018/978-1-60960-863-7.ch008

Reddy, A., & Prasad, G. V. (2012). Consumer perceptions on security, privacy, and trust on e-portals. *International Journal of Online Marketing*, 2(2), 10–24. doi:10.4018/ijom.2012040102

Reeder, F. S., & Pandy, S. M. (2008). Identifying effective funding models for e-government. In A. Anttiroiko (Ed.), *Electronic government: Concepts, methodologies, tools, and applications* (pp. 1108–1138). Hershey, PA: IGI Global. doi:10.4018/978-1-59904-947-2.ch083

Richet, J. (2013). From young hackers to crackers. *International Journal of Technology and Human Interaction*, 9(3), 53–62. doi:10.4018/jthi.2013070104

Riesco, D., Acosta, E., & Montejano, G. (2003). An extension to a UML activity graph from workflow. In L. Favre (Ed.), *UML and the unified process* (pp. 294–314). Hershey, PA: IGI Global. doi:10.4018/978-1-93177-744-5.ch015

**Related References**

Ritzhaupt, A. D., & Gill, T. G. (2008). A hybrid and novel approach to teaching computer programming in MIS curriculum. In S. Negash, M. Whitman, A. Woszczynski, K. Hoganson, & H. Mattord (Eds.), *Handbook of distance learning for real-time and asynchronous information technology education* (pp. 259–281). Hershey, PA: IGI Global. doi:10.4018/978-1-59904-964-9.ch014

Rjaibi, N., Rabai, L. B., Ben Aissa, A., & Mili, A. (2013). Mean failure cost as a measurable value and evidence of cybersecurity: E-learning case study. *International Journal of Secure Software Engineering*, *4*(3), 64–81. doi:10.4018/jsse.2013070104

Roberts, L. D. (2012). Cyber identity theft. In *Cyber crime: Concepts, methodologies, tools and applications* (pp. 21–36). Hershey, PA: IGI Global. doi:10.4018/978-1-61350-323-2.ch103

Roche, E. M. (1993). International computing and the international regime. *Journal of Global Information Management*, *1*(2), 33–44. doi:10.4018/jgim.1993040103

Rocheleau, B. (2007). Politics, accountability, and information management. In G. Garson (Ed.), *Modern public information technology systems: Issues and challenges* (pp. 35–71). Hershey, PA: IGI Global. doi:10.4018/978-1-59904-051-6.ch003

Rodrigues Filho, J. (2010). E-government in Brazil: Reinforcing dominant institutions or reducing citizenship? In C. Reddick (Ed.), *Politics, democracy and e-government: Participation and service delivery* (pp. 347–362). Hershey, PA: IGI Global. doi:10.4018/978-1-61520-933-0.ch021

Rodríguez, J., Fernández-Medina, E., Piattini, M., & Mellado, D. (2011). A security requirements engineering tool for domain engineering in software product lines. In N. Milanovic (Ed.), *Non-functional properties in service oriented architecture: Requirements, models and methods* (pp. 73–92). Hershey, PA: IGI Global. doi:10.4018/978-1-60566-794-2.ch004

Rodriguez, S. R., & Thorp, D. A. (2013). eLearning for industry: A case study of the project management process. In A. Benson, J. Moore, & S. Williams van Rooij (Eds.), Cases on educational technology planning, design, and implementation: A project management perspective (pp. 319-342). Hershey, PA: IGI Global. doi:10.4018/978-1-4666-4237-9.ch017

Roldan, M., & Rea, A. (2011). Individual privacy and security in virtual worlds. In A. Rea (Ed.), *Security in virtual worlds, 3D webs, and immersive environments: Models for development, interaction, and management* (pp. 1–19). Hershey, PA: IGI Global. doi:10.4018/978-1-61520-891-3.ch001

Roman, A. V. (2013). Delineating three dimensions of e-government success: Security, functionality, and transformation. In J. Gil-Garcia (Ed.), *E-government success factors and measures: Theories, concepts, and methodologies* (pp. 171–192). Hershey, PA: IGI Global. doi:10.4018/978-1-4666-4058-0.ch010

Ross, S. C., Tyran, C. K., & Auer, D. J. (2008). Up in smoke: Rebuilding after an IT disaster. In H. Nemati (Ed.), *Information security and ethics: Concepts, methodologies, tools, and applications* (pp. 3659–3675). Hershey, PA: IGI Global. doi:10.4018/978-1-59904-937-3.ch248

Ross, S. C., Tyran, C. K., Auer, D. J., Junell, J. M., & Williams, T. G. (2005). Up in smoke: Rebuilding after an IT disaster. *Journal of Cases on Information Technology*, *7*(2), 31–49. doi:10.4018/jcit.2005040103

Rowe, N. C., Garfinkel, S. L., Beverly, R., & Yannakogeorgos, P. (2011). Challenges in monitoring cyberarms compliance. *International Journal of Cyber Warfare & Terrorism*, *1*(2), 35–48. doi:10.4018/ijcwt.2011040104

Roy, J. (2008). Security, sovereignty, and continental interoperability: Canada's elusive balance. In T. Loendorf & G. Garson (Eds.), *Patriotic information systems* (pp. 153–176). Hershey, PA: IGI Global. doi:10.4018/978-1-59904-594-8.ch007

Rubeck, R. F., & Miller, G. A. (2009). vGOV: Remote video access to government services. In A. Scupola (Ed.), Cases on managing e-services (pp. 253-268). Hershey, PA: IGI Global. doi:10.4018/978-1-60566-064-6.ch017

Rwabutaza, A., Yang, M., & Bourbakis, N. (2012). A comparative survey on cryptology-based methodologies. *International Journal of Information Security and Privacy*, *6*(3), 1–37. doi:10.4018/jisp.2012070101

Sadkhan, S. B., & Abbas, N. A. (2014). Privacy and security of wireless communication networks. In J. Rodrigues, K. Lin, & J. Lloret (Eds.), *Mobile networks and cloud computing convergence for progressive services and applications* (pp. 58–78). Hershey, PA: IGI Global. doi:10.4018/978-1-4666-4781-7.ch004

Saedy, M., & Mojtahed, V. (2011). Machine-to-machine communications and security solution in cellular systems. *International Journal of Interdisciplinary Telecommunications and Networking*, *3*(2), 66–75. doi:10.4018/jitn.2011040105

Saekow, A., & Boonmee, C. (2011). The challenges of implementing e-government interoperability in Thailand: Case of official electronic correspondence letters exchange across government departments. In Y. Charalabidis (Ed.), *Interoperability in digital public services and administration: Bridging e-government and e-business* (pp. 40–61). Hershey, PA: IGI Global. doi:10.4018/978-1-61520-887-6.ch003

*Related References*

Saekow, A., & Boonmee, C. (2012). The challenges of implementing e-government interoperability in Thailand: Case of official electronic correspondence letters exchange across government departments. In *Digital democracy: Concepts, methodologies, tools, and applications* (pp. 1883–1905). Hershey, PA: IGI Global. doi:10.4018/978-1-4666-1740-7.ch094

Sagsan, M., & Medeni, T. (2012). Understanding "knowledge management (KM) paradigms" from social media perspective: An empirical study on discussion group for KM at professional networking site. In M. Cruz-Cunha, P. Gonçalves, N. Lopes, E. Miranda, & G. Putnik (Eds.), *Handbook of research on business social networking: Organizational, managerial, and technological dimensions* (pp. 738–755). Hershey, PA: IGI Global. doi:10.4018/978-1-61350-168-9.ch039

Sahi, G., & Madan, S. (2013). Information security threats in ERP enabled e-governance: Challenges and solutions. In *Enterprise resource planning: Concepts, methodologies, tools, and applications* (pp. 825–837). Hershey, PA: IGI Global. doi:10.4018/978-1-4666-4153-2.ch048

San Nicolas-Rocca, T., & Olfman, L. (2013). End user security training for identification and access management. *Journal of Organizational and End User Computing*, *25*(4), 75–103. doi:10.4018/joeuc.2013100104

Sanford, C., & Bhattacherjee, A. (2008). IT implementation in a developing country municipality: A sociocognitive analysis. *International Journal of Technology and Human Interaction*, *4*(3), 68–93. doi:10.4018/jthi.2008070104

Satoh, F., Nakamura, Y., Mukhi, N. K., Tatsubori, M., & Ono, K. (2011). Model-driven approach for end-to-end SOA security configurations. In N. Milanovic (Ed.), *Non-functional properties in service oriented architecture: Requirements, models and methods* (pp. 268–298). Hershey, PA: IGI Global. doi:10.4018/978-1-60566-794-2.ch012

Saucez, D., Iannone, L., & Bonaventure, O. (2014). The map-and-encap locator/identifier separation paradigm: A security analysis. In M. Boucadair & D. Binet (Eds.), *Solutions for sustaining scalability in internet growth* (pp. 148–163). Hershey, PA: IGI Global. doi:10.4018/978-1-4666-4305-5.ch008

Schelin, S. H. (2003). E-government: An overview. In G. Garson (Ed.), *Public information technology: Policy and management issues* (pp. 120–138). Hershey, PA: IGI Global. doi:10.4018/978-1-59140-060-8.ch006

Schelin, S. H. (2004). Training for digital government. In A. Pavlichev & G. Garson (Eds.), *Digital government: Principles and best practices* (pp. 263–275). Hershey, PA: IGI Global. doi:10.4018/978-1-59140-122-3.ch017

Schelin, S. H. (2007). E-government: An overview. In G. Garson (Ed.), *Modern public information technology systems: Issues and challenges* (pp. 110–126). Hershey, PA: IGI Global. doi:10.4018/978-1-59904-051-6.ch006

Schelin, S. H., & Garson, G. (2004). Theoretical justification of critical success factors. In G. Garson & S. Schelin (Eds.), *IT solutions series: Humanizing information technology: Advice from experts* (pp. 4–15). Hershey, PA: IGI Global. doi:10.4018/978-1-59140-245-9.ch002

Schell, B. H., & Holt, T. J. (2012). A profile of the demographics, psychological predispositions, and social/behavioral patterns of computer hacker insiders and outsiders. In *Cyber crime: Concepts, methodologies, tools and applications* (pp. 1461–1484). Hershey, PA: IGI Global. doi:10.4018/978-1-61350-323-2.ch705

Schmidt, H. (2011). Threat and risk-driven security requirements engineering. *International Journal of Mobile Computing and Multimedia Communications*, *3*(1), 35–50. doi:10.4018/jmcmc.2011010103

Schmidt, H., Hatebur, D., & Heisel, M. (2011). A pattern-based method to develop secure software. In H. Mouratidis (Ed.), *Software engineering for secure systems: Industrial and research perspectives* (pp. 32–74). Hershey, PA: IGI Global. doi:10.4018/978-1-61520-837-1.ch003

Scime, A. (2002). Information systems and computer science model curricula: A comparative look. In M. Dadashzadeh, A. Saber, & S. Saber (Eds.), *Information technology education in the new millennium* (pp. 146–158). Hershey, PA: IGI Global. doi:10.4018/978-1-931777-05-6.ch018

Scime, A. (2009). Computing curriculum analysis and development. In M. Khosrow-Pour (Ed.), *Encyclopedia of information science and technology* (2nd ed.; pp. 667–671). Hershey, PA: IGI Global. doi:10.4018/978-1-60566-026-4.ch108

Scime, A., & Wania, C. (2008). Computing curricula: A comparison of models. In C. Van Slyke (Ed.), *Information communication technologies: Concepts, methodologies, tools, and applications* (pp. 1270–1283). Hershey, PA: IGI Global. doi:10.4018/978-1-59904-949-6.ch088

Seale, R. O., & Hargiss, K. M. (2011). A proposed architecture for autonomous mobile agent intrusion prevention and malware defense in heterogeneous networks. *International Journal of Strategic Information Technology and Applications*, *2*(4), 44–54. doi:10.4018/jsita.2011100104

Seidman, S. B. (2009). An international perspective on professional software engineering credentials. In H. Ellis, S. Demurjian, & J. Naveda (Eds.), *Software engineering: Effective teaching and learning approaches and practices* (pp. 351–361). Hershey, PA: IGI Global. doi:10.4018/978-1-60566-102-5.ch018

Seifert, J. W. (2007). E-government act of 2002 in the United States. In A. Anttiroiko & M. Malkia (Eds.), *Encyclopedia of digital government* (pp. 476–481). Hershey, PA: IGI Global. doi:10.4018/978-1-59140-789-8.ch072

Seifert, J. W., & Relyea, H. C. (2008). E-government act of 2002 in the United States. In A. Anttiroiko (Ed.), *Electronic government: Concepts, methodologies, tools, and applications* (pp. 154–161). Hershey, PA: IGI Global. doi:10.4018/978-1-59904-947-2.ch013

Sen, J. (2013). Security and privacy challenges in cognitive wireless sensor networks. In N. Meghanathan & Y. Reddy (Eds.), *Cognitive radio technology applications for wireless and mobile ad hoc networks* (pp. 194–232). Hershey, PA: IGI Global. doi:10.4018/978-1-4666-4221-8.ch011

Sen, J. (2014). Security and privacy issues in cloud computing. In A. Ruiz-Martinez, R. Marin-Lopez, & F. Pereniguez-Garcia (Eds.), *Architectures and protocols for secure information technology infrastructures* (pp. 1–45). Hershey, PA: IGI Global. doi:10.4018/978-1-4666-4514-1.ch001

Sengupta, A., & Mazumdar, C. (2011). A mark-up language for the specification of information security governance requirements. *International Journal of Information Security and Privacy*, 5(2), 33–53. doi:10.4018/jisp.2011040103

Seufert, S. (2002). E-learning business models: Framework and best practice examples. In M. Raisinghani (Ed.), *Cases on worldwide e-commerce: Theory in action* (pp. 70–94). Hershey, PA: IGI Global. doi:10.4018/978-1-930708-27-3.ch004

Shaqrah, A. A. (2011). The influence of internet security on e-business competence in Jordan: An empirical analysis. In *Global business: Concepts, methodologies, tools and applications* (pp. 1071–1086). Hershey, PA: IGI Global. doi:10.4018/978-1-60960-587-2.ch413

Shareef, M. A., & Archer, N. (2012). E-government service development. In M. Shareef, N. Archer, & S. Dutta (Eds.), *E-government service maturity and development: Cultural, organizational and technological perspectives* (pp. 1–14). Hershey, PA: IGI Global. doi:10.4018/978-1-60960-848-4.ch001

Shareef, M. A., & Archer, N. (2012). E-government initiatives: Review studies on different countries. In M. Shareef, N. Archer, & S. Dutta (Eds.), *E-government service maturity and development: Cultural, organizational and technological perspectives* (pp. 40–76). Hershey, PA: IGI Global. doi:10.4018/978-1-60960-848-4.ch003

Shareef, M. A., Kumar, U., & Kumar, V. (2011). E-government development: Performance evaluation parameters. In M. Shareef, V. Kumar, U. Kumar, & Y. Dwivedi (Eds.), *Stakeholder adoption of e-government services: Driving and resisting factors* (pp. 197–213). Hershey, PA: IGI Global. doi:10.4018/978-1-60960-601-5.ch010

Shareef, M. A., Kumar, U., Kumar, V., & Niktash, M. (2012). Electronic-government vision: Case studies for objectives, strategies, and initiatives. In M. Shareef, N. Archer, & S. Dutta (Eds.), *E-government service maturity and development: Cultural, organizational and technological perspectives* (pp. 15–39). Hershey, PA: IGI Global. doi:10.4018/978-1-60960-848-4.ch002

Shareef, M. A., & Kumar, V. (2012). Prevent/control identity theft: Impact on trust and consumers purchase intention in B2C EC. *Information Resources Management Journal*, *25*(3), 30–60. doi:10.4018/irmj.2012070102

Sharma, K., & Singh, A. (2011). Biometric security in the e-world. In H. Nemati & L. Yang (Eds.), *Applied cryptography for cyber security and defense: Information encryption and cyphering* (pp. 289–337). Hershey, PA: IGI Global. doi:10.4018/978-1-61520-783-1.ch013

Sharma, R. K. (2014). Physical layer security and its applications: A survey. In D. Rawat, B. Bista, & G. Yan (Eds.), *Security, Privacy, Trust, and Resource Management in Mobile and Wireless Communications* (pp. 29–60). Hershey, PA: IGI Global. doi:10.4018/978-1-4666-4691-9.ch003

Shaw, R., Keh, H., & Huang, N. (2011). Information security awareness on-line materials design with knowledge maps. *International Journal of Distance Education Technologies*, *9*(4), 41–56. doi:10.4018/jdet.2011100104

Shebanow, A., Perez, R., & Howard, C. (2012). The effect of firewall testing types on cloud security policies. *International Journal of Strategic Information Technology and Applications*, *3*(3), 60–68. doi:10.4018/jsita.2012070105

Shen, Y., Li, Y., Wu, L., Liu, S., & Wen, Q. (2014). Data protection in the cloud era. In Y. Shen, Y. Li, L. Wu, S. Liu, & Q. Wen (Eds.), *Enabling the new era of cloud computing: Data security, transfer, and management* (pp. 132–154). Hershey, PA: IGI Global. doi:10.4018/978-1-4666-4801-2.ch007

*Related References*

Shen, Y., Li, Y., Wu, L., Liu, S., & Wen, Q. (2014). Enterprise security monitoring with the fusion center model. In Y. Shen, Y. Li, L. Wu, S. Liu, & Q. Wen (Eds.), *Enabling the new era of cloud computing: Data security, transfer, and management* (pp. 116–131). Hershey, PA: IGI Global. doi:10.4018/978-1-4666-4801-2.ch006

Shore, M. (2011). Cyber security and anti-social networking. In *Virtual communities: Concepts, methodologies, tools and applications* (pp. 1286–1297). Hershey, PA: IGI Global. doi:10.4018/978-1-60960-100-3.ch412

Shukla, P., Kumar, A., & Anu Kumar, P. B. (2013). Impact of national culture on business continuity management system implementation. *International Journal of Risk and Contingency Management*, 2(3), 23–36. doi:10.4018/ijrcm.2013070102

Shulman, S. W. (2007). The federal docket management system and the prospect for digital democracy in U S rulemaking. In G. Garson (Ed.), *Modern public information technology systems: Issues and challenges* (pp. 166–184). Hershey, PA: IGI Global. doi:10.4018/978-1-59904-051-6.ch009

Siddiqi, J., Alqatawna, J., & Btoush, M. H. (2011). Do insecure systems increase global digital divide? In *Global business: Concepts, methodologies, tools and applications* (pp. 2102–2111). Hershey, PA: IGI Global. doi:10.4018/978-1-60960-587-2.ch717

Simonovic, S. (2007). Problems of offline government in e-Serbia. In A. Anttiroiko & M. Malkia (Eds.), *Encyclopedia of digital government* (pp. 1342–1351). Hershey, PA: IGI Global. doi:10.4018/978-1-59140-789-8.ch205

Simonovic, S. (2008). Problems of offline government in e-Serbia. In A. Anttiroiko (Ed.), *Electronic government: Concepts, methodologies, tools, and applications* (pp. 2929–2942). Hershey, PA: IGI Global. doi:10.4018/978-1-59904-947-2.ch219

Simpson, J. J., Simpson, M. J., Endicott-Popovsky, B., & Popovsky, V. (2012). Secure software education: A contextual model-based approach. In K. Khan (Ed.), *Security-aware systems applications and software development methods* (pp. 286–312). Hershey, PA: IGI Global. doi:10.4018/978-1-4666-1580-9.ch016

Singh, A. M. (2005). Information systems and technology in South Africa. In M. Khosrow-Pour (Ed.), *Encyclopedia of information science and technology* (pp. 1497–1502). Hershey, PA: IGI Global. doi:10.4018/978-1-59140-553-5.ch263

Singh, S. (2012). Security threats and issues with MANET. In K. Lakhtaria (Ed.), *Technological advancements and applications in mobile ad-hoc networks: Research trends* (pp. 247–263). Hershey, PA: IGI Global. doi:10.4018/978-1-4666-0321-9.ch015

Singh, S., & Naidoo, G. (2005). Towards an e-government solution: A South African perspective. In W. Huang, K. Siau, & K. Wei (Eds.), *Electronic government strategies and implementation* (pp. 325–353). Hershey, PA: IGI Global. doi:10.4018/978-1-59140-348-7.ch014

Snoke, R., & Underwood, A. (2002). Generic attributes of IS graduates: An analysis of Australian views. In F. Tan (Ed.), *Advanced topics in global information management* (Vol. 1, pp. 370–384). Hershey, PA: IGI Global. doi:10.4018/978-1-930708-43-3.ch023

Sockel, H., & Falk, L. K. (2012). Online privacy, vulnerabilities, and threats: A manager's perspective. In *Cyber crime: Concepts, methodologies, tools and applications* (pp. 101–123). Hershey, PA: IGI Global. doi:10.4018/978-1-61350-323-2.ch108

Sommer, L. (2006). Revealing unseen organizations in higher education: A study framework and application example. In A. Metcalfe (Ed.), *Knowledge management and higher education: A critical analysis* (pp. 115–146). Hershey, PA: IGI Global. doi:10.4018/978-1-59140-509-2.ch007

Song, H., Kidd, T., & Owens, E. (2011). Examining technological disparities and instructional practices in English language arts classroom: Implications for school leadership and teacher training. In L. Tomei (Ed.), *Online courses and ICT in education: Emerging practices and applications* (pp. 258–274). Hershey, PA: IGI Global. doi:10.4018/978-1-60960-150-8.ch020

Speaker, P. J., & Kleist, V. F. (2003). Using information technology to meet electronic commerce and MIS education demands. In A. Aggarwal (Ed.), *Web-based education: Learning from experience* (pp. 280–291). Hershey, PA: IGI Global. doi:10.4018/978-1-59140-102-5.ch017

Spitler, V. K. (2007). Learning to use IT in the workplace: Mechanisms and masters. In M. Mahmood (Ed.), *Contemporary issues in end user computing* (pp. 292–323). Hershey, PA: IGI Global. doi:10.4018/978-1-59140-926-7.ch013

Spruit, M., & de Bruijn, W. (2012). CITS: The cost of IT security framework. *International Journal of Information Security and Privacy*, 6(4), 94–116. doi:10.4018/jisp.2012100105

Srinivasan, C., Lakshmy, K., & Sethumadhavan, M. (2011). Complexity measures of cryptographically secure boolean functions. In R. Santanam, M. Sethumadhavan, & M. Virendra (Eds.), *Cyber security, cyber crime and cyber forensics: Applications and perspectives* (pp. 220–230). Hershey, PA: IGI Global. doi:10.4018/978-1-60960-123-2.ch015

**Related References**

Srivatsa, M., Agrawal, D., & McDonald, A. D. (2012). Security across disparate management domains in coalition MANETs. In *Wireless technologies: Concepts, methodologies, tools and applications* (pp. 1494–1518). Hershey, PA: IGI Global. doi:10.4018/978-1-61350-101-6.ch521

Stellefson, M. (2011). Considerations for marketing distance education courses in health education: Five important questions to examine before development. In U. Demiray & S. Sever (Eds.), *Marketing online education programs: Frameworks for promotion and communication* (pp. 222–234). Hershey, PA: IGI Global. doi:10.4018/978-1-60960-074-7.ch014

Stojanovic, M. D., Acimovic-Raspopovic, V. S., & Rakas, S. B. (2013). Security management issues for open source ERP in the NGN environment. In *Enterprise resource planning: Concepts, methodologies, tools, and applications* (pp. 789–804). Hershey, PA: IGI Global. doi:10.4018/978-1-4666-4153-2.ch046

Stoll, M., & Breu, R. (2012). Information security governance and standard based management systems. In M. Gupta, J. Walp, & R. Sharman (Eds.), *Strategic and practical approaches for information security governance: Technologies and applied solutions* (pp. 261–282). Hershey, PA: IGI Global. doi:10.4018/978-1-4666-0197-0.ch015

Straub, D. W., & Loch, K. D. (2006). Creating and developing a program of global research. *Journal of Global Information Management, 14*(2), 1–28. doi:10.4018/jgim.2006040101

Straub, D. W., Loch, K. D., & Hill, C. E. (2002). Transfer of information technology to the Arab world: A test of cultural influence modeling. In M. Dadashzadeh (Ed.), *Information technology management in developing countries* (pp. 92–134). Hershey, PA: IGI Global. doi:10.4018/978-1-931777-03-2.ch005

Straub, D. W., Loch, K. D., & Hill, C. E. (2003). Transfer of information technology to the Arab world: A test of cultural influence modeling. In F. Tan (Ed.), *Advanced topics in global information management* (Vol. 2, pp. 141–172). Hershey, PA: IGI Global. doi:10.4018/978-1-59140-064-6.ch009

Suki, N. M., Ramayah, T., Ming, M. K., & Suki, N. M. (2013). Factors enhancing employed job seekers intentions to use social networking sites as a job search tool. In A. Mesquita (Ed.), *User perception and influencing factors of technology in everyday life* (pp. 265–281). Hershey, PA: IGI Global. doi:10.4018/978-1-4666-1954-8.ch018

Sundaresan, M., & Boopathy, D. (2014). Different perspectives of cloud security. In S. Srinivasan (Ed.), *Security, trust, and regulatory aspects of cloud computing in business environments* (pp. 73–90). Hershey, PA: IGI Global. doi:10.4018/978-1-4666-5788-5.ch004

Suomi, R. (2006). Introducing electronic patient records to hospitals: Innovation adoption paths. In T. Spil & R. Schuring (Eds.), *E-health systems diffusion and use: The innovation, the user and the use IT model* (pp. 128–146). Hershey, PA: IGI Global. doi:10.4018/978-1-59140-423-1.ch008

Swim, J., & Barker, L. (2012). Pathways into a gendered occupation: Brazilian women in IT. *International Journal of Social and Organizational Dynamics in IT*, 2(4), 34–51. doi:10.4018/ijsodit.2012100103

Takabi, H., Joshi, J. B., & Ahn, G. (2013). Security and privacy in cloud computing: Towards a comprehensive framework. In X. Yang & L. Liu (Eds.), *Principles, methodologies, and service-oriented approaches for cloud computing* (pp. 164–184). Hershey, PA: IGI Global. doi:10.4018/978-1-4666-2854-0.ch007

Takabi, H., Zargar, S. T., & Joshi, J. B. (2014). Mobile cloud computing and its security and privacy challenges. In D. Rawat, B. Bista, & G. Yan (Eds.), *Security, privacy, trust, and resource management in mobile and wireless communications* (pp. 384–407). Hershey, PA: IGI Global. doi:10.4018/978-1-4666-4691-9.ch016

Takemura, T. (2014). Unethical information security behavior and organizational commitment. In T. Tsiakis, T. Kargidis, & P. Katsaros (Eds.), *Approaches and processes for managing the economics of information systems* (pp. 181–198). Hershey, PA: IGI Global. doi:10.4018/978-1-4666-4983-5.ch011

Talib, S., Clarke, N. L., & Furnell, S. M. (2011). Establishing a personalized information security culture. *International Journal of Mobile Computing and Multimedia Communications*, 3(1), 63–79. doi:10.4018/jmcmc.2011010105

Talukder, A. K. (2011). Securing next generation internet services. In R. Santanam, M. Sethumadhavan, & M. Virendra (Eds.), *Cyber security, cyber crime and cyber forensics: Applications and perspectives* (pp. 87–105). Hershey, PA: IGI Global. doi:10.4018/978-1-60960-123-2.ch007

Tarafdar, M., & Vaidya, S. D. (2006). Adoption and implementation of IT in developing nations: Experiences from two public sector enterprises in India. In M. Khosrow-Pour (Ed.), *Cases on information technology planning, design and implementation* (pp. 208–233). Hershey, PA: IGI Global. doi:10.4018/978-1-59904-408-8.ch013

Tarafdar, M., & Vaidya, S. D. (2008). Adoption and implementation of IT in developing nations: Experiences from two public sector enterprises in India. In G. Garson & M. Khosrow-Pour (Eds.), *Handbook of research on public information technology* (pp. 905–924). Hershey, PA: IGI Global. doi:10.4018/978-1-59904-857-4.ch076

Tchepnda, C., Moustafa, H., Labiod, H., & Bourdon, G. (2011). Vehicular networks security: Attacks, requirements, challenges and current contributions. In K. Curran (Ed.), *Ubiquitous developments in ambient computing and intelligence: Human-centered applications* (pp. 43–55). Hershey, PA: IGI Global. doi:10.4018/978-1-60960-549-0.ch004

Tereshchenko, N. (2012). US foreign policy challenges of non-state actors cyber terrorism against critical infrastructure. *International Journal of Cyber Warfare & Terrorism*, *2*(4), 28–48. doi:10.4018/ijcwt.2012100103

Thesing, Z. (2007). Zarina thesing, pumpkin patch. In M. Hunter (Ed.), *Contemporary chief information officers: Management experiences* (pp. 83–94). Hershey, PA: IGI Global. doi:10.4018/978-1-59904-078-3.ch007

Thomas, J. C. (2004). Public involvement in public administration in the information age: Speculations on the effects of technology. In M. Malkia, A. Anttiroiko, & R. Savolainen (Eds.), *eTransformation in governance: New directions in government and politics* (pp. 67–84). Hershey, PA: IGI Global. doi:10.4018/978-1-59140-130-8.ch004

Thurimella, R., & Baird, L. C. (2011). Network security. In H. Nemati & L. Yang (Eds.), *Applied cryptography for cyber security and defense: Information encryption and cyphering* (pp. 1–31). Hershey, PA: IGI Global. doi:10.4018/978-1-61520-783-1.ch001

Thurimella, R., & Mitchell, W. (2011). Cloak and dagger: Man-in-the-middle and other insidious attacks. In H. Nemati (Ed.), *Security and privacy assurance in advancing technologies: New developments* (pp. 252–270). Hershey, PA: IGI Global. doi:10.4018/978-1-60960-200-0.ch016

Tiwari, S., Singh, A., Singh, R. S., & Singh, S. K. (2013). Internet security using biometrics. In *IT policy and ethics: Concepts, methodologies, tools, and applications* (pp. 1680–1707). Hershey, PA: IGI Global. doi:10.4018/978-1-4666-2919-6.ch074

Tomaiuolo, M. (2012). Trust enforcing and trust building, different technologies and visions. *International Journal of Cyber Warfare & Terrorism*, *2*(4), 49–66. doi:10.4018/ijcwt.2012100104

Tomaiuolo, M. (2014). Trust management and delegation for the administration of web services. In I. Portela & F. Almeida (Eds.), *Organizational, legal, and technological dimensions of information system administration* (pp. 18–37). Hershey, PA. IGI Global. doi:10.4018/978-1-4666-4526-4.ch002

Touhafi, A., Braeken, A., Cornetta, G., Mentens, N., & Steenhaut, K. (2011). Secure techniques for remote reconfiguration of wireless embedded systems. In M. Cruz-Cunha & F. Moreira (Eds.), *Handbook of research on mobility and computing: Evolving technologies and ubiquitous impacts* (pp. 930–951). Hershey, PA: IGI Global. doi:10.4018/978-1-60960-042-6.ch058

Traore, I., & Woungang, I. (2013). Software security engineering – Part I: Security requirements and risk analysis. In K. Buragga & N. Zaman (Eds.), *Software development techniques for constructive information systems design* (pp. 221–255). Hershey, PA: IGI Global. doi:10.4018/978-1-4666-3679-8.ch012

Treiblmaier, H., & Chong, S. (2013). Trust and perceived risk of personal information as antecedents of online information disclosure: Results from three countries. In F. Tan (Ed.), *Global diffusion and adoption of technologies for knowledge and information sharing* (pp. 341–361). Hershey, PA: IGI Global. doi:10.4018/978-1-4666-2142-8.ch015

Tripathi, M., Gaur, M., & Laxmi, V. (2014). Security challenges in wireless sensor network. In D. Rawat, B. Bista, & G. Yan (Eds.), *Security, privacy, trust, and resource management in mobile and wireless communications* (pp. 334–359). Hershey, PA: IGI Global. doi:10.4018/978-1-4666-4691-9.ch014

Trösterer, S., Beck, E., Dalpiaz, F., Paja, E., Giorgini, P., & Tscheligi, M. (2012). Formative user-centered evaluation of security modeling: Results from a case study. *International Journal of Secure Software Engineering*, *3*(1), 1–19. doi:10.4018/jsse.2012010101

Tsiakis, T. (2013). The role of information security and cryptography in digital democracy: (Human) rights and freedom. In C. Akrivopoulou & N. Garipidis (Eds.), *Digital democracy and the impact of technology on governance and politics: New globalized practices* (pp. 158–174). Hershey, PA: IGI Global. doi:10.4018/978-1-4666-3637-8.ch009

Tsiakis, T., Kargidis, T., & Chatzipoulidis, A. (2013). IT security governance in e-banking. In D. Mellado, L. Enrique Sánchez, E. Fernández-Medina, & M. Piattini (Eds.), *IT security governance innovations: Theory and research* (pp. 13–46). Hershey, PA: IGI Global. doi:10.4018/978-1-4666-2083-4.ch002

*Related References*

Turgeman-Goldschmidt, O. (2011). Between hackers and white-collar offenders. In T. Holt & B. Schell (Eds.), *Corporate hacking and technology-driven crime: Social dynamics and implications* (pp. 18–37). Hershey, PA: IGI Global. doi:10.4018/978-1-61692-805-6.ch002

Tvrdíková, M. (2012). Information system integrated security. In M. Gupta, J. Walp, & R. Sharman (Eds.), *Strategic and practical approaches for information security governance: Technologies and applied solutions* (pp. 158–169). Hershey, PA: IGI Global. doi:10.4018/978-1-4666-0197-0.ch009

Uffen, J., & Breitner, M. H. (2013). Management of technical security measures: An empirical examination of personality traits and behavioral intentions. *International Journal of Social and Organizational Dynamics in IT*, *3*(1), 14–31. doi:10.4018/ijsodit.2013010102

van Grembergen, W., & de Haes, S. (2008). IT governance in practice: Six case studies. In W. van Grembergen & S. De Haes (Eds.), *Implementing information technology governance: Models, practices and cases* (pp. 125–237). Hershey, PA: IGI Global. doi:10.4018/978-1-59904-924-3.ch004

van Os, G., Homburg, V., & Bekkers, V. (2013). Contingencies and convergence in European social security: ICT coordination in the back office of the welfare state. In M. Cruz-Cunha, I. Miranda, & P. Gonçalves (Eds.), *Handbook of research on ICTs and management systems for improving efficiency in healthcare and social care* (pp. 268–287). Hershey, PA: IGI Global. doi:10.4018/978-1-4666-3990-4.ch013

Vance, A., & Siponen, M. T. (2012). IS security policy violations: A rational choice perspective. *Journal of Organizational and End User Computing*, *24*(1), 21–41. doi:10.4018/joeuc.2012010102

Velloso, A. B., Gassenferth, W., & Machado, M. A. (2012). Evaluating IBMEC-RJ's intranet usability using fuzzy logic. In M. Cruz-Cunha, P. Gonçalves, N. Lopes, E. Miranda, & G. Putnik (Eds.), *Handbook of research on business social networking: Organizational, managerial, and technological dimensions* (pp. 185–205). Hershey, PA: IGI Global. doi:10.4018/978-1-61350-168-9.ch010

Veltsos, C. (2011). Mitigating the blended threat: Protecting data and educating users. In D. Kar & M. Syed (Eds.), *Network security, administration and management: Advancing technology and practice* (pp. 20–37). Hershey, PA: IGI Global. doi:10.4018/978-1-60960-777-7.ch002

Venkataraman, R., Pushpalatha, M., & Rao, T. R. (2014). Trust management and modeling techniques in wireless communications. In D. Rawat, B. Bista, & G. Yan (Eds.), *Security, privacy, trust, and resource management in mobile and wireless communications* (pp. 278–294). Hershey, PA: IGI Global. doi:10.4018/978-1-4666-4691-9.ch012

Venkataraman, R., & Rao, T. R. (2012). Security issues and models in mobile ad hoc networks. In K. Lakhtaria (Ed.), *Technological advancements and applications in mobile ad-hoc networks: Research trends* (pp. 219–227). Hershey, PA: IGI Global. doi:10.4018/978-1-4666-0321-9.ch013

Villablanca, A. C., Baxi, H., & Anderson, K. (2009). Novel data interface for evaluating cardiovascular outcomes in women. In A. Dwivedi (Ed.), *Handbook of research on information technology management and clinical data administration in healthcare* (pp. 34–53). Hershey, PA: IGI Global. doi:10.4018/978-1-60566-356-2.ch003

Villablanca, A. C., Baxi, H., & Anderson, K. (2011). Novel data interface for evaluating cardiovascular outcomes in women. In *Clinical technologies: Concepts, methodologies, tools and applications* (pp. 2094–2113). Hershey, PA: IGI Global. doi:10.4018/978-1-60960-561-2.ch806

Viney, D. (2011). Future trends in digital security. In D. Kerr, J. Gammack, & K. Bryant (Eds.), *Digital business security development: Management technologies* (pp. 173–190). Hershey, PA: IGI Global. doi:10.4018/978-1-60566-806-2.ch009

Vinod, P., Laxmi, V., & Gaur, M. (2011). Metamorphic malware analysis and detection methods. In R. Santanam, M. Sethumadhavan, & M. Virendra (Eds.), *Cyber security, cyber crime and cyber forensics: Applications and perspectives* (pp. 178–202). Hershey, PA: IGI Global. doi:10.4018/978-1-60960-123-2.ch013

Virkar, S. (2011). Information and communication technologies in administrative reform for development: Exploring the case of property tax systems in Karnataka, India. In J. Steyn, J. Van Belle, & E. Mansilla (Eds.), *ICTs for global development and sustainability: Practice and applications* (pp. 127–149). Hershey, PA: IGI Global. doi:10.4018/978-1-61520-997-2.ch006

Virkar, S. (2013). Designing and implementing e-government projects: Actors, influences, and fields of play. In S. Saeed & C. Reddick (Eds.), *Human-centered system design for electronic governance* (pp. 88–110). Hershey, PA: IGI Global. doi:10.4018/978-1-4666-3640-8.ch007

von Solms, R., & Warren, M. (2011). Towards the human information security firewall. *International Journal of Cyber Warfare & Terrorism, 1*(2), 10–17. doi:10.4018/ijcwt.2011040102

### Related References

Wall, D. S. (2011). Micro-frauds: Virtual robberies, stings and scams in the information age. In T. Holt & B. Schell (Eds.), *Corporate hacking and technology-driven crime: Social dynamics and implications* (pp. 68–86). Hershey, PA: IGI Global. doi:10.4018/978-1-61692-805-6.ch004

Wallace, A. (2009). E-justice: An Australian perspective. In A. Martínez & P. Abat (Eds.), *E-justice: Using information communication technologies in the court system* (pp. 204–228). Hershey, PA: IGI Global. doi:10.4018/978-1-59904-998-4.ch014

Wang, G. (2012). E-democratic administration and bureaucratic responsiveness: A primary study of bureaucrats' perceptions of the civil service e-mail box in Taiwan. In K. Kloby & M. D'Agostino (Eds.), *Citizen 2.0: Public and governmental interaction through web 2.0 technologies* (pp. 146–173). Hershey, PA: IGI Global. doi:10.4018/978-1-4666-0318-9.ch009

Wang, H., Zhao, J. L., & Chen, G. (2012). Managing data security in e-markets through relationship driven access control. *Journal of Database Management, 23*(2), 1–21. doi:10.4018/jdm.2012040101

Wangpipatwong, S., Chutimaskul, W., & Papasratorn, B. (2011). Quality enhancing the continued use of e-government web sites: Evidence from e-citizens of Thailand. In V. Weerakkody (Ed.), *Applied technology integration in governmental organizations: New e-government research* (pp. 20–36). Hershey, PA: IGI Global. doi:10.4018/978-1-60960-162-1.ch002

Warren, M., & Leitch, S. (2011). Protection of Australia in the cyber age. *International Journal of Cyber Warfare & Terrorism, 1*(1), 35–40. doi:10.4018/ijcwt.2011010104

Weber, S. G., & Gustiené, P. (2013). Crafting requirements for mobile and pervasive emergency response based on privacy and security by design principles. *International Journal of Information Systems for Crisis Response and Management, 5*(2), 1–18. doi:10.4018/jiscrm.2013040101

Wedemeijer, L. (2006). Long-term evolution of a conceptual schema at a life insurance company. In M. Khosrow-Pour (Ed.), *Cases on database technologies and applications* (pp. 202–226). Hershey, PA: IGI Global. doi:10.4018/978-1-59904-399-9.ch012

Wei, J., Lin, B., & Loho-Noya, M. (2013). Development of an e-healthcare information security risk assessment method. *Journal of Database Management, 24*(1), 36–57. doi:10.4018/jdm.2013010103

Weippl, E. R., & Riedl, B. (2012). Security, trust, and privacy on mobile devices and multimedia applications. In *Cyber crime: Concepts, methodologies, tools and applications* (pp. 228–244). Hershey, PA: IGI Global. doi.10.4018/978-1-61350-323-2.ch202

White, G., & Long, J. (2012). Global information security factors. In H. Nemati (Ed.), *Optimizing information security and advancing privacy assurance: New technologies* (pp. 163–174). Hershey, PA: IGI Global. doi:10.4018/978-1-4666-0026-3.ch009

White, S. C., Sedigh, S., & Hurson, A. R. (2013). Security concepts for cloud computing. In X. Yang & L. Liu (Eds.), *Principles, methodologies, and service-oriented approaches for cloud computing* (pp. 116–142). Hershey, PA: IGI Global. doi:10.4018/978-1-4666-2854-0.ch005

Whybrow, E. (2008). Digital access, ICT fluency, and the economically disadvantages: Approaches to minimize the digital divide. In F. Tan (Ed.), *Global information technologies: Concepts, methodologies, tools, and applications* (pp. 1409–1422). Hershey, PA: IGI Global. doi:10.4018/978-1-59904-939-7.ch102

Whybrow, E. (2008). Digital access, ICT fluency, and the economically disadvantages: Approaches to minimize the digital divide. In C. Van Slyke (Ed.), *Information communication technologies: Concepts, methodologies, tools, and applications* (pp. 764–777). Hershey, PA: IGI Global. doi:10.4018/978-1-59904-949-6.ch049

Whyte, B., & Harrison, J. (2011). State of practice in secure software: Experts' views on best ways ahead. In H. Mouratidis (Ed.), *Software engineering for secure systems: Industrial and research perspectives* (pp. 1–14). Hershey, PA: IGI Global. doi:10.4018/978-1-61520-837-1.ch001

Wickramasinghe, N., & Geisler, E. (2010). Key considerations for the adoption and implementation of knowledge management in healthcare operations. In M. Saito, N. Wickramasinghe, M. Fuji, & E. Geisler (Eds.), *Redesigning innovative healthcare operation and the role of knowledge management* (pp. 125–142). Hershey, PA: IGI Global. doi:10.4018/978-1-60566-284-8.ch009

Wickramasinghe, N., & Geisler, E. (2012). Key considerations for the adoption and implementation of knowledge management in healthcare operations. In *Organizational learning and knowledge: Concepts, methodologies, tools and applications* (pp. 1316–1328). Hershey, PA: IGI Global. doi:10.4018/978-1-60960-783-8.ch405

Wickramasinghe, N., & Goldberg, S. (2007). A framework for delivering m-health excellence. In L. Al-Hakim (Ed.), *Web mobile-based applications for healthcare management* (pp. 36–61). Hershey, PA: IGI Global. doi:10.4018/978-1-59140-658-7.ch002

*Related References*

Wickramasinghe, N., & Goldberg, S. (2008). Critical success factors for delivering m-health excellence. In N. Wickramasinghe & E. Geisler (Eds.), *Encyclopedia of healthcare information systems* (pp. 339–351). Hershey, PA: IGI Global. doi:10.4018/978-1-59904-889-5.ch045

Wu, Y., & Saunders, C. S. (2011). Governing information security: Governance domains and decision rights allocation patterns. *Information Resources Management Journal*, 24(1), 28–45. doi:10.4018/irmj.2011010103

Wyld, D. (2009). Radio frequency identification (RFID) technology. In J. Symonds, J. Ayoade, & D. Parry (Eds.), *Auto-identification and ubiquitous computing applications* (pp. 279–293). Hershey, PA: IGI Global. doi:10.4018/978-1-60566-298-5.ch017

Yadav, S. B. (2011). SEACON: An integrated approach to the analysis and design of secure enterprise architecture–based computer networks. In H. Nemati (Ed.), *Pervasive information security and privacy developments: Trends and advancements* (pp. 309–331). Hershey, PA: IGI Global. doi:10.4018/978-1-61692-000-5.ch020

Yadav, S. B. (2012). A six-view perspective framework for system security: Issues, risks, and requirements. In H. Nemati (Ed.), *Optimizing information security and advancing privacy assurance: New technologies* (pp. 58–90). Hershey, PA: IGI Global. doi:10.4018/978-1-4666-0026-3.ch004

Yaghmaei, F. (2010). Understanding computerised information systems usage in community health. In J. Rodrigues (Ed.), *Health information systems: Concepts, methodologies, tools, and applications* (pp. 1388–1399). Hershey, PA: IGI Global. doi:10.4018/978-1-60566-988-5.ch088

Yamany, H. F., Allison, D. S., & Capretz, M. A. (2013). Developing proactive security dimensions for SOA. In *IT policy and ethics: Concepts, methodologies, tools, and applications* (pp. 900–922). Hershey, PA: IGI Global. doi:10.4018/978-1-4666-2919-6.ch041

Yan, G., Rawat, D. B., Bista, B. B., & Chen, L. (2014). Location security in vehicular wireless networks. In D. Rawat, B. Bista, & G. Yan (Eds.), *Security, privacy, trust, and resource management in mobile and wireless communications* (pp. 108–133). Hershey, PA: IGI Global. doi:10.4018/978-1-4666-4691-9.ch006

Yaokumah, W. (2013). Evaluating the effectiveness of information security governance practices in developing nations: A case of Ghana. *International Journal of IT/Business Alignment and Governance*, 4(1), 27–43. doi:10.4018/jitbag.2013010103

Yates, D., & Harris, A. (2011). International ethical attitudes and behaviors: Implications for organizational information security policy. In M. Dark (Ed.), *Information assurance and security ethics in complex systems: Interdisciplinary perspectives* (pp. 55–80). Hershey, PA: IGI Global. doi:10.4018/978-1-61692-245-0.ch004

Yau, S. S., Yin, Y., & An, H. (2011). An adaptive approach to optimizing tradeoff between service performance and security in service-based systems. *International Journal of Web Services Research*, 8(2), 74–91. doi:10.4018/jwsr.2011040104

Yee, G., El-Khatib, K., Korba, L., Patrick, A. S., Song, R., & Xu, Y. (2005). Privacy and trust in e-government. In W. Huang, K. Siau, & K. Wei (Eds.), *Electronic government strategies and implementation* (pp. 145–190). Hershey, PA: IGI Global. doi:10.4018/978-1-59140-348-7.ch007

Yeh, S., & Chu, P. (2010). Evaluation of e-government services: A citizen-centric approach to citizen e-complaint services. In C. Reddick (Ed.), *Citizens and e-government: Evaluating policy and management* (pp. 400–417). Hershey, PA: IGI Global. doi:10.4018/978-1-61520-931-6.ch022

Young-Jin, S., & Seang-tae, K. (2008). E-government concepts, measures, and best practices. In A. Anttiroiko (Ed.), *Electronic government: Concepts, methodologies, tools, and applications* (pp. 32–57). Hershey, PA: IGI Global. doi:10.4018/978-1-59904-947-2.ch004

Yun, H. J., & Opheim, C. (2012). New technology communication in American state governments: The impact on citizen participation. In K. Bwalya & S. Zulu (Eds.), *Handbook of research on e-government in emerging economies: Adoption, e-participation, and legal frameworks* (pp. 573–590). Hershey, PA: IGI Global. doi:10.4018/978-1-4666-0324-0.ch029

Zadig, S. M., & Tejay, G. (2012). Emerging cybercrime trends: Legal, ethical, and practical issues. In A. Dudley, J. Braman, & G. Vincenti (Eds.), *Investigating cyber law and cyber ethics: Issues, impacts and practices* (pp. 37–56). Hershey, PA: IGI Global. doi:10.4018/978-1-61350-132-0.ch003

Zafar, H., Ko, M., & Osei-Bryson, K. (2012). Financial impact of information security breaches on breached firms and their non-breached competitors. *Information Resources Management Journal*, 25(1), 21–37. doi:10.4018/irmj.2012010102

Zapata, B. C., & Alemán, J. L. (2013). Security risks in cloud computing: An analysis of the main vulnerabilities. In D. Rosado, D. Mellado, E. Fernandez-Medina, & M. Piattini (Eds.), *Security engineering for cloud computing: Approaches and tools* (pp. 55–71). Hershey, PA: IGI Global. doi:10.4018/978-1-4666-2125-1.ch004

*Related References*

Zboril, F., Horacek, J., Drahansky, M., & Hanacek, P. (2012). Security in wireless sensor networks with mobile codes. In M. Gupta, J. Walp, & R. Sharman (Eds.), *Threats, countermeasures, and advances in applied information security* (pp. 411–425). Hershey, PA: IGI Global. doi:10.4018/978-1-4666-0978-5.ch021

Zhang, J. (2012). Trust management for VANETs: Challenges, desired properties and future directions. *International Journal of Distributed Systems and Technologies*, *3*(1), 48–62. doi:10.4018/jdst.2012010104

Zhang, N., Guo, X., Chen, G., & Chau, P. Y. (2011). User evaluation of e-government systems: A Chinese cultural perspective. In F. Tan (Ed.), *International enterprises and global information technologies: Advancing management practices* (pp. 63–84). Hershey, PA: IGI Global. doi:10.4018/978-1-60960-605-3.ch004

Zhang, Y., He, L., Shu, L., Hara, T., & Nishio, S. (2012). Security issues on outlier detection and countermeasure for distributed hierarchical wireless sensor networks. In A. Pathan, M. Pathan, & H. Lee (Eds.), *Advancements in distributed computing and internet technologies: Trends and issues* (pp. 182–210). Hershey, PA: IGI Global. doi:10.4018/978-1-61350-110-8.ch009

Zheng, X., & Oleshchuk, V. (2012). Security enhancement of peer-to-peer session initiation. In M. Gupta, J. Walp, & R. Sharman (Eds.), *Threats, countermeasures, and advances in applied information security* (pp. 281–308). Hershey, PA: IGI Global. doi:10.4018/978-1-4666-0978-5.ch015

Zineddine, M. (2012). Is your automated healthcare information secure? In M. Watfa (Ed.), *E-healthcare systems and wireless communications: Current and future challenges* (pp. 128–142). Hershey, PA: IGI Global. doi:10.4018/978-1-61350-123-8.ch006

Zuo, Y., & Hu, W. (2011). Trust-based information risk management in a supply chain network. In J. Wang (Ed.), *Supply chain optimization, management and integration: Emerging applications* (pp. 181–196). Hershey, PA: IGI Global. doi:10.4018/978-1-60960-135-5.ch013

# Compilation of References

Acharjya, D. P., & Mary, A. G. (2014). Privacy preservation in information system. In B. Tripathy & D. Acharjya (Eds.), *Advances in secure computing, internet services, and applications* (pp. 49–72). Hershey, PA: IGI Global. doi:10.4018/978-1-4666-4940-8.ch003

Adeyemo, O. (2013). The nationwide health information network: A biometric approach to prevent medical identity theft. In *User-driven healthcare: Concepts, methodologies, tools, and applications* (pp. 1636–1649). Hershey, PA: IGI Global. doi:10.4018/978-1-4666-2770-3.ch081

Adler, M., & Henman, P. (2009). Justice beyond the courts: The implications of computerisation for procedural justice in social security. In A. Martínez & P. Abat (Eds.), *E-justice: Using information communication technologies in the court system* (pp. 65–86). Hershey, PA: IGI Global. doi:10.4018/978-1-59904-998-4.ch005

Aflalo, E., & Gabay, E. (2013). An information system for coping with student dropout. In L. Tomei (Ed.), *Learning tools and teaching approaches through ICT advancements* (pp. 176–187). Hershey, PA: IGI Global. doi:10.4018/978-1-4666-2017-9.ch016

Agamba, J., & Keengwe, J. (2012). Pre-service teachers perceptions of information assurance and cyber security. *International Journal of Information and Communication Technology Education, 8*(2), 94–101. doi:10.4018/jicte.2012040108

Agarwal, R., & Prasad, J. (1998). A conceptual and operational definition of personal innovativeness in the domain of information technology. *Information Systems Research, 9*(2), 204–215. doi:10.1287/isre.9.2.204

Agarwal, R., Sambamurthy, V., & Stair, R. M. (2000). The evolving relationship between general and specific computer self-efficacy–An empirical assessment. *Information Systems Research, 11*(4), 418–430. doi:10.1287/isre.11.4.418.11876

Aggarwal, R. (2013). Dispute settlement for cyber crimes in India: An analysis. In R. Khurana & R. Aggarwal (Eds.), *Interdisciplinary perspectives on business convergence, computing, and legality* (pp. 160–171). Hershey, PA: IGI Global. doi:10.4018/978-1-4666-4209-6.ch015

Agwu, E. (2013). Cyber criminals on the internet super highways: A technical investigation of different shades and colours within the Nigerian cyber space. *International Journal of Online Marketing*, 3(2), 56–74. doi:10.4018/ijom.2013040104

Ahmad, A. (2012). Security assessment of networks. In *Wireless technologies: Concepts, methodologies, tools and applications* (pp. 208–224). Hershey, PA: IGI Global. doi:10.4018/978-1-61350-101-6.ch111

Ahmed, M. A., Janssen, M., & van den Hoven, J. (2012). Value sensitive transfer (VST) of systems among countries: Towards a framework. *International Journal of Electronic Government Research*, 8(1), 26–42. doi:10.4018/jegr.2012010102

Ahmed, N., & Jensen, C. D. (2012). Security of dependable systems. In L. Petre, K. Sere, & E. Troubitsyna (Eds.), *Dependability and computer engineering: Concepts for software-intensive systems* (pp. 230–264). Hershey, PA: IGI Global. doi:10.4018/978-1-60960-747-0.ch011

Aikins, S. K. (2008). Issues and trends in internet-based citizen participation. In G. Garson & M. Khosrow-Pour (Eds.), *Handbook of research on public information technology* (pp. 31–40). Hershey, PA: IGI Global. doi:10.4018/978-1-59904-857-4.ch004

Aikins, S. K. (2009). A comparative study of municipal adoption of internet-based citizen participation. In C. Reddick (Ed.), *Handbook of research on strategies for local e-government adoption and implementation: Comparative studies* (pp. 206–230). Hershey, PA: IGI Global. doi:10.4018/978-1-60566-282-4.ch011

Aikins, S. K. (2012). Improving e-government project management: Best practices and critical success factors. In *Digital democracy: Concepts, methodologies, tools, and applications* (pp. 1314–1332). Hershey, PA: IGI Global. doi:10.4018/978-1-4666-1740-7.ch065

Akabawi, M. S. (2011). Ghabbour group ERP deployment: Learning from past technology failures. In E. Business Research and Case Center (Ed.), Cases on business and management in the MENA region: New trends and opportunities (pp. 177-203). Hershey, PA: IGI Global. doi:10.4018/978-1-60960-583-4.ch012

Akabawi, M. S. (2013). Ghabbour group ERP deployment: Learning from past technology failures. In *Industrial engineering: Concepts, methodologies, tools, and applications* (pp. 933–958). Hershey, PA: IGI Global. doi:10.4018/978-1-4666-1945-6.ch051

Akbulut, A. Y., & Motwani, J. (2008). Integration and information sharing in e-government. In G. Putnik & M. Cruz-Cunha (Eds.), *Encyclopedia of networked and virtual organizations* (pp. 729–734). Hershey, PA: IGI Global. doi:10.4018/978-1-59904-885-7.ch096

Akers, E. J. (2008). Technology diffusion in public administration. In G. Garson & M. Khosrow-Pour (Eds.), *Handbook of research on public information technology* (pp. 339–348). Hershey, PA: IGI Global. doi:10.4018/978-1-59904-857-4.ch033

Aladwani, A. M. (2002). Organizational actions, computer attitudes and end-user satisfaction in public organizations: An empirical study. In C. Snodgrass & E. Szewczak (Eds.), *Human factors in information systems* (pp. 153–168). Hershey, PA: IGI Global. doi:10.4018/978-1-931777-10-0.ch012

Aladwani, A. M. (2002). Organizational actions, computer attitudes, and end-user satisfaction in public organizations: An empirical study. *Journal of Organizational and End User Computing, 14*(1), 42–49. doi:10.4018/joeuc.2002010104

Al-Ahmad, W. (2011). Building secure software using XP. *International Journal of Secure Software Engineering, 2*(3), 63–76. doi:10.4018/jsse.2011070104

Alavi, R., Islam, S., Jahankhani, H., & Al-Nemrat, A. (2013). Analyzing human factors for an effective information security management system. *International Journal of Secure Software Engineering, 4*(1), 50–74. doi:10.4018/jsse.2013010104

Alazab, A., Abawajy, J. H., & Hobbs, M. (2013). Web malware that targets web applications. In L. Caviglione, M. Coccoli, & A. Merlo (Eds.), *Social network engineering for secure web data and services* (pp. 248–264). Hershey, PA: IGI Global. doi:10.4018/978-1-4666-3926-3.ch012

Alazab, A., Hobbs, M., Abawajy, J., & Khraisat, A. (2013). Malware detection and prevention system based on multi-stage rules. *International Journal of Information Security and Privacy, 7*(2), 29–43. doi:10.4018/jisp.2013040102

Alazab, M., Venkatraman, S., Watters, P., & Alazab, M. (2013). Information security governance: The art of detecting hidden malware. In D. Mellado, L. Enrique Sánchez, E. Fernández-Medina, & M. Piattini (Eds.), *IT security governance innovations: Theory and research* (pp. 293–315). Hershey, PA: IGI Global. doi:10.4018/978-1-4666-2083-4.ch011

Al-Bayatti, A. H., & Al-Bayatti, H. M. (2012). Security management and simulation of mobile ad hoc networks (MANET). In H. Al-Bahadili (Ed.), *Simulation in computer network design and modeling: Use and analysis* (pp. 297–314). Hershey, PA: IGI Global. doi:10.4018/978-1-4666-0191-8.ch014

Al-Bayatti, A. H., Zedan, H., Cau, A., & Siewe, F. (2012). Security management for mobile ad hoc network of networks (MANoN). In I. Khalil & E. Weippl (Eds.), *Advancing the next-generation of mobile computing: Emerging technologies* (pp. 1–18). Hershey, PA: IGI Global. doi:10.4018/978-1-4666-0119-2.ch001

Alhaj, A., Aljawarneh, S., Masadeh, S., & Abu-Taieh, E. (2013). A secure data transmission mechanism for cloud outsourced data. *International Journal of Cloud Applications and Computing, 3*(1), 34–43. doi:10.4018/ijcac.2013010104

Al-Hamdani, W. A. (2011). Three models to measure information security compliance. In H. Nemati (Ed.), *Security and privacy assurance in advancing technologies: New developments* (pp. 351–373). Hershey, PA: IGI Global. doi:10.4018/978-1-60960-200-0.ch022

Al-Hamdani, W. A. (2014). Secure e-learning and cryptography. In K. Sullivan, P. Czigler, & J. Sullivan Hellgren (Eds.), *Cases on professional distance education degree programs and practices: Successes, challenges, and issues* (pp. 331–369). Hershey, PA: IGI Global. doi:10.4018/978-1-4666-4486-1.ch012

Ali, M., & Jawandhiya, P. (2012). Security aware routing protocols for mobile ad hoc networks. In K. Lakhtaria (Ed.), *Technological advancements and applications in mobile ad-hoc networks: Research trends* (pp. 264–289). Hershey, PA: IGI Global. doi:10.4018/978-1-4666-0321-9.ch016

Ali, S. (2012). Practical web application security audit following industry standards and compliance. In J. Zubairi & A. Mahboob (Eds.), *Cyber security standards, practices and industrial applications: Systems and methodologies* (pp. 259–279). Hershey, PA: IGI Global. doi:10.4018/978-1-60960-851-4.ch013

Al-Jaljouli, R., & Abawajy, J. H. (2012). Security framework for mobile agents-based applications. In A. Kumar & H. Rahman (Eds.), *Mobile computing techniques in emerging markets: Systems, applications and services* (pp. 242–269). Hershey, PA: IGI Global. doi:10.4018/978-1-4666-0080-5.ch009

Al-Jaljouli, R., & Abawajy, J. H. (2014). Mobile agents security protocols. In *Crisis management: Concepts, methodologies, tools and applications* (pp. 166–202). Hershey, PA: IGI Global. doi:10.4018/978-1-4666-4707-7.ch007

Aljawarneh, S. (2013). Cloud security engineering: Avoiding security threats the right way. In S. Aljawarneh (Ed.), *Cloud computing advancements in design, implementation, and technologies* (pp. 147–153). Hershey, PA: IGI Global. doi:10.4018/978-1-4666-1879-4.ch010

Allen, A. B., Juillet, L., Paquet, G., & Roy, J. (2001). E-governance and government online in Canada: Partnerships, people and prospects. *Government Information Quarterly, 18*(2), 93–104. doi:10.1016/S0740-624X(01)00063-6

Allen, B., Juillet, L., Paquet, G., & Roy, J. (2005). E-government and private-public partnerships: Relational challenges and strategic directions. In M. Khosrow-Pour (Ed.), *Practicing e-government: A global perspective* (pp. 364–382). Hershey, PA: IGI Global. doi:10.4018/978-1-59140-637-2.ch016

Al, M., & Yoshigoe, K. (2012). Security and attacks in wireless sensor networks. In *Wireless technologies: Concepts, methodologies, tools and applications* (pp. 1811–1846). Hershey, PA: IGI Global. doi:10.4018/978-1-61350-101-6.ch706

Al-Nasrawi, S., & Zoughbi, S. (2014). Information Society, Digital Divide, and E-Governance in Developing Countries. In M. Khosrow-Pour (Ed.), Encyclopedia of Information Science and Technology (3rd ed.; pp. 6525-6533). IGI Global.

Alshaer, H., Muhaidat, S., Shubair, R., & Shayegannia, M. (2014). Security and connectivity analysis in vehicular communication networks. In D. Rawat, B. Bista, & G. Yan (Eds.), *Security, privacy, trust, and resource management in mobile and wireless communications* (pp. 83–107). Hershey, PA: IGI Global. doi:10.4018/978-1-4666-4691-9.ch005

Al-Shafi, S. (2008). Free wireless internet park services: An investigation of technology adoption in Qatar from a citizens perspective. *Journal of Cases on Information Technology, 10*(3), 21–34. doi:10.4018/jcit.2008070103

Al-Shafi, S., & Weerakkody, V. (2009). Implementing free wi-fi in public parks: An empirical study in Qatar. *International Journal of Electronic Government Research, 5*(3), 21–35. doi:10.4018/jegr.2009070102

Alshawaf, A., & Knalil, O. E. (2008). IS success factors and IS organizational impact: Does ownership type matter in Kuwait? *International Journal of Enterprise Information Systems, 4*(2), 13–33. doi:10.4018/jeis.2008040102

Al-Suqri, M. N., & Akomolafe-Fatuyi, E. (2012). Security and privacy in digital libraries: Challenges, opportunities and prospects. *International Journal of Digital Library Systems, 3*(4), 54–61. doi:10.4018/ijdls.2012100103

Alzamil, Z. A. (2012). Information security awareness at Saudi Arabians organizations: An information technology employees perspective. *International Journal of Information Security and Privacy*, 6(3), 38–55. doi:10.4018/jisp.2012070102

Ambali, A. R. (2009). Digital divide and its implication on Malaysian e-government: Policy initiatives. In H. Rahman (Ed.), *Social and political implications of data mining: Knowledge management in e-government* (pp. 267–287). Hershey, PA: IGI Global. doi:10.4018/978-1-60566-230-5.ch016

Amoretti, F. (2007). Digital international governance. In A. Anttiroiko & M. Malkia (Eds.), *Encyclopedia of digital government* (pp. 365–370). Hershey, PA: IGI Global. doi:10.4018/978-1-59140-789-8.ch056

Amoretti, F. (2008). Digital international governance. In A. Anttiroiko (Ed.), *Electronic government: Concepts, methodologies, tools, and applications* (pp. 688–696). Hershey, PA: IGI Global. doi:10.4018/978-1-59904-947-2.ch058

Amoretti, F. (2008). E-government at supranational level in the European Union. In A. Anttiroiko (Ed.), *Electronic government: Concepts, methodologies, tools, and applications* (pp. 1047–1055). Hershey, PA: IGI Global. doi:10.4018/978-1-59904-947-2.ch079

Amoretti, F. (2008). E-government regimes. In A. Anttiroiko (Ed.), *Electronic government: Concepts, methodologies, tools, and applications* (pp. 3846–3856). Hershey, PA: IGI Global. doi:10.4018/978-1-59904-947-2.ch280

Amoretti, F. (2009). Electronic constitution: A Braudelian perspective. In F. Amoretti (Ed.), *Electronic constitution: Social, cultural, and political implications* (pp. 1–19). Hershey, PA: IGI Global. doi:10.4018/978-1-60566-254-1.ch001

Amoretti, F., & Musella, F. (2009). Institutional isomorphism and new technologies. In M. Khosrow-Pour (Ed.), *Encyclopedia of information science and technology* (2nd ed.; pp. 2066–2071). Hershey, PA: IGI Global. doi:10.4018/978-1-60566-026-4.ch325

Analytics & Modelling Division – NIC. (2015). *Business Intelligence and e-Governemnt*. National Informatic Centre, Department of Information Technology, Ministry of Communication & IT. Retrieved from http://www.modelling.nic.in/bi-egov.doc

Andersen, K. V., & Henriksen, H. Z. (2007). E-government research: Capabilities, interaction, orientation, and values. In D. Norris (Ed.), *Current issues and trends in e-government research* (pp. 269–288). Hershey, PA: IGI Global. doi:10.4018/978-1-59904-283-1.ch013

Anderson, K. V., & Henriksen, H. Z. (2005). The first leg of e-government research: Domains and application areas 19982003. *International Journal of Electronic Government Research*, *1*(4), 26–44. doi:10.4018/jegr.2005100102

Anderson, R. (2001). *Security Engineering* (1st ed.). John Wiley & Sons, Inc.

Anttiroiko, A. (2009). Democratic e-governance. In M. Khosrow-Pour (Ed.), *Encyclopedia of information science and technology* (2nd ed.; pp. 990–995). Hershey, PA: IGI Global. doi:10.4018/978-1-60566-026-4.ch158

Anyiwo, D., & Sharma, S. (2011). Web services and e-business technologies: Security issues. In O. Bak & N. Stair (Eds.), *Impact of e-business technologies on public and private organizations: Industry comparisons and perspectives* (pp. 249–261). Hershey, PA: IGI Global. doi:10.4018/978-1-60960-501-8.ch015

Apostolakis, I., Chryssanthou, A., & Varlamis, I. (2011). A holistic perspective of security in health related virtual communities. In *Virtual communities: Concepts, methodologies, tools and applications* (pp. 1190–1204). Hershey, PA: IGI Global. doi:10.4018/978-1-60960-100-3.ch406

Arnett, K. P., Templeton, G. F., & Vance, D. A. (2011). Information security by words alone: The case for strong security policies. In H. Nemati (Ed.), *Security and privacy assurance in advancing technologies: New developments* (pp. 154–159). Hershey, PA: IGI Global. doi:10.4018/978-1-60960-200-0.ch011

Arogundade, O. T., Akinwale, A. T., Jin, Z., & Yang, X. G. (2011). A unified use-misuse case model for capturing and analysing safety and security requirements. *International Journal of Information Security and Privacy*, *5*(4), 8–30. doi:10.4018/jisp.2011100102

Arshad, J., Townend, P., Xu, J., & Jie, W. (2012). Cloud computing security: Opportunities and pitfalls. *International Journal of Grid and High Performance Computing*, *4*(1), 52–66. doi:10.4018/jghpc.2012010104

Asim, M., & Petkovic, M. (2012). Fundamental building blocks for security interoperability in e-business. In E. Kajan, F. Dorloff, & I. Bedini (Eds.), *Handbook of research on e-business standards and protocols: Documents, data and advanced web technologies* (pp. 269–292). Hershey, PA: IGI Global. doi:10.4018/978-1-4666-0146-8.ch013

Askary, S., Goodwin, D., & Lanis, R. (2012). Improvements in audit risks related to information technology frauds. *International Journal of Enterprise Information Systems*, *8*(2), 52–63. doi:10.4018/jeis.2012040104

Aurigemma, S. (2013). A composite framework for behavioral compliance with information security policies. *Journal of Organizational and End User Computing*, *25*(3), 32–51. doi:10.4018/joeuc.2013070103

Avalle, M., Pironti, A., Pozza, D., & Sisto, R. (2011). JavaSPI: A framework for security protocol implementation. *International Journal of Secure Software Engineering*, *2*(4), 34–48. doi:10.4018/jsse.2011100103

Avgerou, C. (2002). *Information Systems and Global Diversity*. New York, NY: Oxford University Press.

Axelrod, C. W. (2012). A dynamic cyber security economic model: incorporating value functions for all involved parties. In M. Gupta, J. Walp, & R. Sharman (Eds.), *Threats, countermeasures, and advances in applied information security* (pp. 462–477). Hershey, PA: IGI Global. doi:10.4018/978-1-4666-0978-5.ch024

Ayanso, A., & Herath, T. (2012). Law and technology at crossroads in cyberspace: Where do we go from here? In A. Dudley, J. Braman, & G. Vincenti (Eds.), *Investigating cyber law and cyber ethics: Issues, impacts and practices* (pp. 57–77). Hershey, PA: IGI Global. doi:10.4018/978-1-61350-132-0.ch004

Baars, T., & Spruit, M. (2012). Designing a secure cloud architecture: The SeCA model. *International Journal of Information Security and Privacy*, *6*(1), 14–32. doi:10.4018/jisp.2012010102

Bachmann, M. (2011). Deciphering the hacker underground: First quantitative insights. In T. Holt & B. Schell (Eds.), *Corporate hacking and technology-driven crime: Social dynamics and implications* (pp. 105–126). Hershey, PA: IGI Global. doi:10.4018/978-1-61692-805-6.ch006

Bachmann, M., & Smith, B. (2012). Internet fraud. In Z. Yan (Ed.), *Encyclopedia of cyber behavior* (pp. 931–943). Hershey, PA: IGI Global. doi:10.4018/978-1-4666-0315-8.ch077

Bai, Y., & Khan, K. M. (2011). Ell secure information system using modal logic technique. *International Journal of Secure Software Engineering*, *2*(2), 65–76. doi:10.4018/jsse.2011040104

Baker, P. M., Bell, A., & Moon, N. W. (2009). Accessibility issues in municipal wireless networks. In C. Reddick (Ed.), *Handbook of research on strategies for local e-government adoption and implementation: Comparative studies* (pp. 569–588). Hershey, PA: IGI Global. doi:10.4018/978-1-60566-282-4.ch030

Baliamoune-Lutz, M. (2003). An analysis of the determinants and effects of ICT diffusion in developing countries. *Information Technology for Development*, *10*(3), 151–169. doi:10.1002/itdj.1590100303

Bandeira, G. S. (2014). Criminal liability of organizations, corporations, legal persons, and similar entities on law of portuguese cybercrime: A brief discussion on the issue of crimes of "false information," the "damage on other programs or computer data," the "computer-software sabotage," the "illegitimate access," the "unlawful interception," and "illegitimate reproduction of the protected program". In I. Portela & F. Almeida (Eds.), *Organizational, legal, and technological dimensions of information system administration* (pp. 96–107). Hershey, PA: IGI Global. doi:10.4018/978-1-4666-4526-4.ch006

Bandura, A. (1977). Self-efficacy: Toward a unifying theory of behavioral change. *Psychological Review*, *84*(2), 191–215. doi:10.1037/0033-295X.84.2.191 PMID:847061

Bandura, A. (1986). *Social foundations of thought and action*. Englewood Cliffs, NJ: Prentice Hall.

Bandura, A. (1997). *Self-efficacy: The exercise of control*. New York: W.H. Freeman &Co.

Barclay, D., Thompson, R., & Higgins, C. (1995). The partial least squares (PLS) approach to causal modeling: Personal computer adoption and use as an illustration. *Technology Studies*, *2*(2), 285–309.

Barjis, J. (2012). Software engineering security based on business process modeling. In K. Khan (Ed.), *Security-aware systems applications and software development methods* (pp. 52–68). Hershey, PA: IGI Global. doi:10.4018/978-1-4666-1580-9.ch004

Basit, F. E., Javed, Y., & Qayyum, U. (2007). Face Recognition using processed histogram and phase only correlation. *3rd IEEE International Conference on Emerging Technology*, 238-242.

Becker, S. A., Keimer, R., & Muth, T. (2012). A case on university and community collaboration: The sci-tech entrepreneurial training services (ETS) program. In Regional development: Concepts, methodologies, tools, and applications (pp. 947-969). Hershey, PA: IGI Global. doi:10.4018/978-1-4666-0882-5.ch507

Becker, S. A., Keimer, R., & Muth, T. (2010). A case on university and community collaboration: The sci-tech entrepreneurial training services (ETS) program. In S. Becker & R. Niebuhr (Eds.), *Cases on technology innovation: Entrepreneurial successes and pitfalls* (pp. 68–90). Hershey, PA: IGI Global. doi:10.4018/978-1-61520-609-4.ch003

Bedi, P., Gandotra, V., & Singhal, A. (2013). Innovative strategies for secure software development. In H. Singh & K. Kaur (Eds.), *Designing, engineering, and analyzing reliable and efficient software* (pp. 217–237). Hershey, PA: IGI Global. doi:10.4018/978-1-4666-2958-5.ch013

Bellare, M., & Rogaway, P. (2005). Introduction. In P. R. Mihir Bellare (Ed.), Introduction to Modern Cryptography, (p. 10). Academic Press.

Belsis, P., Skourlas, C., & Gritzalis, S. (2011). Secure electronic healthcare records management in wireless environments. *Journal of Information Technology Research*, *4*(4), 1–17. doi:10.4018/jitr.2011100101

Bernardi, R. (2012). Information technology and resistance to public sector reforms: A case study in Kenya. In T. Papadopoulos & P. Kanellis (Eds.), *Public sector reform using information technologies: Transforming policy into practice* (pp. 59–78). Hershey, PA: IGI Global. doi:10.4018/978-1-60960-839-2.ch004

Bernardi, R. (2013). Information technology and resistance to public sector reforms: A case study in Kenya. In *User-driven healthcare: Concepts, methodologies, tools, and applications* (pp. 14–33). Hershey, PA: Medical IGI Global. doi:10.4018/978-1-4666-2770-3.ch002

Bernik, I. (2012). Internet study: Cyber threats and cybercrime awareness and fear. *International Journal of Cyber Warfare & Terrorism*, *2*(3), 1–11. doi:10.4018/ijcwt.2012070101

Bhatia, M. S. (2011). World war III: The cyber war. *International Journal of Cyber Warfare & Terrorism*, *1*(3), 59–69. doi:10.4018/ijcwt.2011070104

Blanco, C., Rosado, D., Gutiérrez, C., Rodríguez, A., Mellado, D., Fernández-Medina, E., & Piattini, M. et al. (2011). Security over the information systems development cycle. In H. Mouratidis (Ed.), *Software engineering for secure systems: Industrial and research perspectives* (pp. 113–154). Hershey, PA: IGI Global. doi:10.4018/978-1-61520-837-1.ch005

Bobbert, Y., & Mulder, H. (2012). A research journey into maturing the business information security of mid market organizations. In W. Van Grembergen & S. De Haes (Eds.), *Business strategy and applications in enterprise IT governance* (pp. 236–259). Hershey, PA: IGI Global. doi:10.4018/978-1-4666-1779-7.ch014

Boddington, R. (2011). Digital evidence. In D. Kerr, J. Gammack, & K. Bryant (Eds.), *Digital business security development: Management technologies* (pp. 37–72). Hershey, PA: IGI Global. doi:10.4018/978-1-60566-806-2.ch002

Bolívar, M. P., Pérez, M. D., & Hernández, A. M. (2012). Municipal e-government services in emerging economies: The Latin-American and Caribbean experiences. In Y. Chen & P. Chu (Eds.), *Electronic governance and cross-boundary collaboration: Innovations and advancing tools* (pp. 198–226). Hershey, PA: IGI Global. doi:10.4018/978-1-60960-753-1.ch011

Bommer, M., & Jalajas, D. S. (1999). The threat of organizational downsizing on the innovative propensity of R&D professionals. *R & D Management*, *29*(1), 27–34. doi:10.1111/1467-9310.00114

Borycki, E. M., & Kushniruk, A. W. (2010). Use of clinical simulations to evaluate the impact of health information systems and ubiquitous computing devices upon health professional work. In S. Mohammed & J. Fiaidhi (Eds.), *Ubiquitous health and medical informatics: The ubiquity 2.0 trend and beyond* (pp. 552–573). Hershey, PA: Medical IGI Global. doi:10.4018/978-1-61520-777-0.ch026

Borycki, E. M., & Kushniruk, A. W. (2011). Use of clinical simulations to evaluate the impact of health information systems and ubiquitous computing devices upon health professional work. In *Clinical technologies: Concepts, methodologies, tools and applications* (pp. 532–553). Hershey, PA: Medical IGI Global. doi:10.4018/978-1-60960-561-2.ch220

Bossler, A. M., & Burruss, G. W. (2011). The general theory of crime and computer hacking: Low self-control hackers? In T. Holt & B. Schell (Eds.), *Corporate hacking and technology-driven crime: Social dynamics and implications* (pp. 38–67). Hershey, PA: IGI Global. doi:10.4018/978-1-61692-805-6.ch003

Bouras, C., & Stamos, K. (2011). Security issues for multi-domain resource reservation. In D. Kar & M. Syed (Eds.), *Network security, administration and management: Advancing technology and practice* (pp. 38–50). Hershey, PA: IGI Global. doi:10.4018/978-1-60960-777-7.ch003

Bracci, F., Corradi, A., & Foschini, L. (2014). Cloud standards: Security and interoperability issues. In H. Mouftah & B. Kantarci (Eds.), *Communication infrastructures for cloud computing* (pp. 465–495). Hershey, PA: IGI Global. doi:10.4018/978-1-4666-4522-6.ch020

Brodsky, J., & Radvanovsky, R. (2011). Control systems security. In T. Holt & B. Schell (Eds.), *Corporate hacking and technology-driven crime: Social dynamics and implications* (pp. 187–204). Hershey, PA: IGI Global. doi:10.4018/978-1-61692-805-6.ch010

Brooks, D. (2013). Security threats and risks of intelligent building systems: Protecting facilities from current and emerging vulnerabilities. In C. Laing, A. Badii, & P. Vickers (Eds.), *Securing critical infrastructures and critical control systems: Approaches for threat protection* (pp. 1–16). Hershey, PA: IGI Global. doi:10.4018/978-1-4666-2659-1.ch001

Buchan, J. (2011). Developing a dynamic and responsive online learning environment: A case study of a large Australian university. In B. Czerkawski (Ed.), *Free and open source software for e-learning: Issues, successes and challenges* (pp. 92–109). Hershey, PA: IGI Global. doi:10.4018/978-1-61520-917-0.ch006

Buchsbaum, T. (2004). E-Voting: International Developments and Lessons Learnt. Electronic Voting in Europe – Technology, Law. Lake of Constance: GI, the Gesellschaft für Informatik.

Buenger, A. W. (2008). Digital convergence and cybersecurity policy. In G. Garson & M. Khosrow-Pour (Eds.), *Handbook of research on public information technology* (pp. 395–405). Hershey, PA: IGI Global. doi:10.4018/978-1-59904-857-4.ch038

Bülow, W., & Wester, M. (2012). The right to privacy and the protection of personal data in a digital era and the age of information. In C. Akrivopoulou & N. Garipidis (Eds.), *Human rights and risks in the digital era: Globalization and the effects of information technologies* (pp. 34–45). Hershey, PA: IGI Global. doi:10.4018/978-1-4666-0891-7.ch004

Burkhardt, M. E., & Brass, D. J. (1990). Changing patterns or patterns of change: The effects of a change in technology on social network structure and power. *Administrative Science Quarterly*, *35*(1), 104–127. doi:10.2307/2393552

Burn, J. M., & Loch, K. D. (2002). The societal impact of world wide web - Key challenges for the 21st century. In A. Salehnia (Ed.), *Ethical issues of information systems* (pp. 88–106). Hershey, PA: IGI Global. doi:10.4018/978-1-931777-15-5.ch007

Burn, J. M., & Loch, K. D. (2003). The societal impact of the world wide web-Key challenges for the 21st century. In M. Khosrow-Pour (Ed.), *Advanced topics in information resources management* (Vol. 2, pp. 32–51). Hershey, PA: IGI Global. doi:10.4018/978-1-59140-062-2.ch002

Buyya, Yeo, Venugopal, Broberg, & Brandic. (2009). Cloud Computing and emerging IT platforms: Vision, hype, and reality for delivering computing as the 5th utility. *Future Generation Computer Systems, 25*, 599-616.

Bwalya, K. J., Du Plessis, T., & Rensleigh, C. (2012). The "quicksilver initiatives" as a framework for e-government strategy design in developing economies. In K. Bwalya & S. Zulu (Eds.), *Handbook of research on e-government in emerging economies: Adoption, e-participation, and legal frameworks* (pp. 605–623). Hershey, PA: IGI Global. doi:10.4018/978-1-4666-0324-0.ch031

Byung-Joo, O. (2005). Face Recognition using Radial Basis Function Network based on LDA. World Academy of Science, Engineering and Technology.

Cabotaje, C. E., & Alampay, E. A. (2013). Social media and citizen engagement: Two cases from the Philippines. In S. Saeed & C. Reddick (Eds.), *Human-centered system design for electronic governance* (pp. 225–238). Hershey, PA: IGI Global. doi:10.4018/978-1-4666-3640-8.ch013

Camarinha-Matos, L. M., & Afsarmanesh, H. (2005, October). Collaborative networks: A new scientific discipline. *Journal of Intelligent Manufacturing. Springer.*, *16*(4-5), 439–452. doi:10.1007/s10845-005-1656-3

Camillo, A., Di Pietro, L., Di Virgilio, F., & Franco, M. (2013). Work-groups conflict at PetroTech-Italy, S.R.L.: The influence of culture on conflict dynamics. In B. Christiansen, E. Turkina, & N. Williams (Eds.), *Cultural and technological influences on global business* (pp. 272–289). Hershey, PA: IGI Global. doi:10.4018/978-1-4666-3966-9.ch015

Cano, J., & Hernandez, R. (2013). SCEPYLT: An Information System for Fighting Terrorism. *IEEE Software, 30*(3), 73-79.

Canongia, C., & Mandarino, R. (2014). Cybersecurity: The new challenge of the information society. In Crisis management: Concepts, methodologies, tools and applications (pp. 60-80). Hershey, PA: IGI Global. doi:10.4018/978-1-4666-4707-7.ch003

Cao, X., & Lu, Y. (2011). The social network structure of a computer hacker community. In H. Nemati (Ed.), *Security and privacy assurance in advancing technologies: New developments* (pp. 160–173). Hershey, PA: IGI Global. doi:10.4018/978-1-60960-200-0.ch012

Capra, E., Francalanci, C., & Marinoni, C. (2008). Soft success factors for m-government. In A. Anttiroiko (Ed.), *Electronic government: Concepts, methodologies, tools, and applications* (pp. 1213–1233). Hershey, PA: IGI Global. doi:10.4018/978-1-59904-947-2.ch089

Cardholm, L. (2014). Identifying the business value of information security. In T. Tsiakis, T. Kargidis, & P. Katsaros (Eds.), *Approaches and processes for managing the economics of information systems* (pp. 157–180). Hershey, PA: IGI Global. doi:10.4018/978-1-4666-4983-5.ch010

Cardoso, R. C., & Gomes, A. (2012). Security issues in massively multiplayer online games. In M. Cruz-Cunha (Ed.), *Handbook of research on serious games as educational, business and research tools* (pp. 290–314). Hershey, PA: IGI Global. doi:10.4018/978-1-4666-0149-9.ch016

Carpen-Amarie, A., Costan, A., Leordeanu, C., Basescu, C., & Antoniu, G. (2012). Towards a generic security framework for cloud data management environments. *International Journal of Distributed Systems and Technologies*, *3*(1), 17–34. doi:10.4018/jdst.2012010102

Carpio Cámara, M., León, A., Cano Carrillo, J., & Jiménez, C. E. (2015). *Regulación y ciberseguridad. Contribuciones al modelo de Gobernanza*. Capítulo del libro "Gobernanza de Internet en España", IGF Forum Spain. Retrieved from http://igfspain.com/doc/archivos/Gobernanza_Internet_Spain_2015.pdf

Cartelli, A. (2009). The implementation of practices with ICT as a new teaching-learning paradigm. In A. Cartelli & M. Palma (Eds.), *Encyclopedia of information communication technology* (pp. 413–417). Hershey, PA: IGI Global. doi:10.4018/978-1-59904-845-1.ch055

Caushaj, E., Fu, H., Sethi, I., Badih, H., Watson, D., Zhu, Y., & Leng, S. (2013). Theoretical analysis and experimental study: Monitoring data privacy in smartphone communications. *International Journal of Interdisciplinary Telecommunications and Networking*, *5*(2), 66–82. doi:10.4018/jitn.2013040106

Cepheli, Ö., & Kurt, G. K. (2014). Physical layer security in wireless communication networks. In D. Rawat, B. Bista, & G. Yan (Eds.), *Security, privacy, trust, and resource management in mobile and wireless communications* (pp. 61–81). Hershey, PA: IGI Global. doi:10.4018/978-1-4666-4691-9.ch004

Cetinkaya, O., & Cetinkaya, D. (2007). Verification and Validation Issues in Electronic Voting. The Electronic. *Journal of E-Government*, 117–126.

Chakraborty, P., & Raghuraman, K. (2013). Trends in information security. In K. Buragga & N. Zaman (Eds.), *Software development techniques for constructive information systems design* (pp. 354–376). Hershey, PA: IGI Global. doi:10.4018/978-1-4666-3679-8.ch020

Chandrakumar, T., & Parthasarathy, S. (2012). Enhancing data security in ERP projects using XML. *International Journal of Enterprise Information Systems*, 8(1), 51–65. doi:10.4018/jeis.2012010104

Chapple, M. J., Striegel, A., & Crowell, C. R. (2011). Firewall rulebase management: Tools and techniques. In M. Quigley (Ed.), *ICT ethics and security in the 21st century: New developments and applications* (pp. 254–276). Hershey, PA: IGI Global. doi:10.4018/978-1-60960-573-5.ch013

Charalabidis, Y., Lampathaki, F., & Askounis, D. (2010). Investigating the landscape in national interoperability frameworks. *International Journal of E-Services and Mobile Applications*, 2(4), 28–41. doi:10.4018/jesma.2010100103

Charalabidis, Y., Lampathaki, F., & Askounis, D. (2012). Investigating the landscape in national interoperability frameworks. In A. Scupola (Ed.), *Innovative mobile platform developments for electronic services design and delivery* (pp. 218–231). Hershey, PA: IGI Global. doi:10.4018/978-1-4666-1568-7.ch013

Chen, I. (2005). Distance education associations. In C. Howard, J. Boettcher, L. Justice, K. Schenk, P. Rogers, & G. Berg (Eds.), *Encyclopedia of distance learning* (pp. 599–612). Hershey, PA: IGI Global. doi:10.4018/978-1-59140-555-9.ch087

Chen, I. (2008). Distance education associations. In L. Tomei (Ed.), *Online and distance learning: Concepts, methodologies, tools, and applications* (pp. 562–579). Hershey, PA: IGI Global. doi:10.4018/978-1-59904-935-9.ch048

Chen, L., Hu, W., Yang, M., & Zhang, L. (2011). Security and privacy issues in secure e-mail standards and services. In H. Nemati (Ed.), *Security and privacy assurance in advancing technologies: new developments* (pp. 174–185). Hershey, PA: IGI Global. doi:10.4018/978-1-60960-200-0.ch013

Chen, L., Varol, C., Liu, Q., & Zhou, B. (2014). Security in wireless metropolitan area networks: WiMAX and LTE. In D. Rawat, B. Bista, & G. Yan (Eds.), *Security, privacy, trust, and resource management in mobile and wireless communications* (pp. 11–27). Hershey, PA: IGI Global. doi:10.4018/978-1-4666-4691-9.ch002

Chen, Y. (2008). Managing IT outsourcing for digital government. In A. Anttiroiko (Ed.), *Electronic government: Concepts, methodologies, tools, and applications* (pp. 3107–3114). Hershey, PA: IGI Global. doi:10.4018/978-1-59904-947-2.ch229

Chen, Y. N., Chen, H. M., Huang, W., & Ching, R. K. H. (2006). E-Government strategies in developed and developing countries: An implementation framework and case study. *Journal of Global Information Management*, *14*(1), 23–46. doi:10.4018/jgim.2006010102

Chen, Y., & Dimitrova, D. V. (2006). Electronic government and online engagement: Citizen interaction with government via web portals. *International Journal of Electronic Government Research*, *2*(1), 54–76. doi:10.4018/jegr.2006010104

Chen, Y., & Knepper, R. (2005). Digital government development strategies: Lessons for policy makers from a comparative perspective. In W. Huang, K. Siau, & K. Wei (Eds.), *Electronic government strategies and implementation* (pp. 394–420). Hershey, PA: IGI Global. doi:10.4018/978-1-59140-348-7.ch017

Chen, Y., & Knepper, R. (2008). Digital government development strategies: Lessons for policy makers from a comparative perspective. In H. Rahman (Ed.), *Developing successful ICT strategies: Competitive advantages in a global knowledge-driven society* (pp. 334–356). Hershey, PA: IGI Global. doi:10.4018/978-1-59904-654-9.ch017

Cherdantseva, Y., & Hilton, J. (2014). Information security and information assurance: Discussion about the meaning, scope, and goals. In I. Portela & F. Almeida (Eds.), *Organizational, legal, and technological dimensions of information system administration* (pp. 167–198). Hershey, PA: IGI Global. doi:10.4018/978-1-4666-4526-4.ch010

Cherdantseva, Y., & Hilton, J. (2014). The 2011 survey of information security and information assurance professionals: Findings. In I. Portela & F. Almeida (Eds.), *Organizational, legal, and technological dimensions of information system administration* (pp. 243–256). Hershey, PA: IGI Global. doi:10.4018/978-1-4666-4526-4.ch013

Cherian, E. J., & Ryan, T. W. (2014). Incongruent needs: Why differences in the iron-triangle of priorities make health information technology adoption and use difficult. In C. El Morr (Ed.), *Research perspectives on the role of informatics in health policy and management* (pp. 209–221). Hershey, PA: Medical IGI Global. doi:10.4018/978-1-4666-4321-5.ch012

Chin, W. W. (Ed.). (1998). *The partial least squares approach for structural equation modeling: Modern methods for business research*. Hillsdale, NJ: Lawrence Erlbaum Associates.

Chin, W. W., & Gopal, A. (1995). Adoption intention in GSS: Relative importance of beliefs. *The Data Base for Advances in Information Systems*, *26*(2), 42–63. doi:10.1145/217278.217285

Chin, W. W., Marcolin, B. L., & Newsted, P. R. (2003). A partial least squares latent variable modeling approach for measuring interactions effects: Results from a Monte Carlo simulation study and electronic-mail emotion/adoption study. *Information Systems Research*, *14*(2), 189–217. doi:10.1287/isre.14.2.189.16018

Chiriacescu, I. (2009). *Automatic Emotion Analysis Based on Speech* (MSc Thesis). Faculty of Eng, Mathematics and CS, Delft University of Technology.

Chiristos, Georgiadis, & Stiakakis. (2010). *Extending electronic Government service Measurement Framework to mobile Government.* Academic Press.

Cho, H. J., & Hwang, S. (2010). Government 2.0 in Korea: Focusing on e-participation services. In C. Reddick (Ed.), *Politics, democracy and e-government: Participation and service delivery* (pp. 94–114). Hershey, PA: IGI Global. doi:10.4018/978-1-61520-933-0.ch006

Chongthammakun, R., & Jackson, S. J. (2012). Boundary Objects, Agents, and Organizations: Lessons from E-Document Systems Development in Thailand. *Proceedings of 2012 45th Hawaii International Conference on Systems Sciences*. doi:10.1109/HICSS.2012.133

Chorus, C., & Timmermans, H. (2010). Ubiquitous travel environments and travel control strategies: Prospects and challenges. In M. Wachowicz (Ed.), *Movement-aware applications for sustainable mobility: Technologies and approaches* (pp. 30–51). Hershey, PA: IGI Global. doi:10.4018/978-1-61520-769-5.ch003

Chowdhury, M. U., & Ray, B. R. (2013). Security risks/vulnerability in a RFID system and possible defenses. In N. Karmakar (Ed.), *Advanced RFID systems, security, and applications* (pp. 1–15). Hershey, PA: IGI Global. doi:10.4018/978-1-4666-2080-3.ch001

Chuanshen, R. (2007). E-government construction and China's administrative litigation act. In A. Anttiroiko & M. Malkia (Eds.), *Encyclopedia of digital government* (pp. 507–510). Hershey, PA: IGI Global. doi:10.4018/978-1-59140-789-8.ch077

Ciaghi, A., & Villafiorita, A. (2012). Law modeling and BPR for public administration improvement. In K. Bwalya & S. Zulu (Eds.), *Handbook of research on e-government in emerging economies: Adoption, e-participation, and legal frameworks* (pp. 391–410). Hershey, PA: IGI Global. doi:10.4018/978-1-4666-0324-0.ch019

Ciaramitaro, B. L., & Skrocki, M. (2012). mHealth: Mobile healthcare. In B. Ciaramitaro (Ed.), Mobile technology consumption: Opportunities and challenges (pp. 99-109). Hershey, PA: IGI Global. doi:10.4018/978-1-61350-150-4.ch007

Cofta, P., Lacohée, H., & Hodgson, P. (2011). Incorporating social trust into design practices for secure systems. In H. Mouratidis (Ed.), *Software engineering for secure systems: Industrial and research perspectives* (pp. 260–284). Hershey, PA: IGI Global. doi:10.4018/978-1-61520-837-1.ch010

Comite, U. (2012). Innovative processes and managerial effectiveness of e-procurement in healthcare. In A. Manoharan & M. Holzer (Eds.), *Active citizen participation in e-government: A global perspective* (pp. 206–229). Hershey, PA: IGI Global. doi:10.4018/978-1-4666-0116-1.ch011

Compeau, D. R., & Higgins, C. A. (1995a). Application of social cognitive theory to training for computer skills. *Information Systems Research, 6*(2), 118–143. doi:10.1287/isre.6.2.118

Compeau, D. R., & Higgins, C. A. (1995b). Computer self-efficacy: Development of a measure and initial test. *Management Information Systems Quarterly, 19*(2), 189–211. doi:10.2307/249688

Compeau, D. R., Higgins, C. A., & Huff, S. (1999). Social cognitive theory and individual reactions to computing technology: A longitudinal study. *Management Information Systems Quarterly, 23*(2), 145–158. doi:10.2307/249749

Conway, M. (2012). What is cyberterrorism and how real is the threat? A review of the academic literature, 1996 – 2009. In P. Reich & E. Gelbstein (Eds.), *Law, policy, and technology: Cyberterrorism, information warfare, and internet immobilization* (pp. 279–307). Hershey, PA: IGI Global. doi:10.4018/978-1-61520-831-9.ch011

Cooke R., & Anane, R. (2011). A service-oriented architecture for robust e-voting. *Service Oriented Computing and Applications, 6*(3), 249-266.

Cordella, A. (2013). E-government success: How to account for ICT, administrative rationalization, and institutional change. In J. Gil-Garcia (Ed.), *E-government success factors and measures: Theories, concepts, and methodologies* (pp. 40–51). Hershey, PA: IGI Global. doi:10.4018/978-1-4666-4058-0.ch003

Cormen, T., Leierson, C., & Rivest, R. (1998). *Introduction to Algorithms*. Cambridge, MA: The MIT Press.

Corser, G. P., Arslanturk, S., Oluoch, J., Fu, H., & Corser, G. E. (2013). Knowing the enemy at the gates: Measuring attacker motivation. *International Journal of Interdisciplinary Telecommunications and Networking*, 5(2), 83–95. doi:10.4018/jitn.2013040107

Cropf, R. A. (2009). ICT and e-democracy. In M. Khosrow-Pour (Ed.), *Encyclopedia of information science and technology* (2nd ed.; pp. 1789–1793). Hershey, PA: IGI Global. doi:10.4018/978-1-60566-026-4.ch281

Cropf, R. A. (2009). The virtual public sphere. In M. Pagani (Ed.), *Encyclopedia of multimedia technology and networking* (2nd ed.; pp. 1525–1530). Hershey, PA: IGI Global. doi:10.4018/978-1-60566-014-1.ch206

Crosbie, M. (2013). Hack the cloud: Ethical hacking and cloud forensics. In K. Ruan (Ed.), *Cybercrime and cloud forensics: Applications for investigation processes* (pp. 42–58). Hershey, PA: IGI Global. doi:10.4018/978-1-4666-2662-1.ch002

Curran, K., Carlin, S., & Adams, M. (2012). Security issues in cloud computing. In L. Chao (Ed.), *Cloud computing for teaching and learning: Strategies for design and implementation* (pp. 200–208). Hershey, PA: IGI Global. doi:10.4018/978-1-4666-0957-0.ch014

Czosseck, C., Ottis, R., & Talihärm, A. (2011). Estonia after the 2007 cyber attacks: Legal, strategic and organisational changes in cyber security. *International Journal of Cyber Warfare & Terrorism*, 1(1), 24–34. doi:10.4018/ijcwt.2011010103

Czosseck, C., & Podins, K. (2012). A vulnerability-based model of cyber weapons and its implications for cyber conflict. *International Journal of Cyber Warfare & Terrorism*, 2(1), 14–26. doi:10.4018/ijcwt.2012010102

D'Abundo, M. L. (2013). Electronic health record implementation in the United States healthcare industry: Making the process of change manageable. In V. Wang (Ed.), *Handbook of research on technologies for improving the 21st century workforce: Tools for lifelong learning* (pp. 272–286). Hershey, PA: IGI Global. doi:10.4018/978-1-4666-2181-7.ch018

da Silva, F. A., Moura, D. F., & Galdino, J. F. (2012). Classes of attacks for tactical software defined radios. *International Journal of Embedded and Real-Time Communication Systems*, 3(4), 57–82. doi:10.4018/jertcs.2012100104

Dabcevic, K., Marcenaro, L., & Regazzoni, C. S. (2013). Security in cognitive radio networks. In T. Lagkas, P. Sarigiannidis, M. Louta, & P. Chatzimisios (Eds.), *Evolution of cognitive networks and self-adaptive communication systems* (pp. 301–335). Hershey, PA: IGI Global. doi:10.4018/978-1-4666-4189-1.ch013

Dahbur, K., Mohammad, B., & Tarakji, A. B. (2013). Security issues in cloud computing: A survey of risks, threats and vulnerabilities. In S. Aljawarneh (Ed.), *Cloud computing advancements in design, implementation, and technologies* (pp. 154–165). Hershey, PA: IGI Global. doi:10.4018/978-1-4666-1879-4.ch011

Damurski, L. (2012). E-participation in urban planning: Online tools for citizen engagement in Poland and in Germany. *International Journal of E-Planning Research*, *1*(3), 40–67. doi:10.4018/ijepr.2012070103

Dark, M. (2011). Data breach disclosure: A policy analysis. In M. Dark (Ed.), *Information assurance and security ethics in complex systems: Interdisciplinary perspectives* (pp. 226–252). Hershey, PA: IGI Global. doi:10.4018/978-1-61692-245-0.ch011

Dasgupta, D., & Naseem, D. (2014). A framework for compliance and security coverage estimation for cloud services: A cloud insurance model. In S. Srinivasan (Ed.), *Security, trust, and regulatory aspects of cloud computing in business environments* (pp. 91–114). Hershey, PA: IGI Global. doi:10.4018/978-1-4666-5788-5.ch005

Das, S., Mukhopadhyay, A., & Bhasker, B. (2013). Todays action is better than tomorrows cure - Evaluating information security at a premier indian business school. *Journal of Cases on Information Technology*, *15*(3), 1–23. doi:10.4018/jcit.2013070101

Datta, P. (2011). A preliminary study of ecommerce adoption in developing countries. *Information Systems Journal*, *21*(1), 2–32. doi:10.1111/j.1365-2575.2009.00344.x

Davis, F. D. (1989). Perceived usefulness, perceived ease of use, and user acceptance of information technology. *Management Information Systems Quarterly*, *13*(3), 319–340. doi:10.2307/249008

Davis, F. D., Bagozzi, R. P., & Warshaw, P. R. (1989). User acceptance of computer technology: A comparison of two theoretical models. *Management Science*, *35*(8), 982–1003. doi:10.1287/mnsc.35.8.982

de Almeida, M. O. (2007). E-government strategy in Brazil: Increasing transparency and efficiency through e-government procurement. In M. Gascó-Hernandez (Ed.), *Latin America online: Cases, successes and pitfalls* (pp. 34–82). Hershey, PA: IGI Global. doi:10.4018/978-1-59140-974-8.ch002

De Fuentes, J. M., González-Tablas, A. I., & Ribagorda, A. (2011). Overview of security issues in vehicular ad-hoc networks. In M. Cruz-Cunha & F. Moreira (Eds.), *Handbook of research on mobility and computing: Evolving technologies and ubiquitous impacts* (pp. 894–911). Hershey, PA: IGI Global. doi:10.4018/978-1-60960-042-6.ch056

De Groef, W., Devriese, D., Reynaert, T., & Piessens, F. (2013). Security and privacy of online social network applications. In L. Caviglione, M. Coccoli, & A. Merlo (Eds.), *Social network engineering for secure web data and services* (pp. 206–221). Hershey, PA: IGI Global. doi:10.4018/978-1-4666-3926-3.ch010

de Juana Espinosa, S. (2008). Empirical study of the municipalitites' motivations for adopting online presence. In A. Anttiroiko (Ed.), *Electronic government: Concepts, methodologies, tools, and applications* (pp. 3593–3608). Hershey, PA: IGI Global. doi:10.4018/978-1-59904-947-2.ch262

de Souza Dias, D. (2002). Motivation for using information technology. In C. Snodgrass & E. Szewczak (Eds.), *Human factors in information systems* (pp. 55–60). Hershey, PA: IGI Global. doi:10.4018/978-1-931777-10-0.ch005

Deity. (n.d.). *MSDG*. Retrieved 17 May 2014, from weblink: http://deity.gov.in/content/msdg

Deloitte. (n.d.). *Cloud computing debate*. Retrieved from http://www.deloitte.com

Demediuk, P. (2006). Government procurement ICT's impact on the sustainability of SMEs and regional communities. In S. Marshall, W. Taylor, & X. Yu (Eds.), *Encyclopedia of developing regional communities with information and communication technology* (pp. 321–324). Hershey, PA: IGI Global. doi:10.4018/978-1-59140-575-7.ch056

Denning, D. E. (2011). Cyber conflict as an emergent social phenomenon. In T. Holt & B. Schell (Eds.), *Corporate hacking and technology-driven crime: Social dynamics and implications* (pp. 170–186). Hershey, PA: IGI Global. doi:10.4018/978-1-61692-805-6.ch009

Desai, A. M., & Mock, K. (2013). Security in cloud computing. In A. Bento & A. Aggarwal (Eds.), *Cloud computing service and deployment models: Layers and management* (pp. 208–221). Hershey, PA: IGI Global. doi:10.4018/978-1-4666-2187-9.ch011

Desta. (2010). *M-Government System Service Architecture Using Enterprise Architecture Framework*. Academic Press.

Devonshire, E., Forsyth, H., Reid, S., & Simpson, J. M. (2013). The challenges and opportunities of online postgraduate coursework programs in a traditional university context. In B. Tynan, J. Willems, & R. James (Eds.), *Outlooks and opportunities in blended and distance learning* (pp. 353–368). Hershey, PA: IGI Global. doi:10.4018/978-1-4666-4205-8.ch026

Dhoot, V. (2014). PMO using Big Data techniques on mygov.in to translate popular mood into government action. *The Economic Times*. Retrieved from http://articles. economictimes.indiatimes.com/2014-11-26/news/56490626_1_mygov-digital-india-modi-government

Di Cerbo, F., Scotto, M., Sillitti, A., Succi, G., & Vernazza, T. (2007). Toward a GNU/Linux distribution for corporate environments. In S. Sowe, I. Stamelos, & I. Samoladas (Eds.), *Emerging free and open source software practices* (pp. 215–236). Hershey, PA: IGI Global. doi:10.4018/978-1-59904-210-7.ch010

Dibbern, J., Goles, T., Hirschheim, R., & Jayatilaka, B. (2004, November). Information systems outsourcing: A survey and analysis of the literature. *SIGMIS Database*, *35*(4), 6–102. doi:10.1145/1035233.1035236

Diesner, J., & Carley, K. M. (2005). Revealing social structure from texts: Meta-matrix text analysis as a novel method for network text analysis. In V. Narayanan & D. Armstrong (Eds.), *Causal mapping for research in information technology* (pp. 81–108). Hershey, PA: IGI Global. doi:10.4018/978-1-59140-396-8.ch004

Diffie, W., & Hellman, E. (1976). New directions in cryptography. *IEEE Transactions on Information Theory, 22*(6), 644–654.

Diffie, W. (1988). The first ten years of public-key cryptography.*Proceedings of the IEEE*, 76. doi:10.1109/5.4442

Ding, L., Peristeras, V., & Hausenblas, M. (2012). Linked Open Government Data. *IEEE Intelligent Systems, 27*(3), 11-15.

Dionysiou, I., & Ktoridou, D. (2012). Enhancing dynamic-content courses with student-oriented learning strategies: The case of computer security course. *International Journal of Cyber Ethics in Education*, 2(2), 24–33. doi:10.4018/ijcee.2012040103

Disterer, G. (2012). Attacks on IT systems: Categories of motives. In T. Chou (Ed.), *Information assurance and security technologies for risk assessment and threat management: Advances* (pp. 1–16). Hershey, PA: IGI Global. doi:10.4018/978-1-61350-507-6.ch001

Dologite, D. G., Mockler, R. J., Bai, Q., & Viszhanyo, P. F. (2006). IS change agents in practice in a US-Chinese joint venture. In M. Hunter & F. Tan (Eds.), *Advanced topics in global information management* (Vol. 5, pp. 331–352). Hershey, PA: IGI Global. doi:10.4018/978-1-59140-923-6.ch015

Dougan, T., & Curran, K. (2012). Man in the browser attacks. *International Journal of Ambient Computing and Intelligence, 4*(1), 29–39. doi:10.4018/jaci.2012010103

Drnevich, P., Brush, T. H., & Luckock, G. T. (2011). Process and structural implications for IT-enabled outsourcing. *International Journal of Strategic Information Technology and Applications, 2*(4), 30–43. doi:10.4018/jsita.2011100103

Du Preez, J. (2009). *Assessing the m-government readiness within the provincial government Western Cape* (Unpublished master's thesis). University of Stellenbosch, Cape Town, South Africa.

Du, P., Zhang, Y., & Liu, C. (2002). *Face Recognition using Multi-class SVM.* The 5th Asian Conference on Computer Vision, Melbourne, Australia.

Dubey, R., Sharma, S., & Chouhan, L. (2013). Security for cognitive radio networks. In M. Ku & J. Lin (Eds.), *Cognitive radio and interference management: Technology and strategy* (pp. 238–256). Hershey, PA: IGI Global. doi:10.4018/978-1-4666-2005-6.ch013

Dunkels, E., Frånberg, G., & Hällgren, C. (2011). Young people and online risk. In E. Dunkels, G. Franberg, & C. Hallgren (Eds.), *Youth culture and net culture: Online social practices* (pp. 1–16). Hershey, PA: IGI Global. doi:10.4018/978-1-60960-209-3.ch001

Dunkerley, K., & Tejay, G. (2012). The development of a model for information systems security success. In Z. Belkhamza & S. Azizi Wafa (Eds.), *Measuring organizational information systems success: New technologies and practices* (pp. 341–366). Hershey, PA: IGI Global. doi:10.4018/978-1-4666-0170-3.ch017

Dunkerley, K., & Tejay, G. (2012). Theorizing information security success: Towards secure e-government. In V. Weerakkody (Ed.), *Technology enabled transformation of the public sector: Advances in e-government* (pp. 224–235). Hershey, PA: IGI Global. doi:10.4018/978-1-4666-1776-6.ch014

Dwivedi, A. N. (2009). Handbook of research on information technology management and clinical data administration in healthcare (Vols. 1–2). Hershey, PA: IGI Global. doi:10.4018/978-1-60566-356-2

Eisenga, A., Jones, T. L., & Rodriguez, W. (2012). Investing in IT security: How to determine the maximum threshold. *International Journal of Information Security and Privacy*, *6*(3), 75–87. doi:10.4018/jisp.2012070104

Elbeltagi, I., McBride, N., & Hardaker, G. (2006). Evaluating the factors affecting DSS usage by senior managers in local authorities in Egypt. In M. Hunter & F. Tan (Eds.), *Advanced topics in global information management* (Vol. 5, pp. 283–307). Hershey, PA: IGI Global. doi:10.4018/978-1-59140-923-6.ch013

Eleyan, A., & Demirel, H. (2007). PCA and LDA based neural networks for human face recognition. I-Tech Education and Publishing.

Eli, B., & Adi, S. (1990, January). Differential cryptanalysis of DES-like cryptosystems. *Journal of Cryptology*, *4*, 3–72.

Eom, S., & Fountain, J. E. (2013). Enhancing information services through public-private partnerships: Information technology knowledge transfer underlying structures to develop shared services in the U.S. and Korea. In J. Gil-Garcia (Ed.), *E-government success around the world: Cases, empirical studies, and practical recommendations* (pp. 15–40). Hershey, PA: IGI Global. doi:10.4018/978-1-4666-4173-0.ch002

Esteves, T., Leuenberger, D., & Van Leuven, N. (2012). Reaching citizen 2.0: How government uses social media to send public messages during times of calm and times of crisis. In K. Kloby & M. D'Agostino (Eds.), *Citizen 2.0: Public and governmental interaction through web 2.0 technologies* (pp. 250–268). Hershey, PA: IGI Global. doi:10.4018/978-1-4666-0318-9.ch013

Estevez, E., Fillottrani, P., Janowski, T., & Ojo, A. (2012). Government information sharing: A framework for policy formulation. In Y. Chen & P. Chu (Eds.), *Electronic governance and cross-boundary collaboration: Innovations and advancing tools* (pp. 23–55). Hershey, PA: IGI Global. doi:10.4018/978-1-60960-753-1.ch002

EU European Union. (2015). *Digital Agenda for Europe 2020*. Retrieved from http://ec.europa.eu/information_society/digital-agenda/index_en.htm

Eurodac Supervision Coordination Group Secretariat. (2010). *Coordinated Supervision of Eurodac Activity Report 2008-2009*. Retrieved from http://www.edps.europa.eu/EDPSWEB/edps/Supervision/Eurodac

European Commission. (2014). *DG Enterprise & Industry: ICT TRENDS 2020 Main Trends for Information and Communication Technologies (ICT) and their Implications for e-Leadership Skills*. Retrieved from http://eskills-lead.eu/fileadmin/lead/reports/lead_-_technology_trends_-_august_2014_rev_sep1.pdf

Europol - European Police Office. (2011). *Europol Review*. General Report on Europol Activities.

Eyitemi, M. (2012). Regulation of cybercafés in Nigeria. In *Cyber crime: Concepts, methodologies, tools and applications* (pp. 1305–1313). Hershey, PA: IGI Global. doi:10.4018/978-1-61350-323-2.ch606

Ezumah, B., & Adekunle, S. O. (2012). A review of privacy, internet security threat, and legislation in Africa: A case study of Nigeria, South Africa, Egypt, and Kenya. In J. Abawajy, M. Pathan, M. Rahman, A. Pathan, & M. Deris (Eds.), *Internet and distributed computing advancements: Theoretical frameworks and practical applications* (pp. 115–136). Hershey, PA: IGI Global. doi:10.4018/978-1-4666-0161-1.ch005

Ezz, I. E. (2008). E-governement emerging trends: Organizational challenges. In A. Anttiroiko (Ed.), *Electronic government: Concepts, methodologies, tools, and applications* (pp. 3721–3737). Hershey, PA: IGI Global. doi:10.4018/978-1-59904-947-2.ch269

Fabri, M. (2009). The Italian style of e-justice in a comparative perspective. In A. Martínez & P. Abat (Eds.), *E-justice: Using information communication technologies in the court system* (pp. 1–19). Hershey, PA: IGI Global. doi:10.4018/978-1-59904-998-4.ch001

Fagan, M. H., Stern, N., & Wooldridge, B. R. (2003). An empirical investigation into the relationship between computer self-efficacy, anxiety, experience, support, and usage. *Journal of Computer Information Systems*, *44*(2), 95–104.

Fagbe, T., & Adekola, O. D. (2010). Workplace safety and personnel well-being: The impact of information technology. *International Journal of Green Computing*, *1*(1), 28–33. doi:10.4018/jgc.2010010103

Fagbe, T., & Adekola, O. D. (2011). Workplace safety and personnel well-being: The impact of information technology. In *Global business: Concepts, methodologies, tools and applications* (pp. 1438–1444). Hershey, PA: IGI Global. doi:10.4018/978-1-60960-587-2.ch509

Farmer, L. (2008). Affective collaborative instruction with librarians. In S. Kelsey & K. St.Amant (Eds.), *Handbook of research on computer mediated communication* (pp. 15–24). Hershey, PA: IGI Global. doi:10.4018/978-1-59904-863-5.ch002

Farooq-i-Azam, M., & Ayyaz, M. N. (2014). Embedded systems security. In *Software design and development: Concepts, methodologies, tools, and applications* (pp. 980–998). Hershey, PA: IGI Global. doi:10.4018/978-1-4666-4301-7.ch047

Fauzi, A. H., & Taylor, H. (2013). Secure community trust stores for peer-to-peer e-commerce applications using cloud services. *International Journal of E-Entrepreneurship and Innovation*, 4(1), 1–15. doi:10.4018/jeei.2013010101

Favier, L., & Mekhantar, J. (2007). Use of OSS by local e-administration: The French situation. In K. St.Amant & B. Still (Eds.), *Handbook of research on open source software: Technological, economic, and social perspectives* (pp. 428–444). Hershey, PA: IGI Global. doi:10.4018/978-1-59140-999-1.ch033

FEAF. (2009). *Federal Enterprise Architecture Framework guide by U.S CIO council*. Academic Press.

Fenz, S. (2011). E-business and information security risk management: Challenges and potential solutions. In E. Kajan (Ed.), *Electronic business interoperability: Concepts, opportunities and challenges* (pp. 596–614). Hershey, PA: IGI Global. doi:10.4018/978-1-60960-485-1.ch024

Fernandez, E. B., Yoshioka, N., Washizaki, H., Jurjens, J., VanHilst, M., & Pernu, G. (2011). Using security patterns to develop secure systems. In H. Mouratidis (Ed.), *Software engineering for secure systems: Industrial and research perspectives* (pp. 16–31). Hershey, PA: IGI Global. doi:10.4018/978-1-61520-837-1.ch002

Fernando, S. (2009). Issues of e-learning in third world countries. In M. Khosrow-Pour (Ed.), *Encyclopedia of information science and technology* (2nd ed.; pp. 2273–2277). Hershey, PA: IGI Global. doi:10.4018/978-1-60566-026-4.ch360

Filho, J. R., & dos Santos Junior, J. R. (2009). Local e-government in Brazil: Poor interaction and local politics as usual. In C. Reddick (Ed.), *Handbook of research on strategies for local e-government adoption and implementation: Comparative studies* (pp. 863–878). Hershey, PA: IGI Global. doi:10.4018/978-1-60566-282-4.ch045

Fletcher, P. D. (2004). Portals and policy: Implications of electronic access to U.S. federal government information services. In A. Pavlichev & G. Garson (Eds.), *Digital government: Principles and best practices* (pp. 52–62). Hershey, PA: IGI Global. doi:10.4018/978-1-59140-122-3.ch004

Fletcher, P. D. (2008). Portals and policy: Implications of electronic access to U.S. federal government information services. In A. Anttiroiko (Ed.), *Electronic government: Concepts, methodologies, tools, and applications* (pp. 3970–3979). Hershey, PA: IGI Global. doi:10.4018/978-1-59904-947-2.ch289

Flores, A. E., Win, K. T., & Susilo, W. (2011). Secure exchange of electronic health records. In A. Chryssanthou, I. Apostolakis, & I. Varlamis (Eds.), *Certification and security in health-related web applications: Concepts and solutions* (pp. 1–22). Hershey, PA: Medical IGI Global. doi:10.4018/978-1-61692-895-7.ch001

Fokoue, A., Srivatsa, M., Rohatgi, P., Wrobel, P., & Yesberg, J. (2009). A Decision Support System for Secure Information Sharing. *Proceedings of the 14th ACM Symposium on Access Control Models and Technologies*, 105-114. doi:10.1145/1542207.1542226

Fonseca, J., & Vieira, M. (2014). A survey on secure software development lifecycles. In *Software design and development: Concepts, methodologies, tools, and applications* (pp. 17–33). Hershey, PA: IGI Global. doi:10.4018/978-1-4666-4301-7.ch002

Forlano, L. (2004). The emergence of digital government: International perspectives. In A. Pavlichev & G. Garson (Eds.), *Digital government: Principles and best practices* (pp. 34–51). Hershey, PA: IGI Global. doi:10.4018/978-1-59140-122-3.ch003

Fornell, C., & Larcker, V. F. (1981). Evaluating structural equation models with unobservable variables and measurement error. *JMR, Journal of Marketing Research*, *18*(1), 39–50. doi:10.2307/3151312

Forouzan, B. (2008). *Cryptography and Network Security. McGraw-Hill.*

Fournaris, A. P., Kitsos, P., & Sklavos, N. (2013). Security and cryptographic engineering in embedded systems. In M. Khalgui, O. Mosbahi, & A. Valentini (Eds.), *Embedded computing systems: Applications, optimization, and advanced design* (pp. 420–438). Hershey, PA: IGI Global. doi:10.4018/978-1-4666-3922-5.ch021

Franqueira, V. N., van Cleeff, A., van Eck, P., & Wieringa, R. J. (2013). Engineering security agreements against external insider threat. *Information Resources Management Journal*, *26*(4), 66–91. doi:10.4018/irmj.2013100104

Franzel, J. M., & Coursey, D. H. (2004). Government web portals: Management issues and the approaches of five states. In A. Pavlichev & G. Garson (Eds.), *Digital government: Principles and best practices* (pp. 63–77). Hershey, PA: IGI Global. doi:10.4018/978-1-59140-122-3.ch005

French, T., Bessis, N., Maple, C., & Asimakopoulou, E. (2012). Trust issues on crowd-sourcing methods for urban environmental monitoring. *International Journal of Distributed Systems and Technologies*, *3*(1), 35–47. doi:10.4018/jdst.2012010103

Furnell, S., von Solms, R., & Phippen, A. (2011). Preventative actions for enhancing online protection and privacy. *International Journal of Information Technologies and Systems Approach*, *4*(2), 1–11. doi:10.4018/jitsa.2011070101

Fu, Y., Kulick, J., Yan, L. K., & Drager, S. (2013). Formal modeling and verification of security property in Handel C program. *International Journal of Secure Software Engineering*, *3*(3), 50–65. doi:10.4018/jsse.2012070103

Gaivéo, J. (2011). SMEs e-business security issues. In M. Cruz-Cunha & J. Varajão (Eds.), *Innovations in SMEs and conducting e-business: Technologies, trends and solutions* (pp. 317–337). Hershey, PA: IGI Global. doi:10.4018/978-1-60960-765-4.ch018

Gaivéo, J. M. (2013). Security of ICTs supporting healthcare activities. In M. Cruz-Cunha, I. Miranda, & P. Gonçalves (Eds.), *Handbook of research on ICTs for human-centered healthcare and social care services* (pp. 208–228). Hershey, PA: IGI Global. doi:10.4018/978-1-4666-3986-7.ch011

Garside, A. (2006). *The political genesis and legal impact of proposals for the SIS II: what cost for data protection and security in the EU?*. Sussex Migration Working Paper no. 30. University of Sussex. Retrieved from www.sussex.ac.uk/migration/documents/mwp30.pdf

Garson, G. D. (1999). *Information technology and computer applications in public administration: Issues and trends*. Hershey, PA: IGI Global. doi:10.4018/978-1-87828-952-0

Garson, G. D. (2003). Toward an information technology research agenda for public administration. In G. Garson (Ed.), *Public information technology: Policy and management issues* (pp. 331–357). Hershey, PA: IGI Global. doi:10.4018/978-1-59140-060-8.ch014

Garson, G. D. (2004). The promise of digital government. In A. Pavlichev & G. Garson (Eds.), *Digital government: Principles and best practices* (pp. 2–15). Hershey, PA: IGI Global. doi:10.4018/978-1-59140-122-3.ch001

Garson, G. D. (2007). An information technology research agenda for public administration. In G. Garson (Ed.), *Modern public information technology systems: Issues and challenges* (pp. 365–392). Hershey, PA: IGI Global. doi:10.4018/978-1-59904-051-6.ch018

Gartner Group. (2016). *Top 10 Strategic Technology Trends for 2017*. Retrieved from http://www.gartner.com/newsroom/id/3482617

Gartner. (2015). *Highlights Top 10 Strategic Technology Trends for Government*. Retrieved from http://www.gartner.com/newsroom/id/3069117

Gasco, M. (2007). Civil servants' resistance towards e-government development. In A. Anttiroiko & M. Malkia (Eds.), *Encyclopedia of digital government* (pp. 190–195). Hershey, PA: IGI Global. doi:10.4018/978-1-59140-789-8.ch028

Gasco, M. (2008). Civil servants' resistance towards e-government development. In A. Anttiroiko (Ed.), *Electronic government: Concepts, methodologies, tools, and applications* (pp. 2580–2588). Hershey, PA: IGI Global. doi:10.4018/978-1-59904-947-2.ch190

Gefen, D., & Keil, M. (1998). The impact of developer responsiveness on perceptions of usefulness and ease of use: An extension of the technology acceptance model. *The Data Base for Advances in Information Systems*, *29*(2), 35–49. doi:10.1145/298752.298757

Gefen, D., & Straub, D. W. (1997). Gender differences in the perception and use of e-mail: An extension to the technology acceptance model. *Management Information Systems Quarterly*, *21*(4), 389–400. doi:10.2307/249720

Gelbstein, E. E. (2013). Designing a security audit plan for a critical information infrastructure (CII). In C. Laing, A. Badii, & P. Vickers (Eds.), *Securing critical infrastructures and critical control systems: Approaches for threat protection* (pp. 262–285). Hershey, PA: IGI Global. doi:10.4018/978-1-4666-2659-1.ch011

Ghany, K. K. A., Hefny, H. A., Hassanien, A. E., & Tolba, M. F. (2013). *Kekres Transform for Protecting Fingerprint Template*. The 13th International Conference on Hybrid Intelligent Systems (HIS13), Tunisia.

Ghere, R. K. (2010). Accountability and information technology enactment: Implications for social empowerment. In E. Ferro, Y. Dwivedi, J. Gil-Garcia, & M. Williams (Eds.), *Handbook of research on overcoming digital divides: Constructing an equitable and competitive information society* (pp. 515–532). Hershey, PA: IGI Global. doi:10.4018/978-1-60566-699-0.ch028

Gibson, I. W. (2012). Simulation modeling of healthcare delivery. In A. Kolker & P. Story (Eds.), *Management engineering for effective healthcare delivery: Principles and applications* (pp. 69–89). Hershey, PA: IGI Global. doi:10.4018/978-1-60960-872-9.ch003

Gil-Garcia, J. R. (2007). Exploring e-government benefits and success factors. In A. Anttiroiko & M. Malkia (Eds.), *Encyclopedia of digital government* (pp. 803–811). Hershey, PA: IGI Global. doi:10.4018/978-1-59140-789-8.ch122

Gil-Garcia, J. R., & González Miranda, F. (2010). E-government and opportunities for participation: The case of the Mexican state web portals. In C. Reddick (Ed.), *Politics, democracy and e-government: Participation and service delivery* (pp. 56–74). Hershey, PA: IGI Global. doi:10.4018/978-1-61520-933-0.ch004

Global Security. (2016). *Voice verification*. Retrieved from http://www.globalsecurity.org/security/systems/biometrics-voice.htm

Gódor, G., & Imre, S. (2012). Security aspects in radio frequency identification systems. In D. Saha & V. Sridhar (Eds.), *Next generation data communication technologies: Emerging trends* (pp. 187–225). Hershey, PA: IGI Global. doi:10.4018/978-1-61350-477-2.ch009

Gogolin, G. (2011). Security and privacy concerns of virtual worlds. In B. Ciaramitaro (Ed.), *Virtual worlds and e-commerce: Technologies and applications for building customer relationships* (pp. 244–256). Hershey, PA: IGI Global. doi:10.4018/978-1-61692-808-7.ch014

Gogoulos, F. I., Antonakopoulou, A., Lioudakis, G. V., Kaklamani, D. I., & Venieris, I. S. (2014). Trust in an enterprise world: A survey. In M. Cruz-Cunha, F. Moreira, & J. Varajão (Eds.), *Handbook of research on enterprise 2.0: Technological, social, and organizational dimensions* (pp. 199–219). Hershey, PA: IGI Global. doi:10.4018/978-1-4666-4373-4.ch011

Goldfinch, S. (2012). Public trust in government, trust in e-government, and use of e-government. In Z. Yan (Ed.), *Encyclopedia of cyber behavior* (pp. 987–995). Hershey, PA: IGI Global. doi:10.4018/978-1-4666-0315-8.ch081

Goldman, J. E., & Ahuja, S. (2011). Integration of COBIT, balanced scorecard and SSE-CMM as an organizational & strategic information security management (ISM) framework. In M. Quigley (Ed.), *ICT ethics and security in the 21st century: New developments and applications* (pp. 277–309). Hershey, PA: IGI Global. doi:10.4018/978-1-60960-573-5.ch014

Goldschmidt, C., Dark, M., & Chaudhry, H. (2011). Responsibility for the harm and risk of software security flaws. In M. Dark (Ed.), *Information assurance and security ethics in complex systems: Interdisciplinary perspectives* (pp. 104–131). Hershey, PA: IGI Global. doi:10.4018/978-1-61692-245-0.ch006

Goodyear, M. (2012). Organizational change contributions to e-government project transitions. In S. Aikins (Ed.), *Managing e-government projects: Concepts, issues, and best practices* (pp. 1–21). Hershey, PA: IGI Global. doi:10.4018/978-1-4666-0086-7.ch001

Gordon, S., & Mulligan, P. (2003). Strategic models for the delivery of personal financial services: The role of infocracy. In S. Gordon (Ed.), *Computing information technology: The human side* (pp. 220–232). Hershey, PA: IGI Global. doi:10.4018/978-1-93177-752-0.ch014

Gordon, T. F. (2007). Legal knowledge systems. In A. Anttiroiko & M. Malkia (Eds.), *Encyclopedia of digital government* (pp. 1161–1166). Hershey, PA: IGI Global. doi:10.4018/978-1-59140-789-8.ch175

Graham, J. E., & Semich, G. W. (2008). Integrating technology to transform pedagogy: Revisiting the progress of the three phase TUI model for faculty development. In L. Tomei (Ed.), *Adapting information and communication technologies for effective education* (pp. 1–12). Hershey, PA: IGI Global. doi:10.4018/978-1-59904-922-9.ch001

Grahn, K., Karlsson, J., & Pulkkis, G. (2011). Secure routing and mobility in future IP networks. In M. Cruz-Cunha & F. Moreira (Eds.), *Handbook of research on mobility and computing: Evolving technologies and ubiquitous impacts* (pp. 952–972). Hershey, PA: IGI Global. doi:10.4018/978-1-60960-042-6.ch059

Grandinetti, L., & Pisacane, O. (2012). Web services for healthcare management. In D. Prakash Vidyarthi (Ed.), *Technologies and protocols for the future of internet design: Reinventing the web* (pp. 60–94). Hershey, PA: IGI Global. doi:10.4018/978-1-4666-0203-8.ch004

Greitzer, F. L., Frincke, D., & Zabriskie, M. (2011). Social/ethical issues in predictive insider threat monitoring. In M. Dark (Ed.), *Information assurance and security ethics in complex systems: Interdisciplinary perspectives* (pp. 132–161). Hershey, PA: IGI Global. doi:10.4018/978-1-61692-245-0.ch007

Gritzalis, P. (2002). Secure Electronic Voting. *7th Computer Security Incidents Response Teams Workshop*, (pp. 1-21). Syros, Greece: Kluwer Academic Publishers.

Grobler, M. (2012). The need for digital evidence standardisation. *International Journal of Digital Crime and Forensics*, 4(2), 1–12. doi:10.4018/jdcf.2012040101

Groenewegen, P., & Wagenaar, F. P. (2008). VO as an alternative to hierarchy in the Dutch police sector. In G. Putnik & M. Cruz-Cunha (Eds.), *Encyclopedia of networked and virtual organizations* (pp. 1851–1857). Hershey, PA: IGI Global. doi:10.4018/978-1-59904-885-7.ch245

Gronlund, A. (2001). Building an infrastructure to manage electronic services. In S. Dasgupta (Ed.), *Managing internet and intranet technologies in organizations: Challenges and opportunities* (pp. 71–103). Hershey, PA: IGI Global. doi:10.4018/978-1-878289-95-7.ch006

Gronlund, A. (2002). Introduction to electronic government: Design, applications and management. In Å. Grönlund (Ed.), *Electronic government: Design, applications and management* (pp. 1–21). Hershey, PA: IGI Global. doi:10.4018/978-1-930708-19-8.ch001

Guo, J., Marshall, A., & Zhou, B. (2014). A multi-parameter trust framework for mobile ad hoc networks. In D. Rawat, B. Bista, & G. Yan (Eds.), *Security, privacy, trust, and resource management in mobile and wireless communications* (pp. 245–277). Hershey, PA: IGI Global. doi:10.4018/978-1-4666-4691-9.ch011

Gupta, A., Woosley, R., Crk, I., & Sarnikar, S. (2009). An information technology architecture for drug effectiveness reporting and post-marketing surveillance. In J. Tan (Ed.), *Medical informatics: Concepts, methodologies, tools, and applications* (pp. 631–646). Hershey, PA: Medical IGI Global. doi:10.4018/978-1-60566-050-9.ch047

Gururajan, R., & Hafeez-Baig, A. (2011). Wireless handheld device and LAN security issues: A case study. In D. Kerr, J. Gammack, & K. Bryant (Eds.), *Digital business security development: Management technologies* (pp. 129–151). Hershey, PA: IGI Global. doi:10.4018/978-1-60566-806-2.ch006

Hackbarth, G., Grover, V., & Yi, M. Y. (2003). Computer playfulness and anxiety: Positive and negative mediators of the system experience effect on perceived ease of use. *Information & Management*, *40*(3), 221–232. doi:10.1016/S0378-7206(02)00006-X

Haddadnia, J., Ahmadi, M., & Raahemifar, K. (2003). An effective feature extraction methods for face recognition. *ICIP 2003*.

Hagen, J. M. (2012). The contributions of information security culture and human relations to the improvement of situational awareness. In C. Onwubiko & T. Owens (Eds.), *Situational awareness in computer network defense: Principles, methods and applications* (pp. 10–28). Hershey, PA: IGI Global. doi:10.4018/978-1-4666-0104-8.ch002

Ha, H. (2012). Online security and consumer protection in ecommerce an Australian case. In K. Mohammed Rezaul (Ed.), *Strategic and pragmatic e-business: Implications for future business practices* (pp. 217–243). Hershey, PA: IGI Global. doi:10.4018/978-1-4666-1619-6.ch010

Hai-Jew, S. (2011). The social design of 3D interactive spaces for security in higher education: A preliminary view. In A. Rea (Ed.), *Security in virtual worlds, 3D webs, and immersive environments: Models for development, interaction, and management* (pp. 72–96). Hershey, PA: IGI Global. doi:10.4018/978-1-61520-891-3.ch005

Hair, J. F., Tatham, R. L., Anderson, R. E., & Black, W. (1998). *Multivariate data analysis*. New York, NY: McMillan Publishing Company.

Halder, D., & Jaishankar, K. (2012). Cyber crime against women and regulations in Australia. In *Cyber crime: Concepts, methodologies, tools and applications* (pp. 757–764). Hershey, PA: IGI Global. doi:10.4018/978-1-61350-323-2.ch404

Halder, D., & Jaishankar, K. (2012). Cyber victimization of women and cyber laws in India. In *Cyber crime: Concepts, methodologies, tools and applications* (pp. 742–756). Hershey, PA: IGI Global. doi:10.4018/978-1-61350-323-2.ch403

Halder, D., & Jaishankar, K. (2012). Definition, typology and patterns of victimization. In *Cyber crime: Concepts, methodologies, tools and applications* (pp. 1016–1042). Hershey, PA: IGI Global. doi:10.4018/978-1-61350-323-2.ch502

Hallin, A., & Lundevall, K. (2007). mCity: User focused development of mobile services within the city of Stockholm. In I. Kushchu (Ed.), Mobile government: An emerging direction in e-government (pp. 12-29). Hershey, PA: IGI Global. doi:10.4018/978-1-59140-884-0.ch002

Hallin, A., & Lundevall, K. (2009). mCity: User focused development of mobile services within the city of Stockholm. In D. Taniar (Ed.), Mobile computing: Concepts, methodologies, tools, and applications (pp. 3455-3467). Hershey, PA: IGI Global. doi:10.4018/978-1-60566-054-7.ch253

Hallin, A., & Lundevall, K. (2009). mCity: User focused development of mobile services within the city of Stockholm. In S. Clarke (Ed.), Evolutionary concepts in end user productivity and performance: Applications for organizational progress (pp. 268-280). Hershey, PA: IGI Global. doi:10.4018/978-1-60566-136-0.ch017

Hamlen, K., Kantarcioglu, M., Khan, L., & Thuraisingham, B. (2012). Security issues for cloud computing. In H. Nemati (Ed.), *Optimizing information security and advancing privacy assurance: New technologies* (pp. 150–162). Hershey, PA: IGI Global. doi:10.4018/978-1-4666-0026-3.ch008

Hanson, A. (2005). Overcoming barriers in the planning of a virtual library. In M. Khosrow-Pour (Ed.), *Encyclopedia of information science and technology* (pp. 2255–2259). Hershey, PA: IGI Global. doi:10.4018/978-1-59140-553-5.ch397

Haque, A. (2008). Information technology and surveillance: Implications for public administration in a new word order. In T. Loendorf & G. Garson (Eds.), *Patriotic information systems* (pp. 177–185). Hershey, PA: IGI Global. doi:10.4018/978-1-59904-594-8.ch008

Harnesk, D. (2011). Convergence of information security in B2B networks. In E. Kajan (Ed.), *Electronic business interoperability: Concepts, opportunities and challenges* (pp. 571–595). Hershey, PA: IGI Global. doi:10.4018/978-1-60960-485-1.ch023

Harnesk, D., & Hartikainen, H. (2011). Multi-layers of information security in emergency response. *International Journal of Information Systems for Crisis Response and Management*, *3*(2), 1–17. doi:10.4018/jiscrm.2011040101

Harrison, A., & Rainer, K. Jr. (1992). The influence of individual differences on skills in end-user computing. *Journal of Management Information Systems*, *9*(1), 93–111. doi:10.1080/07421222.1992.11517949

Hassan, B., & Jafar, M. H. (2004). An Empirical Examination of a Model of Computer Learning Performance. *Journal of Computer Information Systems*.

Hatonen, J., & Eriksson, T. (2009). 30+ years of research and practice of outsourcing–Exploring the past and anticipating the future. *Journal of International Management*, *15*(2), 142–155. doi:10.1016/j.intman.2008.07.002

Hauck, R. V., Thatcher, S. M., & Weisband, S. P. (2012). Temporal aspects of information technology use: Increasing shift work effectiveness. In J. Wang (Ed.), *Advancing the service sector with evolving technologies: Techniques and principles* (pp. 87–104). Hershey, PA: IGI Global. doi:10.4018/978-1-4666-0044-7.ch006

Hawk, S., & Witt, T. (2006). Telecommunications courses in information systems programs. *International Journal of Information and Communication Technology Education*, *2*(1), 79–92. doi:10.4018/jicte.2006010107

Hawrylak, P. J., Hale, J., & Papa, M. (2013). Security issues for ISO 18000-6 type C RFID: Identification and solutions. In *Supply chain management: Concepts, methodologies, tools, and applications* (pp. 1565–1581). Hershey, PA: IGI Global. doi:10.4018/978-1-4666-2625-6.ch093

Headayetullah, M., & Pradhan, G. K. (2010). Efficient and Secure Information Sharing For Security Personnels: A Role and Cooperation Based Approach. *International Journal on Computer Science and Engineering*, *2*(3), 2010.

He, B., Tran, T. T., & Xie, B. (2014). Authentication and identity management for secure cloud businesses and services. In S. Srinivasan (Ed.), *Security, trust, and regulatory aspects of cloud computing in business environments* (pp. 180–201). Hershey, PA: IGI Global. doi:10.4018/978-1-4666-5788-5.ch011

Heeks, R. (2003). *Most e-Gov for development projects fail how risks can be reduced.* Academic Press.

Helms, M. M., Moore, R., & Ahmadi, M. (2009). Information technology (IT) and the healthcare industry: A SWOT analysis. In J. Tan (Ed.), *Medical informatics: Concepts, methodologies, tools, and applications* (pp. 134–152). Hershey, PA: IGI Global. doi:10.4018/978-1-60566-050-9.ch012

Hendrickson, S. M., & Young, M. E. (2014). Electronic records management at a federally funded research and development center. In J. Krueger (Ed.), *Cases on electronic records and resource management implementation in diverse environments* (pp. 334–350). Hershey, PA: IGI Global. doi:10.4018/978-1-4666-4466-3.ch020

Henman, P. (2010). Social policy and information communication technologies. In J. Martin & L. Hawkins (Eds.), *Information communication technologies for human services education and delivery: Concepts and cases* (pp. 215–229). Hershey, PA: IGI Global. doi:10.4018/978-1-60566-735-5.ch014

Henrie, M. (2012). Cyber security in liquid petroleum pipelines. In J. Zubairi & A. Mahboob (Eds.), *Cyber security standards, practices and industrial applications: Systems and methodologies* (pp. 200–222). Hershey, PA: IGI Global. doi:10.4018/978-1-60960-851-4.ch011

Herath, T., Rao, H. R., & Upadhyaya, S. (2012). Internet crime: How vulnerable are you? Do gender, social influence and education play a role in vulnerability? In *Cyber crime: Concepts, methodologies, tools and applications* (pp. 1–13). Hershey, PA: IGI Global. doi:10.4018/978-1-61350-323-2.ch101

Hill, T., Smith, N. D., & Mann, M. F. (1987). Role efficacy expectations in predicting the decision to use advanced technologies: The case of computers. *The Journal of Applied Psychology, 72*(2), 307–313. doi:10.1037/0021-9010.72.2.307

Hilmi, M. F., Pawanchik, S., Mustapha, Y., & Ali, H. M. (2013). Information security perspective of a learning management system: An exploratory study. *International Journal of Knowledge Society Research, 4*(2), 9–18. doi:10.4018/jksr.2013040102

Hismanoglu, M. (2011). Important issues in online education: E-pedagogy and marketing. In U. Demiray & S. Sever (Eds.), *Marketing online education programs: Frameworks for promotion and communication* (pp. 184–209). Hershey, PA: IGI Global. doi:10.4018/978-1-60960-074-7.ch012

Ho, K. K. (2008). The e-government development, IT strategies, and portals of the Hong Kong SAR government. In A. Anttiroiko (Ed.), *Electronic government: Concepts, methodologies, tools, and applications* (pp. 715–733). Hershey, PA: IGI Global. doi:10.4018/978-1-59904-947-2.ch060

Holden, S. H. (2003). The evolution of information technology management at the federal level: Implications for public administration. In G. Garson (Ed.), *Public information technology: Policy and management issues* (pp. 53–73). Hershey, PA: IGI Global. doi:10.4018/978-1-59140-060-8.ch003

Holden, S. H. (2007). The evolution of federal information technology management literature: Does IT finally matter? In G. Garson (Ed.), *Modern public information technology systems: Issues and challenges* (pp. 17–34). Hershey, PA: IGI Global. doi:10.4018/978-1-59904-051-6.ch002

Holland, J. W. (2009). Automation of American criminal justice. In M. Khosrow-Pour (Ed.), *Encyclopedia of information science and technology* (2nd ed.; pp. 300–302). Hershey, PA: IGI Global. doi:10.4018/978-1-60566-026-4.ch051

Holloway, K. (2013). Fair use, copyright, and academic integrity in an online academic environment. In *Digital rights management: Concepts, methodologies, tools, and applications* (pp. 917–928). Hershey, PA: IGI Global. doi:10.4018/978-1-4666-2136-7.ch044

Hommel, W. (2012). Security and privacy management for learning management systems. In *Virtual learning environments: Concepts, methodologies, tools and applications* (pp. 1151–1170). Hershey, PA: IGI Global. doi:10.4018/978-1-4666-0011-9.ch602

Hoops, D. S. (2012). Lost in cyberspace: Navigating the legal issues of e-commerce. *Journal of Electronic Commerce in Organizations*, *10*(1), 33–51. doi:10.4018/jeco.2012010103

Horiuchi, C. (2005). E-government databases. In L. Rivero, J. Doorn, & V. Ferraggine (Eds.), *Encyclopedia of database technologies and applications* (pp. 206–210). Hershey, PA: IGI Global. doi:10.4018/978-1-59140-560-3.ch035

Horiuchi, C. (2006). Creating IS quality in government settings. In E. Duggan & J. Reichgelt (Eds.), *Measuring information systems delivery quality* (pp. 311–327). Hershey, PA: IGI Global. doi:10.4018/978-1-59140-857-4.ch014

Houmb, S., Georg, G., Petriu, D., Bordbar, B., Ray, I., Anastasakis, K., & France, R. (2011). Balancing security and performance properties during system architectural design. In H. Mouratidis (Ed.), *Software engineering for secure systems: Industrial and research perspectives* (pp. 155–191). Hershey, PA: IGI Global. doi:10.4018/978-1-61520-837-1.ch006

Hsiao, N., Chu, P., & Lee, C. (2012). Impact of e-governance on businesses: Model development and case study. In *Digital democracy: Concepts, methodologies, tools, and applications* (pp. 1407–1425). Hershey, PA: IGI Global. doi:10.4018/978-1-4666-1740-7.ch070

Huang, E., & Cheng, F. (2012). Online security cues and e-payment continuance intention. *International Journal of E-Entrepreneurship and Innovation, 3*(1), 42–58. doi:10.4018/jeei.2012010104

Huang, G. B., Narayana, M., & Miller, E. (2008). Towards unconstrained face recognition. *Proc. of IEEE Computer Society Workshop on Perceptual Organization in Computer Vision IEEE CVPR.*

Huang, T., & Lee, C. (2010). Evaluating the impact of e-government on citizens: Cost-benefit analysis. In C. Reddick (Ed.), *Citizens and e-government: Evaluating policy and management* (pp. 37–52). Hershey, PA: IGI Global. doi:10.4018/978-1-61520-931-6.ch003

Hung, S. Y., Chia-Ming, C., & Yu, T. J. (2006). Determinants of user acceptance of the e-government services: The case of online tax filing and payment system. *Government Information Quarterly, 23*(1), 97–122. doi:10.1016/j.giq.2005.11.005

Hunter, M. G., Diochon, M., Pugsley, D., & Wright, B. (2002). Unique challenges for small business adoption of information technology: The case of the Nova Scotia ten. In S. Burgess (Ed.), *Managing information technology in small business: Challenges and solutions* (pp. 98–117). Hershey, PA: IGI Global. doi:10.4018/978-1-930708-35-8.ch006

Hu, P. J. H., Clark, T. H. K., & Ma, W. W. (2003). Examining technology acceptance by school teachers: A longitudinal study. *Information & Management, 41*(2), 227–241. doi:10.1016/S0378-7206(03)00050-8

Hurskainen, J. (2003). Integration of business systems and applications in merger and alliance: Case metso automation. In T. Reponen (Ed.), *Information technology enabled global customer service* (pp. 207–225). Hershey, PA: IGI Global. doi:10.4018/978-1-59140-048-6.ch012

Hurt, H. T., Joseph, K., & Cooed, C. D. (1977). Scales for the measurement of innovativeness. *Human Communication Research*, *4*(1), 58–65. doi:10.1111/j.1468-2958.1977.tb00597.x

Iazzolino, G., & Pietrantonio, R. (2011). The soveria.it project: A best practice of e-government in southern Italy. In D. Piaggesi, K. Sund, & W. Castelnovo (Eds.), *Global strategy and practice of e-governance: Examples from around the world* (pp. 34–56). Hershey, PA: IGI Global. doi:10.4018/978-1-60960-489-9.ch003

Ibrahim, S., Kamat, M., Salleh, M., & Abdul Aziz, S. (2003). *Secure E-Voting With Blind*. Johor Bharu, Johor, Malaysia: Signature.

Ifinedo, P. (2011). Relationships between information security concerns and national cultural dimensions: Findings in the global financial services industry. In H. Nemati (Ed.), *Security and privacy assurance in advancing technologies: New developments* (pp. 134–153). Hershey, PA: IGI Global. doi:10.4018/978-1-60960-200-0.ch010

Igbaria, M. (1993). User acceptance of microcomputer technology: An empirical test. *OMEGA International Journal of Management Science*, *21*(1), 73–90. doi:10.1016/0305-0483(93)90040-R

i.    Martinez, A. C. (2008). Accessing administration's information via internet in Spain. In F. Tan (Ed.), *Global information technologies: Concepts, methodologies, tools, and applications* (pp. 2558–2573). Hershey, PA: IGI Global. doi:10.4018/978-1-59904-939-7.ch186

Imran, A., & Gregor, S. (2012). A process model for successful e-government adoption in the least developed countries: A case of Bangladesh. In F. Tan (Ed.), *International comparisons of information communication technologies: Advancing applications* (pp. 321–350). Hershey, PA: IGI Global. doi:10.4018/978-1-61350-480-2.ch014

Inden, U., Lioudakis, G., & Rückemann, C. (2013). Awareness-based security management for complex and internet-based operations management systems. In C. Rückemann (Ed.), *Integrated information and computing systems for natural, spatial, and social sciences* (pp. 43–73). Hershey, PA: IGI Global. doi:10.4018/978-1-4666-2190-9.ch003

Infoplease. (2012). *Election Ballots: Types and History*. Retrieved May 9, 2013, from Infoplease Web site: http://www.infoplease.com/spot/campaign2000ballot.html

Inmitiatiove, A. (2016). *Big Data and Development*. Retrieved from http://www. accountabilityindia.in/accountabilityblog/2580-data-explosion-big-data-and-development

Inoue, Y., & Bell, S. T. (2005). Electronic/digital government innovation, and publishing trends with IT. In M. Khosrow-Pour (Ed.), *Encyclopedia of information science and technology* (pp. 1018–1023). Hershey, PA: IGI Global. doi:10.4018/978-1-59140-553-5.ch180

Ishmatova, D., & Obi, T. (2009). M-government services: User needs and value. *I-Ways Journal of E-Government Policy and Regulation*, *32*(1), 39–46.

Islam, M. M., & Ehsan, M. (2013). Understanding e-governance: A theoretical approach. In M. Islam & M. Ehsan (Eds.), *From government to e-governance: Public administration in the digital age* (pp. 38–49). Hershey, PA: IGI Global. doi:10.4018/978-1-4666-1909-8.ch003

Islam, S., Mouratidis, H., Kalloniatis, C., Hudic, A., & Zechner, L. (2013). Model based process to support security and privacy requirements engineering. *International Journal of Secure Software Engineering*, *3*(3), 1–22. doi:10.4018/jsse.2012070101

Itani, W., Kayssi, A., & Chehab, A. (2012). Security and privacy in body sensor networks: Challenges, solutions, and research directions. In M. Watfa (Ed.), *E-healthcare systems and wireless communications: Current and future challenges* (pp. 100–127). Hershey, PA: Medical IGI Global. doi:10.4018/978-1-61350-123-8.ch005

Jaeger, B. (2009). E-government and e-democracy in the making. In M. Khosrow-Pour (Ed.), *Encyclopedia of information science and technology* (2nd ed.; pp. 1318–1322). Hershey, PA: IGI Global. doi:10.4018/978-1-60566-026-4.ch208

Jain, R. B. (2007). Revamping the administrative structure and processes in India for online diplomacy. In A. Anttiroiko & M. Malkia (Eds.), *Encyclopedia of digital government* (pp. 1418–1423). Hershey, PA: IGI Global. doi:10.4018/978-1-59140-789-8.ch217

Jain, R. B. (2008). Revamping the administrative structure and processes in India for online diplomacy. In A. Anttiroiko (Ed.), *Electronic government: Concepts, methodologies, tools, and applications* (pp. 3142–3149). Hershey, PA: IGI Global. doi:10.4018/978-1-59904-947-2.ch233

Jansen van Vuuren, J., Grobler, M., & Zaaiman, J. (2012). Cyber security awareness as critical driver to national security. *International Journal of Cyber Warfare & Terrorism*, *2*(1), 27–38. doi:10.4018/ijcwt.2012010103

Jansen van Vuuren, J., Leenen, L., Phahlamohlaka, J., & Zaaiman, J. (2012). An approach to governance of CyberSecurity in South Africa. *International Journal of Cyber Warfare & Terrorism*, 2(4), 13–27. doi:10.4018/ijcwt.2012100102

Jauhiainen, J. S., & Inkinen, T. (2009). E-governance and the information society in periphery. In C. Reddick (Ed.), *Handbook of research on strategies for local e-government adoption and implementation: Comparative studies* (pp. 497–514). Hershey, PA: IGI Global. doi:10.4018/978-1-60566-282-4.ch026

Jensen, J., & Groep, D. L. (2012). Security and trust in a global research infrastructure. In J. Leng & W. Sharrock (Eds.), *Handbook of research on computational science and engineering: Theory and practice* (pp. 539–566). Hershey, PA: IGI Global. doi:10.4018/978-1-61350-116-0.ch022

Jensen, M. J. (2009). Electronic democracy and citizen influence in government. In C. Reddick (Ed.), *Handbook of research on strategies for local e-government adoption and implementation: Comparative studies* (pp. 288–305). Hershey, PA: IGI Global. doi:10.4018/978-1-60566-282-4.ch015

Jiao, Y., Hurson, A. R., Potok, T. E., & Beckerman, B. G. (2009). Integrating mobile-based systems with healthcare databases. In J. Erickson (Ed.), *Database technologies: Concepts, methodologies, tools, and applications* (pp. 484–504). Hershey, PA: IGI Global. doi:10.4018/978-1-60566-058-5.ch031

Jiménez, C. E., Falcone, F., Solanas, A., Puyosa, H., Zoughbi, S., & González, F. (2015). Smart Government: Opportunities and Challenges in Smart Cities Development. In Ć. Dolićanin, E. Kajan, D. Randjelović, & B. Stojanović (Eds.), *Handbook of Research on Democratic Strategies and Citizen-Centered E-Government Services* (pp. 1–19). Hershey, PA: Information Science Reference; doi:10.4018/978-1-4666-7266-6.ch001

Johnsen, S. O. (2014). Safety and security in SCADA systems must be improved through resilience based risk management. In *Crisis management: Concepts, methodologies, tools and applications* (pp. 1422–1436). Hershey, PA: IGI Global. doi:10.4018/978-1-4666-4707-7.ch071

Johnston, A. C., Wech, B., & Jack, E. (2012). Engaging remote employees: The moderating role of remote status in determining employee information security policy awareness. *Journal of Organizational and End User Computing*, 25(1), 1–23. doi:10.4018/joeuc.2013010101

Joia, L. A. (2002). A systematic model to integrate information technology into metabusinesses: A case study in the engineering realms. In F. Tan (Ed.), *Advanced topics in global information management* (Vol. 1, pp. 250–267). Hershey, PA: IGI Global. doi:10.4018/978-1-930708-43-3.ch016

Jones, T. H., & Song, I. (2000). Binary equivalents of ternary relationships in entity-relationship modeling: A logical decomposition approach. *Journal of Database Management*, *11*(2), 12–19. doi:10.4018/jdm.2000040102

Juana-Espinosa, S. D. (2007). Empirical study of the municipalitites' motivations for adopting online presence. In L. Al-Hakim (Ed.), *Global e-government: Theory, applications and benchmarking* (pp. 261–279). Hershey, PA: IGI Global. doi:10.4018/978-1-59904-027-1.ch015

Jung, C., Rudolph, M., & Schwarz, R. (2013). Security evaluation of service-oriented systems using the SiSOA method. In K. Khan (Ed.), *Developing and evaluating security-aware software systems* (pp. 20–35). Hershey, PA: IGI Global. doi:10.4018/978-1-4666-2482-5.ch002

Jun, K., & Weare, C. (2012). Bridging from e-government practice to e-government research: Past trends and future directions. In K. Bwalya & S. Zulu (Eds.), *Handbook of research on e-government in emerging economies: Adoption, e-participation, and legal frameworks* (pp. 263–289). Hershey, PA: IGI Global. doi:10.4018/978-1-4666-0324-0.ch013

Junqueira, A., Diniz, E. H., & Fernandez, M. (2010). Electronic government implementation projects with multiple agencies: Analysis of the electronic invoice project under PMBOK framework. In J. Cordoba-Pachon & A. Ochoa-Arias (Eds.), *Systems thinking and e-participation: ICT in the governance of society* (pp. 135–153). Hershey, PA: IGI Global. doi:10.4018/978-1-60566-860-4.ch009

Juntunen, A. (2009). Joint service development with the local authorities. In C. Reddick (Ed.), *Handbook of research on strategies for local e-government adoption and implementation: Comparative studies* (pp. 902–920). Hershey, PA: IGI Global. doi:10.4018/978-1-60566-282-4.ch047

Juwei, L., & Kostantinos, N. (2003, January). Face Recognition Using LDA Based Algorithms. *IEEE Transactions on Neural Networks*, *14*(1), 195–200. doi:10.1109/TNN.2002.806647

Kaiya, H., Sakai, J., Ogata, S., & Kaijiri, K. (2013). Eliciting security requirements for an information system using asset flows and processor deployment. *International Journal of Secure Software Engineering*, *4*(3), 42–63. doi:10.4018/jsse.2013070103

Kalloniatis, C., Kavakli, E., & Gritzalis, S. (2011). Designing privacy aware information systems. In H. Mouratidis (Ed.), *Software engineering for secure systems: Industrial and research perspectives* (pp. 212–231). Hershey, PA: IGI Global. doi:10.4018/978-1-61520-837-1.ch008

Kamel, S. (2001). *Using DSS for crisis management*. Hershey, PA: IGI Global. doi:10.4018/978-1-87828-961-2.ch020

Kamel, S. (2006). DSS for strategic decision making. In M. Khosrow-Pour (Ed.), *Cases on information technology and organizational politics & culture* (pp. 230–246). Hershey, PA: IGI Global. doi:10.4018/978-1-59904-411-8.ch015

Kamel, S. (2009). The software industry in Egypt as a potential contributor to economic growth. In M. Khosrow-Pour (Ed.), *Encyclopedia of information science and technology* (2nd ed.; pp. 3531–3537). Hershey, PA: IGI Global. doi:10.4018/978-1-60566-026-4.ch562

Kamel, S., & Hussein, M. (2008). Xceed: Pioneering the contact center industry in Egypt. *Journal of Cases on Information Technology*, *10*(1), 67–91. doi:10.4018/jcit.2008010105

Kamel, S., & Wahba, K. (2003). The use of a hybrid model in web-based education: "The Global campus project. In A. Aggarwal (Ed.), *Web-based education: Learning from experience* (pp. 331–346). Hershey, PA: IGI Global. doi:10.4018/978-1-59140-102-5.ch020

Kamoun, F., & Halaweh, M. (2012). User interface design and e-commerce security perception: An empirical study. *International Journal of E-Business Research*, *8*(2), 15–32. doi:10.4018/jebr.2012040102

Kamruzzaman, J., Azad, A. K., Karmakar, N. C., Karmakar, G., & Srinivasan, B. (2013). Security and privacy in RFID systems. In N. Karmakar (Ed.), *Advanced RFID systems, security, and applications* (pp. 16–40). Hershey, PA: IGI Global. doi:10.4018/978-1-4666-2080-3.ch002

Kaosar, M. G., & Yi, X. (2011). Privacy preserving data gathering in wireless sensor network. In D. Kar & M. Syed (Eds.), *Network security, administration and management: Advancing technology and practice* (pp. 237–251). Hershey, PA: IGI Global. doi:10.4018/978-1-60960-777-7.ch012

Karadsheh, L., & Alhawari, S. (2011). Applying security policies in small business utilizing cloud computing technologies. *International Journal of Cloud Applications and Computing*, *1*(2), 29–40. doi:10.4018/ijcac.2011040103

Karahanna, E., Straub, D. W., & Chervany, N. L. (1999). Information technology adoption across time: A cross-sectional comparison of pre-adoption and post-adoption beliefs. *Management Information Systems Quarterly*, *23*(2), 183–214. doi:10.2307/249751

Karatsiolis, V., Langer, L., Schmidt, A., Tews, E., & Wiesmaier, A. (2010). *Cryptographic Application Scenarios*. Darmstadt, Germany: Academic Press.

Kar, D. C., Ngo, H. L., Mulkey, C. J., & Sanapala, G. (2011). Advances in security and privacy in wireless sensor networks. In H. Nemati (Ed.), *Security and privacy assurance in advancing technologies: New developments* (pp. 186–213). Hershey, PA: IGI Global. doi:10.4018/978-1-60960-200-0.ch014

Kardaras, D. K., & Papathanassiou, E. A. (2008). An exploratory study of the e-government services in Greece. In G. Garson & M. Khosrow-Pour (Eds.), *Handbook of research on public information technology* (pp. 162–174). Hershey, PA: IGI Global. doi:10.4018/978-1-59904-857-4.ch016

Karimi, O. B., Yousefi, S., Fathy, M., & Mazoochi, M. (2008). Availability measurement in peer to peer network management systems. *IEEE Third International Conference on Digital Information Management*, 745-750.

Karokola, G., Yngström, L., & Kowalski, S. (2012). Secure e-government services: A comparative analysis of e-government maturity models for the developing regions–The need for security services. *International Journal of Electronic Government Research*, *8*(1), 1–25. doi:10.4018/jegr.2012010101

Kassahun, A. E., Molla, A., & Sarkar, P. (2012). Government process reengineering: What we know and what we need to know. In *Digital democracy: Concepts, methodologies, tools, and applications* (pp. 1730–1752). Hershey, PA: IGI Global. doi:10.4018/978-1-4666-1740-7.ch086

Kassim, N. M., & Ramayah, T. (2013). Security policy issues in internet banking in Malaysia. In *IT policy and ethics: Concepts, methodologies, tools, and applications* (pp. 1274–1293). Hershey, PA: IGI Global. doi:10.4018/978-1-4666-2919-6.ch057

Kayem, A. V. (2013). Security in service oriented architectures: Standards and challenges. In *Digital rights management: Concepts, methodologies, tools, and applications* (pp. 50–73). Hershey, PA: IGI Global. doi:10.4018/978-1-4666-2136-7.ch004

Keil, M., Beranek, P. M., & Konsynski, B. R. (1995). Usefulness and ease of use: Field study evidence regarding task considerations. *Decision Support Systems*, *13*(1), 75–91. doi:10.1016/0167-9236(94)E0032-M

Kelarev, A. V., Brown, S., Watters, P., Wu, X., & Dazeley, R. (2011). Establishing reasoning communities of security experts for internet commerce security. In J. Yearwood & A. Stranieri (Eds.), *Technologies for supporting reasoning communities and collaborative decision making: Cooperative approaches* (pp. 380–396). Hershey, PA: IGI Global. doi:10.4018/978-1-60960-091-4.ch020

Kenya National Bureau of Statistics. (2014). *Statistical Abstract 2014.* Nairobi, Kenya: Government Press.

Kerlinger, F. N. (1986). *Foundations of Behavioral Research.* Fort Worth, TX: Holt, Rinehart &Winston Inc.

Kerr, D., Gammack, J. G., & Boddington, R. (2011). Overview of digital business security issues. In D. Kerr, J. Gammack, & K. Bryant (Eds.), *Digital business security development: Management technologies* (pp. 1–36). Hershey, PA: IGI Global. doi:10.4018/978-1-60566-806-2.ch001

Kessler, G. (2013). *An Overview of Cryptography.* Retrieved March 20, 2013, from Gary Kessler: http://www.garykessler.net/library/crypto.html

Khan, B. (2005). Technological issues. In B. Khan (Ed.), *Managing e-learning strategies: Design, delivery, implementation and evaluation* (pp. 154–180). Hershey, PA: IGI Global. doi:10.4018/978-1-59140-634-1.ch004

Khan, K. M. (2011). A decision support system for selecting secure web services. In *Enterprise information systems: Concepts, methodologies, tools and applications* (pp. 1113–1120). Hershey, PA: IGI Global. doi:10.4018/978-1-61692-852-0.ch415

Khan, K. M. (2012). Software security engineering: Design and applications. *International Journal of Secure Software Engineering, 3*(1), 62–63. doi:10.4018/jsse.2012010104

Khasawneh, A., Bsoul, M., Obeidat, I., & Al Azzam, I. (2012). Technology fears: A study of e-commerce loyalty perception by Jordanian customers. In J. Wang (Ed.), *Advancing the service sector with evolving technologies: Techniques and principles* (pp. 158–165). Hershey, PA: IGI Global. doi:10.4018/978-1-4666-0044-7.ch010

Khatibi, V., & Montazer, G. A. (2012). E-research methodology. In A. Juan, T. Daradoumis, M. Roca, S. Grasman, & J. Faulin (Eds.), *Collaborative and distributed e-research: Innovations in technologies, strategies and applications* (pp. 62–81). Hershey, PA: IGI Global. doi:10.4018/978-1-4666-0125-3.ch003

Kidd, T. (2011). The dragon in the school's backyard: A review of literature on the uses of technology in urban schools. In L. Tomei (Ed.), *Online courses and ICT in education: Emerging practices and applications* (pp. 242–257). Hershey, PA. IGI Global. doi:10.4018/978-1-60960-150-8.ch019

Kidd, T. T. (2010). My experience tells the story: Exploring technology adoption from a qualitative perspective - A pilot study. In H. Song & T. Kidd (Eds.), *Handbook of research on human performance and instructional technology* (pp. 247–262). Hershey, PA: IGI Global. doi:10.4018/978-1-60566-782-9.ch015

Kieley, B., Lane, G., Paquet, G., & Roy, J. (2002). e-Government in Canada: Services online or public service renewal? In Å. Grönlund (Ed.), Electronic government: Design, applications and management (pp. 340-355). Hershey, PA: IGI Global. doi:10.4018/978-1-930708-19-8.ch016

Kiiski, C., & Matti, P. (2002). Cross country diffusion of the internet. *Information Economics and Policy, 14*(2), 297–310. doi:10.1016/S0167-6245(01)00071-3

Kilger, M. (2011). Social dynamics and the future of technology-driven crime. In T. Holt & B. Schell (Eds.), *Corporate hacking and technology-driven crime: Social dynamics and implications* (pp. 205–227). Hershey, PA: IGI Global. doi:10.4018/978-1-61692-805-6.ch011

Kim, P. (2012). "Stay out of the way! My kid is video blogging through a phone!": A lesson learned from math tutoring social media for children in underserved communities. In *Wireless technologies: Concepts, methodologies, tools and applications* (pp. 1415–1428). Hershey, PA: IGI Global. doi:10.4018/978-1-61350-101-6.ch517

Kim, Y., Yoon, J., Park, S., & Han, J. (2004). *Architecture for Implementing the Mobile Government Services in Korea.* doi:10.1007/978-3-540-30466-1_55

King, R.S. (2011). How 5 technologies fared after 9/11. *IEEE Spectrum, 48*(9), 13.

Kinzie, M. B., Delcourt, M. A. B., & Powers, S. M. (1994). Computer technologies: Attitudes and self-efficacy across undergraduate disciplines. *Research in Higher Education, 35*(6), 745–768. doi:10.1007/BF02497085

Kirlidog, M. (2010). Financial aspects of national ICT strategies. In S. Kamel (Ed.), *E-strategies for technological diffusion and adoption: National ICT approaches for socioeconomic development* (pp. 277–292). Hershey, PA: IGI Global. doi:10.4018/978-1-60566-388-3.ch016

Kirwan, G., & Power, A. (2012). Hacking: Legal and ethical aspects of an ambiguous activity. In A. Dudley, J. Braman, & G. Vincenti (Eds.), *Investigating cyber law and cyber ethics: Issues, impacts and practices* (pp. 21–36). Hershey, PA: IGI Global. doi:10.4018/978-1-61350-132-0.ch002

Kishore, K., Krishna, & Varma, G. (2010). Hybrid Face Recognition System using Multi Feature Neural Network. *Journal of Computing, 2*(7).

Kisielnicki, J. (2006). Transfer of information and knowledge in the project management. In E. Coakes & S. Clarke (Eds.), *Encyclopedia of communities of practice in information and knowledge management* (pp. 544–551). Hershey, PA: IGI Global. doi:10.4018/978-1-59140-556-6.ch091

Kittner, M., & Van Slyke, C. (2006). Reorganizing information technology services in an academic environment. In M. Khosrow-Pour (Ed.), *Cases on the human side of information technology* (pp. 49–66). Hershey, PA: IGI Global. doi:10.4018/978-1-59904-405-7.ch004

Kline, D. M., He, L., & Yaylacicegi, U. (2011). User perceptions of security technologies. *International Journal of Information Security and Privacy, 5*(2), 1–12. doi:10.4018/jisp.2011040101

Knoell, H. D. (2008). Semi virtual workplaces in German financial service enterprises. In P. Zemliansky & K. St.Amant (Eds.), *Handbook of research on virtual workplaces and the new nature of business practices* (pp. 570–581). Hershey, PA: IGI Global. doi:10.4018/978-1-59904-893-2.ch041

Kohno, T., Stubblefield, A., Rubin, A., & Wallach, D. (2004). Analysis of an Electronic Voting System.*IEEE Symposium on Security and Privacy*, (pp. 1-23). IEEE Computer Society Press.

Koh, S. L., & Maguire, S. (2009). Competing in the age of information technology in a developing economy: Experiences of an Indian bank. In S. Koh & S. Maguire (Eds.), *Information and communication technologies management in turbulent business environments* (pp. 326–350). Hershey, PA: IGI Global. doi:10.4018/978-1-60566-424-8.ch018

Koica, S. K. (2006). *Mongolian ICT Development e-Gov Framework Project Report*. Academic Press.

Kolkowska, E., Hedström, K., & Karlsson, F. (2012). Analyzing information security goals. In M. Gupta, J. Walp, & R. Sharman (Eds.), *Threats, countermeasures, and advances in applied information security* (pp. 91–110). Hershey, PA: IGI Global. doi:10.4018/978-1-4666-0978-5.ch005

Kollmann, T., & Häsel, M. (2009). Competence of information technology professionals in internet-based ventures. In A. Cater-Steel (Ed.), *Information technology governance and service management: Frameworks and adaptations* (pp. 239–253). Hershey, PA: IGI Global. doi:10.4018/978-1-60566-008-0.ch013

Kollmann, T., & Häsel, M. (2009). Competence of information technology professionals in internet-based ventures. In I. Lee (Ed.), *Electronic business: Concepts, methodologies, tools, and applications* (pp. 1905–1919). Hershey, PA: IGI Global. doi:10.4018/978-1-60566-056-1.ch118

Kollmann, T., & Häsel, M. (2010). Competence of information technology professionals in internet-based ventures. In *Electronic services: Concepts, methodologies, tools and applications* (pp. 1551–1565). Hershey, PA: IGI Global. doi:10.4018/978-1-61520-967-5.ch094

Korhonen, J. J., Hiekkanen, K., & Mykkänen, J. (2012). Information security governance. In M. Gupta, J. Walp, & R. Sharman (Eds.), *Strategic and practical approaches for information security governance: Technologies and applied solutions* (pp. 53–66). Hershey, PA: IGI Global. doi:10.4018/978-1-4666-0197-0.ch004

Korovessis, P. (2011). Information security awareness in academia. *International Journal of Knowledge Society Research*, 2(4), 1–17. doi:10.4018/jksr.2011100101

Koskosas, I., & Sariannidis, N. (2011). Project commitment in the context of information security. *International Journal of Information Technology Project Management*, 2(3), 17–29. doi:10.4018/jitpm.2011070102

Kotsonis, E., & Eliakis, S. (2013). Information security standards for health information systems: The implementer's approach. In *User-driven healthcare: Concepts, methodologies, tools, and applications* (pp. 225–257). Hershey, PA: Medical IGI Global. doi:10.4018/978-1-4666-2770-3.ch013

Kraemer, K., & King, J. L. (2006). Information technology and administrative reform: Will e-government be different? *International Journal of Electronic Government Research*, 2(1), 1–20. doi:10.4018/jegr.2006010101

Kraemer, K., & King, J. L. (2008). Information technology and administrative reform: Will e-government be different? In D. Norris (Ed.), *E-government research: Policy and management* (pp. 1–20). Hershey, PA: IGI Global. doi:10.4018/978-1-59904-913-7.ch001

Krishna, A. V. (2014). A randomized cloud library security environment. In S. Dhamdhere (Ed.), *Cloud computing and virtualization technologies in libraries* (pp. 278–296). Hershey, PA: IGI Global. doi:10.4018/978-1-4666-4631-5.ch016

Kruck, S. E., & Teer, F. P. (2011). Computer security practices and perceptions of the next generation of corporate computer users. In H. Nemati (Ed.), *Pervasive information security and privacy developments: Trends and advancements* (pp. 255–265). Hershey, PA: IGI Global. doi:10.4018/978-1-61692-000-5.ch017

Kumar, Hanumanthappa, & Reddy. (2008). *Security issues in m-government.* Academic Press.

Kumar, M., Sareen, M., & Chhabra, S. (2011). Technology related trust issues in SME B2B E-Commerce. *International Journal of Information Communication Technologies and Human Development, 3*(4), 31–46. doi:10.4018/jicthd.2011100103

Kumar, P. S., Ashok, M. S., & Subramanian, R. (2012). A publicly verifiable dynamic secret sharing protocol for secure and dependable data storage in cloud computing. *International Journal of Cloud Applications and Computing, 2*(3), 1–25. doi:10.4018/ijcac.2012070101

Kumar, P., & Mittal, S. (2012). The perpetration and prevention of cyber crime: An analysis of cyber terrorism in India. *International Journal of Technoethics, 3*(1), 43–52. doi:10.4018/jte.2012010104

Kumar, S., & Dutta, K. (2014). Security issues in mobile ad hoc networks: A survey. In D. Rawat, B. Bista, & G. Yan (Eds.), *Security, privacy, trust, and resource management in mobile and wireless communications* (pp. 176–221). Hershey, PA: IGI Global. doi:10.4018/978-1-4666-4691-9.ch009

Kushchu, I., & Kuscu, H. M. (2003). From e-government to m-government: Facing the inevitable. In *Proceeding of European Conference on E-Government (ECEG).* Trinity College.

Kushchu. (2003). *From e-Government to m-Government Facing the Inevitable.* Academic Press.

Lallan, E. (2003). *e-Government for development, m-Government definitions and models.* Retrieved from http://www.egov4dev.org/mgovernment/index.shtml

Lampathaki, F., Tsiakaliaris, C., Stasis, A., & Charalabidis, Y. (2011). National interoperability frameworks: The way forward. In Y. Charalabidis (Ed.), *Interoperability in digital public services and administration: Bridging e-government and e-business* (pp. 1–24). Hershey, PA: IGI Global. doi:10.4018/978-1-61520-887-6.ch001

Lan, Z., & Scott, C. R. (1996). The relative importance of computer-mediated information versus conventional non-computer-mediated information in public managerial decision making. *Information Resources Management Journal, 9*(1), 27–0. doi:10.4018/irmj.1996010103

Lawson, S. (2013). Motivating cybersecurity: Assessing the status of critical infrastructure as an object of cyber threats. In C. Laing, A. Badii, & P. Vickers (Eds.), *Securing critical infrastructures and critical control systems: Approaches for threat protection* (pp. 168–189). Hershey, PA: IGI Global. doi:10.4018/978-1-4666-2659-1.ch007

Law, W. (2004). *Public sector data management in a developing economy*. Hershey, PA: IGI Global. doi:10.4018/978-1-59140-259-6.ch034

Law, W. K. (2005). Information resources development challenges in a cross-cultural environment. In M. Khosrow-Pour (Ed.), *Encyclopedia of information science and technology* (pp. 1476–1481). Hershey, PA: IGI Global. doi:10.4018/978-1-59140-553-5.ch259

Law, W. K. (2009). Cross-cultural challenges for information resources management. In M. Khosrow-Pour (Ed.), *Encyclopedia of information science and technology* (2nd ed.; pp. 840–846). Hershey, PA: IGI Global. doi:10.4018/978-1-60566-026-4.ch136

Law, W. K. (2011). Cross-cultural challenges for information resources management. In *Global business: Concepts, methodologies, tools and applications* (pp. 1924–1932). Hershey, PA: IGI Global. doi:10.4018/978-1-60960-587-2.ch704

Leitch, S., & Warren, M. (2011). The ethics of security of personal information upon Facebook. In M. Quigley (Ed.), *ICT ethics and security in the 21st century: New developments and applications* (pp. 46–65). Hershey, PA: IGI Global. doi:10.4018/978-1-60960-573-5.ch003

Lewis, W., Agarwal, R., & Sambamurthy, V. (2003). Sources of influence on beliefs about information technology use: An empirical study of knowledge workers. *Management Information Systems Quarterly, 27*(4), 657–679.

Liaw, S. S. (2002). Understanding user perceptions of World-Wide Web environments. *Journal of Computer Assisted Learning, 18*(2), 137–148. doi:10.1046/j.0266-4909.2001.00221.x

Liaw, S. S. (2007). Computers and the Internet as a job assisted tool: Based on the three-tier use model approach. *Computers in Human Behavior, 23*(1), 399–414. doi:10.1016/j.chb.2004.10.018

Ligaarden, O. S., Refsdal, A., & Stølen, K. (2013). Using indicators to monitor security risk in systems of systems: How to capture and measure the impact of service dependencies on the security of provided services. In D. Mellado, L. Enrique Sánchez, E. Fernández-Medina, & M. Piattini (Eds.), *IT security governance innovations: Theory and research* (pp. 256–292). Hershey, PA: IGI Global. doi:10.4018/978-1-4666-2083-4.ch010

Li, M. (2013). Security terminology. In A. Miri (Ed.), *Advanced security and privacy for RFID technologies* (pp. 1–13). Hershey, PA: IGI Global. doi:10.4018/978-1-4666-3685-9.ch001

Lim, J. S., Chang, S., Ahmad, A., & Maynard, S. (2012). Towards an organizational culture framework for information security practices. In M. Gupta, J. Walp, & R. Sharman (Eds.), *Strategic and practical approaches for information security governance: Technologies and applied solutions* (pp. 296–315). Hershey, PA: IGI Global. doi:10.4018/978-1-4666-0197-0.ch017

Lindström, J., & Hanken, C. (2012). Security challenges and selected legal aspects for wearable computing. *Journal of Information Technology Research, 5*(1), 68–87. doi:10.4018/jitr.2012010104

Lin, X., & Luppicini, R. (2011). Socio-technical influences of cyber espionage: A case study of the GhostNet system. *International Journal of Technoethics, 2*(2), 65–77. doi:10.4018/jte.2011040105

Lobo, S. (2015). *Government Will Adopt Big Data on a Massive Scale. Analytics Training*. Retrieved from http://analyticstraining.com/2015/jigsaw-academys-predictions-analytics-big-data-industry-2015/

Löhmoeller, J. B. (1984). *LVPS 1.6 program manual: Latent variable path analysis with partial least squares estimation*. Universitaetzu Koehn, Zentralarchivfuer EmpirischeSozialforschung.

Lonergan, A. (2007). Dependability of Electronic Voting Machines. Galway, Ireland: Academic Press.

Lu, J., Yao, J. E., & Yu, C. S. (2005). Personal innovativeness, social influences and adoption of wireless internet services via mobile technology. *The Journal of Strategic Information Systems, 14*(3), 245–268. doi:10.1016/j.jsis.2005.07.003

Maheshwari, H., Hyman, H., & Agrawal, M. (2012). A comparison of cyber-crime definitions in India and the United States. In *Cyber crime: Concepts, methodologies, tools and applications* (pp. 714–726). Hershey, PA: IGI Global. doi:10.4018/978-1-61350-323-2.ch401

Malcolmson, J. (2014). The role of security culture. In I. Portela & F. Almeida (Eds.), *Organizational, legal, and technological dimensions of information system administration* (pp. 225–242). Hershey, PA: IGI Global. doi:10.4018/978-1-4666-4526-4.ch012

Malkia, M., & Savolainen, R. (2004). eTransformation in government, politics and society: Conceptual framework and introduction. In M. Malkia, A. Anttiroiko, & R. Savolainen (Eds.), eTransformation in governance: New directions in government and politics (pp. 1-21). Hershey, PA: IGI Global. doi:10.4018/978-1-59140-130-8.ch001

Mandal, T., Jonathan, Q. M., & Yuan, Y. (2009). Curvelet based face recognition via dimension reduction. Elsevier.

Mandujano, S. (2011). Network manageability security. In D. Kar & M. Syed (Eds.), *Network security, administration and management: Advancing technology and practice* (pp. 158–181). Hershey, PA: IGI Global. doi:10.4018/978-1-60960-777-7.ch009

Mantas, G., Lymberopoulos, D., & Komninos, N. (2011). Security in smart home environment. In A. Lazakidou, K. Siassiakos, & K. Ioannou (Eds.), *Wireless technologies for ambient assisted living and healthcare: Systems and applications* (pp. 170–191). Hershey, PA: Medical IGI Global. doi:10.4018/978-1-61520-805-0.ch010

Maple, C., Short, E., Brown, A., Bryden, C., & Salter, M. (2012). Cyberstalking in the UK: Analysis and recommendations. *International Journal of Distributed Systems and Technologies*, *3*(4), 34–51. doi:10.4018/jdst.2012100104

Maqousi, A., & Balikhina, T. (2011). Building security awareness culture to serve e-government initiative. In A. Al Ajeeli & Y. Al-Bastaki (Eds.), *Handbook of research on e-services in the public sector: E-government strategies and advancements* (pp. 304–311). Hershey, PA: IGI Global. doi:10.4018/978-1-61520-789-3.ch024

Marich, M. J., Schooley, B. L., & Horan, T. A. (2012). A normative enterprise architecture for guiding end-to-end emergency response decision support. In M. Jennex (Ed.), *Managing crises and disasters with emerging technologies: Advancements* (pp. 71–87). Hershey, PA: IGI Global. doi:10.4018/978-1-4666-0167-3.ch006

Markov, R., & Okujava, S. (2008). Costs, benefits, and risks of e-government portals. In G. Putnik & M. Cruz-Cunha (Eds.), *Encyclopedia of networked and virtual organizations* (pp. 354–363). Hershey, PA: IGI Global. doi:10.4018/978-1-59904-885-7.ch047

Martinez de la Cruz, V. (n.d.). *Something about clouds*. Retrieved from http://vmartinezdelacruz.com

Martin, N., & Rice, J. (2013). Evaluating and designing electronic government for the future: Observations and insights from Australia. In V. Weerakkody (Ed.), *E-government services design, adoption, and evaluation* (pp. 238–258). Hershey, PA: IGI Global. doi:10.4018/978-1-4666-2458-0.ch014

Martin, N., & Rice, J. (2013). Spearing high net wealth individuals: The case of online fraud and mature age internet users. *International Journal of Information Security and Privacy*, *7*(1), 1–15. doi:10.4018/jisp.2013010101

Martino, L., & Bertino, E. (2012). Security for web services: Standards and research issues. In L. Jie-Zhang (Ed.), *Innovations, standards and practices of web services: Emerging research topics* (pp. 336–362). Hershey, PA: IGI Global. doi:10.4018/978-1-61350-104-7.ch015

Massonet, P., Michot, A., Naqvi, S., Villari, M., & Latanicki, J. (2013). Securing the external interfaces of a federated infrastructure cloud. In *IT policy and ethics: Concepts, methodologies, tools, and applications* (pp. 1876–1903). Hershey, PA: IGI Global. doi:10.4018/978-1-4666-2919-6.ch082

Mathieson, K. (1991). Predicting user intention: Comparing the technology acceptance model with theory of planned behavior. *Information Systems Research*, *2*(3), 173–191. doi:10.1287/isre.2.3.173

Maumbe, B., & Owei, V. T. (2013). Understanding the information security landscape in South Africa: Implications for strategic collaboration and policy development. In B. Maumbe & C. Patrikakis (Eds.), *E-agriculture and rural development: Global innovations and future prospects* (pp. 90–102). Hershey, PA: IGI Global. doi:10.4018/978-1-4666-2655-3.ch009

Mazumdar, C. (2011). Enterprise information system security: A life-cycle approach. In *Enterprise information systems: Concepts, methodologies, tools and applications* (pp. 154–168). Hershey, PA: IGI Global. doi:10.4018/978-1-61692-852-0.ch111

Mbarika, V. W., Meso, P. N., & Musa, P. F. (2006). A disconnect in stakeholders' perceptions from emerging realities of teledensity growth in Africa's least developed countries. In M. Hunter & F. Tan (Eds.), *Advanced topics in global information management* (Vol. 5, pp. 263–282). Hershey, PA: IGI Global. doi:10.4018/978-1-59140-923-6.ch012

Mbarika, V. W., Meso, P. N., & Musa, P. F. (2008). A disconnect in stakeholders' perceptions from emerging realities of teledensity growth in Africa's least developed countries. In F. Tan (Ed.), *Global information technologies: Concepts, methodologies, tools, and applications* (pp. 2948–2962). Hershey, PA: IGI Global. doi:10.4018/978-1-59904-939-7.ch209

McCune, J., & Haworth, D. A. (2012). Securing America against cyber war. *International Journal of Cyber Warfare & Terrorism*, 2(1), 39–49. doi:10.4018/ijcwt.2012010104

McKeown, B., & Thomas, D. (1988). *Q Methodology*. Newbury Park, CA: Sage Publications, Inc. doi:10.4135/9781412985512

McKinsey & Company (2015). *The Internet of Things: Mapping the Value behind the Hype*. Author.

McKinsey Global Institute. (2015). *Unlocking the potential of the Internet of Things*. Retrieved from http://www.mckinsey.com/business-functions/digital-mckinsey/our-insights/the-internet-of-things-the-value-of-digitizing-the-physical-world

Means, T., Olson, E., & Spooner, J. (2013). Discovering ways that don't work on the road to success: Strengths and weaknesses revealed by an active learning studio classroom project. In A. Benson, J. Moore, & S. Williams van Rooij (Eds.), *Cases on educational technology planning, design, and implementation: A project management perspective* (pp. 94–113). Hershey, PA: IGI Global. doi:10.4018/978-1-4666-4237-9.ch006

Megh, R. (2015). *GI Cloud– A Cloud Computing Initiative of MeitY*. Ministry of Electronics and Information Technology, India. Retrieved from http://deity.gov.in/content/e-governance

Melitski, J., Holzer, M., Kim, S., Kim, C., & Rho, S. (2008). Digital government worldwide: An e-government assessment of municipal web sites. In G. Garson & M. Khosrow-Pour (Eds.), *Handbook of research on public information technology* (pp. 790–804). Hershey, PA: IGI Global. doi:10.4018/978-1-59904-857-4.ch069

Mell, P., & Grance, T. (2009). The NIST Definition of Cloud Computing, National Institute of Standards and Technology, Information Technology Laboratory. *Technical Report Version*, 15, 2009.

Melvin, A. O., & Ayotunde, T. (2011). Spirituality in cybercrime (Yahoo Yahoo) activities among youths in south west Nigeria. In E. Dunkels, G. Franberg, & C. Hallgren (Eds.), *Youth culture and net culture: Online social practices* (pp. 357–380). Hershey, PA: IGI Global. doi:10.4018/978-1-60960-209-3.ch020

Memmola, M., Palumbo, G., & Rossini, M. (2009). Web & RFID technology: New frontiers in costing and process management for rehabilitation medicine. In L. Al-Hakim & M. Memmola (Eds.), *Business web strategy: Design, alignment, and application* (pp. 145–169). Hershey, PA: IGI Global. doi:10.4018/978-1-60566-024-0.ch008

Mengistu, H., & Rho, J. (2009). *M-Government opportunities and Challenges to Deliver Mobile Government Services in Developing Countries*. Academic Press.

Meng, Z., Fahong, Z., & Lei, L. (2008). Information technology and environment. In Y. Kurihara, S. Takaya, H. Harui, & H. Kamae (Eds.), *Information technology and economic development* (pp. 201–212). Hershey, PA: IGI Global. doi:10.4018/978-1-59904-579-5.ch014

Mentzingen de Moraes, A. J., Ferneda, E., Costa, I., & Spinola, M. D. (2011). Practical approach for implementation of governance process in IT: Information technology areas. In N. Shi & G. Silvius (Eds.), *Enterprise IT governance, business value and performance measurement* (pp. 19–40). Hershey, PA: IGI Global. doi:10.4018/978-1-60566-346-3.ch002

Merwin, G. A. Jr, McDonald, J. S., & Odera, L. C. (2008). Economic development: Government's cutting edge in IT. In M. Raisinghani (Ed.), *Handbook of research on global information technology management in the digital economy* (pp. 1–37). Hershey, PA: IGI Global. doi:10.4018/978-1-59904-875-8.ch001

Meso, P. N., & Duncan, N. B. (2002). Can national information infrastructures enhance social development in the least developed countries? In F. Tan (Ed.), *Advanced topics in global information management* (Vol. 1, pp. 207–226). Hershey, PA: IGI Global. doi:10.4018/978-1-930708-43-3.ch014

Meso, P., & Duncan, N. (2002). Can national information infrastructures enhance social development in the least developed countries? An empirical investigation. In M. Dadashzadeh (Ed.), *Information technology management in developing countries* (pp. 23–51). Hershey, PA: IGI Global. doi:10.4018/978-1-931777-03-2.ch002

Middleton, M. (2008). Evaluation of e-government web sites. In G. Garson & M. Khosrow-Pour (Eds.), *Handbook of research on public information technology* (pp. 699–710). Hershey, PA: IGI Global. doi:10.4018/978-1-59904-857-4.ch063

Miller, J. M., Higgins, G. E., & Lopez, K. M. (2013). Considering the role of e-government in cybercrime awareness and prevention: Toward a theoretical research program for the 21st century. In *Digital rights management: Concepts, methodologies, tools, and applications* (pp. 789–800). Hershey, PA: IGI Global. doi:10.4018/978-1-4666-2136-7.ch036

Millman, C., Whitty, M., Winder, B., & Griffiths, M. D. (2012). Perceived criminality of cyber-harassing behaviors among undergraduate students in the United Kingdom. *International Journal of Cyber Behavior, Psychology and Learning*, 2(4), 49–59. doi:10.4018/ijcbpl.2012100104

Minami, N. A. (2012). Employing dynamic models to enhance corporate IT security policy. *International Journal of Agent Technologies and Systems*, *4*(2), 42–59. doi:10.4018/jats.2012040103

Mingers, J. (2010). Pluralism, realism, and truth: The keys to knowledge in information systems research. In D. Paradice (Ed.), *Emerging systems approaches in information technologies: Concepts, theories, and applications* (pp. 86–98). Hershey, PA: IGI Global. doi:10.4018/978-1-60566-976-2.ch006

Ministry of Electronics and Information Technology. (2015). *National e-Governance Plan of India*. Retrieved from http://deity.gov.in/content/national-e-governance-plan

Mirante, D. P., & Ammari, H. M. (2014). Wireless sensor network security attacks: A survey. In *Crisis management: Concepts, methodologies, tools and applications* (pp. 25–59). Hershey, PA: IGI Global. doi:10.4018/978-1-4666-4707-7.ch002

Mishra, A., & Mishra, D. (2013). Cyber stalking: A challenge for web security. In J. Bishop (Ed.), *Examining the concepts, issues, and implications of internet trolling* (pp. 32–42). Hershey, PA: IGI Global. doi:10.4018/978-1-4666-2803-8.ch004

Mishra, S. (2011). Wireless sensor networks: Emerging applications and security solutions. In D. Kar & M. Syed (Eds.), *Network security, administration and management: Advancing technology and practice* (pp. 217–236). Hershey, PA: IGI Global. doi:10.4018/978-1-60960-777-7.ch011

Mital, K. M. (2012). ICT, unique identity and inclusive growth: An Indian perspective. In A. Manoharan & M. Holzer (Eds.), *E-governance and civic engagement: Factors and determinants of e-democracy* (pp. 584–612). Hershey, PA: IGI Global. doi:10.4018/978-1-61350-083-5.ch029

Mitra, S., & Padman, R. (2012). Privacy and security concerns in adopting social media for personal health management: A health plan case study. *Journal of Cases on Information Technology*, *14*(4), 12–26. doi:10.4018/jcit.2012100102

Mizell, A. P. (2008). Helping close the digital divide for financially disadvantaged seniors. In F. Tan (Ed.), *Global information technologies: Concepts, methodologies, tools, and applications* (pp. 2396–2402). Hershey, PA: IGI Global. doi:10.4018/978-1-59904-939-7.ch173

Modares, H., Lloret, J., Moravejosharieh, A., & Salleh, R. (2014). Security in mobile cloud computing. In J. Rodrigues, K. Lin, & J. Lloret (Eds.), *Mobile networks and cloud computing convergence for progressive services and applications* (pp. 79–91). Hershey, PA: IGI Global. doi:10.4018/978-1-4666-4781-7.ch005

Mohammadi, S., Golara, S., & Mousavi, N. (2012). Selecting adequate security mechanisms in e-business processes using fuzzy TOPSIS. *International Journal of Fuzzy System Applications*, 2(1), 35–53. doi:10.4018/ijfsa.2012010103

Mohammed, L. A. (2012). ICT security policy: Challenges and potential remedies. In *Cyber crime: Concepts, methodologies, tools and applications* (pp. 999–1015). Hershey, PA: IGI Global. doi:10.4018/978-1-61350-323-2.ch501

Molinari, F., Wills, C., Koumpis, A., & Moumtzi, V. (2011). A citizen-centric platform to support networking in the area of e-democracy. In H. Rahman (Ed.), *Cases on adoption, diffusion and evaluation of global e-governance systems: Impact at the grass roots* (pp. 282–302). Hershey, PA: IGI Global. doi:10.4018/978-1-61692-814-8.ch014

Molinari, F., Wills, C., Koumpis, A., & Moumtzi, V. (2013). A citizen-centric platform to support networking in the area of e-democracy. In H. Rahman (Ed.), *Cases on progressions and challenges in ICT utilization for citizen-centric governance* (pp. 265–297). Hershey, PA: IGI Global. doi:10.4018/978-1-4666-2071-1.ch013

Molok, N. N., Ahmad, A., & Chang, S. (2012). Online social networking: A source of intelligence for advanced persistent threats. *International Journal of Cyber Warfare & Terrorism*, 2(1), 1–13. doi:10.4018/ijcwt.2012010101

Monteleone, S. (2011). Ambient intelligence: Legal challenges and possible directions for privacy protection. In C. Akrivopoulou & A. Psygkas (Eds.), *Personal data privacy and protection in a surveillance era: Technologies and practices* (pp. 201–221). Hershey, PA: IGI Global. doi:10.4018/978-1-60960-083-9.ch012

Monteverde, F. (2010). The process of e-government public policy inclusion in the governmental agenda: A framework for assessment and case study. In J. Cordoba-Pachon & A. Ochoa-Arias (Eds.), *Systems thinking and e-participation: ICT in the governance of society* (pp. 233–245). Hershey, PA: IGI Global. doi:10.4018/978-1-60566-860-4.ch015

Moodley, S. (2008). Deconstructing the South African government's ICT for development discourse. In A. Anttiroiko (Ed.), *Electronic government: Concepts, methodologies, tools, and applications* (pp. 622–631). Hershey, PA: IGI Global. doi:10.4018/978-1-59904-947-2.ch053

Moodley, S. (2008). Deconstructing the South African government's ICT for development discourse. In C. Van Slyke (Ed.), *Information communication technologies: Concepts, methodologies, tools, and applications* (pp. 816–825). Hershey, PA: IGI Global. doi:10.4018/978-1-59904-949-6.ch052

MoPAS & NIA of Korea. (2011). *Smart Government Implementation Plan*. Retrieved from http://www.mospa.go.kr/

MoPAS. NIA of Korea. (2013). m-Government of Korea. Author.

Moralis, A., Pouli, V., Grammatikou, M., Kalogeras, D., & Maglaris, V. (2012). Security standards and issues for grid computing. In N. Preve (Ed.), *Computational and data grids: Principles, applications and design* (pp. 248–264). Hershey, PA: IGI Global. doi:10.4018/978-1-61350-113-9.ch010

Mora, M., Cervantes-Perez, F., Gelman-Muravchik, O., Forgionne, G. A., & Mejia-Olvera, M. (2003). DMSS implementation research: A conceptual analysis of the contributions and limitations of the factor-based and stage-based streams. In G. Forgionne, J. Gupta, & M. Mora (Eds.), *Decision-making support systems: Achievements and challenges for the new decade* (pp. 331–356). Hershey, PA: IGI Global. doi:10.4018/978-1-59140-045-5.ch020

Mörtberg, C., & Elovaara, P. (2010). Attaching people and technology: Between e and government. In S. Booth, S. Goodman, & G. Kirkup (Eds.), *Gender issues in learning and working with information technology: Social constructs and cultural contexts* (pp. 83–98). Hershey, PA: IGI Global. doi:10.4018/978-1-61520-813-5.ch005

Mouratidis, H., & Kang, M. (2011). Secure by design: Developing secure software systems from the ground up. *International Journal of Secure Software Engineering*, 2(3), 23–41. doi:10.4018/jsse.2011070102

Murphy, J., Harper, E., Devine, E. C., Burke, L. J., & Hook, M. L. (2011). Case study: Lessons learned when embedding evidence-based knowledge in a nurse care planning and documentation system. In A. Cashin & R. Cook (Eds.), *Evidence-based practice in nursing informatics: Concepts and applications* (pp. 174–190). Hershey, PA: IGI Global. doi:10.4018/978-1-60960-034-1.ch014

Murthy, A. S., Nagadevara, V., & De', R. (2012). Predictive models in cybercrime investigation: An application of data mining techniques. In J. Wang (Ed.), *Advancing the service sector with evolving technologies: Techniques and principles* (pp. 166–177). Hershey, PA: IGI Global. doi:10.4018/978-1-4666-0044-7.ch011

Mutula, S. M. (2013). E-government's role in poverty alleviation: Case study of South Africa. In H. Rahman (Ed.), *Cases on progressions and challenges in ICT utilization for citizen-centric governance* (pp. 44–68). Hershey, PA: IGI Global. doi:10.4018/978-1-4666-2071-1.ch003

Nabi, S. I., Al-Ghmlas, G. S., & Alghathbar, K. (2012). Enterprise information security policies, standards, and procedures: A survey of available standards and guidelines. In M. Gupta, J. Walp, & R. Sharman (Eds.), *Strategic and practical approaches for information security governance: Technologies and applied solutions* (pp. 67–89). Hershey, PA: IGI Global. doi:10.4018/978-1-4666-0197-0.ch005

Nachtigal, S. (2011). E-business and security. In O. Bak & N. Stair (Eds.), *Impact of e-business technologies on public and private organizations: Industry comparisons and perspectives* (pp. 262–277). Hershey, PA: IGI Global. doi:10.4018/978-1-60960-501-8.ch016

Nahm, A. Y., Solis-Galvan, L. E., & Rao, S. S. (2002). The Q-Sort method: Assessing reliability and construct validity of questionnaire items at a pre-testing stage. *Journal of Modern Applied Statistical Methods; JMASM, 1*(1), 114–125. doi:10.22237/jmasm/1020255360

Namal, S., & Gurtov, A. (2012). Security and mobility aspects of femtocell networks. In R. Saeed, B. Chaudhari, & R. Mokhtar (Eds.), *Femtocell communications and technologies: Business opportunities and deployment challenges* (pp. 124–156). Hershey, PA: IGI Global. doi:10.4018/978-1-4666-0092-8.ch008

Naqvi, D. E. (2011). Designing efficient security services infrastructure for virtualization oriented architectures. In H. Nemati (Ed.), *Pervasive information security and privacy developments: Trends and advancements* (pp. 149–171). Hershey, PA: IGI Global. doi:10.4018/978-1-61692-000-5.ch011

Nath, R., & Angeles, R. (2005). Relationships between supply characteristics and buyer-supplier coupling in e-procurement: An empirical analysis. *International Journal of E-Business Research, 1*(2), 40–55. doi:10.4018/jebr.2005040103

Ndou, V. (2004). E-government for developing countries: Opportunities and challenges. *Electronic Journal on Information Systems in Developing Countries, 18*(1), 1–24.

Neto, A. A., & Vieira, M. (2011). Security gaps in databases: A comparison of alternative software products for web applications support. *International Journal of Secure Software Engineering, 2*(3), 42–62. doi:10.4018/jsse.2011070103

Ngugi, B., Mana, J., & Segal, L. (2011). Evaluating the quality and usefulness of data breach information systems. *International Journal of Information Security and Privacy, 5*(4), 31–46. doi:10.4018/jisp.2011100103

Nhlabatsi, A., Bandara, A., Hayashi, S., Haley, C., Jurjens, J., & Kaiya, H. … Yu, Y. (2011). Security patterns: Comparing modeling approaches. In H. Mouratidis (Ed.), *Software engineering for secure systems: Industrial and research perspectives* (pp. 75-111). Hershey, PA: IGI Global. doi:10.4018/978-1-61520-837-1.ch004

NIC Data Centers. (2014). *Core of e-Governance Infrastructure of India*. Retrieved from http://datacentres.nic.in/ndcshastripark.html

Nicho, M. (2013). An information governance model for information security management. In D. Mellado, L. Enrique Sánchez, E. Fernández-Medina, & M. Piattini (Eds.), *IT security governance innovations: Theory and research* (pp. 155–189). Hershey, PA: IGI Global. doi:10.4018/978-1-4666-2083-4.ch007

Nicho, M., Fakhry, H., & Haiber, C. (2011). An integrated security governance framework for effective PCI DSS implementation. *International Journal of Information Security and Privacy*, *5*(3), 50–67. doi:10.4018/jisp.2011070104

Nissen, M. E. (2006). Application cases in government. In M. Nissen (Ed.), *Harnessing knowledge dynamics: Principled organizational knowing & learning* (pp. 152–181). Hershey, PA: IGI Global. doi:10.4018/978-1-59140-773-7.ch008

NIST. (2011). *Cloud computing definition publication*. NIST.

Nobelis, N., Boudaoud, K., Delettre, C., & Riveill, M. (2012). Designing security properties-centric communication protocols using a component-based approach. *International Journal of Distributed Systems and Technologies*, *3*(1), 1–16. doi:10.4018/jdst.2012010101

Norris, D. F. (2003). Leading-edge information technologies and American local governments. In G. Garson (Ed.), *Public information technology: Policy and management issues* (pp. 139–169). Hershey, PA: IGI Global. doi:10.4018/978-1-59140-060-8.ch007

Norris, D. F. (2008). Information technology among U.S. local governments. In G. Garson & M. Khosrow-Pour (Eds.), *Handbook of research on public information technology* (pp. 132–144). Hershey, PA: IGI Global. doi:10.4018/978-1-59904-857-4.ch013

Northrop, A. (1999). The challenge of teaching information technology in public administration graduate programs. In G. Garson (Ed.), *Information technology and computer applications in public administration: Issues and trends* (pp. 1–22). Hershey, PA: IGI Global. doi:10.4018/978-1-87828-952-0.ch001

Northrop, A. (2003). Information technology and public administration: The view from the profession. In G. Garson (Ed.), *Public information technology: Policy and management issues* (pp. 1–19). Hershey, PA: IGI Global. doi:10.4018/978-1-59140-060-8.ch001

Northrop, A. (2007). Lip service? How PA journals and textbooks view information technology. In G. Garson (Ed.), *Modern public information technology systems: Issues and challenges* (pp. 1–16). Hershey, PA: IGI Global. doi:10.4018/978-1-59904-051-6.ch001

Ntaliani, M. (2006). *M-Government challenges for agriculture*. Academic Press.

Null, E. (2013). Legal and political barriers to municipal networks in the United States. In A. Abdelaal (Ed.), *Social and economic effects of community wireless networks and infrastructures* (pp. 27–56). Hershey, PA: IGI Global. doi:10.4018/978-1-4666-2997-4.ch003

Nunnally, J. C. (1978). *Psychometric Theory*. New York: McGraw-Hill.

Odongo, A. O. (2009). *Electronic Government system architecture design directed by an e-Government development process*. Academic Press.

Ofori-Dwumfuo, G., & Paatey, E. (2011). *The Design of an Electronic Voting System. Research Journal of Information Technology*.

Ohashi, M., & Hori, M. (2011). Security management services based on authentication roaming between different certificate authorities. In M. Cruz-Cunha & J. Varajao (Eds.), *Enterprise information systems design, implementation and management: Organizational applications* (pp. 72–84). Hershey, PA: IGI Global. doi:10.4018/978-1-61692-020-3.ch005

Okubo, T., Kaiya, H., & Yoshioka, N. (2012). Analyzing impacts on software enhancement caused by security design alternatives with patterns. *International Journal of Secure Software Engineering, 3*(1), 37–61. doi:10.4018/jsse.2012010103

Okunoye, A., Frolick, M., & Crable, E. (2006). ERP implementation in higher education: An account of pre-implementation and implementation phases. *Journal of Cases on Information Technology, 8*(2), 110–132. doi:10.4018/jcit.2006040106

Olasina, G. (2012). A review of egovernment services in Nigeria. In A. Tella & A. Issa (Eds.), *Library and information science in developing countries: Contemporary issues* (pp. 205–221). Hershey, PA: IGI Global. doi:10.4018/978-1-61350-335-5.ch015

Oost, D., & Chew, E. K. (2012). Investigating the concept of information security culture. In M. Gupta, J. Walp, & R. Sharman (Eds.), *Strategic and practical approaches for information security governance: Technologies and applied solutions* (pp. 1–12). Hershey, PA: IGI Global. doi:10.4018/978-1-4666-0197-0.ch001

Orgeron, C. P. (2008). A model for reengineering IT job classes in state government. In G. Garson & M. Khosrow-Pour (Eds.), *Handbook of research on public information technology* (pp. 735–746). Hershey, PA: IGI Global. doi:10.4018/978-1-59904-857-4.ch066

Ostberg, O. (2003). A Swedish view on 'mobile government'. *Proceedings of International Symposium on E- & M-Government.*

Otero, A. R., Ejnioui, A., Otero, C. E., & Tejay, G. (2013). Evaluation of information security controls in organizations by grey relational analysis. *International Journal of Dependable and Trustworthy Information Systems, 2*(3), 36–54. doi:10.4018/jdtis.2011070103

Ouedraogo, M., Mouratidis, H., Dubois, E., & Khadraoui, D. (2011). Security assurance evaluation and IT systems context of use security criticality. *International Journal of Handheld Computing Research, 2*(4), 59–81. doi:10.4018/jhcr.2011100104

Owsinski, J. W., & Pielak, A. M. (2011). Local authority websites in rural areas: Measuring quality and functionality, and assessing the role. In Z. Andreopoulou, B. Manos, N. Polman, & D. Viaggi (Eds.), *Agricultural and environmental informatics, governance and management: Emerging research applications* (pp. 39–60). Hershey, PA: IGI Global. doi:10.4018/978-1-60960-621-3.ch003

Owsiński, J. W., Pielak, A. M., Sęp, K., & Stańczak, J. (2014). Local web-based networks in rural municipalities: Extension, density, and meaning. In Z. Andreopoulou, V. Samathrakis, S. Louca, & M. Vlachopoulou (Eds.), *E-innovation for sustainable development of rural resources during global economic crisis* (pp. 126–151). Hershey, PA: IGI Global. doi:10.4018/978-1-4666-4550-9.ch011

Pagani, M., & Pasinetti, C. (2008). Technical and functional quality in the development of t-government services. In A. Anttiroiko (Ed.), *Electronic government: Concepts, methodologies, tools, and applications* (pp. 2943–2965). Hershey, PA: IGI Global. doi:10.4018/978-1-59904-947-2.ch220

Palanisamy, R., & Mukerji, B. (2012). Security and privacy issues in e-government. In M. Shareef, N. Archer, & S. Dutta (Eds.), *E-government service maturity and development: Cultural, organizational and technological perspectives* (pp. 236–248). Hershey, PA: IGI Global. doi:10.4018/978-1-60960-848-4.ch013

Pal, S. (2013). Cloud computing: Security concerns and issues. In A. Bento & A. Aggarwal (Eds.), *Cloud computing service and deployment models: Layers and management* (pp. 191–207). Hershey, PA: IGI Global. doi:10.4018/978-1-4666-2187-9.ch010

Pani, A. K., & Agrahari, A. (2005). On e-markets in emerging economy: An Indian experience. In M. Khosrow-Pour (Ed.), *Advanced topics in electronic commerce* (Vol. 1, pp. 287–299). Hershey, PA: IGI Global. doi:10.4018/978-1-59140-819-2.ch015

Pan, Y., Yuan, B., & Mishra, S. (2011). Network security auditing. In D. Kar & M. Syed (Eds.), *Network security, administration and management: Advancing technology and practice* (pp. 131–157). Hershey, PA: IGI Global. doi:10.4018/978-1-60960-777-7.ch008

Papadopoulos, T., Angelopoulos, S., & Kitsios, F. (2011). A strategic approach to e-health interoperability using e-government frameworks. In A. Lazakidou, K. Siassiakos, & K. Ioannou (Eds.), *Wireless technologies for ambient assisted living and healthcare: Systems and applications* (pp. 213–229). Hershey, PA: IGI Global. doi:10.4018/978-1-61520-805-0.ch012

Papadopoulos, T., Angelopoulos, S., & Kitsios, F. (2013). A strategic approach to e-health interoperability using e-government frameworks. In *User-driven healthcare: Concepts, methodologies, tools, and applications* (pp. 791–807). Hershey, PA: IGI Global. doi:10.4018/978-1-4666-2770-3.ch039

Papaleo, G., Chiarella, D., Aiello, M., & Caviglione, L. (2012). Analysis, development and deployment of statistical anomaly detection techniques for real e-mail traffic. In T. Chou (Ed.), *Information assurance and security technologies for risk assessment and threat management: Advances* (pp. 47–71). Hershey, PA: IGI Global. doi:10.4018/978-1-61350-507-6.ch003

Papazoglou, M. P. (1990). Distributed database architectures. *IEEE International Conference on Databases, Parallel Architectures and Their Applications, PARBASE-90*. doi:10.1109/PARBSE.1990.77215

Papp, R. (2003). Information technology & FDA compliance in the pharmaceutical industry. In M. Khosrow-Pour (Ed.), *Annals of cases on information technology* (Vol. 5, pp. 262–273). Hershey, PA: IGI Global. doi:10.4018/978-1-59140-061-5.ch017

Parsons, T. W. (2007). Developing a knowledge management portal. In A. Tatnall (Ed.), *Encyclopedia of portal technologies and applications* (pp. 223–227). Hershey, PA: IGI Global. doi:10.4018/978-1-59140-989-2.ch039

Passaris, C. E. (2007). Immigration and digital government. In A. Anttiroiko & M. Malkia (Eds.), *Encyclopedia of digital government* (pp. 988–994). Hershey, PA: IGI Global. doi:10.4018/978-1-59140-789-8.ch148

Patel, A., Taghavi, M., Júnior, J. C., Latih, R., & Zin, A. M. (2012). Safety measures for social computing in wiki learning environment. *International Journal of Information Security and Privacy, 6*(2), 1–15. doi:10.4018/jisp.2012040101

Pathan, A. K. (2012). Security management in heterogeneous distributed sensor networks. In S. Bagchi (Ed.), *Ubiquitous multimedia and mobile agents: Models and implementations* (pp. 274–294). Hershey, PA: IGI Global. doi:10.4018/978-1-61350-107-8.ch012

Paul, C., & Porche, I. R. (2011). Toward a U.S. army cyber security culture. *International Journal of Cyber Warfare & Terrorism, 1*(3), 70–80. doi:10.4018/ijcwt.2011070105

Pavlichev, A. (2004). The e-government challenge for public administration. In A. Pavlichev & G. Garson (Eds.), *Digital government: Principles and best practices* (pp. 276–290). Hershey, PA: IGI Global. doi:10.4018/978-1-59140-122-3.ch018

Pavlidis, M., Mouratidis, H., & Islam, S. (2012). Modelling security using trust based concepts. *International Journal of Secure Software Engineering, 3*(2), 36–53. doi:10.4018/jsse.2012040102

Pendegraft, N., Rounds, M., & Stone, R. W. (2012). Factors influencing college students' use of computer security. In H. Nemati (Ed.), *Optimizing information security and advancing privacy assurance: New technologies* (pp. 225–234). Hershey, PA: IGI Global. doi:10.4018/978-1-4666-0026-3.ch013

Penrod, J. I., & Harbor, A. F. (2000). Designing and implementing a learning organization-oriented information technology planning and management process. In L. Petrides (Ed.), *Case studies on information technology in higher education: Implications for policy and practice* (pp. 7–19). Hershey, PA: IGI Global. doi:10.4018/978-1-878289-74-2.ch001

Petkovic, M., & Ibraimi, L. (2011). Privacy and security in e-health applications. In C. Röcker & M. Ziefle (Eds.), *E-health, assistive technologies and applications for assisted living: Challenges and solutions* (pp. 23–48). Hershey, PA: IGI Global. doi:10.4018/978-1-60960-469-1.ch002

Pfleeger, C., & Pfleeger, S. (2007). *Security in Computing* (4th ed.). Upper Saddle River, NJ: Prentice Hall.

Picazo-Sanchez, P., Ortiz-Martin, L., Peris-Lopez, P., & Hernandez-Castro, J. C. (2013). Security of EPC class-1. In P. Lopez, J. Hernandez-Castro, & T. Li (Eds.), *Security and trends in wireless identification and sensing platform tags: Advancements in RFID* (pp. 34–63). Hershey, PA: IGI Global. doi:10.4018/978-1-4666-1990-6.ch002

Pieters, W., Probst, C. W., Lukszo, Z., & Montoya, L. (2014). Cost-effectiveness of security measures: A model-based framework. In T. Tsiakis, T. Kargidis, & P. Katsaros (Eds.), *Approaches and processes for managing the economics of information systems* (pp. 139–156). Hershey, PA: IGI Global. doi:10.4018/978-1-4666-4983-5.ch009

Pirim, T., James, T., Boswell, K., Reithel, B., & Barkhi, R. (2011). Examining an individual's perceived need for privacy and security: Construct and scale development. In H. Nemati (Ed.), *Pervasive information security and privacy developments: Trends and advancements* (pp. 1–13). Hershey, PA: IGI Global. doi:10.4018/978-1-61692-000-5.ch001

Planas-Silva, M. D., & Joseph, R. C. (2011). Perspectives on the adoption of electronic resources for use in clinical trials. In M. Guah (Ed.), *Healthcare delivery reform and new technologies: Organizational initiatives* (pp. 19–28). Hershey, PA: IGI Global. doi:10.4018/978-1-60960-183-6.ch002

Podhradsky, A., Casey, C., & Ceretti, P. (2012). The bluetooth honeypot project: Measuring and managing bluetooth risks in the workplace. *International Journal of Interdisciplinary Telecommunications and Networking*, *4*(3), 1–22. doi:10.4018/jitn.2012070101

Pomazalová, N., & Rejman, S. (2013). The rationale behind implementation of new electronic tools for electronic public procurement. In N. Pomazalová (Ed.), *Public sector transformation processes and internet public procurement: Decision support systems* (pp. 85–117). Hershey, PA: IGI Global. doi:10.4018/978-1-4666-2665-2.ch006

Pomponiu, V. (2011). Security in e-health applications. In C. Röcker & M. Ziefle (Eds.), *E-health, assistive technologies and applications for assisted living: Challenges and solutions* (pp. 94–118). Hershey, PA: IGI Global. doi:10.4018/978-1-60960-469-1.ch005

Pomponiu, V. (2014). Securing wireless ad hoc networks: State of the art and challenges. In *Crisis management: Concepts, methodologies, tools and applications* (pp. 81–101). Hershey, PA: IGI Global. doi:10.4018/978-1-4666-4707-7.ch004

Pope, M. B., Warkentin, M., & Luo, X. R. (2012). Evolutionary malware: Mobile malware, botnets, and malware toolkits. *International Journal of Wireless Networks and Broadband Technologies*, 2(3), 52–60. doi:10.4018/ijwnbt.2012070103

Postorino, M. N. (2012). City competitiveness and airport: Information science perspective. In M. Bulu (Ed.), *City competitiveness and improving urban subsystems: Technologies and applications* (pp. 61–83). Hershey, PA: IGI Global. doi:10.4018/978-1-61350-174-0.ch004

Poupa, C. (2002). Electronic government in Switzerland: Priorities for 2001-2005 - Electronic voting and federal portal. In Å. Grönlund (Ed.), *Electronic government: Design, applications and management* (pp. 356–369). Hershey, PA: IGI Global. doi:10.4018/978-1-930708-19-8.ch017

Powell, S. R. (2010). Interdisciplinarity in telecommunications and networking. In *Networking and telecommunications: Concepts, methodologies, tools and applications* (pp. 33–40). Hershey, PA: IGI Global. doi:10.4018/978-1-60566-986-1.ch004

Prakash, S., Vaish, A., Coul, N. G. S., Srinidhi, T., & Botsa, J. (2013). Child security in cyberspace through moral cognition. *International Journal of Information Security and Privacy*, 7(1), 16–29. doi:10.4018/jisp.2013010102

Priya, P. S., & Mathiyalagan, N. (2011). A study of the implementation status of two e-governance projects in land revenue administration in India. In M. Shareef, V. Kumar, U. Kumar, & Y. Dwivedi (Eds.), *Stakeholder adoption of e-government services: Driving and resisting factors* (pp. 214–230). Hershey, PA: IGI Global. doi:10.4018/978-1-60960-601-5.ch011

Prysby, C. L., & Prysby, N. D. (2003). Electronic mail in the public workplace: Issues of privacy and public disclosure. In G. Garson (Ed.), *Public information technology: Policy and management issues* (pp. 271–298). Hershey, PA: IGI Global. doi:10.4018/978-1-59140-060-8.ch012

Prysby, C. L., & Prysby, N. D. (2007). You have mail, but who is reading it? Issues of e-mail in the public workplace. In G. Garson (Ed.), *Modern public information technology systems: Issues and challenges* (pp. 312–336). Hershey, PA: IGI Global. doi:10.4018/978-1-59904-051-6.ch016

Prysby, C., & Prysby, N. (2000). Electronic mail, employee privacy and the workplace. In L. Janczewski (Ed.), *Internet and intranet security management: Risks and solutions* (pp. 251–270). Hershey, PA: IGI Global. doi:10.4018/978-1-878289-71-1.ch009

Pye, G. (2011). Critical infrastructure systems: Security analysis and modelling approach. *International Journal of Cyber Warfare & Terrorism*, *1*(3), 37–58. doi:10.4018/ijcwt.2011070103

Radl, A., & Chen, Y. (2005). Computer security in electronic government: A state-local education information system. *International Journal of Electronic Government Research*, *1*(1), 79–99. doi:10.4018/jegr.2005010105

Rahman, H. (2008). Information dynamics in developing countries. In C. Van Slyke (Ed.), *Information communication technologies: Concepts, methodologies, tools, and applications* (pp. 104–114). Hershey, PA: IGI Global. doi:10.4018/978-1-59904-949-6.ch008

Rahman, M. M., & Rezaul, K. M. (2012). Information security management: Awareness of threats in e-commerce. In M. Gupta, J. Walp, & R. Sharman (Eds.), *Threats, countermeasures, and advances in applied information security* (pp. 66–90). Hershey, PA: IGI Global. doi:10.4018/978-1-4666-0978-5.ch004

Rajagopalan, M. R. (2013). Big Data Framework for National e-Governance Plan. *IEEE 2013 Eleventh International Conference on ICT and Knowledge Engineering.*

Rak, M., Ficco, M., Luna, J., Ghani, H., Suri, N., Panica, S., & Petcu, D. (2012). Security issues in cloud federations. In M. Villari, I. Brandic, & F. Tusa (Eds.), *Achieving federated and self-manageable cloud infrastructures: Theory and practice* (pp. 176–194). Hershey, PA: IGI Global. doi:10.4018/978-1-4666-1631-8.ch010

Ramachandran, M., & Mahmood, Z. (2011). A framework for internet security assessment and improvement process. In M. Ramachandran (Ed.), *Knowledge engineering for software development life cycles: Support technologies and applications* (pp. 244–255). Hershey, PA: IGI Global. doi:10.4018/978-1-60960-509-4.ch013

Ramachandran, S., Mundada, R., Bhattacharjee, A., Murthy, C., & Sharma, R. (2011). Classifying host anomalies: Using ontology in information security monitoring. In R. Santanam, M. Sethumadhavan, & M. Virendra (Eds.), *Cyber security, cyber crime and cyber forensics: Applications and perspectives* (pp. 70–86). Hershey, PA: IGI Global. doi:10.4018/978-1-60960-123-2.ch006

Ramamurthy, B. (2014). Securing business IT on the cloud. In S. Srinivasan (Ed.), *Security, trust, and regulatory aspects of cloud computing in business environments* (pp. 115–125). Hershey, PA: IGI Global. doi:10.4018/978-1-4666-5788-5.ch006

Ramanathan, J. (2009). Adaptive IT architecture as a catalyst for network capability in government. In P. Saha (Ed.), *Advances in government enterprise architecture* (pp. 149–172). Hershey, PA: IGI Global. doi:10.4018/978-1-60566-068-4.ch007

Ramos, I., & Berry, D. M. (2006). Social construction of information technology supporting work. In M. Khosrow-Pour (Ed.), *Cases on information technology: Lessons learned* (Vol. 7, pp. 36–52). Hershey, PA: IGI Global. doi:10.4018/978-1-59140-673-0.ch003

Raspotnig, C., & Opdahl, A. L. (2012). Improving security and safety modelling with failure sequence diagrams. *International Journal of Secure Software Engineering, 3*(1), 20–36. doi:10.4018/jsse.2012010102

Ray, D., Gulla, U., Gupta, M. P., & Dash, S. S. (2009). Interoperability and constituents of interoperable systems in public sector. In V. Weerakkody, M. Janssen, & Y. Dwivedi (Eds.), *Handbook of research on ICT-enabled transformational government: A global perspective* (pp. 175–195). Hershey, PA: IGI Global. doi:10.4018/978-1-60566-390-6.ch010

Reddick, C. G. (2007). E-government and creating a citizen-centric government: A study of federal government CIOs. In G. Garson (Ed.), *Modern public information technology systems: Issues and challenges* (pp. 143–165). Hershey, PA: IGI Global. doi:10.4018/978-1-59904-051-6.ch008

Reddick, C. G. (2010). Citizen-centric e-government. In C. Reddick (Ed.), *Homeland security preparedness and information systems: Strategies for managing public policy* (pp. 45–75). Hershey, PA: IGI Global. doi:10.4018/978-1-60566-834-5.ch002

Reddick, C. G. (2010). E-government and creating a citizen-centric government: A study of federal government CIOs. In C. Reddick (Ed.), *Homeland security preparedness and information systems: Strategies for managing public policy* (pp. 230–250). Hershey, PA: IGI Global. doi:10.4018/978-1-60566-834-5.ch012

Reddick, C. G. (2010). Perceived effectiveness of e-government and its usage in city governments: Survey evidence from information technology directors. In C. Reddick (Ed.), *Homeland security preparedness and information systems: Strategies for managing public policy* (pp. 213–229). Hershey, PA: IGI Global. doi:10.4018/978-1-60566-834-5.ch011

Reddick, C. G. (2012). Customer relationship management adoption in local governments in the United States. In S. Chhabra & M. Kumar (Eds.), *Strategic enterprise resource planning models for e-government: Applications and methodologies* (pp. 111–124). Hershey, PA: IGI Global. doi:10.4018/978-1-60960-863-7.ch008

Reddy, A., & Prasad, G. V. (2012). Consumer perceptions on security, privacy, and trust on e-portals. *International Journal of Online Marketing, 2*(2), 10–24. doi:10.4018/ijom.2012040102

Reeder, F. S., & Pandy, S. M. (2008). Identifying effective funding models for e-government. In A. Anttiroiko (Ed.), *Electronic government: Concepts, methodologies, tools, and applications* (pp. 1108–1138). Hershey, PA: IGI Global. doi:10.4018/978-1-59904-947-2.ch083

Remmert, M. (2004). Towards European Standards on Electronic Voting. Electronic Voting in Europe – Technology, Law. Lake of Constance: GI, the Gesellschaft für Informatik.

Richet, J. (2013). From young hackers to crackers. *International Journal of Technology and Human Interaction*, *9*(3), 53–62. doi:10.4018/jthi.2013070104

Riesco, D., Acosta, E., & Montejano, G. (2003). An extension to a UML activity graph from workflow. In L. Favre (Ed.), *UML and the unified process* (pp. 294–314). Hershey, PA: IGI Global. doi:10.4018/978-1-93177-744-5.ch015

Ritzhaupt, A. D., & Gill, T. G. (2008). A hybrid and novel approach to teaching computer programming in MIS curriculum. In S. Negash, M. Whitman, A. Woszczynski, K. Hoganson, & H. Mattord (Eds.), *Handbook of distance learning for real-time and asynchronous information technology education* (pp. 259–281). Hershey, PA: IGI Global. doi:10.4018/978-1-59904-964-9.ch014

Rivest, R. (2001). *Electronic Voting*. Cambridge, MA: Academic Press.

Rjaibi, N., Rabai, L. B., Ben Aissa, A., & Mili, A. (2013). Mean failure cost as a measurable value and evidence of cybersecurity: E-learning case study. *International Journal of Secure Software Engineering*, *4*(3), 64–81. doi:10.4018/jsse.2013070104

Roberts, L. D. (2012). Cyber identity theft. In *Cyber crime: Concepts, methodologies, tools and applications* (pp. 21–36). Hershey, PA: IGI Global. doi:10.4018/978-1-61350-323-2.ch103

Roche, E. M. (1993). International computing and the international regime. *Journal of Global Information Management*, *1*(2), 33–44. doi:10.4018/jgim.1993040103

Rocheleau, B. (2007). Politics, accountability, and information management. In G. Garson (Ed.), *Modern public information technology systems: Issues and challenges* (pp. 35–71). Hershey, PA: IGI Global. doi:10.4018/978-1-59904-051-6.ch003

Rodrigues Filho, J. (2010). E-government in Brazil: Reinforcing dominant institutions or reducing citizenship? In C. Reddick (Ed.), *Politics, democracy and e-government: Participation and service delivery* (pp. 347–362). Hershey, PA: IGI Global. doi:10.4018/978-1-61520-933-0.ch021

Rodriguez, L. & Li, X. (2011). A dynamic vertical partitioning approach for distributed database system. *IEEE International Conference on Systems, Man, and Cybernetics (SMC)*, 1853-1858.

Rodriguez, S. R., & Thorp, D. A. (2013). eLearning for industry: A case study of the project management process. In A. Benson, J. Moore, & S. Williams van Rooij (Eds.), Cases on educational technology planning, design, and implementation: A project management perspective (pp. 319-342). Hershey, PA: IGI Global. doi:10.4018/978-1-4666-4237-9.ch017

Rodríguez, J., Fernández-Medina, E., Piattini, M., & Mellado, D. (2011). A security requirements engineering tool for domain engineering in software product lines. In N. Milanovic (Ed.), *Non-functional properties in service oriented architecture: Requirements, models and methods* (pp. 73–92). Hershey, PA: IGI Global. doi:10.4018/978-1-60566-794-2.ch004

Roldan, M., & Rea, A. (2011). Individual privacy and security in virtual worlds. In A. Rea (Ed.), *Security in virtual worlds, 3D webs, and immersive environments: Models for development, interaction, and management* (pp. 1–19). Hershey, PA: IGI Global. doi:10.4018/978-1-61520-891-3.ch001

Roman, A. V. (2013). Delineating three dimensions of e-government success: Security, functionality, and transformation. In J. Gil-Garcia (Ed.), *E-government success factors and measures: Theories, concepts, and methodologies* (pp. 171–192). Hershey, PA: IGI Global. doi:10.4018/978-1-4666-4058-0.ch010

Ross, S. C., Tyran, C. K., & Auer, D. J. (2008). Up in smoke: Rebuilding after an IT disaster. In H. Nemati (Ed.), *Information security and ethics: Concepts, methodologies, tools, and applications* (pp. 3659–3675). Hershey, PA: IGI Global. doi:10.4018/978-1-59904-937-3.ch248

Ross, S. C., Tyran, C. K., Auer, D. J., Junell, J. M., & Williams, T. G. (2005). Up in smoke: Rebuilding after an IT disaster. *Journal of Cases on Information Technology*, 7(2), 31–49. doi:10.4018/jcit.2005040103

Rowe, N. C., Garfinkel, S. L., Beverly, R., & Yannakogeorgos, P. (2011). Challenges in monitoring cyberarms compliance. *International Journal of Cyber Warfare & Terrorism*, 1(2), 35–48. doi:10.4018/ijcwt.2011040104

Roy, J. (2008). Security, sovereignty, and continental interoperability: Canada's elusive balance. In T. Loendorf & G. Garson (Eds.), *Patriotic information systems* (pp. 153–176). Hershey, PA: IGI Global. doi:10.4018/978-1-59904-594-8.ch007

Rubeck, R. F., & Miller, G. A. (2009). vGOV: Remote video access to government services. In A. Scupola (Ed.), Cases on managing e-services (pp. 253-268). Hershey, PA: IGI Global. doi:10.4018/978-1-60566-064-6.ch017

Rubin, A. (2001). *Security Considerations for Remote Electronic Voting over the Internet*. Florham Park, NJ: Academic Press.

Rubin, D. (2001). *The Security of Remote Online Voting*. University of Virginia.

Rwabutaza, A., Yang, M., & Bourbakis, N. (2012). A comparative survey on cryptology-based methodologies. *International Journal of Information Security and Privacy*, 6(3), 1–37. doi:10.4018/jisp.2012070101

Sadkhan, S. B., & Abbas, N. A. (2014). Privacy and security of wireless communication networks. In J. Rodrigues, K. Lin, & J. Lloret (Eds.), *Mobile networks and cloud computing convergence for progressive services and applications* (pp. 58–78). Hershey, PA: IGI Global. doi:10.4018/978-1-4666-4781-7.ch004

Saedy, M., & Mojtahed, V. (2011). Machine-to-machine communications and security solution in cellular systems. *International Journal of Interdisciplinary Telecommunications and Networking*, 3(2), 66–75. doi:10.4018/jitn.2011040105

Saekow, A., & Boonmee, C. (2011). The challenges of implementing e-government interoperability in Thailand: Case of official electronic correspondence letters exchange across government departments. In Y. Charalabidis (Ed.), *Interoperability in digital public services and administration: Bridging e-government and e-business* (pp. 40–61). Hershey, PA: IGI Global. doi:10.4018/978-1-61520-887-6.ch003

Saekow, A., & Boonmee, C. (2012). The challenges of implementing e-government interoperability in Thailand: Case of official electronic correspondence letters exchange across government departments. In *Digital democracy: Concepts, methodologies, tools, and applications* (pp. 1883–1905). Hershey, PA: IGI Global. doi:10.4018/978-1-4666-1740-7.ch094

Sagsan, M., & Medeni, T. (2012). Understanding "knowledge management (KM) paradigms" from social media perspective: An empirical study on discussion group for KM at professional networking site. In M. Cruz-Cunha, P. Gonçalves, N. Lopes, E. Miranda, & G. Putnik (Eds.), *Handbook of research on business social networking: Organizational, managerial, and technological dimensions* (pp. 738–755). Hershey, PA: IGI Global. doi:10.4018/978-1-61350-168-9.ch039

Sahi, G., & Madan, S. (2013). Information security threats in ERP enabled e-governance: Challenges and solutions. In *Enterprise resource planning: Concepts, methodologies, tools, and applications* (pp. 825–837). Hershey, PA: IGI Global. doi:10.4018/978-1-4666-4153-2.ch048

Sahoolizadeh, A. H., & Heidari, B. Z. (2008). A New Face Recognition Method using PCA,LDA and Neural Network, World Academy of Science. *Engineering and Technology, 41*, 7–12.

San Nicolas-Rocca, T., & Olfman, L. (2013). End user security training for identification and access management. *Journal of Organizational and End User Computing, 25*(4), 75–103. doi:10.4018/joeuc.2013100104

Sanford, C., & Bhattacherjee, A. (2008). IT implementation in a developing country municipality: A sociocognitive analysis. *International Journal of Technology and Human Interaction, 4*(3), 68–93. doi:10.4018/jthi.2008070104

Satell, G. (2013). 5 Trends That Will Drive the Future of Technology. *Forbes*. Retrieved from http://www.forbes.com/sites/gregsatell/2013/03/12/5-trends-that-will-drive-the-future-of-technology/#12af5e1a4cf5

Satoh, F., Nakamura, Y., Mukhi, N. K., Tatsubori, M., & Ono, K. (2011). Model-driven approach for end-to-end SOA security configurations. In N. Milanovic (Ed.), *Non-functional properties in service oriented architecture: Requirements, models and methods* (pp. 268–298). Hershey, PA: IGI Global. doi:10.4018/978-1-60566-794-2.ch012

Satpathy, B. N., & Chanana, A. K. (2014). Open Data Initiative of Government of India – Fostering Innovations, Creating Opportunities. Planning Commission. Retrieved from http://www.unece.org/fileadmin/DAM/stats/documents/ece/ces/ge.50/2014/Topic_3_India.pdf

Saucez, D., Iannone, L., & Bonaventure, O. (2014). The map-and-encap locator/identifier separation paradigm: A security analysis. In M. Boucadair & D. Binet (Eds.), *Solutions for sustaining scalability in internet growth* (pp. 148–163). Hershey, PA: IGI Global. doi:10.4018/978-1-4666-4305-5.ch008

Schelin, S. H. (2003). E-government: An overview. In G. Garson (Ed.), *Public information technology: Policy and management issues* (pp. 120–138). Hershey, PA: IGI Global. doi:10.4018/978-1-59140-060-8.ch006

Schelin, S. H. (2004). Training for digital government. In A. Pavlichev & G. Garson (Eds.), *Digital government: Principles and best practices* (pp. 263–275). Hershey, PA: IGI Global. doi:10.4018/978-1-59140-122-3.ch017

Schelin, S. H. (2007). E-government: An overview. In G. Garson (Ed.), *Modern public information technology systems: Issues and challenges* (pp. 110–126). Hershey, PA: IGI Global. doi:10.4018/978-1-59904-051-6.ch006

Schelin, S. H., & Garson, G. (2004). Theoretical justification of critical success factors. In G. Garson & S. Schelin (Eds.), *IT solutions series: Humanizing information technology: Advice from experts* (pp. 4–15). Hershey, PA: IGI Global. doi:10.4018/978-1-59140-245-9.ch002

Schell, B. H., & Holt, T. J. (2012). A profile of the demographics, psychological predispositions, and social/behavioral patterns of computer hacker insiders and outsiders. In *Cyber crime: Concepts, methodologies, tools and applications* (pp. 1461–1484). Hershey, PA: IGI Global. doi:10.4018/978-1-61350-323-2.ch705

Schmidt, H. (2011). Threat and risk-driven security requirements engineering. *International Journal of Mobile Computing and Multimedia Communications*, *3*(1), 35–50. doi:10.4018/jmcmc.2011010103

Schmidt, H., Hatebur, D., & Heisel, M. (2011). A pattern-based method to develop secure software. In H. Mouratidis (Ed.), *Software engineering for secure systems: Industrial and research perspectives* (pp. 32–74). Hershey, PA: IGI Global. doi:10.4018/978-1-61520-837-1.ch003

Scime, A. (2002). Information systems and computer science model curricula: A comparative look. In M. Dadashzadeh, A. Saber, & S. Saber (Eds.), *Information technology education in the new millennium* (pp. 146–158). Hershey, PA: IGI Global. doi:10.4018/978-1-931777-05-6.ch018

Scime, A. (2009). Computing curriculum analysis and development. In M. Khosrow-Pour (Ed.), *Encyclopedia of information science and technology* (2nd ed.; pp. 667–671). Hershey, PA: IGI Global. doi:10.4018/978-1-60566-026-4.ch108

Scime, A., & Wania, C. (2008). Computing curricula: A comparison of models. In C. Van Slyke (Ed.), *Information communication technologies: Concepts, methodologies, tools, and applications* (pp. 1270–1283). Hershey, PA: IGI Global. doi:10.4018/978-1-59904-949-6.ch088

Seale, R. O., & Hargiss, K. M. (2011). A proposed architecture for autonomous mobile agent intrusion prevention and malware defense in heterogeneous networks. *International Journal of Strategic Information Technology and Applications*, *2*(4), 44–54. doi:10.4018/jsita.2011100104

Seidman, S. B. (2009). An international perspective on professional software engineering credentials. In H. Ellis, S. Demurjian, & J. Naveda (Eds.), *Software engineering: Effective teaching and learning approaches and practices* (pp. 351–361). Hershey, PA: IGI Global. doi:10.4018/978-1-60566-102-5.ch018

Seifert, J. W. (2007). E-government act of 2002 in the United States. In A. Anttiroiko & M. Malkia (Eds.), *Encyclopedia of digital government* (pp. 476–481). Hershey, PA: IGI Global. doi:10.4018/978-1-59140-789-8.ch072

Seifert, J. W., & Relyea, H. C. (2008). E-government act of 2002 in the United States. In A. Anttiroiko (Ed.), *Electronic government: Concepts, methodologies, tools, and applications* (pp. 154–161). Hershey, PA: IGI Global. doi:10.4018/978-1-59904-947-2.ch013

Sengupta, A., & Mazumdar, C. (2011). A mark-up language for the specification of information security governance requirements. *International Journal of Information Security and Privacy*, *5*(2), 33–53. doi:10.4018/jisp.2011040103

Sen, J. (2013). Security and privacy challenges in cognitive wireless sensor networks. In N. Meghanathan & Y. Reddy (Eds.), *Cognitive radio technology applications for wireless and mobile ad hoc networks* (pp. 194–232). Hershey, PA: IGI Global. doi:10.4018/978-1-4666-4221-8.ch011

Sen, J. (2014). Security and privacy issues in cloud computing. In A. Ruiz-Martinez, R. Marin-Lopez, & F. Pereniguez-Garcia (Eds.), *Architectures and protocols for secure information technology infrastructures* (pp. 1–45). Hershey, PA: IGI Global. doi:10.4018/978-1-4666-4514-1.ch001

Serenko, A., & Bontis, N. (2004). A model of user adoption of mobile portals. *Quarterly Journal of Electronic Commerce*, *4*(1), 64–98.

Seufert, S. (2002). E-learning business models: Framework and best practice examples. In M. Raisinghani (Ed.), *Cases on worldwide e-commerce: Theory in action* (pp. 70–94). Hershey, PA: IGI Global. doi:10.4018/978-1-930708-27-3.ch004

Seva, M. (2014). *What is Mobile Seva*. Retrieved from https://mgov.gov.in/msdp-basic.jsp

Shaqrah, A. A. (2011). The influence of internet security on e-business competence in Jordan: An empirical analysis. In *Global business: Concepts, methodologies, tools and applications* (pp. 1071–1086). Hershey, PA: IGI Global. doi:10.4018/978-1-60960-587-2.ch413

Shareef, M. A., & Archer, N. (2012). E-government initiatives: Review studies on different countries. In M. Shareef, N. Archer, & S. Dutta (Eds.), *E-government service maturity and development: Cultural, organizational and technological perspectives* (pp. 40–76). Hershey, PA: IGI Global. doi:10.4018/978-1-60960-848-4.ch003

Shareef, M. A., & Archer, N. (2012). E-government service development. In M. Shareef, N. Archer, & S. Dutta (Eds.), *E-government service maturity and development: Cultural, organizational and technological perspectives* (pp. 1–14). Hershey, PA: IGI Global. doi:10.4018/978-1-60960-848-4.ch001

Shareef, M. A., Kumar, U., & Kumar, V. (2011). E-government development: Performance evaluation parameters. In M. Shareef, V. Kumar, U. Kumar, & Y. Dwivedi (Eds.), *Stakeholder adoption of e-government services: Driving and resisting factors* (pp. 197–213). Hershey, PA: IGI Global. doi:10.4018/978-1-60960-601-5.ch010

Shareef, M. A., Kumar, U., Kumar, V., & Niktash, M. (2012). Electronic-government vision: Case studies for objectives, strategies, and initiatives. In M. Shareef, N. Archer, & S. Dutta (Eds.), *E-government service maturity and development: Cultural, organizational and technological perspectives* (pp. 15–39). Hershey, PA: IGI Global. doi:10.4018/978-1-60960-848-4.ch002

Shareef, M. A., & Kumar, V. (2012). Prevent/control identity theft: Impact on trust and consumers purchase intention in B2C EC. *Information Resources Management Journal*, 25(3), 30–60. doi:10.4018/irmj.2012070102

Sharma, P., & Swami, S. (2013). Digital Image Watermarking Using 3 level Discrete Wavelet Transform. *Conference on Advances in Communication and Control Systems* (CAC2S2013), 129-133.

Sharma, K., & Singh, A. (2011). Biometric security in the e-world. In H. Nemati & L. Yang (Eds.), *Applied cryptography for cyber security and defense: Information encryption and cyphering* (pp. 289–337). Hershey, PA: IGI Global. doi:10.4018/978-1-61520-783-1.ch013

Sharma, R. K. (2014). Physical layer security and its applications: A survey. In D. Rawat, B. Bista, & G. Yan (Eds.), *Security, Privacy, Trust, and Resource Management in Mobile and Wireless Communications* (pp. 29–60). Hershey, PA: IGI Global. doi:10.4018/978-1-4666-4691-9.ch003

Shaw, R., Keh, H., & Huang, N. (2011). Information security awareness on-line materials design with knowledge maps. *International Journal of Distance Education Technologies*, 9(4), 41–56. doi:10.4018/jdet.2011100104

Shebanow, A., Perez, R., & Howard, C. (2012). The effect of firewall testing types on cloud security policies. *International Journal of Strategic Information Technology and Applications*, *3*(3), 60–68. doi:10.4018/jsita.2012070105

Shen, Y., Li, Y., Wu, L., Liu, S., & Wen, Q. (2014). Data protection in the cloud era. In Y. Shen, Y. Li, L. Wu, S. Liu, & Q. Wen (Eds.), *Enabling the new era of cloud computing: Data security, transfer, and management* (pp. 132–154). Hershey, PA: IGI Global. doi:10.4018/978-1-4666-4801-2.ch007

Shen, Y., Li, Y., Wu, L., Liu, S., & Wen, Q. (2014). Enterprise security monitoring with the fusion center model. In Y. Shen, Y. Li, L. Wu, S. Liu, & Q. Wen (Eds.), *Enabling the new era of cloud computing: Data security, transfer, and management* (pp. 116–131). Hershey, PA: IGI Global. doi:10.4018/978-1-4666-4801-2.ch006

Shore, M. (2011). Cyber security and anti-social networking. In *Virtual communities: Concepts, methodologies, tools and applications* (pp. 1286–1297). Hershey, PA: IGI Global. doi:10.4018/978-1-60960-100-3.ch412

Shukla, P., Kumar, A., & Anu Kumar, P. B. (2013). Impact of national culture on business continuity management system implementation. *International Journal of Risk and Contingency Management*, *2*(3), 23–36. doi:10.4018/ijrcm.2013070102

Shulman, S. W. (2007). The federal docket management system and the prospect for digital democracy in U S rulemaking. In G. Garson (Ed.), *Modern public information technology systems: Issues and challenges* (pp. 166–184). Hershey, PA: IGI Global. doi:10.4018/978-1-59904-051-6.ch009

Siddiqi, J., Alqatawna, J., & Btoush, M. H. (2011). Do insecure systems increase global digital divide? In *Global business: Concepts, methodologies, tools and applications* (pp. 2102–2111). Hershey, PA: IGI Global. doi:10.4018/978-1-60960-587-2.ch717

Simonovic, S. (2007). Problems of offline government in e-Serbia. In A. Anttiroiko & M. Malkia (Eds.), *Encyclopedia of digital government* (pp. 1342–1351). Hershey, PA: IGI Global. doi:10.4018/978-1-59140-789-8.ch205

Simonovic, S. (2008). Problems of offline government in e-Serbia. In A. Anttiroiko (Ed.), *Electronic government: Concepts, methodologies, tools, and applications* (pp. 2929–2942). Hershey, PA: IGI Global. doi:10.4018/978-1-59904-947-2.ch219

Simpson, J. J., Simpson, M. J., Endicott-Popovsky, B., & Popovsky, V. (2012). Secure software education: A contextual model-based approach. In K. Khan (Ed.), *Security-aware systems applications and software development methods* (pp. 286–312). Hershey, PA: IGI Global. doi:10.4018/978-1-4666-1580-9.ch016

Singh, A. M. (2005). Information systems and technology in South Africa. In M. Khosrow-Pour (Ed.), *Encyclopedia of information science and technology* (pp. 1497–1502). Hershey, PA: IGI Global. doi:10.4018/978-1-59140-553-5.ch263

Singh, S. (2012). Security threats and issues with MANET. In K. Lakhtaria (Ed.), *Technological advancements and applications in mobile ad-hoc networks: Research trends* (pp. 247–263). Hershey, PA: IGI Global. doi:10.4018/978-1-4666-0321-9. ch015

Singh, S., & Naidoo, G. (2005). Towards an e-government solution: A South African perspective. In W. Huang, K. Siau, & K. Wei (Eds.), *Electronic government strategies and implementation* (pp. 325–353). Hershey, PA: IGI Global. doi:10.4018/978-1-59140-348-7.ch014

Smuts, H., van der Merwe, A., Paula Kotzé, P., & Loock, M. (2010). Critical success factors for information systems outsourcing management: a software development lifecycle view. In *Proceedings of the 2010 Annual Research Conference of the South African Institute of Computer Scientists and Information Technologists (SAICSIT '10)*. ACM. doi:10.1145/1899503.1899537

Snoke, R., & Underwood, A. (2002). Generic attributes of IS graduates: An analysis of Australian views. In F. Tan (Ed.), *Advanced topics in global information management* (Vol. 1, pp. 370–384). Hershey, PA: IGI Global. doi:10.4018/978-1-930708-43-3.ch023

Sockel, H., & Falk, L. K. (2012). Online privacy, vulnerabilities, and threats: A manager's perspective. In *Cyber crime: Concepts, methodologies, tools and applications* (pp. 101–123). Hershey, PA: IGI Global. doi:10.4018/978-1-61350-323-2.ch108

Sommer, L. (2006). Revealing unseen organizations in higher education: A study framework and application example. In A. Metcalfe (Ed.), *Knowledge management and higher education: A critical analysis* (pp. 115–146). Hershey, PA: IGI Global. doi:10.4018/978-1-59140-509-2.ch007

Song, X., & Zhang, R. (2011). Research on constructing distributed large database based on J2EE. *IEEE 3rd International Conference on Communication Software and Networks (ICCSN)*, 704-707. doi:10.1109/ICCSN.2011.6014989

Song, H., Kidd, T., & Owens, E. (2011). Examining technological disparities and instructional practices in English language arts classroom: Implications for school leadership and teacher training. In L. Tomei (Ed.), *Online courses and ICT in education: Emerging practices and applications* (pp. 258–274). Hershey, PA: IGI Global. doi:10.4018/978-1-60960-150-8.ch020

Speaker, P. J., & Kleist, V. F. (2003). Using information technology to meet electronic commerce and MIS education demands. In A. Aggarwal (Ed.), *Web-based education: Learning from experience* (pp. 280–291). Hershey, PA: IGI Global. doi:10.4018/978-1-59140-102-5.ch017

Spitler, V. K. (2007). Learning to use IT in the workplace: Mechanisms and masters. In M. Mahmood (Ed.), *Contemporary issues in end user computing* (pp. 292–323). Hershey, PA: IGI Global. doi:10.4018/978-1-59140-926-7.ch013

Spruit, M., & de Bruijn, W. (2012). CITS: The cost of IT security framework. *International Journal of Information Security and Privacy*, 6(4), 94–116. doi:10.4018/jisp.2012100105

Srinivasan, C., Lakshmy, K., & Sethumadhavan, M. (2011). Complexity measures of cryptographically secure boolean functions. In R. Santanam, M. Sethumadhavan, & M. Virendra (Eds.), *Cyber security, cyber crime and cyber forensics: Applications and perspectives* (pp. 220–230). Hershey, PA: IGI Global. doi:10.4018/978-1-60960-123-2.ch015

Srivatsa, M., Agrawal, D., & McDonald, A. D. (2012). Security across disparate management domains in coalition MANETs. In *Wireless technologies: Concepts, methodologies, tools and applications* (pp. 1494–1518). Hershey, PA: IGI Global. doi:10.4018/978-1-61350-101-6.ch521

Stellefson, M. (2011). Considerations for marketing distance education courses in health education: Five important questions to examine before development. In U. Demiray & S. Sever (Eds.), *Marketing online education programs: Frameworks for promotion and communication* (pp. 222–234). Hershey, PA: IGI Global. doi:10.4018/978-1-60960-074-7.ch014

Stojanovic, M. D., Acimovic-Raspopovic, V. S., & Rakas, S. B. (2013). Security management issues for open source ERP in the NGN environment. In *Enterprise resource planning: Concepts, methodologies, tools, and applications* (pp. 789–804). Hershey, PA: IGI Global. doi:10.4018/978-1-4666-4153-2.ch046

Stoll, M., & Breu, R. (2012). Information security governance and standard based management systems. In M. Gupta, J. Walp, & R. Sharman (Eds.), *Strategic and practical approaches for information security governance: Technologies and applied solutions* (pp. 261–282). Hershey, PA: IGI Global. doi:10.4018/978-1-4666-0197-0.ch015

Straub, D. W., & Loch, K. D. (2006). Creating and developing a program of global research. *Journal of Global Information Management*, 14(2), 1–28. doi:10.4018/jgim.2006040101

Straub, D. W., Loch, K. D., & Hill, C. E. (2002). Transfer of information technology to the Arab world: A test of cultural influence modeling. In M. Dadashzadeh (Ed.), *Information technology management in developing countries* (pp. 92–134). Hershey, PA: IGI Global. doi:10.4018/978-1-931777-03-2.ch005

Straub, D. W., Loch, K. D., & Hill, C. E. (2003). Transfer of information technology to the Arab world: A test of cultural influence modeling. In F. Tan (Ed.), *Advanced topics in global information management* (Vol. 2, pp. 141–172). Hershey, PA: IGI Global. doi:10.4018/978-1-59140-064-6.ch009

Suki, N. M., Ramayah, T., Ming, M. K., & Suki, N. M. (2013). Factors enhancing employed job seekers intentions to use social networking sites as a job search tool. In A. Mesquita (Ed.), *User perception and influencing factors of technology in everyday life* (pp. 265–281). Hershey, PA: IGI Global. doi:10.4018/978-1-4666-1954-8.ch018

Sundaresan, M., & Boopathy, D. (2014). Different perspectives of cloud security. In S. Srinivasan (Ed.), *Security, trust, and regulatory aspects of cloud computing in business environments* (pp. 73–90). Hershey, PA: IGI Global. doi:10.4018/978-1-4666-5788-5.ch004

Suomi, R. (2006). Introducing electronic patient records to hospitals: Innovation adoption paths. In T. Spil & R. Schuring (Eds.), *E-health systems diffusion and use: The innovation, the user and the use IT model* (pp. 128–146). Hershey, PA: IGI Global. doi:10.4018/978-1-59140-423-1.ch008

Swim, J., & Barker, L. (2012). Pathways into a gendered occupation: Brazilian women in IT. *International Journal of Social and Organizational Dynamics in IT*, *2*(4), 34–51. doi:10.4018/ijsodit.2012100103

Szajna, B. (1996). Empirical evaluation of the revised technology acceptance model. *Management Science*, *42*(1), 85–92. doi:10.1287/mnsc.42.1.85

Takabi, H., Joshi, J. B., & Ahn, G. (2013). Security and privacy in cloud computing: Towards a comprehensive framework. In X. Yang & L. Liu (Eds.), *Principles, methodologies, and service-oriented approaches for cloud computing* (pp. 164–184). Hershey, PA: IGI Global. doi:10.4018/978-1-4666-2854-0.ch007

Takabi, H., Zargar, S. T., & Joshi, J. B. (2014). Mobile cloud computing and its security and privacy challenges. In D. Rawat, B. Bista, & G. Yan (Eds.), *Security, privacy, trust, and resource management in mobile and wireless communications* (pp. 384–407). Hershey, PA: IGI Global. doi:10.4018/978-1-4666-4691-9.ch016

Takemura, T. (2014). Unethical information security behavior and organizational commitment. In T. Tsiakis, T. Kargidis, & P. Katsaros (Eds.), *Approaches and processes for managing the economics of information systems* (pp. 181–198). Hershey, PA: IGI Global. doi:10.4018/978-1-4666-4983-5.ch011

Talbot, E.B., Frincke, D., & Bishop, M. (2010). Demythifying Cybersecurity. *IEEE Security & Privacy, 8*(3), 56-59.

Talib, S., Clarke, N. L., & Furnell, S. M. (2011). Establishing a personalized information security culture. *International Journal of Mobile Computing and Multimedia Communications, 3*(1), 63–79. doi:10.4018/jmcmc.2011010105

Talukder, A. K. (2011). Securing next generation internet services. In R. Santanam, M. Sethumadhavan, & M. Virendra (Eds.), *Cyber security, cyber crime and cyber forensics: Applications and perspectives* (pp. 87–105). Hershey, PA: IGI Global. doi:10.4018/978-1-60960-123-2.ch007

Tambouris, E., Loutas, N., Peristeras, V., & Tarabanis, K. (2008). The role of interoperability in eGovernment applications: An investigation of obstacles and implementation decisions. *Digital Information Management, 2008. ICDIM 2008. Third International Conference on*, 381-386. doi:10.1109/ICDIM.2008.4746798

Tarafdar, M., & Vaidya, S. D. (2006). Adoption and implementation of IT in developing nations: Experiences from two public sector enterprises in India. In M. Khosrow-Pour (Ed.), *Cases on information technology planning, design and implementation* (pp. 208–233). Hershey, PA: IGI Global. doi:10.4018/978-1-59904-408-8.ch013

Tarafdar, M., & Vaidya, S. D. (2008). Adoption and implementation of IT in developing nations: Experiences from two public sector enterprises in India. In G. Garson & M. Khosrow-Pour (Eds.), *Handbook of research on public information technology* (pp. 905–924). Hershey, PA: IGI Global. doi:10.4018/978-1-59904-857-4.ch076

Taylor, S., & Todd, P. A. (1995). Assessing IT usage: The role of prior experience. *Management Information Systems Quarterly, 19*(4), 561–570. doi:10.2307/249633

Tchepnda, C., Moustafa, H., Labiod, H., & Bourdon, G. (2011). Vehicular networks security: Attacks, requirements, challenges and current contributions. In K. Curran (Ed.), *Ubiquitous developments in ambient computing and intelligence: Human-centered applications* (pp. 43–55). Hershey, PA: IGI Global. doi:10.4018/978-1-60960-549-0.ch004

Tereshchenko, N. (2012). US foreign policy challenges of non-state actors cyber terrorism against critical infrastructure. *International Journal of Cyber Warfare & Terrorism, 2*(4), 28–48. doi:10.4018/ijcwt.2012100103

Thatcher, J. B., & Perrewé, P. L. (2002). An empirical examination of individual traits as antecedents to computer anxiety and computer self-efficacy. *Management Information Systems Quarterly*, *26*(4), 381–396. doi:10.2307/4132314

The Earth Institute Columbia University. (2016). *ICT and the SDGs: How Information and Communications Technology Can Achieve The Sustainable Development Goals*. Retrieved from: https://www.ericsson.com/res/docs/2015/ict-and-sdg-interim-report.pdf

The Register. (2010). *Citizens rail against government data sharing*. Retrieved from: http://www.theregister.co.uk/2010/02/23/public_data_shari ng_poll/

Thesing, Z. (2007). Zarina thesing, pumpkin patch. In M. Hunter (Ed.), *Contemporary chief information officers: Management experiences* (pp. 83–94). Hershey, PA: IGI Global. doi:10.4018/978-1-59904-078-3.ch007

Thomas, J. C. (2004). Public involvement in public administration in the information age: Speculations on the effects of technology. In M. Malkia, A. Anttiroiko, & R. Savolainen (Eds.), *eTransformation in governance: New directions in government and politics* (pp. 67–84). Hershey, PA: IGI Global. doi:10.4018/978-1-59140-130-8.ch004

Thomson, S. (2015). *What are the Sustainable Development Goals? From World Economic Forum*. Retrieved from: https://www.weforum.org/agenda/2015/09/what-are-the-sustainable-development-goals/

Thuraisingham, B., Rubinovitz, H., Foti, D., & Abreu, A. (1993). Design and implementation of a distributed database. *IEEE COMPSAC 93 Proceedings,Seventeenth Annual International Computer Software and Applications Conference*, 152-158. doi:10.1109/CMPSAC.1993.404229

Thurimella, R., & Baird, L. C. (2011). Network security. In H. Nemati & L. Yang (Eds.), *Applied cryptography for cyber security and defense: Information encryption and cyphering* (pp. 1–31). Hershey, PA: IGI Global. doi:10.4018/978-1-61520-783-1.ch001

Thurimella, R., & Mitchell, W. (2011). Cloak and dagger: Man-in-the-middle and other insidious attacks. In H. Nemati (Ed.), *Security and privacy assurance in advancing technologies: New developments* (pp. 252–270). Hershey, PA: IGI Global. doi:10.4018/978-1-60960-200-0.ch016

Tian-shi, L., Jiao, L,m Gao, R.-F., & Gang, M. (2010). Overview of P2P Distributed Database System. *IEEE International Conference on Web Information Systems and Mining (WISM)*, *2*, 192-197.

Tiwari, N., & Sharma, M.K. (2013). Cloud based Working Concept for E-Governance Citizen Charter. *International Journal of Advanced Research in Computer Science and Software Engineering, 3*(6).

Tiwari, S., Singh, A., Singh, R. S., & Singh, S. K. (2013). Internet security using biometrics. In *IT policy and ethics: Concepts, methodologies, tools, and applications* (pp. 1680–1707). Hershey, PA: IGI Global. doi:10.4018/978-1-4666-2919-6.ch074

Tomaiuolo, M. (2012). Trust enforcing and trust building, different technologies and visions. *International Journal of Cyber Warfare & Terrorism, 2*(4), 49–66. doi:10.4018/ijcwt.2012100104

Tomaiuolo, M. (2014). Trust management and delegation for the administration of web services. In I. Portela & F. Almeida (Eds.), *Organizational, legal, and technological dimensions of information system administration* (pp. 18–37). Hershey, PA: IGI Global. doi:10.4018/978-1-4666-4526-4.ch002

Touhafi, A., Braeken, A., Cornetta, G., Mentens, N., & Steenhaut, K. (2011). Secure techniques for remote reconfiguration of wireless embedded systems. In M. Cruz-Cunha & F. Moreira (Eds.), *Handbook of research on mobility and computing: Evolving technologies and ubiquitous impacts* (pp. 930–951). Hershey, PA: IGI Global. doi:10.4018/978-1-60960-042-6.ch058

Traore, I., & Woungang, I. (2013). Software security engineering – Part I: Security requirements and risk analysis. In K. Buragga & N. Zaman (Eds.), *Software development techniques for constructive information systems design* (pp. 221–255). Hershey, PA: IGI Global. doi:10.4018/978-1-4666-3679-8.ch012

Treiblmaier, H., & Chong, S. (2013). Trust and perceived risk of personal information as antecedents of online information disclosure: Results from three countries. In F. Tan (Ed.), *Global diffusion and adoption of technologies for knowledge and information sharing* (pp. 341–361). Hershey, PA: IGI Global. doi:10.4018/978-1-4666-2142-8.ch015

Tripathi, M., Gaur, M., & Laxmi, V. (2014). Security challenges in wireless sensor network. In D. Rawat, B. Bista, & G. Yan (Eds.), *Security, privacy, trust, and resource management in mobile and wireless communications* (pp. 334–359). Hershey, PA: IGI Global. doi:10.4018/978-1-4666-4691-9.ch014

Trösterer, S., Beck, E., Dalpiaz, F., Paja, E., Giorgini, P., & Tscheligi, M. (2012). Formative user-centered evaluation of security modeling: Results from a case study. *International Journal of Secure Software Engineering, 3*(1), 1–19. doi:10.4018/jsse.2012010101

Tsiakis, T. (2013). The role of information security and cryptography in digital democracy: (Human) rights and freedom. In C. Akrivopoulou & N. Garipidis (Eds.), *Digital democracy and the impact of technology on governance and politics: New globalized practices* (pp. 158–174). Hershey, PA: IGI Global. doi:10.4018/978-1-4666-3637-8.ch009

Tsiakis, T., Kargidis, T., & Chatzipoulidis, A. (2013). IT security governance in e-banking. In D. Mellado, L. Enrique Sánchez, E. Fernández-Medina, & M. Piattini (Eds.), *IT security governance innovations: Theory and research* (pp. 13–46). Hershey, PA: IGI Global. doi:10.4018/978-1-4666-2083-4.ch002

Turgeman-Goldschmidt, O. (2011). Between hackers and white-collar offenders. In T. Holt & B. Schell (Eds.), *Corporate hacking and technology-driven crime: Social dynamics and implications* (pp. 18–37). Hershey, PA: IGI Global. doi:10.4018/978-1-61692-805-6.ch002

Tvrdíková, M. (2012). Information system integrated security. In M. Gupta, J. Walp, & R. Sharman (Eds.), *Strategic and practical approaches for information security governance: Technologies and applied solutions* (pp. 158–169). Hershey, PA: IGI Global. doi:10.4018/978-1-4666-0197-0.ch009

Uffen, J., & Breitner, M. H. (2013). Management of technical security measures: An empirical examination of personality traits and behavioral intentions. *International Journal of Social and Organizational Dynamics in IT*, *3*(1), 14–31. doi:10.4018/ijsodit.2013010102

Umble, E. J., Haft, R. R., & Umble, M. M. (2003). Enterprise resource planning: Implementation procedures and critical success factors. *European Journal of Operational Research, 146*(2), 241-257. 10.1016/S0377-2217(02)00547-7

UN General Assmebly. (2014). *Report of the Open Working Group of the General Assembly on Sustainable Development Goals* (A/68/970). Retrieved from: http://www.un.org/ga/search/view_doc.asp?symbol=A/68/970&Lang=E

UN Secretary-General's Expert Advisory Group on Data Revolution. (2014). *Ref: 2 "A World That Counts"*. Retrieved from: http://www.unglobalpulse.org/IEAG-Data-Revolution-Report-A-World-That-Counts

UN United Nations. (2010). *E-Government Survey 2010: Leveraging e-government at a time of financial and economic crisis*. Retrieved from http://www2.unpan.org/egovkb/documents/2010/E_Gov_2010_Complete.pdf

UN United Nations. (2012). *The Post-2015 Agenda*. Retrieved from http://www.undp. org/content/dam/undp/library/Poverty Reduction/Realizing the future we want. pdf

UN United Nations. (2013). *Report of the UN System Task Team on the Post-2015 Development Agenda*. Retrieved from http://www.un.org/en/development/desa/ policy/untaskteam_undf/report.shtml

Urbaczewski & Mrdalj. (2007). *A comparison of EAFs*. Academic Press.

US Government. (1996). *Summary: Information Technology Management Reform Act*. Retrieved from http://govinfo.library.unt.edu/npr/library/misc/itref.html

van Grembergen, W., & de Haes, S. (2008). IT governance in practice: Six case studies. In W. van Grembergen & S. De Haes (Eds.), *Implementing information technology governance: Models, practices and cases* (pp. 125–237). Hershey, PA: IGI Global. doi:10.4018/978-1-59904-924-3.ch004

van Os, G., Homburg, V., & Bekkers, V. (2013). Contingencies and convergence in European social security: ICT coordination in the back office of the welfare state. In M. Cruz-Cunha, I. Miranda, & P. Gonçalves (Eds.), *Handbook of research on ICTs and management systems for improving efficiency in healthcare and social care* (pp. 268–287). Hershey, PA: IGI Global. doi:10.4018/978-1-4666-3990-4.ch013

Vance, A., & Siponen, M. T. (2012). IS security policy violations: A rational choice perspective. *Journal of Organizational and End User Computing, 24*(1), 21–41. doi:10.4018/joeuc.2012010102

Vaquero, L.M., Rodero-Merino, L., Caceres, J., & Lindner, M. (2009). A break in the clouds: Towards a cloud definition. *SIGCOMM Computer Communications Review, 39*, 50-55.

Velloso, A. B., Gassenferth, W., & Machado, M. A. (2012). Evaluating IBMEC-RJ's intranet usability using fuzzy logic. In M. Cruz-Cunha, P. Gonçalves, N. Lopes, E. Miranda, & G. Putnik (Eds.), *Handbook of research on business social networking: Organizational, managerial, and technological dimensions* (pp. 185–205). Hershey, PA: IGI Global. doi:10.4018/978-1-61350-168-9.ch010

Veltsos, C. (2011). Mitigating the blended threat: Protecting data and educating users. In D. Kar & M. Syed (Eds.), *Network security, administration and management: Advancing technology and practice* (pp. 20–37). Hershey, PA: IGI Global. doi:10.4018/978-1-60960-777-7.ch002

Venkataraman, R., Pushpalatha, M., & Rao, T. R. (2014). Trust management and modeling techniques in wireless communications. In D. Rawat, B. Bista, & G. Yan (Eds.), *Security, privacy, trust, and resource management in mobile and wireless communications* (pp. 278–294). Hershey, PA: IGI Global. doi:10.4018/978-1-4666-4691-9.ch012

Venkataraman, R., & Rao, T. R. (2012). Security issues and models in mobile ad hoc networks. In K. Lakhtaria (Ed.), *Technological advancements and applications in mobile ad-hoc networks: Research trends* (pp. 219–227). Hershey, PA: IGI Global. doi:10.4018/978-1-4666-0321-9.ch013

Venkatesh, V., & Davis, F. D. (2000). A theoretical extension of the technology acceptance model: Four longitudinal field studies. *Management Science, 46*(2), 186–204. doi:10.1287/mnsc.46.2.186.11926

Venkatesh, V., Morris, M. G., Davis, G. B., & Davis, F. D. (2003). User acceptance of information technology: Toward a unified view. *Management Information Systems Quarterly, 27*(3), 425–478.

Verizon. (2015). *State of the Market: Internet of Things 2016: Accelerating innovation, productivity and value.* Retrieved from http://www.verizon.com/about/sites/default/files/state-of-the-internet-of-things-market-report-2016.pdf

Vetterli, C., Brenner, W., Uebernickel, F., & Petrie, C. (2013). From Palaces to Yurts: Why Requirements Engineering Needs Design Thinking. *IEEE Internet Computing, 17*(2), 91-94.

Villablanca, A. C., Baxi, H., & Anderson, K. (2009). Novel data interface for evaluating cardiovascular outcomes in women. In A. Dwivedi (Ed.), *Handbook of research on information technology management and clinical data administration in healthcare* (pp. 34–53). Hershey, PA: IGI Global. doi:10.4018/978-1-60566-356-2.ch003

Villablanca, A. C., Baxi, H., & Anderson, K. (2011). Novel data interface for evaluating cardiovascular outcomes in women. In *Clinical technologies: Concepts, methodologies, tools and applications* (pp. 2094–2113). Hershey, PA: IGI Global. doi:10.4018/978-1-60960-561-2.ch806

Villegas, M., & Paredes, R. (2005). Comparison of illumination normalization methods for face recognition. In *Third COST 275 Workshop - Biometrics on the Internet*. University of Hertfordshire.

Viney, D. (2011). Future trends in digital security. In D. Kerr, J. Gammack, & K. Bryant (Eds.), *Digital business security development: Management technologies* (pp. 173–190). Hershey, PA: IGI Global. doi:10.4018/978-1-60566-806-2.ch009

Vinod, P., Laxmi, V., & Gaur, M. (2011). Metamorphic malware analysis and detection methods. In R. Santanam, M. Sethumadhavan, & M. Virendra (Eds.), *Cyber security, cyber crime and cyber forensics: Applications and perspectives* (pp. 178–202). Hershey, PA: IGI Global. doi:10.4018/978-1-60960-123-2.ch013

Virkar, S. (2011). Information and communication technologies in administrative reform for development: Exploring the case of property tax systems in Karnataka, India. In J. Steyn, J. Van Belle, & E. Mansilla (Eds.), *ICTs for global development and sustainability: Practice and applications* (pp. 127–149). Hershey, PA: IGI Global. doi:10.4018/978-1-61520-997-2.ch006

Virkar, S. (2013). Designing and implementing e-government projects: Actors, influences, and fields of play. In S. Saeed & C. Reddick (Eds.), *Human-centered system design for electronic governance* (pp. 88–110). Hershey, PA: IGI Global. doi:10.4018/978-1-4666-3640-8.ch007

von Solms, R., & Warren, M. (2011). Towards the human information security firewall. *International Journal of Cyber Warfare & Terrorism, 1*(2), 10–17. doi:10.4018/ijcwt.2011040102

Walker, A. (2014). *Trends in Big Data: A Forecast for 2014, Big Data & Analytics*. Retrieved from http://www.csc.com/big_data/publications/91710/105057-big_data_trends_2014_prediction

Wallace, A. (2009). E-justice: An Australian perspective. In A. Martínez & P. Abat (Eds.), *E-justice: Using information communication technologies in the court system* (pp. 204–228). Hershey, PA: IGI Global. doi:10.4018/978-1-59904-998-4.ch014

Wall, D. S. (2011). Micro-frauds: Virtual robberies, stings and scams in the information age. In T. Holt & B. Schell (Eds.), *Corporate hacking and technology-driven crime: Social dynamics and implications* (pp. 68–86). Hershey, PA: IGI Global. doi:10.4018/978-1-61692-805-6.ch004

Wang, G. (2012). E-democratic administration and bureaucratic responsiveness: A primary study of bureaucrats' perceptions of the civil service e-mail box in Taiwan. In K. Kloby & M. D'Agostino (Eds.), *Citizen 2.0: Public and governmental interaction through web 2.0 technologies* (pp. 146–173). Hershey, PA: IGI Global. doi:10.4018/978-1-4666-0318-9.ch009

Wang, H., Zhao, J. L., & Chen, G. (2012). Managing data security in e-markets through relationship driven access control. *Journal of Database Management, 23*(2), 1–21. doi:10.4018/jdm.2012040101

Wangpipatwong, S., Chutimaskul, W., & Papasratorn, B. (2011). Quality enhancing the continued use of e-government web sites: Evidence from e-citizens of Thailand. In V. Weerakkody (Ed.), *Applied technology integration in governmental organizations: New e-government research* (pp. 20–36). Hershey, PA: IGI Global. doi:10.4018/978-1-60960-162-1.ch002

Warren, M., & Leitch, S. (2011). Protection of Australia in the cyber age. *International Journal of Cyber Warfare & Terrorism, 1*(1), 35–40. doi:10.4018/ijcwt.2011010104

Weber, S. G., & Gustiené, P. (2013). Crafting requirements for mobile and pervasive emergency response based on privacy and security by design principles. *International Journal of Information Systems for Crisis Response and Management, 5*(2), 1–18. doi:10.4018/jiscrm.2013040101

Wedemeijer, L. (2006). Long-term evolution of a conceptual schema at a life insurance company. In M. Khosrow-Pour (Ed.), *Cases on database technologies and applications* (pp. 202–226). Hershey, PA: IGI Global. doi:10.4018/978-1-59904-399-9.ch012

Wei, J., Lin, B., & Loho-Noya, M. (2013). Development of an e-healthcare information security risk assessment method. *Journal of Database Management, 24*(1), 36–57. doi:10.4018/jdm.2013010103

Weippl, E. R., & Riedl, B. (2012). Security, trust, and privacy on mobile devices and multimedia applications. In *Cyber crime: Concepts, methodologies, tools and applications* (pp. 228–244). Hershey, PA: IGI Global. doi:10.4018/978-1-61350-323-2.ch202

White, G., & Long, J. (2012). Global information security factors. In H. Nemati (Ed.), *Optimizing information security and advancing privacy assurance: New technologies* (pp. 163–174). Hershey, PA: IGI Global. doi:10.4018/978-1-4666-0026-3.ch009

White, S. C., Sedigh, S., & Hurson, A. R. (2013). Security concepts for cloud computing. In X. Yang & L. Liu (Eds.), *Principles, methodologies, and service-oriented approaches for cloud computing* (pp. 116–142). Hershey, PA: IGI Global. doi:10.4018/978-1-4666-2854-0.ch005

Whybrow, E. (2008). Digital access, ICT fluency, and the economically disadvantages: Approaches to minimize the digital divide. In F. Tan (Ed.), *Global information technologies: Concepts, methodologies, tools, and applications* (pp. 1409–1422). Hershey, PA: IGI Global. doi:10.4018/978-1-59904-939-7.ch102

Whybrow, E. (2008). Digital access, ICT fluency, and the economically disadvantages: Approaches to minimize the digital divide. In C. Van Slyke (Ed.), *Information communication technologies: Concepts, methodologies, tools, and applications* (pp. 764–777). Hershey, PA: IGI Global. doi:10.4018/978-1-59904-949-6.ch049

Whyte, B., & Harrison, J. (2011). State of practice in secure software: Experts' views on best ways ahead. In H. Mouratidis (Ed.), *Software engineering for secure systems: Industrial and research perspectives* (pp. 1–14). Hershey, PA: IGI Global. doi:10.4018/978-1-61520-837-1.ch001

Wickramasinghe, N., & Geisler, E. (2010). Key considerations for the adoption and implementation of knowledge management in healthcare operations. In M. Saito, N. Wickramasinghe, M. Fuji, & E. Geisler (Eds.), *Redesigning innovative healthcare operation and the role of knowledge management* (pp. 125–142). Hershey, PA: IGI Global. doi:10.4018/978-1-60566-284-8.ch009

Wickramasinghe, N., & Geisler, E. (2012). Key considerations for the adoption and implementation of knowledge management in healthcare operations. In *Organizational learning and knowledge: Concepts, methodologies, tools and applications* (pp. 1316–1328). Hershey, PA: IGI Global. doi:10.4018/978-1-60960-783-8.ch405

Wickramasinghe, N., & Goldberg, S. (2007). A framework for delivering m-health excellence. In L. Al-Hakim (Ed.), *Web mobile-based applications for healthcare management* (pp. 36–61). Hershey, PA: IGI Global. doi:10.4018/978-1-59140-658-7.ch002

Wickramasinghe, N., & Goldberg, S. (2008). Critical success factors for delivering m-health excellence. In N. Wickramasinghe & E. Geisler (Eds.), *Encyclopedia of healthcare information systems* (pp. 339–351). Hershey, PA: IGI Global. doi:10.4018/978-1-59904-889-5.ch045

Wimmer, M. A., & Traunmuller, R. (2008). Perspectives e-Government 2020: Results and Conclusions from the EC Roadmap 2020 Project. *Information and Communication Technologies: From Theory to Applications, 2008. ICTTA 2008. 3rd International Conference on.* doi:10.1109/ICTTA.2008.4529941

World Bank. (2014). *Open data for Sustainable Development.* Retrieved from http://pubdocs.worldbank.org/en/741081441230716917/Open-Data-for-Sustainable-development-PN-FINAL-ONLINE-September1.pdf

Wu, J. H., Tennyson, R. D., & Hsia, T. L. (2010). A study of student satisfaction in a blended e-learning system environment. *Computers & Education, 55*(1), 155–164. doi:10.1016/j.compedu.2009.12.012

Wu, Y., & Saunders, C. S. (2011). Governing information security: Governance domains and decision rights allocation patterns. *Information Resources Management Journal, 24*(1), 28–45. doi:10.4018/irmj.2011010103

Wyld, D. (2009). Radio frequency identification (RFID) technology. In J. Symonds, J. Ayoade, & D. Parry (Eds.), *Auto-identification and ubiquitous computing applications* (pp. 279–293). Hershey, PA: IGI Global. doi:10.4018/978-1-60566-298-5.ch017

Xiaoyan, M., Watta, P., & Hassoun, M. H. (2006). A Weighted Voting and Sequential Combination of Classifiers Scheme for Human Face Recognition. *IEEE Conferences, Neural Networks*, 3929 – 3935.

Yadav, S. B. (2011). SEACON: An integrated approach to the analysis and design of secure enterprise architecture–based computer networks. In H. Nemati (Ed.), *Pervasive information security and privacy developments: Trends and advancements* (pp. 309–331). Hershey, PA: IGI Global. doi:10.4018/978-1-61692-000-5.ch020

Yadav, S. B. (2012). A six-view perspective framework for system security: Issues, risks, and requirements. In H. Nemati (Ed.), *Optimizing information security and advancing privacy assurance: New technologies* (pp. 58–90). Hershey, PA: IGI Global. doi:10.4018/978-1-4666-0026-3.ch004

Yaghmaei, F. (2010). Understanding computerised information systems usage in community health. In J. Rodrigues (Ed.), *Health information systems: Concepts, methodologies, tools, and applications* (pp. 1388–1399). Hershey, PA: IGI Global. doi:10.4018/978-1-60566-988-5.ch088

Yamany, H. F., Allison, D. S., & Capretz, M. A. (2013). Developing proactive security dimensions for SOA. In *IT policy and ethics: Concepts, methodologies, tools, and applications* (pp. 900–922). Hershey, PA: IGI Global. doi:10.4018/978-1-4666-2919-6.ch041

Yan, G., Rawat, D. B., Bista, B. B., & Chen, L. (2014). Location security in vehicular wireless networks. In D. Rawat, B. Bista, & G. Yan (Eds.), *Security, privacy, trust, and resource management in mobile and wireless communications* (pp. 108–133). Hershey, PA: IGI Global. doi:10.4018/978-1-4666-4691-9.ch006

Yang, J., Frangi, A. F., Yang, J., Zhang, D., & Jin, Z. (2005, February). KPCA Plus LDA: A Complete Kernel Fisher Discriminant Framework for Feature Extraction and Recognition. *IEEE Transactions on Pattern Analysis and Machine Intelligence*, 27(2), 230–244. doi:10.1109/TPAMI.2005.33 PMID:15688560

Yaokumah, W. (2013). Evaluating the effectiveness of information security governance practices in developing nations: A case of Ghana. *International Journal of IT/Business Alignment and Governance*, 4(1), 27–43. doi:10.4018/jitbag.2013010103

Yates, D., & Harris, A. (2011). International ethical attitudes and behaviors: Implications for organizational information security policy. In M. Dark (Ed.), *Information assurance and security ethics in complex systems: Interdisciplinary perspectives* (pp. 55–80). Hershey, PA: IGI Global. doi:10.4018/978-1-61692-245-0.ch004

Yau, S. S., Yin, Y., & An, H. (2011). An adaptive approach to optimizing tradeoff between service performance and security in service-based systems. *International Journal of Web Services Research*, 8(2), 74–91. doi:10.4018/jwsr.2011040104

Yee, G., El-Khatib, K., Korba, L., Patrick, A. S., Song, R., & Xu, Y. (2005). Privacy and trust in e-government. In W. Huang, K. Siau, & K. Wei (Eds.), *Electronic government strategies and implementation* (pp. 145–190). Hershey, PA: IGI Global. doi:10.4018/978-1-59140-348-7.ch007

Yeh, S., & Chu, P. (2010). Evaluation of e-government services: A citizen-centric approach to citizen e-complaint services. In C. Reddick (Ed.), *Citizens and e-government: Evaluating policy and management* (pp. 400–417). Hershey, PA: IGI Global. doi:10.4018/978-1-61520-931-6.ch022

Young-Jin, S., & Seang-tae, K. (2008). E-government concepts, measures, and best practices. In A. Anttiroiko (Ed.), *Electronic government: Concepts, methodologies, tools, and applications* (pp. 32–57). Hershey, PA: IGI Global. doi:10.4018/978-1-59904-947-2.ch004

Yun, H. J., & Opheim, C. (2012). New technology communication in American state governments: The impact on citizen participation. In K. Bwalya & S. Zulu (Eds.), *Handbook of research on e-government in emerging economies: Adoption, e-participation, and legal frameworks* (pp. 573–590). Hershey, PA: IGI Global. doi:10.4018/978-1-4666-0324-0.ch029

Zadig, S. M., & Tejay, G. (2012). Emerging cybercrime trends: Legal, ethical, and practical issues. In A. Dudley, J. Braman, & G. Vincenti (Eds.), *Investigating cyber law and cyber ethics: Issues, impacts and practices* (pp. 37–56). Hershey, PA: IGI Global. doi:10.4018/978-1-61350-132-0.ch003

Zafar, H., Ko, M., & Osei-Bryson, K. (2012). Financial impact of information security breaches on breached firms and their non-breached competitors. *Information Resources Management Journal*, 25(1), 21–37. doi:10.4018/irmj.2012010102

Zapata, B. C., & Alemán, J. L. (2013). Security risks in cloud computing: An analysis of the main vulnerabilities. In D. Rosado, D. Mellado, E. Fernandez-Medina, & M. Piattini (Eds.), *Security engineering for cloud computing: Approaches and tools* (pp. 55–71). Hershey, PA: IGI Global. doi:10.4018/978-1-4666-2125-1.ch004

Zboril, F., Horacek, J., Drahansky, M., & Hanacek, P. (2012). Security in wireless sensor networks with mobile codes. In M. Gupta, J. Walp, & R. Sharman (Eds.), *Threats, countermeasures, and advances in applied information security* (pp. 411–425). Hershey, PA: IGI Global. doi:10.4018/978-1-4666-0978-5.ch021

Zhang, J. (2012). Trust management for VANETs: Challenges, desired properties and future directions. *International Journal of Distributed Systems and Technologies*, 3(1), 48–62. doi:10.4018/jdst.2012010104

Zhang, N., Guo, X., Chen, G., & Chau, P. Y. (2011). User evaluation of e-government systems: A Chinese cultural perspective. In F. Tan (Ed.), *International enterprises and global information technologies: Advancing management practices* (pp. 63–84). Hershey, PA: IGI Global. doi:10.4018/978-1-60960-605-3.ch004

Zhang, Q., Guo, L., & Wei, X. (2010). Image encryption using DNA addition combining with chaotic maps. *Mathematical and Computer Modelling*, 52(11-12), 2028–2035. doi:10.1016/j.mcm.2010.06.005

Zhang, Y., He, L., Shu, L., Hara, T., & Nishio, S. (2012). Security issues on outlier detection and countermeasure for distributed hierarchical wireless sensor networks. In A. Pathan, M. Pathan, & H. Lee (Eds.), *Advancements in distributed computing and internet technologies: Trends and issues* (pp. 182–210). Hershey, PA: IGI Global. doi:10.4018/978-1-61350-110-8.ch009

Zhao, W., Chellappa, R., Phillips, J., & Rosenfeld, A. (2003, December). Face Recognition in Still and Video Images: A Literature Survey. *ACM Computing Surveys*, 35(4), 399–458. doi:10.1145/954339.954342

Zheng, X., & Oleshchuk, V. (2012). Security enhancement of peer-to-peer session initiation. In M. Gupta, J. Walp, & R. Sharman (Eds.), *Threats, countermeasures, and advances in applied information security* (pp. 281–308). Hershey, PA: IGI Global. doi:10.4018/978-1-4666-0978-5.ch015

Zhifeng, L., & Tang, X. (2004). Bayesian Face Recognition Using Support Vector Machine and Face Clustering. *IEEE Computer Society Conference on Computer Vision and Pattern Recognition* (CVPR'04).

Zhifeng, L., & Tang, X. (2007). *Using Support Vector Machines to Enhance the Performance of Bayesian Face Recognition. IEEE Transactions on Information Forensics And Security, 2*, 174–180.

Zineddine, M. (2012). Is your automated healthcare information secure? In M. Watfa (Ed.), *E-healthcare systems and wireless communications: Current and future challenges* (pp. 128–142). Hershey, PA: IGI Global. doi:10.4018/978-1-61350-123-8.ch006

Zuo, Y., & Hu, W. (2011). Trust-based information risk management in a supply chain network. In J. Wang (Ed.), *Supply chain optimization, management and integration: Emerging applications* (pp. 181–196). Hershey, PA: IGI Global. doi:10.4018/978-1-60960-135-5.ch013

# About the Contributors

**Saleem Zoughbi** is an international advisor for ICT. He has been providing technical assistance and advisory services to over 30 countries. His focus is on development and has been assisting governments on the strategic and policy levels on e-governance, smart cities, national strategies and ICT development. He conducts consultancies for major consulting firms such as Booze, PricewaterhouseCoopers and others in technical missions and projects. He is active in international community of e-governance, strategies and policies of smart governance, mobile government, smart cities and smart sectors, and ICT for development. He previously held post of ICT regional adviser in UN-ESCWA, and then moved to UNU IIST. Currently he is engaged in Enterprise Architecture work with UN ESCAP. Recently he helped develop Change Management and Capacity Building strategic plans for all ministries of Libya according to eLibya Strategy. He is also the IEEE STC e-Gov committee secretary and officer in charge of e-Gov development projects.

\* \* \*

**Jesus Cano Carrillo** is an engineer who has worked in public sector for seventeen years. He is an officer with military rank at the Spanish Civil Guard and currently working in the Constitutional Court as Head of Area of Computing. Before that he worked as Head of Development Area, Systems Architect and Project Management in Computer Services at the Civil Guard Headquarter in Madrid. In addition, he collaborates as a visiting professor of Criminology in the Faculty of Law at the Universidad San Pablo CEU and in School of Computer Science at the Universidad Nacional de Educación a Distancia (UNED – The Spanish University of Distance Education) where he has taught cryptography for the past 6 years.

**Tumennast Erdenebold** graduated Master of Arts in IT Management (MA), Global Information Telecommunication Technology Program of Korean Advanced Institute of Science and Technology, Daejeon city, Korea in 2014. And Bachelor of Computer Science in Hardware and Software Engineering, Computer Science and Management's School at Mongolian University of Science and Technology, Ulaanbaatar, Mongolia. Worked as Deputy Director, Policy Implementation and Regulatory Department of the Information, Communications Technology and Post Authority, the Government of Mongolia between 2008-2012.

**Kareem Kamal A. Ghany** received the B.Sc. degree in Information Systems from Sadat Academy in 2002. Also he got his Master Degree in Computer Sciences & Information from Cairo University with Thesis Title "Data Integration in Data Warehousing". Now he is almost finishing his PhD Degree in Computer Sciences & Information from Cairo University. Kareem has been focused on Information Security, Data Warehousing, Biometrics Technologies, big data and Image Processing. He has published about 15 papers in Peer Reviewed International Conferences and journals and still working on more. Kareem has participated in the committees of many International Conferences, also he participated as an Editorial Board Member for many International Journals. He is working as an Assistant Professor at the Faculty of Computers and Information.

**Roberto Hernández** is an associate professor at the Control and Communication Systems Department at UNED. He has been Dean at School of Computer Science at UNED for eighth years. His research interests include e-government, quality of service support in distributed systems and development of infrastructures for e-learning, software quality and architecture systems engineering. He is a senior member of IEEE and he has co-authored more than 80 publications in international journals and conferences.

**Gilbert Mwirigi**, as the Senior ICT officer in the Office of the President, Ministry of Interior and Coordination of National Government in the Republic of Kenya, is both diligent in his work and committed to upholding professionalism. He joined the Ministry in 2012 after seven years of service as an ICT Officer at the National Treasury. Gilbert Mwirigi was born and raised in Meru County. He graduated with First class Honors in Bsc. IT from Jomo Kenyatta University of Agriculture and Technology in 2009 and his Master's degree in Information and Telecommunication Technology from Korea Advanced Institute of Science and Technology in 2012. Upon completion of his Master's degree he went back to continue with civil service at the Ministry.

# Index

3D 129, 131

## A

academia 121
algorithm 28, 41, 43, 45-47, 51, 54
alignment 128
Authentication 16, 37-39, 52, 56-58, 98, 110
averaging 47, 57

## B

Behavior Intention 63, 65, 67, 69, 71, 76, 78-82
Biometrics 37-38, 60
bureaucratic procedures 5, 8, 13-14, 21-22
buzzword 105

## C

civil servants 13, 16
Cloud Computing 91, 95, 98, 101-108, 110, 112-114, 129
comparative study 28, 35
Cooperation 7-9, 16, 126
correlation 46, 57, 59, 80

## D

deployment 64, 83, 104-105, 109, 112, 114
developing countries 1, 3, 22-23, 62-66, 78-85, 88, 92, 95, 103, 115-116, 118, 121-122, 124-125, 127, 133
digital information 24-25

Distributed Systems 1
DNA encoding 37-38, 52-53

## E

E-Governance 23, 27, 30-32, 34-36, 84, 104, 110-111, 113-114
e-Government 1, 13, 22, 24-31, 33-35, 62-65, 84, 86-88, 90-94, 96, 100-104, 110-111, 117, 119
embedding 37, 52, 54, 57, 128
encryption 61, 98
Enterprise Architecture 90, 92-94, 98, 100, 102, 124, 134
EU 1, 8, 21, 23-24, 134
extracting 52, 55

## F

face recognition 37-41, 44, 56, 59-61
facial images 40, 46
Facilitating Conditions 62-63, 66, 71-72, 78, 81-82
Feature Extraction 37-38, 40-41, 46, 59-61
frequency 38, 45, 54

## G

global database 17, 19-20
government data 23, 116-118, 120-129, 131-134
government services 32, 34, 63-65, 93, 97, 102-103, 111, 113

# H

hardware 82, 105-107, 115, 128, 130, 134
hidden meaning 31
Histogram Quantization 37, 45, 55, 59
holistic 94, 96, 124

# I

ICT 1, 3, 36, 84, 90-94, 100-102, 107, 117,
    120, 124, 126-128, 130-131, 133-134
India 27, 30-31, 36, 91-92, 97-98, 101,
    104-105, 111-114
Information Systems 2-6, 9, 23-25, 62,
    65-67, 69, 76, 79, 81, 83-89
innovativeness 69, 78-81, 83, 86, 88
integrity 32, 123
Internet 6, 13, 16, 18, 22-23, 26, 29, 31-32,
    60, 63-64, 69-70, 72, 78-81, 87-88,
    91, 98, 105, 110-111, 114, 117, 129,
    131-132, 135
interventions 81, 83
IT Management 1

# K

Korea 62, 90-93, 96, 98, 101-103

# L

lighting 38, 40, 44

# M

m-government 62-67, 69, 71-72, 75-76, 78-
    81, 83, 85-88, 92-93, 96, 98, 101-104
Mobile Application Self-efficacy 69-72,
    76, 78-81
mobile application services 90-92, 94, 98,
    100-101

# N

nature 7, 13, 16, 38, 73, 125, 131
node 16-20, 34

# O

Ontologies 16
operating systems 106, 110, 130

# P

participation 4, 8, 13, 30, 92-93, 110, 122
penetration 63-64, 91
perception 69-70, 80, 86, 93
Performance Expectation 68-72, 76, 78-82
personal innovativeness 69, 78-81, 83, 88
platform 7, 35, 95-97, 100-101, 106, 108,
    110, 112, 114-115, 121, 128, 132, 134
policy makers 63, 65-66, 81-83, 94, 100-101
portfolio 128
possible drivers 65, 81, 83
Principal component analysis 37, 41
protocols 15-16, 125, 130
public key 96

# Q

quantization 37, 45, 55, 59

# R

resolution 42, 57, 59
risk 5-6, 34, 69, 114, 120, 128, 131

# S

sector 1-4, 7-10, 13-14, 21-23, 28, 33, 116,
    122-123, 128
Secure Communications 14
self-efficacy 64, 67-72, 76, 78-81, 83-85,
    87-88
signal 38, 55
Social Cognitive Theory 66, 85
Support Vector Machines 46, 48, 61

# T

technology development 128-130, 133
Telecommunications 90, 98, 115, 128, 130
template 44, 46, 52, 54, 58, 60

# U

UN 1, 3-4, 7-8, 25, 118, 126
United Nations 1, 3-4, 10, 25, 116, 118-
    119, 127
University 1, 24, 27, 37, 59-60, 84-85, 104,
    115, 126-127
unrest 125

# V

virtualization 106-108

# W

Watermarking 37-38, 54, 60

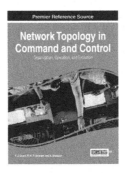

Stay Current on the Latest Emerging Research Developments

# Become an IGI Global Reviewer for Authored Book Projects

Premier Reference Source

Solutions for High-Touch Communications in a High-Tech World

Premier Reference Source

Advanced Research on Biologically Inspired Cognitive Architectures

Premier Reference Source

Workforce Development Theory and Practice in the Mental Health Sector

Premier Reference Source

Resource Management and Efficiency in Cloud Computing Environments

## The overall success of an authored book project is dependent on quality and timely reviews.

In this competitive age of scholarly publishing, constructive and timely feedback significantly decreases the turnaround time of manuscripts from submission to acceptance, allowing the publication and discovery of progressive research at a much more expeditious rate. Several IGI Global authored book projects are currently seeking highly qualified experts in the field to fill vacancies on their respective editorial review boards:

## Applications may be sent to:
development@igi-global.com

Applicants must have a doctorate (or an equivalent degree) as well as publishing and reviewing experience. Reviewers are asked to write reviews in a timely, collegial, and constructive manner. All reviewers will begin their role on an ad-hoc basis for a period of one year, and upon successful completion of this term can be considered for full editorial review board status, with the potential for a subsequent promotion to Associate Editor.

If you have a colleague that may be interested in this opportunity, we encourage you to share this information with them.